T0338416

Knowledge LTD

Randy Martin

Knowledge LTD

Toward a Social Logic of the Derivative

TEMPLE UNIVERSITY PRESS
Philadelphia • Rome • Tokyo

TEMPLE UNIVERSITY PRESS
Philadelphia, Pennsylvania 19122
www.temple.edu/tempress

Library of Congress Cataloging-in-Publication Data

Martin, Randy, 1957–
  Knowledge Ltd : toward a social logic of the derivative / Randy Martin.
     pages cm
  Includes bibliographical references and index.
  ISBN 978-1-4399-1223-2 (hardback : alk. paper) — ISBN 978-1-4399-1224-9
(paper : alk. paper) — ISBN 978-1-4399-1225-6 (e-book) 1. Finance—Social
aspects—United States. 2. Economics—United States. I. Title.
  HG181.M3153 2015
  306.3—dc23

                                                          2014023737

∞ The paper used in this publication meets the requirements of the American
National Standard for Information Sciences—Permanence of Paper for Printed
Library Materials, ANSI Z39.48-1992

For Ginger,
The Love of My Life

Contents

Acknowledgments   ix

Introduction: Who Knew?   1

1 After Economy?   13

2 Public Quandary   80

3 De-centered Social Kinesthetics   143

   Conclusion: Derivative Knowledge   213

   Notes   225

   Index   253

Acknowledgments

This book brings together three long-standing concerns. The first is an interest in how the protocols and perquisites of finance have reoriented and reorganized capitalism as we know and live it (a concern that has captivated my attention for the past fifteen years). The second is an interest in how to think about politics so that it is an expansive capacity in our midst rather than a threshold whose expectations are never met (a formative concern of mine since my college days). The third is a commitment to examine social life from the perspective of the performing arts in general and dance in particular (a concern that launched with my doctoral dissertation, based on my experience as a dancer in New York, where I went to pursue professional training more than thirty years ago).

Over the years, to my great fortune, a range of inspiring situations and interlocutors have provided the means to bring these disparate streams together. My work at New York University directing the graduate program in arts politics has brought me in contact with not only an amazing array of students from around the world and with all manner of engagements with what constitutes the relation between activism and esthetic practice but also cherished colleagues such as Kathy Engel, Karen Finley, Pato Hebert, Ella Shohat, Marta Moreno Vega, and my fellow travelers at Social Text, the Cultural Studies Association, and Imagining America, where we have tried to create openings for these kinds of crossings and shared attentions.

This book has also been nurtured by a very special collaboration with the Cultures of Finance Group that includes Arjun Appadurai, Peter Dimock, Benjamin Lee, Edward Lipuma, Robert Meister, and Robert Wosnitzer. Together, especially over the past several years, we have been pushing on the prospects of where a critical appraisal of derivatives might lead, and we are undertaking a series of writing and convening projects—an incredibly enriching and expansive ground that has provided a profound learning experience altogether too rare among well-published scholars. My understanding of these matters has been enlarged considerably through the critical engagements of Patricia Clough and Dick Bryan and through the important work coming out of Australia from Fiona Allon, Melinda Cooper, Martijn Konings, and Mike Rafferty. Through generous invitations from Mark Deputter, Joyce Goggin, Stefano Harney, Stefan Holscher, Victoria Lamont, and Jan Ritsema, among many others, I have greatly benefited from the opportunity to share these ideas with artists, activists, and critical thinkers of myriad dispositions at a variety of venues.

Some of the ideas presented in Chapter 1 were originally published in Randy Martin, "After Economy: Social Logics of the Derivative," *Social Text* 114 (Spring 2013). Portions of Chapter 3 were originally published in Randy Martin, "A Precarious Dance, a Derivative Sociality," *TDR: The Drama Review* 56, no. 4, T216 (Winter 2012). I thank the editors of these journals. It is also a pleasure to be able to sustain my link to Temple University Press, where Micah Kleit and the very capable staff shepherded two prior explorations of these themes: *Financialization of Daily Life* and *Under New Management: Universities, Administrative Labor, and the Professional Turn*. This manuscript has benefited especially from the expert editorial attentions of Joan Vidal and Susan Deeks, and I am deeply appreciative of their efforts. I would also like to acknowledge Victor Peterson for stepping in and completing the work on this book with his usual professional plum, as well as Dean Allyson Green of the Tisch School of the Arts at New York University.

On the home front, my life has been considerably enlarged by my partner, Ginger Gillespie, and our children, Oliver and Sophia, who teach us every day what it is all about.

Knowledge LTD

Introduction

Who Knew?

A story has been told. It has been told again and again in the hope that the retelling would make it so. Out of darkness would come light, if only we could see. Out of ignorance would come knowledge, if only we could understand. Out of mastery would come progress, if only we placed our faith in the future. This was a tragic but ultimately hopeful tale, full of heartbreak and distraction, setbacks and frustration. Each chastening episode made the will stronger until, eventually, uncertainty itself could be managed by powerful instruments for anticipating and acting on what might come to pass. While it was possible that events might overtake these models, such unexpected occurrences were rare and unlikely. Knowledge, focused through expertise and formalized through models, crafted a world of its own design in which thought was translated into action and departures from expectation could be tamed through the precision of mathematical prediction. But the highly unlikely has become increasingly familiar, the perfect storm a normal weather pattern.

This, at least, is the new ode to disaster. The methods of forecasting meant to render the world safe increased volatility and fomented overwhelming danger. In the multiple travesties of financial markets, the quantitative models devised to insure against unactionable risk succumbed to the interlocking debt instruments of their own creation. On April 20, 2010, the Deepwater Horizon well in the Gulf of Mexico exploded and leaked uncontrollably when the layered systems of engineers, the output demands of executives, and the safety protocols on-site suffered a massive pile-up. The earthquake and tsunami that struck northern Japan on March 20, 2011, breached the myriad warning and protective devices that would prevent and contain a nuclear accident. In New Orleans in the wake of the landfall of Hurricane Katrina on August 29, 2005, the levees broke, left unfortified by the engineering corps charged with their management yet discharged from the means of their maintenance. Wars against terror, in the aftermath of the hijacking of four jets-turned-suicide bombs on September 11, 2001, were ushered in based on unrivaled technologies of command, control, communication, and computation, only to become ensnarled in the most forthright failure of intelligence regarding the presumed predicates for intervention.

While it may seem tendentious at best to link these various episodes together, and while their particular stories remain distinct, they each report on a limit to knowledge with catastrophic consequences where refined modes of expertise were most assiduously applied. Beyond the anxiety that the exceptional has become commonplace, apocalyptic terms applied to various instances of crisis, such as "meltdown," "tsunami," "bailout," and "disaster," blur the sacred and profane, the natural and artificial, to suggest a scale of problem that transcends human efforts of comprehension, let alone containment or redress. In each case, a question recurs: "If they were the smartest ones in the room, how could their intelligence have failed them so?" If the behavior was as extreme as the events they fomented and confronted were supposed to be unlikely, then the villains could be readily punished and the outliers banished. The normal order of things would be restored, and crisis would be put behind us, at least until the next installment of extreme occurrences converged on an unsuspecting public. What are we to make of so many rare occurrences that pile on top of one another? How are we to respond to extreme behavior that, on closer inspection, appears as a professional norm? Certainly, knowledge has always had its limits. The unknown has served as the beckoning call of inquiry. But what happens when that horizon of the unknown no longer looks approachable? How are we to orient to knowledge when the unknown threatens to overwhelm its very efficacy and reasonableness?

For centuries, the horizon of the unknown was a beacon to further discovery. Expertise, while subject to skepticism from within and without, was generally taken to be in short supply. The knowledge economy was predicated on a scarcity of labor even if knowledge itself was potentially infinite. The credentials and offices through which it was formalized and bequeathed were jealously kept as perquisites of rule. Credentials remain expensive for many, but by historical measure they have never been more plentiful. Just as enclosure and dispossession provided the hands for bountiful industrialization, now kindred processes operate across those once autonomous fields of the professions. As with the prior proletarianization, this amalgamation and association of the work of expertise has been part and parcel of the expansion of what is now referred to as a knowledge economy. As we now live it, this ascent of capitalism generated vast surplus, some of it in the form of further wealth and another share that went to waste, whether as externalities, byproducts, and such, or the ruination of the very inputs on which it had so relied.

Can a similar story be told of the industrialization of knowledge and proletarianization of its production? Despite the best efforts of current rationalizers, gains in knowledge-based productivity are notoriously difficult to measure. Yet clearly more realms of human endeavor—more aspects of the planet and cosmos, whether large or small—are objects of knowledge. More people, more time, more space is dedicated to an expansive share of such materializations. But if knowledge presents its own challenges of measure, it is above all in what are the corresponding realms of surplus or excess, not simply of what remains to be put to use, but of what lies beyond utility. The unknown is the equivalent domain of waste in knowledge production.

The strong constructivist version of this argument would be that the myriad protocols of risk management evident across professional fields, from financial to energy engineering and from public health to homeland security, generate, foment, and constitute the very volatility they seek to master and profit from. A cursory glance at the revenue streams of hedge funds, energy companies, and security firms would seem to confirm this speculation. But if knowledge were so straightforward a translation from other modes of industrial production, then the challenges of accounting for its products might present no more than a minor conceptual nuisance. For the social and political observers of the prior great transformation, it was the shift in the very process by which life was lived—the forms of solidarity, the logics of rationalization, the character of association and interdependence—that was the most profound and abiding aspect of a new order devoted to maximizing the expansion of wealth, not simply how much gilt was created or who most attended its commandments. After all, from proletarianization sprang potent movements to lay claim to the very end of history; to craft the organizational means by which society might be fashioned; to imbue daily life with endowments of leisure, pleasure, and inventiveness.

And now, if knowledge itself is abundant—excessively, even dangerously, so—how might we understand the commensurate forms of solidarity, rationalization, and association? If the prior expression was that of a growing mass, occupying ever more space and accelerating forward in time (in a neat logarithm of progress and development), what social principles of space and time now obtain? More difficultly still, what if knowledge is now produced in such abundance that it cannot all be used, absorbed, applied, that its excess can generate crisis, catastrophe, disaster? What if the aggregated surplus of knowledge, the unknown, acts as a force of its own beyond the particular domains of requisite expertise? Just as the various forms of waste force an awareness of our planetary co-presence, the excesses of knowledge impose a sense of mutual indebtedness beyond the separate spheres of specialization in a neatly ordered division of labor. Regardless of whether the unknown that is the consequent surplus of knowledge production eludes measure, how might we understand the ways it shapes, connects, distributes our habits of being together?

Knowledge may be extended as a kind of credit, a promise of what is to come, but the unknown circulates as a type of debt, a way in which we are implicated in the works and lives of one another. My project here is to rethink the relation between contemporary ways of making wealth and rendering society, to pick up from what has been widely observed as a crisis of knowledge in an economy based on making it serviceable. As a consequence, the very architecture by which knowledge of the social has been made legible—the grand trinity that partitions economy, polity and culture—has come undone, and from these ruins issue all manner of challenge and possibility. I take seriously the approach laid out by Karl Marx in his critique of capital, where he opens his critique of political economy by asking what capital would say if it could indeed speak.

But capital today is not merely attributed the power to speak; it is presented as something that senses, touches, feels, embodies. Thus, a knowledge society is not simply about knowing. It also engenders ways of being that are key to the manners of affective, embodied, kinesthetic association. Much important work has now been done to bring these other materialities into the domain of politics, to demonstrate that what was once considered private is deeply implicated in what we realize as the public. But these contributions to a politics of value have been in scant communication with the value forms made familiar through the conventions of political economy. I want to think about this double relation of value as ways of knowing and being, thinking and embodied, indebted and associated, through what I take to be the current edge of capital and the contemporary transformation of the commodity relation—namely, that of the derivative.

More so than the commodity of the nineteenth century, the derivative appears as a magical or fictitious object, an ephemeral, chimerical specter that references a world that has become unmoored from underlying value, that cannot orient itself to what is real, that is obsessed with all that is spectacular and speculative. Yet as a means of bundling together attributes from disparate values, the derivative holds the key to the most salient mode of sociality of our moment, one that makes the future actionable in the present, that connects what is near and far, that assembles bits and moments together for appreciable gain, that melds circulation with production, that hedges knowledge against the unknown in ever more intricate indices of risk, that enables movement together from what is already in motion without first insisting on unity. Derivatives, the instruments of risk management that generated unmanageable risk, have been pinned with the blame for the puncture in our knowledge economy. Across an ideological spectrum, calls for returning to the real, to underlying value, can be heard. But lost in this din is a consideration of the principles of sociality that this pervasive derivative logic now visits upon us. If the derivative as the quintessential expression of commodified knowledge can bring us to the brink of disaster, can it also disclose what might rise from these very ruins, what is being assembled in our midst, what sensibilities and socialities it moves through and makes this life we know? Therein lies the aim in this book to press against the limits of knowledge, to divine in its excesses otherwise illegible principles of sociality that can be discerned and disclosed by tracing certain social logics of the derivative.

This book is in some ways the summa of the work I have undertaken over the past twenty-five years. It draws together the analytic approach I developed in my first three books to employ the performing arts (dance and theater specifically) as an optic or analytic lens to engage the inner movement of politics that is not readily detectable by standard social science frameworks and my subsequent effort to negotiate the aporias and divides through a rereading of Marx with interest in the operations of finance and knowledge as a feature of daily life, global reach, and higher education that I have considered in my last three books. *Knowledge LTD* treats as its point of departure the predicates and entailments of a series of disasters that have come to prominence since the massive bailout of the U.S. banking sector in 2008. There have been the subprime meltdown, the storms and tsunamis, but also the sovereign debt crisis of Europe, the impasse of governability in the United States, the seeming cancellation of the American dream for so many, the imperial retreats in Iraq and Afghanistan—all of which would seem to point to not only the limits of knowledge to master its conditions but also a waywardness with respect to mastery as such.

Many have been harmed by these events, and more doubtless will be placed in danger as the prevailing frameworks for devising and applying knowledge come to ruin. This is not to say that all is new or different, that all is ruptured, and there are no continuities. Quite the contrary: Old historical forces never seem to fully disappear. Rather, their intensities vary, with their efficacies rearranged. Some three billion people work the land as peasants and nearly an equal number undertake wage labor, while those engaging emergent forms of value creation and circulation—networked, independent, do-it-yourselfers—are but a small slice of the global population, even as the fates of these constituencies are entangled in unprecedented ways. So much of disaster and crisis is told as a story of rescue and recovery, an orientation that yields a desired return to normalcy, even as the underlying norms and references shift. Divining what is different and what can be made of those differences is the greater analytic challenge. Hence, while not ignoring the disastrous events, the focus here is on the effects those events have on architectures of knowledge as such.

Rather than assuming that the levees can be repaired and rebuilt, this book explores what the terrain of the social looks like when the waters have over-spilled their banks. This, it should be noted, is the etymological root of derivative—from the French *de-rive*—for the flow of water to exceed the limits of its embankments. After the waters have receded, the ground has stopped shaking, the winds have abated, and the leaks have been plugged, the landscape is certainly changed. More pointedly, our access to the social, our way of giving it shape and design as an object of knowledge of our actual and imagined condition of being together, of being an "us" or "we" that is oriented and orients activity at scales both too small and too large to see, may also have become dramatically reconfigured. The relation of how to what we know that enables us to know ourselves in our interconnections, interdependencies, and mutualities of debt describes what is meant here by a social logic.

Treating the derivative as a social logic invites an approach to knowledge after its boundaries have been breached, its means of enclosure violated. It is in this regard that we can inquire into what the state of affairs is after economy, polity, and culture—not that activities of production and circulation have disappeared, or that power no longer exists, or that there are no more expressive means for making sense of the world. Instead, there is an abundance of wealth amid a scarcity of generalizing its availability; political sovereignty appears stymied and occluded against a mobilization of myriad critical dispositions, a fracturing of shared values and common norms in the face of a proliferation of means for making sense and creating forms and flows of life.

Giving a name to these dynamics and the conjuncture that forms the present is always unwieldy and never unproblematic. On the one hand, if knowledge always has limits, how can we understand the consequences for politics and society today? In terms of conjuncture, of an assemblage of factors and forces that slice through the present with connections to larger processes of social transformation, finance as we know it emerges from the ruins of the financial arrangements that came undone in the early 1970s. In terms of rationalizing economic activity, finance has been ascendant over these past forty years, and derivatives themselves are taken as financial instruments used to manage risks to enhance return on investments. During this time, not only corporate strategy but also domestic and foreign policy and cultural and creative innovation have been oriented around various approaches to rendering risk generative and productive. In this respect, daily life seems to have undergone a process of financialization, where what once belonged to bankers' boardrooms now seems to have escaped and colonized the rest of the world.

Yet derivatives as ways to hedge against variable future economic outcomes have antecedents that extend back thousands of years. The term itself is used in many fields, from mathematics and music to medicine, with various meanings. But if derivatives at their root have to do with some kind of overflow, with the disassembly of some whole into parts and the bundling together of those attributes into something that moves away from or independently of its source, then finance may turn out to be less the originator of this social logic than a particularly prominent expression of derivative principles at work. Careful scrutiny of finance, just like Marx's attention to capital itself, yields this double session. Finance not only focuses, articulates, and disseminates a social logic of the derivative but also achieves its potency as a consequence of that very sociality. The social logic of the derivative is therefore a kind of epistemological hedge against the claim that a form of capital is the first cause of all social life, but that it rests on and discloses a mutual indebtedness, a sociality that it requires but that it can neither abide nor sustain.

In the subprime mortgage debacle, hitherto excluded populations—especially women and minorities—would be enlisted in debt relations and then abandoned to foreclosure when their participation no longer proved profitable. This flight of capital from where once it nested and propagated is a persistent feature of its history of accumulation and expansion. The migration is usually activated by some demands or contestation from those enlisted in the wealth-making scheme—be it slavery, industrial manufacture, or debt bondage. It is surely too soon to assay the political ramifications of these precarious and debt-distressed populations, but it is evident that the problems of credit and debt—of who can demand it, of who deserves it, of what purposes it can serve—are now features of the political horizon.

The most common way to understand these changes has been through the critique of neoliberalism, a triumphant ideology that replaces state with markets, public with private values, and a liberal consensus with a conservative hegemony. While the critique has been potent in naming a wholesale shift of political and economic culture that has spread from Anglophone roots to global dominance, it has frequently proved a tragic narrative. Neoliberalism laminates together an ideological formulation, a means for its institutional accomplishment (deregulation and privatization), and a capture of the popular imagination. For this reason, it has proved impervious to recognizing the very alternative and oppositional currents it seeks or to see such politics as always insufficient to its conditions and predicaments. By seeing in capitalism only disaster and crisis, this analysis, while compelling and comprehensive, has suffered its own crisis of value in thinking through the difference it might make to the existing state of affairs.

My concern is not to ignore these contributions to political thought but to engage a reenergized critique of capital in its derivative form to generate a view of the immanence of association and political potentiality that the present knowledge economy posits as its own limit.

The presentation of the book operates on these limits. Three long, perhaps excessively so, chapters stage a scene (set in the United States but gazing out at the rest of the world) by which the conceptual and practical integrity and autonomy of economy, polity, and culture is complicated and, in certain aspects, undone by forces unleashed through the social logic of the derivative. Chapter 1, "After Economy?" takes the architects of the financial bailout at their word, that what they knew to be the economy was on the verge of disappearing. By "economy," they meant a means by which price making and profit taking—the inner life of the market—was self-regulating, separate, and distinct from the political realm of which they were the presumptive delegates. Of course, the very need for a bailout belied this claim, but the apparent restriction of the benefits of collateralizing tax coffers to the private interests who held fiduciary claims on depreciated corporate holdings compromised the notion that economy integrates and aligns the interests and activities of the whole population—across the divide of labor and capital. From this perspective, the bailout is not a rescue of the economy, but an escape from it for those who once reaped its greatest rewards. Derivatives were at once the unmaking of this unity called economy and the means through which cardinal relations of price making and profit taking, information and regulation, wealth and population would be reconfigured.

Rather than its origin, the financial bailout could be taken as the apotheosis of the scrambling of public and private interest. No doubt, the effacement of the clear boundary that separates general will from particular need—if, indeed, it was ever intact—has been decades in the making. Winning presidential candidates were promising to end government as we know it long before they woke up to the horror that this dream had come true. If the political had rested on the distinctiveness of a public domain, then it has become increasingly evident that the public is a quandary. Chapter 2, "Public Quandary," considers three quandaries that are in common but also contrary use across economy, culture, and polity. The public is a kind of good made in a certain place, the nonprofit sector. It is a perspective on the people that situates a way of knowing all through the measure of a few (either at the volatile center or the shifting outlier). It is also, in its political expression, an interest, a value given to gathering, a capacity for critique.

The public in many ways is now a derivative of private values. Yet what is called private relies on and crafts all manner of public presence, whether to expand markets, maintain a healthy business climate, or enlist further participation in the glistening malls of subjectivity. The institutional expression of public goods, the so-called third sector situated between state and market, lies in nonprofit organizations. Yet on closer inspection, much of this autonomy for nonprofits belies the very manner in which they articulate a relation between government and business and, by means of tax-exempt philanthropy, place citizens in the situation of acting in judgment as to what merits public attention. A similar antinomy is evident in the evocation of the people through means of ongoing assessment and measure through such devices as public opinion polling. While such devices purportedly aggregate populations into the central tendencies of their common dispositions, the suffusion of the public sphere with these technologies of measure has yielded an emphasis on outliers, exception, and celebrity. This effacement of public opinion in favor of an orientation toward celebrity does not quell critical dispositions or render the populace quiescent. Rather, incessant measure without reference to underlying value yields a volatility of public opinion, the profusion of voices that noisily occupy our deliberative domains, and fueled by manifold claims to expertise, to means of representing and generating voices to be heard, the contours of this public body are manifest as a kind of excess criticality. Rather than seeing the public imagination truncated in defeat through what has been called the culture wars, I want to treat the surplus of knowledge production as generating a form of excess criticality. Making sense of this critical presence is full of traps and perils. Here too, the standard measures of public voice, statistical measures from opinion polls, still what is otherwise critical or excessive in the very voicing of the public.

Finally, I show that these alternative sensibilities are legible in embodied movement-based practice but not restricted to it. To do so, I turn to a related range of movement practices that emerges with the destruction of the old financial architecture in the early 1970s. I play on the shift between lost currency sovereignty and new forms of distributed sovereignty that derivatives make concrete. These movement practices—postmodern dance, boarding culture, hip-hop—do not share an esthetic or genealogical link. Instead, they are connected in derivative fashion through what I term a "de-centered social kinesthetic." In privileging a dance analytics to sketch the terms of a historical conjuncture, Chapter 3, "De-centered Social Kinesthetics," examines what I call a social kinesthetic that emanates from a decolonization of the body. Western concert dance incorporated features of sovereignty; King Louis XIV formalized ballet steps by commanding his vassals to imitate his very moves as a descendant of God. Martha Graham fashioned a modernist esthetic based on a technique, the contraction that signaled an infinite depth in her self-making genius. In both cases, verticality ruled as a universalist conception of bodily sovereignty was promulgated.

The decolonization movements that swept north and south in the long sixties (1956–1975) were palpable in a range of innovative movement practices as well. Postmodern dance flourished amid abandoned industrial loft spaces of lower Manhattan; hip-hop emerged from decaying social housing and infrastructure in the Bronx; boarding culture moved from the collapsed beachfront play lands and precincts of Santa Monica and Venice (California) suburbia. Finance as we now live it also emerged from the ruin of the colonial order, not simply the loss of currency sovereignty in the form of the dollar with the breakup of what had been the international financial architecture (1971–1973), but also the creation of options-based revenue streams, mutual funds, and other financial instruments. The financial and movement practices responded to the collapsed verticality with an emphasis on lateral mobility, which is particularly evident in the three movement practices named earlier.

Rather than sharing a style or influence, these movement forms are derived from other practices (the pedestrian, slave dances, and the indigenous Hawaiian practice of surfing), but they are also connected and animated in derivative fashion through their bundled attributes of flying low, reversibility (on hands and feet), ensemble-distributed esthetics, and an embrace of risk as reward. This non-probabalistic, non-stochastic conception of risk, grounded in other notions of self-appreciation, mutual indebtedness, and distributed possession, makes legible a range of outcomes for this social logic of the derivative that differs from the ones that take finance itself as its only means of account. I trace the ways in which this other way to make value through movement emerges from the ruins of the old financial order, one that also, in the cases of these particular practices, affects urban space in the form of deindustrialization, suburban decay, and the collapse of social housing.

Finance has as its root the French word *fin*, the end, or to bring a transaction to an end. Its history has been one of ruin, of persistent and recurrent crisis from which the provenance of wealth is restored. From these ruins have arisen not only species of precarity and human misery as populations have been cleaved from their means of social life but also new means of association in which population might emerge as sovereign in its own right. The etymology of the word "population" bears meanings of both "to ruin" and "to people." This book aims to derive the value of the latter from the unwanted conditions of the unknown that accompany the former.

After Economy?

On the Thursday evening of September 18, 2008, Ben Bernanke, chairman of the Federal Reserve, and Henry Paulson, Secretary of the Treasury, convened a meeting in House Speaker Nancy Pelosi's office with congressional leaders who included senators Charles Schumer, Chris Dodd, and Richard Shelby. In the previous thirty-six hours, large institutional investors and hedge fund managers had been pulling billions of dollars from leading investment houses such as Goldman Sachs and Morgan Stanley. Bernanke and Paulson, the two men with the greatest responsibility for federal financial policy, had decided that the moment had come for the $700 billion rescue plan they had been preparing but holding off until they could wait no longer. Bernanke informed the handful of elected representatives assembled in the room, "If we don't do this, we may not have an economy on Monday."[1]

That Monday came and went, but Bernanke's prognostication came to be referred to only retroactively. The presumption was that the economy had been saved by allowing some corporate houses to fall (notably, Lehman Brothers) while fortifying the stores of others through large government purchases of their stock (from the insurer AIG to the automobile industry). A few years on, those targeted businesses remained largely rescued, but the fate of the economy remained uncertain. Conventional wisdom held that the economy was intact, albeit diminished in a state of crisis, depression, or recession. But the other possibility raised by Bernanke's comment and never really entertained is that the economy as it had been known saw its delimiting boundaries breached so that it changed into something else. Economy as it has come to be understood rests on an exclusion from the political and an inclusion of a national population. Crisis seemed to have reversed what was included and what excluded, to have drawn the political realm deeply into a world that normally disavows its dependence on anything but its own capacities for keeping itself going and to unravel the claims to integrate the wealthiest and poorest through lives directed by common principles of rationality and a shared promise of prosperity.

Such a change doubtless would elude those very measures that establish what economy is and does, for none of those markers and protocols have gone away, any more than businesses have ceased to pursue profit and people have been compelled to seek employment. Stuff still gets made and sold, even if through thickets of debt and credit; some continue to get more and others, less; economic indicators rise and fall. But perhaps it all does not add up in the same way, is no longer stitched seamlessly together. Maybe the big ideas of reason, progress, and prosperity no longer hold everyone in their place. Surely, it is not credible that the economy could have disappeared over the course of a weekend, as if kidnapped and secreted away in the middle of the night. But what if Bernanke was right—that he saw a change coming, likely was well on its way, that what he was considering for the future had already arrived in the present. Clearly, such a prospect is so rife with problems as to be difficult even to contemplate. Is the demise of economy as we have known it beyond what can be treated as knowable? Or, how would we know a limit to knowledge itself? Let us see. If the established habits of perception no longer yield the same clarity and insight, what kind of attention now needs to be paid to make sense of what is different in our midst?

The closed meeting with Bernanke and Paulson was reported by the *New York Times* two weeks later, and a year afterward, suits were still being filed by public interest groups to determine who exactly had been in the room. These two were odd messengers of doom, as only months before both had issued assurances that all would settle back to normal without need of extraordinary measures. In 2007, Bernanke had testified before Congress, "At this juncture, however, the impact on the broader economy and financial markets of the problems in the subprime markets seems likely to be contained." Later that year, Paulson said of those same "problems" with subprime mortgages, "I don't think it poses any threat to the overall economy."[2] The inadequate political preparation for a major bipartisan alignment doomed the initial version of the bailout bill. In the months to come, $12 trillion, practically the entire gross domestic product (GDP) of the United States, would be effectively pledged to save the economy from what was taken to be its imminent demise. On the authority of a few that the bailout of financial services would be a rescue for all, many would be asked to make sacrifices in what was promised as a recovery to come. The credit crisis would become entangled with questions of credibility over the ability of expert knowledge to rule for the common good.

Just two days after the meeting in Pelosi's office, Paulson made an appeal to the Senate for the funds based on a three-page memo drafted by his office. This document authorized him to purchase mortgage-backed securities or other financial assets that had become illiquid or unsalable because they had either suffered a steep drop in price or could no longer be priced by the market. In effect, the bad debts would be removed from the balance sheets of the investment houses, allowing them to appear solvent again, while holding these depreciated assets in separate accounts or secondary markets in the hope that their value would return and provide revenue for both the banks and the government. The powers for an officer of the government to do what the market could not positioned the Secretary of the Treasury as a kind of Ur-investor who could exercise his discretion as he saw fit to prevent the financial markets and banking system from being disrupted.

Paulson promised he would make his investment decisions in a manner so as to protect taxpayers, who by proxy would now have the same interests as investors in these companies. In return, the Senate would grant him immunity from any potential harm that might come from any of his decisions: "Decisions by the Secretary pursuant to the authority of this Act are non-reviewable and committed to agency discretion, and may not be reviewed by any court of law or any administrative agency."[3] The visible hand of regulation was to be beyond regulation. The lack of account for the funds and accountability for their disbursal factored into the initial rejection of what came to be called the Troubled Asset Relief Program (TARP) when it was first brought to the House of Representatives on September 28, 2008, under the aegis of the Emergency Economic Stabilization Act. It was resubmitted and passed into law a few days later. The law authorized two disbursements of $350 billion (one on October 3, 2008, and the other on January 15, 2009, which the Senate would have fifteen days to disapprove) and established the Office of Financial Stability to manage the funds.

Days before, in testimony before the Senate to explain the need for the bill, Paulson said that credit markets had frozen when financial institutions stopped lending money and that his aim was to restore confidence in the markets: "We must now take further, decisive action to fundamentally and comprehensively address the root cause of this turmoil. And that root cause is the housing correction which has resulted in illiquid mortgage-related assets that are choking off the flow of credit which is so vitally important to our economy. We must address this underlying problem, and restore confidence in our financial markets and financial institutions so they can perform their mission of supporting future prosperity and growth."[4] If markets had frozen out of fear of their own correction, government aid would allow market actors to trust one another once again. Government was being charged with a mandate less to fix economic mechanisms than to change public feelings toward key institutions. This restoration of confidence was to be affected by the magnitude of the bailout itself, as one Treasury official was quoted as saying at the time: "It's not based on any particular data point. We just wanted to choose a really large number."[5]

This decisive and prodigious action, meant to instill the confidence that would make the economy move again, instead generated considerable doubt. Popular outrage that private interests who had assumed excessive risk were being rescued with public money were echoed by economists who defended the integrity of the market to punish bad risk with failure. Government reward for bad behavior in the marketplace distorts the natural balance of risk and reward and promotes what is known as moral hazard, in which the expectation of rescue encourages excessive risk. To make matters worse, public money was being put up without the kinds of authority or voting rights on publicly owned shares that typically would be provided to a major shareholder or investor. In this way, collective protection would come to taxpayers through the performance of private companies rather than by realization of some public interest in how monies were allocated. Shareholder value was being defined as the public interest. The purposes of the act were defined so as to calibrate protection and accountability as a function of overall returns such that public interest and market measure became one. Hence, the act "protects home values, college funds, retirement accounts, and life savings; preserves homeownership and promotes jobs and economic growth; maximizes overall returns to the taxpayers of the United States; and provides public accountability for the exercise of such authority."[6]

Years later, the record is rather mixed. At best, defenders will claim—in the face of depleted home, retirement, and college fund value and diminished homeownership rates—that it could have been worse without the support. Of course, critics still seize on the lack of public accountability. The Congressional Oversight Panel, charged with monitoring but not altering relief decisions, concluded in its last of thirty reports that TARP had been effective in saving banks, but rather than protecting the integrity of the Secretary, it had created a "public stigma" for Treasury Department intervention that would make future assistance less likely.

As TARP evolved, the Treasury Department found its policy choices increasingly constrained by public anger about the program. The program is now widely perceived as having restored stability to the financial sector by bailing out Wall Street banks and domestic automotive manufacturers while doing little for the 13.9 million workers who are unemployed, the 2.4 million homeowners who are at immediate risk of foreclosure, and the countless families who otherwise are struggling to make ends meet. The Treasury Department acknowledges that, as a result of this perception, TARP is burdened by a public "stigma." Nonetheless, the fact that the same people who contributed to the crisis were charged with ending it abetted a perception that the government was quietly helping banking insiders at the expense of accountability and transparency.[7]

The public career of regulation would position it as self-liquidating, an exceptional intervention that could not be replicated in the future. Yet perhaps the most fully realized purpose has been to leave the banks and businesses on their own to maximize returns to taxpayers on the investment. The government bought tens of billions of dollars of stock in Citigroup, Bank of America, AIG, JPMorgan Chase, Wells Fargo, General Motors (just to name the largest investments). Indeed, much of the TARP money has already been paid back, with billions returned in revenues to government coffers. Of the $700 billion figure, $462 billion was allocated, the Congressional Budget Office estimates, and the cost of the program will be about $19 billion: "Overall, the outcomes of most transactions made through the TARP were favorable for the federal government."[8]

While the actual money provided to these businesses is less than the guarantee and the return is less than the lost revenue, the notion that TARP itself was set up as a kind of private investment without a federal hand in what the money would need to be used for is perhaps its most striking feature. For business generally, 2010 was a year of record profits, and thanks to gains in productivity by refraining from hiring and investing, the bailout effectively transferred funds from public to private coffers. For banks alone, the amount of "non-borrowed" funds increased from just over $1 trillion in May 2010 to more than $1.6 trillion in May 2011.[9] In the aftermath of the bailout, banks went from having what was subsequently considered inadequate reserves to cover credit exposure (about $40 billion in the years leading to the crash) to holding an excess that could readily constitute a stimulus the government is said to be incapable of funding.[10]

The language of frozen markets, housing corrections, and restored confidence suggested an agency to the movement of money beyond policymakers' grasp. If banks had stopped lending to one another, what would make them begin again? The bailout program provided not so much an explanation for how or why it would work as a declaration, based on decisions that themselves were not subject to scrutiny, that markets had to be made to move, and if they could be, all would benefit. As is now apparent, little was built into the conveyance of public credit to private entities that would compel them to attend to what constituted taxpayer protection or future prosperity beyond limits to liability on the part of the recipient institutions.

Yet if there was considerable doubt about what was broken and how it might be fixed, the urgency to do something was posed as a kind of threat. If nothing was done, there might not be an economy as such. The response to emergency was reminiscent of the September 11 attacks. There was no time to wait for all of the information to come in. Not knowing that there was a threat was at the root of the problem. The only safety lay in assuming that what was unknown would indeed cause further pain. The only prudent course was to hit hard, effect shock and awe, imagine that the unknown would be driven away. No less an authority than Queen Elizabeth of England had demanded to know why no expert had foreseen the crisis, despite abundant signs that were there for the reading.[11] Alan Greenspan, Bernanke's predecessor, whose much praised views on the self-correcting powers of markets oriented toward profit taking were treated as the most potent ideas of the age, testified before Congress after the bailout was passed. He was "distressed," he confessed, to have found a "flaw in the model that I perceived is the critical functioning structure that defines how the world works, so to speak."[12]

But it would seem that a good measure of the free market economics theory rested on unchallenged or unchallengeable assertion. Sheila Bair, the head of the Federal Deposit Insurance Corporation, whose mandate is to regulate banks to protect depositors large and small, voiced frustration about being sidelined on major decisions and about the absence of evidentiary deliberation in the course of decision making. "They would bring me in after they'd made their decision on what needed to be done," she said about her relation to Paulson and Bernanke, "and without giving me any information, they would say, 'You have to do this or the system will go down.' If I heard that once, I heard it a thousand times. . . . No analysis, no meaningful discussion. It was very frustrating."[13] The assertion that intervention was necessary in the name of a general interest in preserving the system was presented as self-evident. While belated, intervention was posed as preemptive, a temporal logic shared by monetary policy aimed to stop inflation that was Greenspan's signature legacy and the foreign policy crafted to join the global war on terror.

What had previously been normal practices of economics and politics now became speculation and terror, respectively. In the hands of Paulson and Bernanke, regulation was speculative in the double sense of placing a wager on a desired outcome and being exploratory without a clear understanding of how it might work. Like a terrorist threat, each individual act was posed as a prevention of the unthinkable, which, if it were to take place, would quickly become contagious and spread. These terms seemed to name the unknowable, the unforeseeable, the unpredictable. While uncertainty may be generalized as a condition for amplifying the consequences of the unknown, the risks—that is, the measurable differences of these departures from expected norms—are borne unevenly in a vast sorting machine of the "haves" and the "have-nots." Some will profit handsomely from this state of affairs, while others will suffer miserably from what is taken to be their own failure to master the risks of their environment.

Given how quickly financial and industrial organizations returned to profitability and how much suffering was sustained by taxpayers and the populace at large, it would be easy to dismiss the claims of crisis as so much hyperbole. For the rich, things are looking good again; for others, not so much. In one way, this is standard issue inequality to which economy as both concept and operation provides the mechanism and the rationalization by which an entire population is fit and functions within a unified national space. The economy will provide each a place according to his or her capacity and ambition, will distribute spoils on the basis of mastering its terms of reason, will absorb all inputs and convert these to available outputs, and will create the boundaries by which one nation can be measured against the wealth of others.

The economy by this reckoning would be precisely the device that converts knowing into being, that parlays belief that it is all that is worthy of knowing to a world of worth. This is the neoclassical image of the market as the supreme and omniscient machine, a computer or information processor that imbibes all inputs of what can be known about economic activity and converts this into a price. The result is a steady state of harmony or equilibrium. When the market, which sees all with the equivalent of God's eye, detects a discrepancy between an assigned price and an underlying value, it makes a "correction." Recall that this is precisely the term that Paulson used to account for the precipitating events in housing. Humans may have failed to assess their risk exposure adequately, but the market as a whole was correcting for these foibles of individuals by adjusting housing prices, interest rates, and credit instruments. With patience, this realm of reason will return. Individuals may be taken by surprise, but in the end, the economy knows best, and its actions, however painful for some, will reflect the truth of the moment.

At this point, it would seem that Paulson and Bernanke were not so much riding to the rescue of the economy as a dynamic duo as speaking from the fault lines of their respective positions as manager and engineer. The Treasury Department is charged with keeping the faith in a money-based economy; the Federal Reserve must maintain the flow or current—actually, currency—that keeps the market machinery running. Paulson's message in his initial terse memo on the bailout was to restore faith by investing himself with an authority without oversight. Bernanke was informing the assembled political leaders that the metrics he possessed to model the economy had made what he was looking for illegible. There was a possibility that the computer could simply be rebooted and run again. There was also the chance that its operation would fail to do what it had done in the past. After the approval of the various bailout bills and the return of the surviving institutions to solvency, the assumption went, the economy as it had been known and knowable had been restored.

Another possibility is that what Bernanke imagined as the unimaginable consequence of not intervening in some ways came to pass. From this perspective, he was making what would have to be considered the mother of all predictions, which for economists is precisely what makes economies: an orientation to price based on available knowledge. In etymological terms, "crisis" refers to a point of decision, inflection, or consequential change in the course of a cycle or disease. Yet in its own terms, the economic crisis seemed to reference an impossibility of knowing, an inadequacy of explanation, a suspension of confidence in certain beliefs by which all could be governed. It was a colossal knowledge failure not because it eluded prediction or concealed an undetected flaw, as Queen Elizabeth and Alan Greenspan, respectively, implied, but because the prediction of its demise could not find a stable referent. Business returned to profitability while the rest of us were turned toward something else. The conventional opposition named by "crisis" between a return to normal health and a terminus or total collapse itself has been undone. If the economy met its end, in some regard it did so because it became unknowable in ways that exceeded the conviction that more appropriate or better knowledge could be found.

The aftermath of a rescue without recovery seems to have opened up the chasm between managing or governability and engineering or modeling that Paulson and Bernanke sought to put a brave united face on that early fall evening of 2008. At the time, Paulson's travails seemed to get displaced onto the Republican Party, whose candidate John McCain had surged in the polls in September, only to be tarred with the brush of the incumbent party's mismanagement. While governance would get a hopeful new start with Timothy Geithner (who as head of the New York Federal Reserve was deeply implicated in the events), Bernanke would be reappointed as chair of the Federal Reserve, reprising the bipartisan support of his predecessor, Greenspan, and lending credence to the claim that the position of chief economic engineer was outside party politics.

The bailout effectively reengineered banks' profitability partly by freeing them from the obligation to service those with (now) bad credit. It seems to have done little, however, to alleviate the knowledge crisis or public stigma associated with government itself. Rather than being credited with applying expert knowledge that saved people from a ruined economy and averted a catastrophe worse than the one that befell them, the unknown shape-shifted into the ungovernable. The massive debt held by government, which effectively transferred a public surplus into private hands, presents the national account as antithetical to productive activity—hence, the bipartisan refusal to throw good money after bad by increasing tax revenues. If the thing called "the economy" is ungovernable, this must be the fault of government, which represents not the people but the failure of disinterested expert rule.

Here, then, is a double bind. If the government actively manages the economy, it is violating the boundary that keeps politics and economics separate fields so that property can be the measure of personal liberty that government is charged to protect. If government is positioned as lacking the knowledge of how the economy works, of being unable to foresee or fix what is broken, it affirms its own inadequacy to do anything other than turn management over to the economy. Such a conundrum shrinks the realm of what could be considered effective regulation. But it also leaves the impression that the economic machinery is still weaving together a world of people and prices, of translating human needs into effective demand. Chronic foreclosure, unemployment, debt, and lost retirement, public services, and access to education and health care would all seem to suggest otherwise.

The aftermath of the bailout leaves a profound irony. The infusion of trillions of dollars of public monies into the coffers of private corporations is a clear statement of how much economic activity depends on political intervention. The ongoing refusal to raise taxes that might compromise certain perquisites of accumulation; to cut public services, labor, and pensions as a sacrifice to prosperity; and to squeeze social needs to contain debt and deliver credit to financial institutions are evidence of the hyperactivity of political intervention, regulation, and management in the heart of what is termed "economy." The hyperactivity of the political in the midst of an economy that needs ever more attention but complains bitterly about its dependence approximates the tone of antigovernment governmental activism proclaimed as the new common sense several years after the crisis. The sighting at a Tea Party rally of a placard proclaiming "Don't Cut My Social Security" may be apocryphal, but by a margin of two to one, its constituents consider such cuts unacceptable.[14]

This is not to say that the orientation toward private gain typically understood as capitalism suddenly came to an end. Rather, the creature devised to make that process self-evident and necessary, which goes by a more restricted and technical term of the economy, somehow morphed into something else. The analogy of economy to a system of interdependent parts that worked together as a machine was an achievement of twentieth-century social science, whose theories spoke of integration and attended to assimilation of immigrant populations to a single rational order. Clearly, capitalism as a means of privatizing wealth through socializing production preceded and evidently follows its systemic expression as economy—or, at least, that is a premise that is examined here. Traces of system and measures of economy still abound, even as their historical project and ability to control society lose their grip.

Without doubt, the crisis authorized categorical and terminal judgment made without necessarily reconsidering criteria of assessment. This was true of the very tissue of terminology found in an expansive literature of apologia and *explanandum* that oscillated between metaphors of natural disaster (tsunami, perfect storm, flood) and millenarian retribution (Armageddon, apocalypse) and technological malfunction (meltdown, implosion).[15] Less clear is how crisis altered analytic approaches, terms of understanding, or conceptions of the operations of knowledge as such. Rescue was aimed at recovery that would restore normalcy. From this perspective, crisis was a reset button that would convert the threat of total obliteration into a resumption of prosperity. If crises are periodic, endemic, inevitable—views shared by apologists for and critics of capitalism—then the lessons they provide will be affirmations of convictions already held. For apologists, norms will resume, while the fact that the world did not end will silence critics until the next crisis comes along. Instead, crisis may be the momentary response to questions that have yet to be formulated, to problems not yet understood. If so, crisis would need to be sustained beyond its moment to see how it might transform knowledge itself.[16]

Bernanke's worry that the economy could come to an end suggests as much about a failure to know the economy as a failure of knowledge as it had been implicated in the very notion and operation of what made for an economy. It is possible to see in that crisis moment of September 2008 a whole array of knowledge failures, even though their predicates and consequences extend far beyond that particular event. These could be named as a knowledge failure in the price mechanism; a collapse of prediction and theory; an evacuation of expert authority; an unmaking of what contains or bounds the economy as a distinct domain; and a shift in the relation between knowledge and its presumed opposite, nonknowledge. Treating each of these in turn would then allow consideration of what is doing the work of economy; of what kinds of relations bridge the continuities and breaks in the relations of production, circulation, force, and difference by which processes of value and social wealth can now be understood.

Knowledge and Price

The very conception of the economy as a self-regulating system for setting prices rests on an understanding of how knowledge is distributed among individuals so that each uses information to establish a hierarchy of preferences. Thus, a first technical notion of the crisis would be a condition in which knowledge cannot make prices, a breakdown in what was taken as the fundamental relation of individuals, decisions, and allocation of resources or objects. The brief for the economy itself as knowledge machinery was articulated forcefully in Frederick Hayek's address "The Use of Knowledge in Society" of 1945.[17] The utility of knowledge is to optimize the use of resources through variations in their price, which becomes its own information signal so as to coordinate among individuals where that good is best distributed. The decisions that make for these allocations Hayek terms "planning," and economic systems can be distinguished by whether planning is undertaken by a single entity (centralized in the state), by industrial organizations (monopoly), or by individuals (competition). His concern is to counter the logic of socialism by a usurpation of its claim to achieve rational allocation through planning. In this respect, the market is the sum of all knowledge that individuals provide but that they cannot master because it is incomplete, dispersed, contradictory. "The economic problem of society is thus not merely a problem of how to allocate 'given' resources—if 'given' is taken to mean given to a single mind which deliberately solves the problem set by these 'data,'" Hayek writes. "It is rather a problem of how to secure the best use of resources known to any of the members of society, for ends whose relative importance only these individuals know. Or, to put it briefly, it is a problem of the utilization of knowledge which is not given to anyone in its totality."[18]

Knowledge here is of two kinds: a formal and abstract kind possessed by experts that can be aggregated statistically and another unorganized kind based on circumstances of the moment. Expert knowledge on which state planning depends can be unreliable insofar as it lumps together the local variations based on direct observation and therefore misses the rapid adaptation to change available only to those who are directly confronting the circumstances at hand. Hence, state planning is destined to fail and competition is destined to succeed in translating by means of the market the collective intelligence of this direct decision making aggregated as price. When knowledge is equally dispersed, the market operates as a noncoercive expression of the totality of the best that can be known. The result is order without command as each individual submits to rules of reason by which his or her knowledge is best applied. "The problem is precisely how to extend the span of our utilization of resources beyond the span of the control of any one mind," according to Hayek, "and therefore, how to dispense with the need of conscious control, and how to provide inducements which will make the individuals do the desirable things without anyone having to tell them what to do."[19]

Hayek calls his nonexpert the man on the spot, but what he has in mind is the distinction between economists and managers. It is, after all, the latter who are making the decisions of allocation that are being described. The totality named by the market selects out most kinds of labor and much of the tacit knowledge that is not oriented toward or registered in price-making activity. But even among the industrial managers who constitute individuals who count in an economy, it is their proximity to variation that affects the equality of knowledge particularity that is reflected in the God's-eye capacity for decision making that gives the market its integrative force.

That the market is the answer to the problem of consensually based order and that state involvement in planning yields only inefficiency became a staple of the very assumptions in which finance became ascendant. Financial markets would seem to be the exercise of the universe of knowledge in its purest form, a mechanism for prices to oscillate continuously in response to the information inputs of men and women on the spot without interference by nonmarket agents. The ascent of finance itself would be a key signal that knowledge had triumphed in society—indeed, what came to be known as the neoclassical paradigm, which, as Philip Mirowski so comprehensively has shown, came to dominate twentieth-century economics. The neoclassical approach adopted notions of system and mechanism derived from the physical sciences and relied on a privileging of information as the input that fueled its operations. Yet as Mirowski demonstrates, the fathers of this idea came to no consensus as to what information meant and seemed indifferent to this inconsistency at the core of their foundational claim for an economics of knowledge. From its formulation, mid-century information was treated variously as a thing, an inductive index, and a symbolic computation. The epistemic incoherence was finessed by a notion of economics as a marketplace of ideas without a means to negotiate key differences in underlying assumption. "It suffers from the bad habit of presuming what it cannot demonstrate," Mirowski writes. "The very notion that austere utility maximization could induce economists to develop a naturalized epistemology and a rich cognitive psychology smacks too much of magic realism. Yet many economists find it perfectly natural to shrug off such paradoxes of self-reference: they have yet to suffer the consequences of their insouciance."[20] At issue here is whether Bernanke's statement suggests otherwise, even if the economists themselves would, according to script, refuse to admit it.

The limits to knowledge were, however, part of the initial formulation undertaken by Hayek. Mirowski elsewhere pinpoints how this limitation was meant to operate to preserve its own kind of equilibrium:

> Hayek should be read as one of a long line of social theorists who praise the unanticipated and unintended consequences of social action as promoting the public interest, but who takes it one crucial step further by insisting upon the indispensable role of ignorance in guaranteeing that the greater good is served. For Hayek, the conscious attempt to conceive of the nature of public interest is the ultimate hubris, and to concoct stratagems to achieve it is to fall into Original Sin. True organic solidarity can only be obtained when people believe (correctly or not) they are only following their own selfish idiosyncratic ends, or perhaps don't have any clear idea at all of what they are doing, when in fact they are busily (re)producing beneficent evolutionary regularities beyond their ken and imagination. Thus *ignorance helps promote social order*, or as Hayek said, "knowledge and ignorance are relative concepts.[21]

Submission to the authority of the market requires an embrace of one's own ignorance, a trade on conscious assertion for a noncognitive cooperation that does not require dialogue. Self-limitation or ignorance must be welcomed, if the ultimate wisdom of the market is to be affirmed, as a kind of automation of thought, an intimately capable information processor or computer. To the extent that the values of the competitive price system are internalized by all, people are drawn into the logic of momentary and positional differences in the name of the good of an order that is not of their making. This information asymmetry is both structural and self-erasing. Exclusion from meaningful decision, omission from the criteria for conscious control, is to be experienced as a kind of freedom whereby people behave desirably without having to be told what to do.

In this schema, the market principle is sustained through a tautology of knowledge equilibrium. By accepting the superior intelligence of the price system, values are inculcated among individuals, market knowledge achieves rational efficiency, civilization advances as a progressively embodied ideal, and competition is demonstrated as best realizing human aspirations. As with any circular reasoning, a break in the chain causes the whole fence to collapse. The potential for ignorance to fall out of balance with knowledge is there every step of the way. The select market makers can send false signals about what they know or misread what the market is telling them; the market itself could collect ignorance instead of knowledge; the values, trust, and faith could dissipate in a massive run on credit and a public disbelief in economic sovereignty so constituted. Herein lies the anxiety over panic attributed to flaws in human nature that distort or corrupt the machinery's continued operation, a preoccupation of what is called behavioral finance.[22]

Precisely because the economy is a machine that runs on belief, it is subject to sudden cessation, failure, dysfunction. The specter that the music and the magic would suddenly stop, the very motivation for keeping knowledge of the economy private or proprietary, secreted from the public, is what necessitates keeping the hand of coordination invisible. Hayek at least is clear that the triumph of the form of interconnected sociality embodied in the market is but one form among many. The failure of the market can be precisely the moment in which other principles of a sociality or coordination beyond individual decision become legible. Bernanke's comment disclosed what the unspoken and unseen looked like. After the naked had been redressed and sent on their way, the on-the-spot folk could again be merry, but the curious balance of knowledge and ignorance that would keep the many aligned to the few remained out of step and in tatters.

Chancing Prediction

If the economy could end on a single day, we would witness Armageddon. With the end would come reckoning, judgment day. The very cry that the end is nigh occasioned a litany of blame, a desire for retribution, a lust for blood that has yet to be satisfied. These biblical trappings would make it difficult for a mere mortal to point the finger. Closer to God than most, if not privy to the omniscience of the market, the queen's query to the lords of economy, "Why did no one see it coming?" would have to be taken ironically, if Hayek is to be believed, since no one could. But the queen was also impugning the powers of prediction of thought to be the very bread and butter of the market makers. In this light, Bernanke's statement would be a template for further predictions, one he was making without attendant falsification. Again, if in some respect he was correct that the culprit itself had disappeared, no exercise in finger pointing would be suitable to the task of restoration—or, at least, the question of what was to be restored would itself be begged.

The failure of prediction and the confusion that ensued over how to restore accountability point beyond the normative behavioral claims of how life should be organized in a sphere of competition to the manner in which economic thought became operationalized and applied in finance. A frequently observed predicate of the debacle was that the very mathematical models meant to control risk wound up making the markets unsustainably risky. The purported overreliance on models harbors an unexamined assumption of the normal functioning of economic theory as such. Prices can be modeled in the first place because the economy, like the natural world, operates according to deterministic laws that, like gravity, are independent of the bodies on which they act. The model in question is the normal distribution that allows events to be predicted with pre-given probabilities.

The vast complexes of the financial services industry, with their seemingly endless product lines of options, swaps, swaptions, collateralized debt obligations (CDOs), and CDO-squareds, arose on the grounds that expected outcomes could be calculated and assigned a price, irrespective of the kinds of debt they were made of and how they were combined. If prices conformed to models of randomness, risk could be spread through diversification—the premise of portfolio theory. For the models to be implemented, it was necessary to demonstrate that variations in price remained smooth over time, for if prices were subject to extreme departures from expectation, investors would lose confidence that the factors that had brought them to an investment would still apply, prompting massive capital flight or systemic risk. But because this volatility is indeed a feature of investing, the models rely on data taken from the short term. Longer appraisals of price variation disclose that the unexpected event is far more common than a random model would have predicted, so that supposed outliers actually occupy substantial space among actual occurrences—hence, the phenomena known as fat tails. The world, in short, was a more chaotic place than the economists had imagined when they devised their models of well-ordered distributions.[23]

The view of the world as chaotic and nonlinear but still able to be modeled was what allowed the mathematician Benoit Mandelbrot to deploy a different mimetic faculty between the domain of economics and the physical world. His notion of fractals turned continuous distribution on its side and explored the ways in which the patterned geometries of measurable events repeated at different scales. Fractals opened a new consideration of previously intractable problems such as the length of a coastline, which would yield different results depending on whether the units of measure were very large or very small: the smaller the measure, the more surface area covered by the jigs and jags of the perimeter, and the greater the distance. Yet the different scales of measure had certain ratios in common. Nasim Nicholas Taleb and others applied this logic to investment by claiming to engineer models for unexpected but still statistically possible occurrences, the outliers or catastrophes that Taleb terms "black swans." Taleb became an outspoken critic of the models and their inventors, known as quants, presumably trumping their math based on normal distributions with his own based on fractals. Yet for all of his vociferous criticism, his motive was the same as theirs: to profit from properly managed risk. The unwillingness of events to obey the ideals of either order or chaos could lead to a call for better models or a more focused skepticism toward the costs of relying so heavily on them.

One version of this doubt derives from the distinction made by Frank Knight, a contemporary of Hayek's, between risk and uncertainty in "The Limitations of the Scientific Method in Economics."[24] Recognizing these limits was crucial if life was not to be reduced to a mere matter of mechanics governed by a technique of prediction; inferences were more likely to be false than true; and at bottom, getting along with others requires more common sense than theory, a matter that belongs to esthetics not science. Ultimately, Knight was validating the judgment of executives to navigate the otherwise inscrutable intuition of practical decision making to transform conditions of uncertainty into profit in the face of limitations to knowledge. Uncertainty would also imply that government would need to be standing by in the event that the world became too risky a place, a view that fit with the Keynesian perspective that would keep Hayek and his legacy in the shadows for decades to come. The paradox Knight finds is that "the existence of a problem of knowledge depends on the future being different from the past, while the possibility of the solution of the problem depends on the future being like the past."[25] Change in a static world maintains the measurability that can predict risk, but uncertainty springs from an unknowable world in which intuitive decision is riddled with error. The effective present, which keeps at bay this antinomy between future and past, opens a space for the wealthy individual, the beneficiary of uncertainty turned into fruitful decision.

The disclosed limits of the models and the detected flaws in the theories have delivered few professional economists to the role of explaining what happened. While Professor Paul Krugman of Princeton University won a Nobel Prize in Economics, ostensibly for his work in understanding the Great Depression of the 1930s, it is hard to see a mere coincidence in his role as a *New York Times* columnist railing against the shortcomings of his profession. For all of the hearings and disclosures, the larger story of crisis has been told by journalists. Joe Nocera is one of business's more formidable raconteurs. He was responsible for an early diagnosis of "how the middle class joined the money class" and has been there to describe what it means to lose club membership.[26] While presidents have offered assurance that "there is plenty of blame to go around," Nocera has tried to parse responsibility within the dens of professional economic practice itself. Indeed, contemporary finance would seem to be the influence-minded academic's dream, a world in which theory is practice and abstract mathematical modeling that garners professional respect gains widespread application.

The model in question is called value at risk (VaR). Its virtue is to take all manner of financial instruments (stocks, bonds, securities, derivatives) held by an individual or firm and translate the net exposure to loss in terms of a single dollar amount. A latter-day alchemy, this VaR promised the ability to spin information into gold. From the mid-1990s into the next decade, risk was spread not simply through a firm but throughout all manner of financial services—including, notoriously, the subprime real estate market—through the expansion of what amounted to a form of insurance against loss called derivatives. By June 2008, contracts covering more than $1 quadrillion ($1,140,000,000,000,000) of exchanged-based and interparty or over-the-counter derivatives were issued with the confidence that continued hedging of risk would defer unmanageable outcomes indefinitely and the economy would be all good, or what was called a virtuous cycle.[27] As is the case in business, what is all good for some is quite nasty for many. Nocera shares the tale of the one that got away, the success among failures lionized in management studies as a "best practice." For a while, at least, that was Goldman Sachs, the investment bank that Paulson had led two years before he became Treasury Secretary:

> Reporters wanted to understand how Goldman had somehow side-stepped the disaster that had befallen everyone else. What they discovered was that in December 2006, Goldman's various indicators, including VaR and other risk models, began suggesting that something was wrong. Not hugely wrong, mind you, but wrong enough to warrant a closer look.
>
> "We look at the P.&L. of our businesses every day," said Goldman Sachs's chief financial officer, David Viniar, when I went to see him recently to hear the story for myself. (P.&L. stands for profit and loss.) "We have lots of models here that are important, but none are more important than the P.&L., and we check every day to make sure our P.&L. is consistent with where our risk models say it should be. In December our mortgage business lost money for 10 days in a row. It wasn't a lot of money, but by the 10th day we thought that we should sit down and talk about it."
>
> So Goldman called a meeting of about 15 people, including several risk managers and the senior people on the various trading desks. They examined a thick report that included every trading position the firm held. For the next three hours, they pored over everything. They examined their VaR numbers and their other risk models. They talked about how the mortgage-backed securities market "felt." "Our guys said that it felt like it was going to get worse before it got better," Viniar recalled. "So we made a decision: let's get closer to home."[28]

Subjective feeling that inhabits experienced managerial judgment trumps coldhearted reliance on quantification. The early warning system worked perfectly. The alarm sounded, and all escaped safely. The risky exposures (later to become toxic assets) were shed, and the partners found comfort and safety back at "home." A hard day spent, the good men put the good tools to rest. An effective *oikos* entails sensing what belongs to art and what to science, giving subject and object each its due, building a marriage of anima and animas, the rational and the affective. Before leading us to this unmarked gender of the gift—where each knows her or his place and contributes to the commonweal of the bonus pool from her or his distinct ability—Nocera tours us through the ethical incompleteness of those who are not able to recognize this golden mean.

While mathematical models are attributed with powers of seeing the future, in practice they operate in the moment of their available data streams. More, what they see in the present is what they take to be most likely to happen. Accordingly, the meltdown was not so much unforesee-able as improbable when probabilities were being forged out of institutional investors' adhering to their own forecasts. While this has been derided in studies of investor psychology as a herd mentality that makes for animal-istic "irrational exuberance," a less charged phrase, "clustering around the mean," describes that most normal of statistical figures: the bell curve. The VaR model slayer that Nocera brings into his picture is none other than Taleb, who casts the question of probability in terms of black and white swans, with black swans describing an ideal condition of the improbable and the white swans describing a perfect fit with expected forecasts. "Because we don't know what a black swan might look like or when it might appear and therefore don't plan for it, it will always get us in the end," according to Nocera. "'Any system susceptible to a black swan will eventually blow up,' Taleb says. The modern system of world finance, complex and interrelated and opaque, where what happened yesterday can and does affect what hap-pens tomorrow, and where one wrong tug of the thread can cause it all to unravel, is just such a system."[29]

The figure of a black swan follows a pattern in which imagined meta-phor collides with observed measure. Until these rare birds were spotted by the Dutch explorer Willem de Vlamingh in western Australia at the end of the seventeenth century, the term was used metaphorically to describe what people believed, on the basis of their own experience, could not exist. The discovery becomes a signal event that upends prior assumption but restores the power of explanation. Taleb wants the world to know that the quants are wrong, but his engineering is right. Between black and white there is a third possibility: Events do not simply shift their likelihood of occur-rence on a fixed plane of distribution, but the context, the very surface onto which the events are inscribed, is subject to change. For the adventurous trader, this new context presents an opportunity for writing afresh, not simply seizing what hitherto was unlikely. This third prospect is described by the financial trader Elie Ayache in an inversion of Taleb as a blank swan. Like Taleb, Ayache aims to profit from opportunities that others miss, but instead of using mathematical models to explain his approach, he draws on poststructuralist theorists such as Jacques Derrida and Gilles Deleuze to recognize what is left out of conventional schemes of representation. He sees his own work as writing on a blank page a new context for the complex financial contracts or derivatives that seek to benefit from what the future might bring. White and black swans are based on anticipated and predictive knowledge of where prices will go; derivatives, however, are written by traders such as Ayache in the hope that his action on what he does not know will yield pecuniary gain:

> We had to wait until the advent of derivatives and derivatives markets for the exchange to really acquire the rank of substitute of knowledge instead of accessory to knowledge, and to pull the market away from equilibrium or collapse instead of driving it towards them. To repeat, derivatives weren't created because we knew something but because we didn't know something. We didn't know the future; we didn't know the probability distribution of the underlying. They weren't created either in order that we may value them (as if the exercise could merely stop at the totalization of possibilities and the replication of derivatives). Derivatives are intended for trading. They are the un-knowledge of the future, made market. They are the market. They have no existence outside the market. To me, derivatives and exchange are the same.[30]

In imagining a context for making money after prediction has ceased to deliver reliably on its promises, Ayache is asserting the power of a financial trader to make a market by and for himself or herself without concern about what is known, what the political effects may be, or how a market of exchange in his or her terms might affect the universe of knowing exchange by which the term "economy" was once known. It is certainly disquieting to see ideas developed to explicate the limits of dominant knowledge schemes of capitalism applied to a reaffirmation of a yet more restrictive conception of who might benefit from the economy's disarray. At the same time, this readiness to gain from others' loss, to harvest uncertainty's crop, to flee the ruins of what once was encumbering is utterly consistent with the longer *durée* of capital's progress. What is different here is the exhilarating particularism of these claims to find profit in un-knowledge and market demise, not for a generalizable horizon called the economy, but for the derivative writer and the circuit of exchange that writes on its own behalf.

From this perspective, Bernanke's statement might look more like a blank swan than a white or black one. The bailout was indeed a kind of blank check to the banks, an effort to bring about a sudden shift of context without responsibility for what had come before. The banks could be free to write their own ticket or not, to refuse to disclose what they were doing, or to hold for themselves the money that was meant to unfreeze the markets and get the economy going. Indicative is the position of one of the largest recipients of TARP monies in the aftermath of the bailout. When asked to account for how JPMorgan Chase had spent the $25 billion in emergency funds it had received to that point, Thomas Kelly, a spokesman for the firm, said, "We've lent some of it. We've not lent some of it. . . . We have not disclosed that to the public. We're declining to."[31] This absence of accountability, the inability to provide even an account, links together those officials—both public and private—thought to be in the know. Whether they knew and would not say or did not know and could not say is neatly annulled in these circumstances. Either position would hold out hope for knowledge to regain its footing once things returned to normal. More worrisome, then, would be the prospect that expertise itself had lost its conditions of rule over what it was supposed to know.

Lost Expertise

Beyond the venalities of greed, which can be quickly subsumed to narratives of a few bad actors that can be expunged from an otherwise healthy state of affairs, the subtext that expertise can no longer stabilize society and deliver prosperity discloses a deeper anxiety. Granted, this disquiet is of long standing. Plato's *Republic* is a cautionary tale about letting the wrong kind of knowledge into the polis. Mistrust of experts has accompanied their rise through the secular pathways known as modern society over the past five hundred years.[32] Recall that Hayek's doubt consists in a concern that experts would interfere with the collective wisdom of the market. Hayek would not be one to recognize the labor that goes into making a knowledge society, but the decades that followed World War II generalized a social compact organized around a specific authority associated with the proliferation of professional expertise. Accordingly, higher education would pass from a self-affirming privilege for the elite to a metric of meritocratic advancement based on expanded access to professional credentials, now treated as a public good. Investment in this infrastructure, fueled by the Cold War race to knowledge dominance, resulted in massive expansion of campuses and programs like Pell Grants that would fund access for those whose futures were once confined to harvests and assembly lines.

The most ambitious of these initiatives for credential-fueled mobility, the California Master Plan, envisioned universal access to a hierarchy of junior colleges, state colleges, and universities, with universities holding a monopoly on doctorates and research capacities. Even where government grants were involved, research would be governed by disciplinary norms and priorities—a pure pursuit of fundamental knowledge undistracted by instrumental demands of utility or profit. The partition between the protocols of governance that disciplines reserved for themselves and the judgment of worth of the resulting knowledge by various claimants from government and business to popular opinion maintained the core value of autonomy in an increasingly complex division of knowledge labor.[33] Accordingly, specialists would be left to their own devices, protected by academic freedom, professional associations, or institutional differentiation. So successful was the process of class formation that by the 1970s, concerns were being raised that the self-interest of professionals would undermine their call to service and that technical reason would undercut the substantive basis for shared values by which society should be oriented. Instead, society would be subordinated to the particular concerns of these new mandarins, referred to as the professional managerial class.[34]

But if the architecture of the professional managerial class was the result of massive public works, the continued expansion of its ranks would not be sufficient to assure its prevailing social epistemology. Margaret Thatcher, with her pronouncement that "there is no such thing as society"—only individuals and families—and Ronald Reagan, with his anti-tax, supply-side, monetarist, "voodoo economics," would signal a Hayekian turn among heads of state.[35] They would voice a government assault on its own credibility, a skepticism toward the trustworthiness of those who would claim to know better than what people knew about the conduct of their affairs. If the market knew better than the experts, then everyone could be invited to judge for himself or herself whether specialists were worth the cost and added to general measures of the commonwealth. Knowledge that once had only to judge for itself now had to demonstrate that it could add value for others.

A technical logic colonized the values of communal living along the lines of this rampant managerialism, unmoored from its particular professional domain. In a reversal of Hayek's circumscribed realm of managerial prerogative, all were to be positioned on the spot, even if the greatest benefit would still be reserved for a few. Indeed, if all were to stand in judgment of legislation or of knowledge that was thought to control access to resources such as proper health care or education, then the consequences of making better or worse decisions would be enjoyed or suffered alone. For people to have access to maximum benefit, they would need to undertake risks. Government should be seen not as guaranteeing security for all but as assuring that those best able to maximize the returns on risk can deliver the greatest prosperity. This was, of course, the financial understanding of risk management, and as finance came to stand for the engine of prosperity, some version of this logic was inscribed in the daily affairs of a knowledge populace whose efforts at planning would be cast in terms of maximizing competition to ensure personal liberty.

The escape of this financial reason from its rarefied precincts of investment bankers and arbitrageurs and the larger question of whether the vectors of influence move toward or away from a putative center or ideal type of the financial actor or arbitrageur are discussed in much more detail later. Suffice it to say for now that what had been identified as a culture in finance would become a culture of finance. For professionals reared on promises of autonomy, the shift in knowledge terms compelled them to attend to a master who was indifferent to their fate. The phrase "the smartest ones in the room," connected first to the implosion of Enron, then repeated as investment houses fell, reports on a general failure of knowledge to sustain its conditions of prosperity.[36] The division of labor by which each expert in tending to his or her own garden summed to a bountiful harvest saw its basic units of value erode. But for experts who lost their particular critical distance, accountants who moved into Enron headquarters, ratings agencies that did not want to disappoint those who had paid for their services, journalists beholden to their sources, and quants whose models could work only to affirm the firm's risk strategy, the dilemma was internal.

In the annals of crisis, these failings were momentary lapses, pressed by greed and opportunity that caused reasonable folk to lose grip of their senses. In actuality, this loss of sensibility had been decades in the making. The loss in trust among those charged with managing the particular risks that applied to all was the popular manifestation of a knowledge-based capital that depended on a blankness to rewrite its conditions of accumulation. The great mass of specialized knowledge on which finance rested became an unbearable impediment to further amassing of wealth. Getting closer to home meant not only getting away from particular risk exposures to invest in others but also disengaging from the specialized knowledges that had produced the risk profiles to begin with. The efficacy of expertise would be assessed by the external standard, the managerialism that would erode its internal capacities for decision on the basis of what it knew best.

The professional managerial class turned out not to be a class in and for itself in the manner that this was imagined for the nineteenth-century masses whose association would translate into unions, political parties, and other organizational forms that could direct society. As governance came to reflect a coalition of benefit between the smaller strata of partners, stars, managing directors, and owners over and against the majorities of knowledge producers in a given field—the researchers and adjuncts, primary care providers, and inspectors—the professional compact-turned-compromise would prove incapable of collecting and pursuing a shared interest or organizational capacity that would increase its authority along with its numbers. Though far more numerous than the industrial proletariat it replaced, the professional managerial class discloses a different principle of association. If autonomy was being eroded with the rise of this new class, then the circumstances of the past forty years would bear more of a resemblance to the transformation of an agrarian peasantry into industrial workers, a move from discrete productive entities to mounting interdependence among associated producers.

Marx had likened this condition of class decomposition to potatoes in a sack of potatoes: "Their mode of production isolates them from one another, instead of bringing them into mutual intercourse. . . . They are consequently incapable of enforcing their class interest in their own name, whether through a parliament or through convention. They cannot represent themselves, they must be represented."[37] The difficulty in finding a vehicle for a common voice has its own paradoxical echo in the state, whose representative voice is despotic (the farcical authority Marx terms "Bonapartism") while its techniques of governance proceed through a self-destructive "demolition of the state machine."[38] While much divides peasant potatoes and professional expertise, the political chaos he described, the sense that government might short itself—that it might prove ungovernable or bet on its depreciation at the same time that it exerts an iron hand over errant populations—invites some compelling resonance between this account of a society at the crossroads and our own. Marx, of course, was seeing the formation of a new class through the decomposition of the old. Professional autonomy erodes in favor of an endemic incompleteness where expertise serves a master indifferent to it. Knowledge workers cannot contain the uncertainty they unleash and produce an ungovernable surplus of the unknown. The principles of association that make for an emergent class may be detectable only on its own ruins.

This is a situation in which all have some specialized knowledge at the same time that all claim the authority to judge others through managerial protocols of performance assessment, diffusion of information, and doubt regarding the disinterestedness of expertise. Capital flees the strictures of the democratization of knowledge from which it could once profit, as seen in the defunding of public education and enclosure of commons through intellectual property. Changes in the constitution of a general will of public opinion or the formation of capital point to the ways in which the division of labor implied in the rule of experts has run its course. What is less clear is the principle of sovereignty that emerges when rule itself has become so thoroughly discredited a notion, as in the case of bipartisanism, where neither party can claim a majority of support for its exercise of power. When those charged with ruling the economy—with delivering its rules but also proclaiming its viability—can do neither, they are reporting on their own demise as rulers. This interplay between ruler and what is ruled is complex, to say the least, but "the economy" may be the most specific way to name this intersection of activity and effect. The economy is, after all, the effect of the sum total of self-guided decisions. If the terms of autonomy for producing decision failed, it would make sense that the conditions of possibility for the economy would be compromised as well.

Ends of Economy

The birth of the economy as a universal object was predicated on a generalizing way of knowing but also on a new kind of being, homo economicus, a rational, calculating subject. If the economy has shifted away from what once rendered it a distinctive subject and object—both ways of knowing and the work of knowledge—then the placement of subjects in the world and their operations as agents (to say nothing of subjectivity and agency) would also be transformed. If economy triumphed under the aegis of a knowledge society and knowledge itself failed, or was unable to exercise its authority within its specified domains, then the problems associated with the economic crisis would be legible in other crisis forms as well. The environmental disasters of the Deepwater Horizon rig in the Gulf of Mexico in the spring of 2010 and the Fukushima Daiichi nuclear reactor in Japan nearly a year later, with their serial failures of risk management protocols and engineering operations, would be important places to look for evidence of this shift.[39] Surely, this unbounding of information, decision, and utility did not happen over the course of a weekend, but the odd and mysterious array of predicates and consequences now understood as and consolidated under the nomenclature of the crisis may have fundamentally altered what was meant by the term "economy" or robbed the domain it once described of its internal coherence.

The emergence of the market as a distinct realm and purpose of human association constitutes the historical, political, and ideological project that

Karl Polanyi terms "The Great Transformation." Polanyi argues that there have always been some kind of market relations for the distribution of goods, but these values of exchange were subordinated to other cultural, religious, or political ends. Whereas economy was once embedded in society, its dominance over human affairs entailed dis-embedding its procedures and requirements so that they became ends in themselves. This is the basis for the autonomy of the economic sphere from the political at the same time that economy assumes the mantle of broader social purposes. While Polanyi understands well that in practice, the state continues to play an active role in the management, regulation, and organization of economic relations, dis-embeddedness is a promise of what the future will look like when individuals become fully rational economically; hence, it constitutes the utopian horizon of capitalist development. The rise of fascism at a global scale provides Polanyi's historical counterfactual to the myth of the self-regulating market: "Our thesis is that the idea of a self-adjusting market implied a stark utopia. Such an institution could not exist for any length of time without annihilating the human and natural substance of society; it would have physically destroyed man and transformed his surroundings into a wilderness."[40]

The present failure of the market would seem to stand for an abdication of that utopian aspect altogether, as the end of the market entails not only that an expansive future in the form of social benefits such as health care and pensions has been canceled, but also that the future is a debt to be paid for now. The liberty that would be delivered by the full autonomy of the market was itself predicated on the manufacture of a credible conviction that the future would be an improvement over the present. Yet utopia also requires that the future be seen as another time, discontinuous from the present, in which the hope of emancipation might be realized. Since this other time would need to be sustained as an article of faith, continuous improvement or growth would have to stand for the possibility of a utopian break to full prosperity and the good life. Instead, there is mounting anxiety when the home ownership that has become a cognate for both participation (literally owning a piece of the nation) and prosperity (seeing the value of one's holdings expand) begins to decline. Similarly, after stocks lost half their value from the 2007 peak, many would come to realize that they would never accumulate sufficient funds on which to retire through their stock-based defined-contribution pension schemes.

For the already affluent third of retirees, especially those who saw gains through the 1980s and 1990s, options were open. But for the rest, the pursuit of freedom from work would be put on hold, perhaps indefinitely.

Declining wages, increasing college costs, and an uncertain prospect for career advancement would contribute to unprecedented intergenerational downward mobility.[41] Canceling this prospect of a utopian future would not entail eliminating growth per se but decoupling these various continuities or material entailments of expansion from the promised land of progress through mobility. Certainly, it is possible that any of these measures of decline could be reversed. What is less clear is that the particular time sense that underwrites the utopian aspect of economy could be resurrected as a practical universal that encompasses the aspirations of an entire population. Already strained by their logical contradiction, the hinge between the year-to-year continuities of a self-expanding market and the temporal discontinuity of a market utopia in which prosperity is self-realizing could be exposed for its fragility through a transformative event.

That society itself could be understood in terms of its different ways to order knowledge or epistemes led Michel Foucault to speculate in *The Order of Things* that the modern form of abstract classification that produced the individual subject of history called "man" might already be over. What had emerged as "the effect of a change in the fundamental arrangements of knowledge" could fade as a consequence of some cataclysmic event: "If those arrangements were to disappear as they appeared, if some event of which we can at the moment do no more than sense the possibility—without knowing either what its form will be or what it promises—were to cause them to crumble, as the ground of Classical thought did, at the end of the eighteenth century, then one can certainly wager that man would be erased, like a face drawn in sand at the edge of the sea."[42] The event of erasure comes at the limit of knowledge. Neither its form nor its effects appear as something tangible and positive. Instead, they appear as what we can do no more than sense.

Far from the consequence of a natural history, the calculative agent that represents the zero degree of decision, the individual or being that cannot be further divided, was the result of a particular logic that employed universal rules to generate hierarchies of value. This pursuit of the boundary conditions by which calculative agents would see themselves as distinct entities competing is a circumscribed sphere of the economy. This is what led Michel Callon to formulate the embeddedness of economics as a specific knowledge practice in the delimited arena of action known as the economy. The content of this embeddedness is indeed the expertise enacted by these agents to constitute the domain of market activity—or as he puts it, "Economics, in the broad sense of the term, performs, shapes, and formats the economy rather than observing how it functions."[43] For

Callon, the economy is at once what economists do, the relations of market exchange, and the general discursive space referenced by the term. His concept separates distribution from production—there is decision but not labor, agents but not organizations or movements of workers, contestation over terms of control but not coercion of who is included or excluded from the workplace or national labor market, as in the case of immigration.

Knowledge is borne not simply by agents but among the objects in their environment—the various devices ranging from computers, to furniture and spatial layouts that incorporate the tacit understandings of a network. The image of embeddedness is all about how people act according to particular logics under given circumstances that are maintained or kept in place by a frame. The frame serves not only to partition what economy can claim as its own, but also to exclude that which would undermine its operation. The external forces, including and incorporating other ways of understanding and acting on the situation by those outside the frame, or consequences not in the control of the enframed, constantly threaten to seep into or out of the frame. These overflows, then, are the contested, negotiated terms of the political. Politics, for Callon, takes places in the disputes between buyers and sellers and in the overflows of the frame, both of which are normal features that sustain the autonomy of the economic itself. The internal differences among calculative agents are resolved through the adjudications of the price mechanism, and the external challenges of overflow lead to new pricing opportunities and efforts to reassert control. In both cases, the political affirms the boundaries that sustain the economic as such. Given this, it would be difficult for Callon (despite his frequent association with Foucault) to entertain the Foucauldian proposition that the economy itself might be brought to an end.

This entanglement between expertise and economy is developed most elegantly in Tim Mitchell's *The Rule of Experts*, a study of the process of modernization in Egypt during the middle of the twentieth century. The promise of national development by which a nationally bounded economy would be exported for imitation through the work of techno-scientific expertise was to force native populations into a state of modernity by treating their existing conditions of life as a litany of ills and missed potential in need of repair—hence, a fixing of the economy. The work of expertise operated on the gap opened between oppositions such as that of nature and technology, backwardness and development. Yet paradoxically, these binaries are never fully achieved or achievable; hence, expertise must insinuate itself into this very gap between the problems they bring to notice and the solutions deemed worthy of attention with all the force of a self-justifying rationality of capitalist development. The problem that the idea of the economy was meant to fix, then, lay in ways to see and organize the world by means of a few simple measures such as fiscal and monetary balances that would delimit as inevitable progress what was an otherwise fragile and uncertain accomplishment. Mitchell's grasp of these contradictory dynamics bears quoting at length:

> Thus the simple idea of "externality" rests upon the operation of complex and mobile forms of law, international convention, government, corporate power, and economics. These multiple arrangements make possible the economy. Property rights, tax rules, contract and criminal law, administrative regulation, and policing all contribute to fixing the difference between the formal and the informal, between the act of exchange and its externalities, between those with rights and those without, between measurable values and the unmeasurable. . . . To apply a rule, for example, one must negotiate its limits and exceptions, since no rule contains its own interpretation. These negotiations become part of the act of exchange they are supposed to regulate. To act according to an implicit understanding, or an accepted norm, one must engage over time in a series of exchanges, economic and noneconomic, out of which the norm or understanding emerges. To enforce a regulation involves all the expense and interactions of adjudication, resort to force, and monitoring. At every one of these points the "frame" opens up and reveals its dual nature. Instead of acting as a limit, containing the economic, it becomes a series of exchanges and connections that involve the act of exchange in a potentially limitless series of further interactions. Thus the problem of fixing the economy is not a residual one of accounting for informal and clandestine activities, or turning externalities into internal costs. The problem is that the frame or border of the economy is not a line on a map, but a horizon that at every point opens up into other territories.[44]

Here we have a process already mired in uncertainty, one constantly negotiating the relation between its inside and outside, where the external is already internal and the prior assumption is already anticipated in the consequence.

The question then would become: At what point is this very border no longer visible from this moving horizon? When do the other territories make their very scene of origin illegible? Granted, from within this vertiginous and volatile relation of expertise and knowledge, it would be difficult to mark a single moment in which sovereignty could no longer be presumed. When frames, boundaries, partitions no longer do their work, the array of relations and practices they had organized and classified do not simply cease to exist, but they cannot add up in the same way. The world looks to be moving differently. It is tough to say where. The new queasiness would look much like the old, and the experts would continue on their way acting as if they still ruled the world (but, perhaps, for their own admission to the contrary). If economists and other calculating agents were the motor for the economy and not simply the recorders of something outside themselves—in Donald MacKenzie's terms, "an engine, not a camera"—then these experts' inability to make markets from what they knew and did would spell the economy's demise.[45]

Yet if crisis and conflict are normative, it would be hard to discern when a series of misfires would no longer have a mark to find. All manner of economic agency and market activity would continue even as the target was lost. If economists could not fix the economy any longer; if their rules and devices seemed unreasonable and dysfunctional; if the restoration of profitability and bonuses, the repayment of credit and accelerated productivity did not convince people that health for anyone but financiers had been restored, what would count as evidence that the economists were no longer capable of working their magic? One measure might be the extent to which economists, by virtue of their own externality to the formal domain of political decision, could claim that their prognostications were grounded in nature-like laws.

A consequence of the terms of dispute after the bailout was the report that economists no longer occupied this partitioned terrain. During the debates over the debt ceiling that took place in the summer of 2011, the *New York Times* reported from what could easily look like a moment after the frame or horizon of economy was gone:

> The politicians grappling over how to pay the nation's debts have been contributing to the heat of summer with back-and-forth charges that their opponents are disregarding the laws of economics. Such laws, unfortunately, do not exist. . . . The absence of a clear mainstream is one underappreciated reason for the standoff between the Obama administration and Congressional Republicans over raising the federal debt limit. . . . "I just don't think economists have any comparative advantage" in answering these questions, said Joel Slemrod, a University of Michigan professor and a

leading expert on taxation. "There are a lot of reasons why sensible people might disagree about the answers to the fiscal questions that we face. It's a value judgment that the citizens of the country have to make."[46]

This political dispute both relies on an economic truth, which is presented as indeterminate, and treats the economy as a referent of uncertain effect, as if it very well could be a corpse. The proposal to refuse to provide revenue for existing commitments stands both as a suggestion that the economy be brought (again) into crisis and a refusal to believe that it could be placed in default if its debt capacity is not increased. A part of this public presentation is the refusal to recognize that economists have any special purchase on "fiscal questions," a predicament in which contrary views of economists, rather than being matters of internal dispute, are treated as canceling the privileged perspective of the discipline in directing economic decision. Economists now have to share their calculative agency with all manner of public personae, including politicians who came to office through a conservative critique of the bailout.

The Tea Party representatives and congressional novices whose voices are amplified to majority status apply their own investment-based strategy of shorting government or betting that it will fail or depreciate in value. The wager that government will lose its traction over policy and influence over popular imagination is based more on a moral right and effort to assert political will than any claim to have privileged expert knowledge about how economies work. The downgrade of U.S. government debt from the perfect AAA it had held since 1941 to a AA+ on August 5, 2011, by Standard and Poor's, one of three major ratings agencies, was made due to the bipartisan conflicts over the debt ceiling and budget balancing. Standard and Poor's cited "political risks" as the basis for its economic decision, a sign of how explicit the embedding of the political in the economic had become.[47] That programs would be unfunded or that future generations would be left out of a set of benefits enjoyed by their forebears departs measurably from the promises of expert-led development and knowledge-shared prosperity that Mitchell so perceptively described.

Nonknowledge

The conceit of economy as claimed thus far is that all can know themselves through the actions of those who know the market. Economy, then, is the successful completion of a syllogism: If economists make economies and others apply their knowledge in the same way, then economy must be what we all make together, which makes us together. The market frees knowledge from the minds of experts to our common expertise. The economy, then, would be the achievement of this singularity, the common sense of purpose that comes when all act as if their calculative agency would indeed redound to their benefit. Without this equilibration of decision, capitalism might just be lived as if it were the "-ism" or society of capital and not a society of producers. If the economy named this particular suspension of disbelief, knowledge is what rendered shared sensibility through participation believable. If all possessed knowledge, could wield it to their benefit or detriment under conditions free of force and coercion or distraction from external consequences or complications, that happy state neoliberals like to refer to as freedom might just be achieved.

Hence, if the matter of economy is knowledge, its antimatter would be nonknowledge. If knowledge cannot fix the economy, nonknowledge would have its moment to come rushing in. What this other to knowledge amounts to is complex and varied. As Mirowski noted, nonknowledge could be consistent with the economists' program if it were merely an information asymmetry, either because some had privileged access or because ignorance was engendered through deliberate withholding of damaging data, like the deleterious effects of smoking tobacco. Nonknowledge could simply stand for what still needs to be learned to correct present insufficiencies. Failure leads us to try again, come up with better solutions to problems, and turn ignorance back to a source of inspiration for progress. Indeed, this version of nonknowledge is also the basis of techno-scientific sovereignty—the engineers who build better bridges when the existing ones collapse.[48]

Nonknowledge could, in a different meaning, announce a limit on what can be still discoverable. Physicists, who once imagined that they could get any experiment funded and built, now realize that from an empirical perspective, many of their most revered questions may have to go unanswered. The physicist Russell Stannard notes that string theory aimed to unlock the limits of quantum mechanics by positing yet smaller particles that displayed the properties that the hypothesis regarding the origins of the universe would predict. "It would be a physical impossibility to build an accelerator capable of probing such distances; it would have to be the size of a galaxy," he writes. "This whole question of point-like particles or strings may well turn out to be unsolvable." He goes on to note that his field has pursued a kind of Holy Grail that would provide an explanation of all imaginable phenomena, a theory of everything: "If one is a reductionist, then one holds that the physical is all that there is, and hence the theory does indeed cover everything. But if one believes that even a complete theory of the physical world would still not account for everything—consciousness, free will, aesthetics, morals, the spiritual—then such a claim is without foundation."[49]

The first kind of nonknowledge would be an unknown known, something discoverable by application of expertise. The second type would be a known unknown, something imaginable but impossible to verify through observation. A third kind of nonknowledge would be an unknown unknown, a formulation keyed to former U.S. Secretary of Defense Donald Rumsfeld. When Rumsfeld was asked at a press conference at North Atlantic Treaty Organization headquarters in Brussels on June 6, 2002, about why the situation regarding terrorism and weapons of mass destruction was worse than the facts showed, he responded:

> Sure. All of us in this business read intelligence information. And we read it daily and we think about it and it becomes, in our minds, essentially what exists. And that's wrong. It is not what exists.
>
> I say that because I have had experiences where I have gone back and done a great deal of work and analysis on intelligence information and looked at important countries, target countries, looked at important subject matters with respect to those target countries and asked, probed deeper and deeper and kept probing until I found out what it is we knew, and when we learned it, and when it actually had existed. And I found that, not to my surprise, but I think anytime you look at it that way what you find is that there are very important pieces of intelligence information that countries, that spend a lot of money, and a lot of time with a lot of wonderful people trying to learn more about what's going in the world, did not know some significant event for two years after it happened, for four years after it happened, for six years after it happened, in some cases 11 and 12 and 13 years after it happened.
>
> Now what is the message there? The message is that there are no "knowns." There are things we know that we know. There are known unknowns. That is to say there are things that we now know we don't know. But there are also unknown unknowns. There are things we don't know we don't know. So when we do the best we can and we pull all this information together, and we then say well that's basically what we see as the situation, that is really only the known knowns and the known unknowns. And each year, we discover a few more of those unknown unknowns.

It sounds like a riddle. It isn't a riddle. It is a very serious, important matter.

There's another way to phrase that and that is that the absence of evidence is not evidence of absence. It is basically saying the same thing in a different way. Simply because you do not have evidence that something exists does not mean that you have evidence that it doesn't exist. And yet almost always, when we make our threat assessments, when we look at the world, we end up basing it on the first two pieces of that puzzle, rather than all three.

Yes, sir.[50]

Rumsfeld was in Brussels to garner support for the global war on terror, a conflict based on a doctrine of preemptive and open-ended engagement that combines what expert intelligence discloses with what it cannot. Risk and uncertainty here encounter a third term, a generative absence that constitutes the environment of threat. Without factoring in unknown unknowns, threats can simply be identified when they arise and can then be eliminated or prepared for and defended against. The need to strike militarily before the threat has materialized and after it seemingly has been eliminated attends to the ongoing production of the unknown in the midst of knowledge. This is to be the specificity of terror— namely, that attacking it through unprecedented collections of information is a condition of its very multiplication both in terms of measurable acts, which increased seven-fold once the war on terror began, but also as a matter of creating enormous fields of volatility that spilled out of the national territories of Afghanistan and Iraq.[51] The collateral damage in Iraq—one million dead, five million displaced, shattered political and civil infrastructure—are treated not as genocide, which similar disruptions in, say, Rwanda and Sudan have been formally designated, but as a puzzle for an imperial intelligence to ponder while rendering inexhaustible its very conditions of perpetuation.[52] The intelligence failure that led the United States to invade and occupy the wrong country and then to continue to prosecute a war as if the initial mistake did not matter combined willful misrepresentation regarding the existence of weapons of mass destruction and links to al-Qaeda, a refusal to learn about local political circumstances that would affect pacification, and an indifference toward the consequences of long-term occupation either for Iraq or for the United States and its relations to other nations.[53] Knowledge failure, here mistaking the absence of evidence for the evidence of absence, ensures a problem that knowledge will be obliged to address but will never master.

This generalized condition of knowledge failure translates into a world that becomes an ever riskier place. The long histories of imperial war-fare and colonial usurpation, of environmental devastation and deple-tion, increase the frequency and scope of catastrophic events. The shift onto individuals for the burdens and consequences of these externalities contributes to a state of manufactured uncertainty in which institutions themselves become sources rather than managers of risk and experts are mistrusted even as demands increase on their performance. This is Ulrich Beck's vision of a world risk society, which he has developed to incorporate an ever expansive palette of sites and conditions for dangerous and unwant-ed consequences of human assertions over their environments. "Manufac-tured uncertainties make society more reliant than ever on security and control," Beck writes. "The combination of knowledge and non-knowing of global risks, in particular, destabilizes the established systems of national and international 'relations of definition.' It may sound ironic, but it is pre-cisely the unknown unknowns which provoke the major conflicts over the definition and construction of political rules and responsibilities—with the aim of preventing the worst."[54]

The preemptive strike for which Rumsfeld served as the apologist acted in anticipation of what could be observed or what there was adequate evi-dence for—in that case, war against Iraq. The anticipatory action could not in actuality be preventative, as the purported harm had already occurred in the form of the formation of a terrorist state. The premise of the war on terror was that targeted intervention against specific risks could stave off larger uncertainty if violence spread around the world through the shad-owy networks such as al-Qaeda in which it was conveyed. The financial crisis presented itself in a similar aspect, where now intervention was to be affirmative rather than destructive, to identify those institutions too big to fail that would spread contagion elsewhere but whose targeted rescue could stanch generalized collapse. Although the crisis was already under way, just as the terror war had already been joined, intervention in the form of bailout was positioned preemptively. Naming the end of the economy rendered it otherwise impossible to contemplate. From Beck's perspective, this collision between preemptive action and the impossibility of its success stages a turn in the social order: "World risk society is a *non*-knowledge society in a very precise sense. In contrast to the premodern era, it can-not be overcome by more and better knowledge, more and better science; rather precisely the opposite holds: it is the *product* of more and better sci-ence. Non-knowledge rules in the world risk society. Hence, living in the milieu of manufactured non-knowing means seeking unknown answers to questions that nobody can clearly formulate."[55]

For Beck, nonknowledge and uncertainty have the effect of equalizing expert and nonexpert decision-making preferences and abilities beyond national and state authority, hence contributing to a cosmopolitan global civil society as a kind of pluralistic ideal in which allowing dissent over knowledge yields a more robust consensus. Society, in this view, still bears traces of the collective mind and supreme decision maker that runs from the legacies of nineteenth-century sociology to Hayek's conception of the market. If the nonknowledge sanctioned by world risk society normalizes anxious pronouncements of mounting danger while embracing some mechanism of decision making as the best means of distributing this inescapably fearful state, then the social may prove more constraining a realm of freedom than the economic turned out to be. Ultimately and despite claims to the contrary, this is a tragic reading of risk and nonknowledge, where they result in disruptive externalities whose deleterious consequences need to be shared more equitably but nonetheless accepted as a feature of the new order. That risk society is in some ways isomorphic with the market may explain the cognitive emphasis in society and the paucity of attention given to questions of production, labor, creativity, corporality, or other means in which risk itself could be taken as internally generative.

This very different understanding of nonknowledge and economy is found in the work of Georges Bataille. His comparison of various general economies suggested some occult or unabsorbable part he termed "the accursed share," the expenditure in any society of an "excess energy, translated into the effervescence of life"[56] If nonknowledge paradoxically gets instrumentalized through the closed systems-based conceptions of economy and society, Bataille is willing to consider it as a capacity of deinstrumentalization, as in his remark that nonknowledge is "knowledge that brings me to nothing."[57] Far from a tragic emptiness, he sees in this a condition in which there is not necessarily movement toward something determinate but also "there is not even any guarantee as to the limits of the movements that can occur."[58] Beyond the telos of cognitive decision making that drives collective action toward the norms of a perfectible decision-making machinery, nonknowledge opens what can be done together and elicits a visceral response, something that takes in excess and yields a moment of joy:

> One of the most remarkable aspects of the domain of the unforeseeable unknown is given in the laughable, in the objects that excite in us this effect of intimate overturning, of suffocating surprise, that we call laughter.

We would laugh, not for a reason that we would not happen to know, for lack of information, or for want of sufficient penetration, but because *the unknown makes us laugh*.

In sum, it makes us laugh to pass very abruptly, all of a sudden from a world in which each thing is well qualified, in which each thing is given in its stability, generally in a stable order, to a world in which our assurance is suddenly overthrown, in which we perceive that this assurance is deceptive, and where we believed that everything was strictly anticipated, an unforeseeable and upsetting element appeared unexpectedly from the unforeseeable, that reveals to us in sum a final truth: that superficial appearances conceal a perfect lack of response to our anticipation.

We see that finally, given the exercise of knowledge, the world is likewise situated completely out of the reach of this exercise, and even that not only the world, but the being that we are, is out of reach. There is, in us and in the world, something that reveals that knowledge was not given to us, and that situates itself uniquely as being unable to be attained by knowledge. This, it seems to me, is that at which we laugh. And fundamentally, one must to say it immediately, when it is a question of a theory of laughter, this is what illuminates us and what fills us with joy.[59]

Given the misery that finance and other manufactured uncertainties have visited on us, it might seem especially untoward and uncritically irreverent to shift appropriate affect from fear and rage to laughter and joy. But Bataille is not talking about laughing at people's misery or taking joy in their misfortune. Rather than laughing all the way to the bank, this affective shift would ask what joy might spring when something else is taken away from the bank and its conventional means of account. This is a politics made from a condition of ignorance, what Robert Proctor calls "agnotology," which leads us back to the fateful relation between knowledge and human interest: "Decisions about what kind of knowledge 'we' want to support are also decisions about what kinds of ignorance should remain in place. . . . People have extracted very different things from different kinds of unknowns, and will no doubt continue to mix suspect with admirable reasons for letting those flourish or disappear."[60]

But Bataille seems to be inviting something different by opening a more active channel of response to what otherwise appears as a loss of control and certainty that leads to a desire for more of what yielded that dilemma to begin with. The unavailability of surplus funds; the scarcity of food, water, fuel; the instabilities of war need not be presented as the inevitable outcome of knowledge limits or risk. Something else would need to be found in both of these conditions to see what other directions of movement may be among us but not necessarily upon us. Such a shift in register might require that we move more directly into the space once occupied by economy, the claims on a "we," a public, a capacity for wealth, and a purpose for prosperity. The gambit here is that these conditions are matters of immanence rather than transcendence; that in the smoke and mirrors, decks of cards, confusion and outrage that has gone by the name of the financial crisis, we might just be able to locate some joy if we know how to look and what to do with what we miss.

From Nonknowledge to Derivative Logics

If economy has an afterlife that is more than the sum of its ruins, it will now be necessary to tell the story forward. To break the conceptual stranglehold of inevitable crisis in which destruction begets its own creative renewal and leaves the precepts of economy intact, other forces will need to be given value. An alternative framework will need to move beyond nostalgia for the lost island of blissfully knowable equilibrium and toward grasping the presence of those logics that prosper when nonknowledge assumes the mantle of a prevailing productive force. We have already heard a tale of societies of risk, uncertainty, and nonknowledge whose financial interface lies with the evanescence of the derivative. Derivatives are typically described as technical features of finance that, in turn, are but an adjunct to the real economy. Disaster ensued when derivatives escaped from their rightful place and inundated other quarters. Derivatives made something out of nothing as a greedy few took advantage while regulators looked away.

While this is the standard story, it begs many questions, not the least of which is where this logic of the derivative came from and how it came to be predominant. If derivatives broke the economy, were they simply an internal contradiction of utility maximizing or pursuit of profits? Accordingly, excising or containing derivatives would allow the damaging flood waters to recede from the social lowlands and return to the higher ground of an economy whose integrity had been restored. But if derivatives are not essentially economic but feature in all manner of social relations, sites, and forms, containing how and where their logic is expressed may be as difficult as reassembling economy from its tousled shards. While derivative principles have been applied in economic settings for thousands of years, albeit without the materiality or impact they currently exercise, their logic has a presence in many fields.[61] Despite entering august dictionary listings and public discourse only in the past decade, derivatives actually have a long history and complex genealogy that incorporates meanings from law, medicine, geology, engineering, chemistry, music, calculus, and grammar. In all of these senses, derivatives are a transmission of some value from a source to something else, an attribute of that original expression that can be combined with like characteristics, a variable factor that can move in harmony or dissonance with others.[62]

In the technical sense that obtains within financial services, derivatives are conventionally understood as contracts to exchange a certain amount of something at a determinate future time at an agreed-on price. For example, a furniture manufacturer in Europe is making tables for a U.S. retailer that will be ready in six months and will charge a million euros at an exchange rate of a euro and a half to the dollar. But should that rate change if the dollar appreciates or goes up against the euro, the manufacturer stands to lose money when the tables are ready for shipment and so is willing to spend a thousand euros for the right to exchange at the agreed-on rate rather than losing more money if the exchange rate becomes, say, 1.6 euros to the dollar. On the other side of the pond, for the purchaser, the impact would be reversed; the U.S. retailer would get the tables for fewer dollars but might readily want to protect itself from appreciation of the dollar against the euro. The agreement to exchange at a fixed rate acts as insurance that hedges against this risk. By so doing, the risk, or possibility of a deviant but predictable outcome, is also priced through a contract that can be exchanged and therefore becomes an instrument of investment that hedges against a range of possible gains or losses. In this case, there are derivatives contracts in circulation for currency fluctuations in both directions based on the same sale. But risks and occasions to create derivatives for various eventualities that emanate from a single exchange abound. For example, the sale of tables can be subject not only to currency fluctuations but also to the possible cancellation of the order or a bank's inability to pay. As a consequence, the sum total of all derivative contracts far exceeds the actual or underlying price of the assets being traded. As global transactions have increased, more and more kinds of risk are priced—from exchange and interest rates to changes in temperature and the weather.

While derivative contracts for agricultural prices have been in existence for thousands of years, derivatives in their current guise date from the 1970s and began to be traded extensively on formal exchanges in the 1990s. The quantity of publicly traded derivatives is exceeded by over-the-counter contracts made directly between parties. The contracts do not terminate the exchange; only small percentages are actually paid when they come due. Rather, the contracts are kept open or in ongoing exchange through what are called clearinghouses. The result is a continuous circulation of debt instruments and an integration of local production into global markets and chances to make money whether prices on those markets rise or fall. While derivatives reap tens of billions in revenue for traders and, if cashed in, would be worth tens of trillions (specifically, $27 trillion—that is, less than the stock and bond markets, which globally have a market capitalization of some $200 trillion, but more than the annual global GDP of some $75 trillion), the face or notional value of all derivative contracts in 2012 continued to increase since the effective bailout and was $.15 quadrillion.[63]

Capital had claimed "economy" as the name of its social relations. The task here is to explore what social logic is disclosed through the derivative that would account for its expansion and impact beyond profit-taking exchange or as a mere succession in an unbroken chain of ever more effective regimes of accumulation. Here "logic" will need to be a point of departure, not closure or completion—a mode of account, a means of telling and counting (*lego*); hence, a sensibility that draws things together in a particular way while moving beyond itself. Capital accumulation has also generated an abundance of social relations, mutualities, and encumbrances that it could not abide. It flees the socialities it engenders and moves toward those of which it wants but a part. The derivative is no different. It draws on all manner of value forms that are already in motion, if not already to hand.

Beyond the pervasiveness of the phenomenon, however, the question arises as to why it is useful analytically and politically to think the social through the lens of the derivative. Demonstrating these various resonances will require a wide-ranging approach, but a few provisional points can be made at the outset. First, we could say that a derivative logic speaks to what is otherwise balefully named fragmentation, dispersion, or isolation by allowing us to recognize ways in which the concrete particularities—the specific engagements, commitments, and interventions we tender and expend—might be interconnected without first or ultimately needing to appear as a single whole or unity of practice or perspective. Second, derivatives articulate what is made in motion, how production is inside circulation, and, as such, how to notice the value of our work in the midst of volatility. Third, derivatives work through the agency of arbitrage, of small interventions that make significant difference, of a generative risk in the face of generalized failure but on behalf of desired ends. To recognize and realize these other kinds of gains that might issue from a more fully elaborated social logic of the derivative, we must pull it from the wreckage of the economic where its conventional meanings are interred.

Far from Equilibrium Regulation

What appeared to be a forecast for what might take place over a weekend turned out to resemble more closely a reflection on changes under way for the prior thirty years. "Economy" thus names the harmonious state of a national population whose internal balance can be held in account through common growth and individual prosperity. As a category of inclusion, the term permits differences generated by inequality, unemployment, and surplus populations, or that between labor and capital, to be contained and unified as matters of degree subject to its common laws and measures. This notion of economy launched in the nineteenth century as a mechanism by which energy could be profitably conserved in the form of utility achieves a massive edifice of implementation during the twentieth century that is modeled mathematically as information processing that yields equilibrium.[64] Economy stood as the effective lamination between a logical and a social tautology. The logic of machine-like efficiency of markets held that they would be populated by rational information processors, where information was visible to all and the impact of decisions were readily transparent and sublimely reflected in prices. Anyone behaving irrationally by pulling markets away from their state of equilibrium would be punished by losses. Economy generalizes the particular condition of profit taking enjoyed by those with private property to all people who approach life as a process of maximizing gain to themselves. Since these actions took place within a national space to which all belonged by virtue of acting within them, the self-regulating virtues of economy were a cognate of democracy, or universal participation.

Knowledge was key to this slippage between quantity and quality, between inputs that could be measured and modeled and intrinsic properties such as being nonexcludable (i.e., it escapes control by producers) and nonrival (i.e., it can be used by many at once without being used up) that made knowledge nonproprietary or a public good, an expression of what was held in common, like the air.[65] The initial challenges to charging for information have been steadily overcome through emerging protocols of intellectual property. As markets emerge to draw revenue from what was once considered unprofitable, the distinctive space, quality, and character of public goods are diminished. Education is measured according to tests of productivity, and even air quality is now priced through such mechanisms as cap and trade, which treats pollution as a property right whose levels will be ameliorated through exchange between those who produce more and those who make less.[66] The mechanics of equilibrium claimed an alignment with the balanced scales of justice. For economy to be sustained, all relevant information by which markets were made would need to pertain to all who would be subject to the national account. What was billed as the ascent of the market to realize the true workings of the economy in actuality had unglued the former from the latter. There was still plenty of evidence that the mechanisms and operations associated with an economy were around. Indeed, the machinery that turned out the evidence remained in place, and the surfeit of data would readily leave the impression that the economy was damaged but intact. The validity of these particular measures would become a much harder sell if economy lost its demotic calling and ceased to do the work of stitching together the many and the few under the felicitous sign of knowledge. Experts' insistence that people would need to sacrifice their livelihoods to rescue the national economy from default consequently would be met with increasing incredulity.

The limits that had always been the boundary condition for knowledge production now threatened to overwhelm the rule that knowledge had set in place. Indeed, the first flush of crisis explanations pin their hopes on a return of regulation and transparency, as if rules per se had been absent and they could be applied like cement to fill in a hole. But contrary to the fable of triumphant neoliberalism in which capital was freed from the strictures of government interference, the generalization of knowledge elaborated the machinery of regulation not only as an apparent externality delivered by the state, but also as an internal condition for financial engineering.[67] As the conditions for capital's success become increasingly complex, more regulation, not less, is required and must be taken ever more deeply into the process of accumulation. Freeing capital from the state is neither possible nor desirable, yet the best course and outcome for regulatory intervention is unknown. As both the government actions to restructure mortgage and financial services and the bailout that ensued, business asks for more, not less, even as it protests this assistance as so much interference in its affairs. Here, taxpayers, citizens, immigrants, social movements, the poor, and the at-risk would be wise to take their lead from business self-confidence regarding government entitlements.

The wealth of nations is a political project whose welfare and sustainability cannot be left to its prime beneficiaries. This was, of course, the point of political economy before it became dismembered into politics and economics. In the hands of the social scientists who staked their own knowledge claims on this partition, the differentiation and specialization was a hallmark of the process of rationalization or rule governance that propelled modern society forward. At their most general expression, rules mark the scene of conflict or contestation. They are the material residue of a dispute that, in turn, shapes terms of opposition, conditions of resolution, and strategies of benefit. Indeed, the very model of a rational actor optimizing information to make decisions that maximize benefits and minimizes costs assumes that human behavior abides by predictable laws such that rules are both constitutive and the consequence of deliberative activity.[68]

By many measures, there are more rules for corporations and individuals than ever before. The *Federal Register*, which records all nonclassified proposed and final regulations, presidential decrees and proclamations, and announcements of government actions had swelled to more than eighty thousand pages by the end of the Bush presidency in 2008, and the cumulative *Code of Federal Regulations* grew by some five thousand pages during his tenure, to 145,816 pages.[69] Beyond page count and the dull facts of mounting regulatory density, at issue is not simply the sheer volume of rules but what they are for and what they produce.[70] Even what is called "deregulation" rewrites rather than erases extant statutes. As finance becomes more prevalent in scope and scale, more complex in its applications, it is implicated in ever wider webs of regulatory attention and reaction; it creates conflicts that require resolution; and it incorporates existing rules in ways that make its operations even more volatile.

Financialization, the process by which perquisites of finance increasingly come to orient the expansion of wealth and the metrics of daily life, entails a shift in policy emphasis from providing security to managing risk.[71] The former is a condition for which citizenship prequalifies one, whereas the latter is earned on the basis of performance assessment. Stripping away security from citizens in the name of unleashing their productivity implements force through the rule of law. Enabling a pervasive environment of risk benefit requires active support for business initiatives that range from relocation and retooling to litigation and negotiation over jurisdiction in local and global markets. Before there was a bailout, government policy was persistently directed at laws that would create incentives for certain capital flows and agglomerations through tax abatement, credits, subventions, and international treaties such as the General Agreement on Tariffs and Trade. The conservative complaint about increasing the size of government is not based on a mistaken observation of trends. Instead, it makes a consideration of public qualities or capacities all the more inaccessible. The regime of intellectual property, from informatics and biotechnology to education and

finance, is itself a rulemaking machinery that requires increasing regulation for its operation. This surfeit of rules contributes to the incoherence
by which knowledge becomes excessed as nonknowledge, by which the surplus of the unknown that inhabits uncertainty is borne insufficiently and
inadequately in models of risk. The swelling risks that need to be hedged
contributed to the climate for the mounting creation of derivatives, whose
face value increased tenfold between 1998 and 2007—from less than $100
trillion to more than $1 quadrillion.[72]

While the florescence of derivatives has been accompanied by a massive expansion and concentration of the rulemaking capacities and expressions of the state, the past thirty years have also been characterized by
what could be called regulatory disintermediation. That markets are to be
self-regulating hints at what they make, but it also refers to the spread of
regulatory capacity from a state monopoly over individual actors and firms
to become the province of sectors, associations, and industries. Not only are
more entities at different scales engaged in rulemaking, but also different
professionals may operate on the same rules to markedly different effect.
Describing what has been a formalization of regulatory frameworks over
the past several decades from a "bottom-up social norm of business practice" to a "top-down prescription" Shyam Sunder, an accounting professor
at Yale, describes the "unequal battle" waged between financial reporting
and engineering:

> It may take a few years for the FASB [the U.S. Financial Account-
> ing Standards Board] or IASB [International Accounting Standards
> Board] to make its policy in the form of a rule on an accounting
> issue (unless it is under pressure from the U.S. Congress or a Gallic
> politician, in which case years are compressed into days). It takes
> mere hours or days for the financial engineer to circumvent the new
> accounting rules intended to put constraints on managers. While
> accountants are limited to doing the accounting for transactions
> chosen by the managers, the latter are free to devise the transac-
> tions, instruments, and even organizations (recall Enron's three
> thousand special purpose entities) to circumvent the intent of the
> financial accounting rules. The history of leases and various kinds
> of financial derivatives and securitization provides a wealth of evi-
> dence. . . . Yet financial engineering has played a critical role not
> only in defeating the intent of financial accounting rules, but also
> pushing the rules toward increasing detail in fruitless attempts to
> plug the holes. Ironically, the more specific the rules get, the easier

is the job of the financial engineer: specificity reduces uncertainty about violating the rules.[73]

Here the violation of the rules is the basis for crafting new financial products, which themselves take the form of contracts or terms of agreement directly between parties. The removal of go-betweens, or disintermediation, is evident in banking and government, as well as in more kinds of regulatory contracts that are crafted and placed in circulation. The symbiosis between accountants and engineers is a matter of not shared intent but interdependence of consequence, for the labors of each are made possible by the gaps in the work of the other. The resulting derivative sustains the temporal and spatial displacement—namely, what takes place over years versus hours and out of sight but in anticipation of what others will do. The enhanced regulatory environment has been driven by and readily incorporated into financial engineering practices. While specificity of regulation becomes a factor of production in directing where new products need to be developed, it is also a condition for future demand based on the increased uncertainty as to what escalating violation will yield.

This paradox of regulation in a knowledge economy is that it is derided as unnecessary for transparently knowable markets yet essential for them to work to price nonknowledge of the future. The disdain for regulation that one depends on for benefit fits the Tea Party temperament but also describes the situation of arbitrage, of one whose opportunity derives from the gap between momentary price differences and fundamental value. Arbitrage is conventionally understood as risk-free, or a free lunch, because it entails a privileged identification of a discrepancy between a price for the same product found in two different market settings or exchanges. Say, for example, a derivative contract such as an agreement to exchange currencies at a given price and point in time is selling for $20.15 on the Mexican Derivatives Exchange and for $20.18 on the Turkish Derivatives Exchange. Buying ten million of these futures contract at the lower price and selling at the higher price would yield an immediate gain of $300,000. From this perspective, arbitrage opportunities presumably would be self-dissolving, as they would signal the price difference and close the gap, thereby restoring equilibrium to a market that tends toward an arbitrage-free state. But hedging is a deliberate strategy for creating arbitrage opportunities by leveraging a small discrepancy in price into a large gain.

Here the moment of disclosure would come if there was a large loss that affected the related positions—in this case, the investment would be termed speculative. Besides moral evaluation of what constitutes ethical and unethical bases of profit, true and speculative arbitrage rest on a stable partition of knowledge between private and public. This is the distinction made in the seminal 1954 paper on social prediction by Emile Grunberg and Franco Modigliani that asserts that the distorting effects of private information asymmetries will be balanced through public disclosure as expectations for outcomes are discrete in number, thereby constituting what is termed a "bounded rationality." Rather than distorting predictive action by changing how people perceive what is likely to come to pass, information feedback aligns what they decide with what they expect. This is, of course, the familiar tautology of equilibrium; what disallows this condition, in their view, is "speculation": "This is the case where individuals may find a *general climate of uncertainty* desirable and therefore set out to make prediction in general—rather than specific predictions only—impossible by systemic falsification." This they deem an unrealistic scenario that is formally possible but not "empirically important." This environment would be unsustainable because signaling a prediction would foreclose other choices. The predictor, even though he knows the agents' intentions, must publish his prediction—that is, commit himself—while the agents remain free to choose their own actions afterward in full knowledge of what has been predicted."[74]

If a general climate of uncertainty has become desirable because it is now empirically important, the portrayal of agency as decision that can be formally or mathematically modeled (what Grunberg and Modigliani undertake) cannot be explained away as an instance of collusion. The logically incompatible maneuver of committing to one decision and keeping open others is what derivatives make possible, general, and desirable. The focus on this paper among a suite of seminal treatments that will establish the basis for the derivatives pricing model is meant to show that the understanding of the problem that derivatives both solve and abet is already imagined at the inception of what will come to serve as their logic.

Whereas transparency initially was to be the norm and opacity the special case, the expansion of derivatives effectively encourages these two values to trade places. The result is the rise of "shadow banks" and "dark pools" that seek to shield risk from the market and regulatory body's scrutiny. This capacity to hedge against what supervisory bodies require is called regulatory arbitrage. Accordingly, a bank could decide that its risk of defaulting is actually lower (or higher) than what would be covered by its mandated capital reserves. It could create a derivative contract that would enable it to profit from this risk calculation. In 1998, Alan Greenspan anticipated such responses to reserve requirements established by the

Basel Accords, which in his mind arbitrarily set an 8 percent capital standard that applied to all corporate loans, irrespective of their particular risk characteristics. Since some banks would seek greater holdings and others less, there was an incentive for arbitrage trading among them to align the regulation's expectation of their exposure with their own internal assessments.[75] Yet what was before the bailout another tool for profiting from a given knowledge assessment was in the aftermath labeled by some economists a purposeful avoidance or evasion of the rules and the scrutiny of regulators in pursuit of profits at any cost.[76]

Paradoxically, this evasion took the form of rendering their investments more subject to common forces and factors beyond their own authorship precisely in a manner like the regulatory environment they were said to be avoiding. The securitization process that accompanied the growth in subprime mortgages managed risk by removing debts more likely to default from the accounts of the lending institutions, which at the same time rendered those risks and who, precisely, held or controlled them equally opaque. Accordingly, risk that prices an outcome based on the probability of foreseeable expectations is converted into uncertainty in which both inputs and outcomes are unknown. In the case of the implosion of the subprime mortgage market, not being able to calculate precise risk exposures made it impossible to distinguish banks that momentarily did not have sufficient reserves or lines of credit to cover immediate losses (illiquidity) from those institutions that had no equity or collateral that could be drawn on (insolvency). The result was a flight from the unknown.

Capitalism with Derivatives

Whereas what has been described as the economy imagines that price is the moment of a resolution of difference, the derivative operates through the conditions of generalized uncertainty as a bearer of this ongoing contestation over value in which the relation between knowledge and nonknowledge is governed. This is key to the pathbreaking contribution of Dick Bryan and Mike Rafferty in their analysis of what they term "capitalism with derivatives," which might here be taken as shorthand for what follows upon the economy. Unlike most accounts of finance from the perspective of political economy, theirs is neither a sectoral nor a stage theory. Granted, derivatives are now "with" capitalism in a way they were not before, but they do much of the work once covered by economy without the same forms of anchoring equivalence or geopolitical integration. Their innovative work merits due attention—both for how it allows a rethinking of finance and for what it opens for a consideration of social logics. Derivatives first appear as a mechanism for securing the price of a commodity whose production, like a crop, will be delivered at some point in the future, as with nonsubsistence agriculture and the formation of ancient cities such as Babylon. They came to apply to other commodities, from raw materials to finished goods, where an option to purchase a certain amount at a fixed price could be set, or to swap one risk exposure for another. After the fall of the Bretton Woods system, derivatives gained increasing importance as ways to implement what would be the new financial order when there was no currency anchor to render all exchange transactions across the globe commensurate with one another.

The call of economy is that we can return to what is true, what lies close to home, what is fundamental regarding value. Accordingly, if finance was a veil of representation, restoring economy allows a return of and to what can be considered real. Yet for Bryan and Rafferty, the very notion that this real economy of values can be separated from financial markets is countermanded by derivatives trading. They observe that prices are formed in options and futures markets before they are set in cash markets. The core operation of derivatives is to bind the future to the present through a range of contractual opportunities and to make all manner of capital across disparate spheres of place, sector, and characteristic commensurate with one another. In this respect, derivatives provide some of the anchoring functions of currency sovereignty once provided by gold and dollar standards. They introduce a highly dynamic but comprehensively convertible measure of prices across time and space to stand as a form of meta-capital. They therefore elaborate and transform a process of abstracting and recalibrating concrete instances and capacities for production to conditions of universal exchange that Marx identified with the accumulation of commodities as such. Yet if commodities appeared as a unit of wealth that could abstract parts into a whole, derivatives are a still more complex process by which parts are no longer unitary but are continuously disassembled and reassembled as various attributes are bundled and their notional value exceeds the whole economy to which they may once have been summed. Shifts in scale from concrete to abstract or local to global are no longer external yardsticks of equivalence. They are internal to the circulation of the bundled attributes that derivative transactions multiply and set in motion.

But capital still bore the limitations of its concrete circumstances denominated as a national currency, fixed to particular investments in productive factors or technology, or attached to determinate conditions of labor. Each of these specific forms of capital would display indifference toward the material circumstances on which it relied: people, places, institutional surroundings with given characteristics that would place limits on how that capital could move toward more profitable circumstances. The archetypal instance would be automobile manufacturing through most of the twentieth century. Firms such as Ford would develop not only through a stable and relatively well-paid workforce secured through collective bargaining that enabled workers to afford to purchase cars and homes and receive pensions and health care, but also through an expanding tax-base for urban infrastructure and public amenities such as parks and education and federal foreign policy that delivered cheap oil and raw materials. Car makers' flight from the workers and environments that they had rendered affluent combined outsourcing parts and assembly with increased attention to financing as wages, job security, and productivity fell, but without the promise of enhanced prosperity that was restored by government investment in firms rather than a social compact.

The mass assembly line gathered all its inputs in one place to build a tightly integrated commodity that was more than the sum of its parts. Financial engineering played this process in reverse, disassembling a commodity into its constituent and variable elements and dispersing these attributes to be bundled together with the elements of other commodities of interest to a globally oriented market for risk-managed exchange. Each of these moveable parts is reassembled by risk attribute so that they become worth more as derivatives than their individual commodities, leveraged as they are for the further purchase of credit instruments. By abstracting capital from its own body, carving it up into more and less productive aspects that can be applied toward gain or loss, dispossessing any given capital of those attributes which are of greatest interest to aggregates of wealth making or terms of exchange (such as currency exchange or interest rates), derivatives do to capital what capital itself has been doing to concrete forms of money and productive conditions such as labor, raw materials, and the physical plant.

Hence, while derivatives serve as a globally exchangeable money form, they also break down the distinction between money and capital. At the same time, they make available to capital accumulation what would be considered new materialities of ideas and perceptions, weather and war, bits of code stripped from tele-technology or DNA, the microscopic and cosmic. If once derivatives required some underlying source of value—a physical commodity whose completion or delivery such as a crop or animal product their expected term of exchange was based on—now such instruments could be cooked up out of a singer's potential future earnings, or a slew of tornados that might never make landfall, or a new medicine that might never get approved for patients' use. Whatever their discrete sources or eventual realization, all manner of hitherto localized production would be converted into globally comparable variable risk profiles while at the same time inscribing all of these potential sources of value into complex schemas of pricing representation written as financial contracts.

For all their powers of integrating an ever enlarging conception of what can be considered a source of value and how price can be represented across wide spans of time and space, derivatives deliver neither equilibrium of value nor stability of price. The conceit of the system metaphor is that the relation of parts to whole is known beforehand, and that each retains its integrity, which fixes its position, interest, and contribution. Derivatives, on the other hand, disassemble and bundle attributes of commodities, thereby removing the presumption of functionality on which the machine-like metaphor of system is based. While prices are formed in futures, options, and swap markets, those prices are treated always not only provisionally but also as persistently falsifiable. At any given moment, someone else can always do better—and is doing better. Subjecting the world to the logic of derivatives means acting as if no transaction is final and there is always a globally realizable potential for improved performance. (Think of spot and futures markets for oil on which prices are constantly being renegotiated on the basis of spatially dispersed differentiated grades of oil and hedged on future movements of price based on how markets will respond to these representations of difference.)

Not only do derivatives increase opacity as they spread ownership; they also enhance volatility as they amplify risk—in both cases converting what was known and containable in its impact to what is dispersed, conflicted, and unknown. Rather than doing away with some ideal underlying or fundamental value, price is contested at every moment of its articulation. Derivatives stand as an enhanced medium of this open and ceaseless contestation. By removing one array of risk circumstances, derivatives engender a hyperactive manufacture of risk conditions insofar as they treat the volatility they produce as their general horizon of opportunity. Constant comparison in search of better opportunities makes for negotiation without end where a partner one moment is an antagonist the next while every sign of movement is grounds for anxious anticipation. As Bryan and Rafferty observe, "Derivatives are thereby the bearers of contestability. So they are crucial to the link between money, price and fundamental value not because they *actually* determine fundamental values (for there are no truths here) but because they are the way in which the market judges or perceives fundamental value.

They turn *the contestability* of fundamental value into a tradable commodity. In so doing, they provide a market benchmark for an unknowable value."[77]

Crucial in this account is the relation between contestability and unknowability, for it is the self-generating volatility that creates a measure for what cannot be known. A benchmark is a point of reference after the fact that is treated as intentional, a target to be hit based on something that has already occurred—hence, a momentary conversion of an unknown into a measure that cannot hold. The derivative serves as a kind of shuttle between the particular risk factors it bundles together and the general glare of optimum market performance as an imaginary horizon to which the measure is subject. As opposed to the fixed relation between part and whole that informs the system metaphysic, the derivative acts as the movement between these polarities that are rendered unstable through its very contestation of accurate price and fundamental value—in effect, the truth of the commodity and that of the market that economy served to bind together. Contestability is not simply what capital does to itself. It also becomes reinscribed in the managerial pressures for ever increasing productivity performance from labor. From this view, labor everywhere and at every moment is subject to a point of reference or benchmark that comes from what is now treated as a global standard of general market indicators.

Certainly, in the aftermath of the bailout when banks have refused to lend and industries have declined to hire, the spike in profits has been driven by precisely these conceptions of productivity whereby employees have been let go and those who remain are asked to make up the difference of their absent parts and partners. This is another reason that Bryan and Rafferty refuse to accept a partition between real and financial economies, as it is the financial logics that have entered the workplace and not only the externalities imposed by financial woes that have heightened contestability of the value of labor itself at the point of production. The coercive impact of heightened unemployment may make those who remain employed grateful and or the newly hired willing to work for wages a fraction of what peers receive (as was the case for newly hired autoworkers at General Motors, Ford, and Chrysler in 2011, whose $14 hourly rate is half what others in the United Auto Workers bargaining unit received).[78] In its first iteration, at least, contestability looks to be a property borne by derivatives rather than a principle that provides a means to oppose or resist their effects, which would be consistent with conventional accounts of class struggle.[79] Insofar as labor assimilates this logic, it could readily absorb the increased productivity while not experiencing itself as a part of the whole that its increased efforts are said to be serving.

If derivatives undo the mechanics of part and whole, they also undermine the relation between the visible and the invisible by which the known and the unknown had been partitioned. Since derivatives do not result in a transfer of possession or ownership, they are not recorded in accounts of assets and liabilities; therefore, they are entered as "off-balance sheet" investments. In one respect, taking assets off-book is what makes it impossible to read market signals and to know firm exposures that increase the dangers of financial traffic. Yet in a more fundamental sense, derivatives affect this movement or circulation between what can be seen but not acted on and what cannot be taken hold of but that enables activity. In terms of the firm that increasingly places bets on risks with its own capital holdings (what is termed "proprietary trading"), ownership now appears as a range of financial claims that are of variable worth because their value is linked to corporate and other assets. These amount to ownership rights associated with attributes of capital rather than goods or shares based on performance. But the discrepancy between actual prices under these circumstances and what the model of the efficient market hypothesis would predict—namely, that prices reflect all relevant information—has been noted by the most prominent economists responsible for overseeing monetary policy (Lawrence Summers, Treasury Secretary under President Bill Clinton and director of the President's Economic Council under Barack Obama) and measuring housing markets (Robert Shiller, who developed the now standard Case Shiller index and went on to share the Nobel Prize in 2013).[80] Oversight in this regard might be said to have gone off-book, as those responsible for verifying indicators falsified what would count as verification when their fees were paid by those they would claim to monitor independently and therefore provided the sterling AAA ratings on securities composed of bundles of mortgages that on their own would be considered likely to default.

Bryan and Rafferty take this rupture of the economy tautology as posing the dilemma of regulation that has been used to suggest that an extraeconomic force could restore trust and credibility in the economy. "Posed in the framework of empowering the gatekeepers, we stay entrapped in (domestic) market efficiency, an innately nationalist, conception of regulation. If, instead, we see state regulation as facilitating the global integration of financial markets, derivatives show up in different (additional) light. Derivatives in this context are not the extreme case of deregulation, but on the contrary, part of a newly emerging regulatory process."[81] What was written on the eve of the financial meltdown becomes all the more prescient today. If derivatives, unlike an autonomous object domain called "the economy," do not come at us from outside so that a wall could be built for protection but are constitutive of what is treated as protection (risk management), as such simply saying no to them, sorting the good from the bad or the known from the unknown will not be such an easy task. On the other side, if the regulators assume their positions as financial engineers in their own right, the notion that there is a political outside the economic may be the very fantasy structure that the derivative puts to rest.

Once we begin to see that the derivative is not simply an economic object that should and can be regulated by some political body that stands outside it but a figure of regulatory capacity in its own right, we have moved outside the binary that made economy possible. Rather than proving the realization of the fantasy of economy as governed by an invisible hand, the regulatory operations internal to production and circulation of value are fraught with the conflict, contestation, and assertions of power relegated to the political. If derivatives bear politics into the world and are not simply political in the sense of containable disagreements, then the integrative functions associated with economy and population will also begin to dissipate. The focus on fat tails and outliers, of stars and winners-taking-all makes it difficult to sustain rational optimizers at the center. The place where consensus is formed and the people gather to participate in civil society, again conceived along the lines of a well-functioning distributive market, will also need to be rethought accordingly as an interior of exclusion, critique, and contest.

If risk and uncertainty can no longer stand for the partition between economy and polity, then we may also need to rethink the interactions between the presumptively unproductive domain of nonknowledge from the sunny view of knowledge as economic utility maximization. While these binaries are undone, the derivative does more than point us toward some reinvigorated framework of political economy. Though no doubt such a move is crucial, the derivative also points toward the missing third term that is otherwise suppressed in current conceptions of possessive individualism realized through market participation—namely, that of the social.[82] The derivative solves some of the challenges to liquidity or revenue streams posed by what had been conceived as a public good. Knowledge that was once viewed as nonexcludable and nonrival and therefore difficult to treat as a discrete commodified object that can be priced is now converted into a contingency that can be traded in its own terms. Derivatives both price uncertainty—that is, they address the unknowable future as an array of possible outcomes that can be acted on in the present—and render the distinction between risk and uncertainty indecipherable. Opacity, volatility, and nonknowledge are obstacles not simply to controlled decision making but also to its general conditions of production and possibility.

Rather than these conditions of uncertainty overwhelming action in a cloud of doubt, price movements are imputed to have a clarity of motive that engenders overconfidence and thus increases systemic risk, as was amply in evidence in the case of failed arbitrage investments. In an ethnographic study of traders whose decisions are made individually in anticipation of what their colleagues are secretly thought to be doing, David Stark and Daniel Beunza show the traders using sophisticated models reflexively. These arbitrageurs check their own estimates as to anticipated prices against those of rival traders with whom they are in competition, a practice known as backing out. While this continuous surveillance of price volatility to divine what others are doing gives a sense of the market, it poses dangers of a false threat when the interdependence among these actors cannot be accessed and generates sudden collective moves and precipitous losses or arbitrage disasters. They conclude:

> Reflexive modeling works by providing traders with dissonance whenever their estimates are different from the majority . . . and therefore, possibly mistaken. Conversely, traders take the absence of dissonance to mean they have the correct estimate. And, critically, this modus operandi gives rise to the possibility of widespread failure: if enough traders miss a key variable, their mistake will reverberate to the others through the implied probability. Traders will develop a false confidence that their variables are sufficient, leading them to increase their positions and eventually their losses. We refer to this mechanism as resonance.[83]

This false confidence that reads their ungovernable sociality or interdependence as an affirmation of the individual decision authority that normal market conditions produce speaks to the sudden appearance of what is otherwise closeted in their routine trading activity. What appear as the coherent signals of individual decision, of seemingly zero-sum competition that keeps them apart, in actuality point to a more disruptive sociality that bears their deeper interdependence. While these traders are in a strict sense peers in terms of holding cognate positions and exercising equivalent judgment based on specialized expertise, their review of one another is not affirmative in the conventional sense. Instead, it organizes a constant anticipation of the decisions of others to which they are subject indirectly and in the aggregate. Knowledge failure here speaks to the incompleteness through which their professional competence is exercised. The acts of arbitrage that treat derivatives as detachable instances of decision regarding buying and selling reveals that scope of mutual indebtedness. While disastrous in its immediate effects, these residues of arbitrage open the horizon of an ungovernable externality that binds people together even as they live their lives and expend their labors apart.

Before Economy

A deep aspect of the economic fix was to render the problems of capital accumulation everyone's problem—or, at least, the problem of those legitimated as actors endowed with the capacities of decision to inhabit this putative sphere of freedom. Inclusion within this bounded realm, which would be organized along national lines, was realized through various processes of coercion and exclusion, from incorporation of native peoples in the case of settler colonies to dispossession and enclosure for those undergoing the transition to economy. As agency was attached to property, disqualification through servitude or slavery by which race was constructed, the unpaid labor of domesticity that partitioned gender and childhood were perquisites of economy's reign. Yet, as Polanyi observed, if economy was conceived as a space apart from the political, it would not have to be answerable to the violence that was its condition of possibility and expansion. If economic liberty relied on an elaboration of force, then freedom would need to be a property still to come—hence, economy would rely for its generalized legitimacy on a utopian promise that the future would be different from the history that rendered economy dominant.

Yet so many accounts of the financial crisis report that the future had gone missing, that a commitment to long-term growth had been replaced by an imperative for short-term returns, that decision making and ownership based on shareholder value and bonuses traded revenue capacity over the long haul for immediate liquidity and profit squeeze. Derivatives, after all, made future outcomes actionable in the present, and models such as VaR squeezed the immediate past into a barometer of the present, foreshortening the horizon of progressive transformation in both directions. Economy sorted whole people as being inside or outside its attentions, as bearing capacities for optimizing utility through decision or being excluded from bearing effective demand or interest. In contrast, derivatives treat people not as whole but in parts, less as subjects who must meet a threshold for participation than as attributes of risk that can be profiled, collected, and ranked. From the perspective of derivatives, no deficiency is grounds for exclusion; it is only a basis of pricing in combination with other factors. No opportunity need be missed on the basis of poverty or lack, given that default and failure are simply revenue opportunities to be identified, quantified, and hedged. As with subprime or microcredit, racial division and national exclusion still operate to discount or blemish as rating, but this only becomes a pricing mechanism that sets escalating payments and expected returns.

When the bailout came, it was to loosen frozen credit and to reanimate financial markets, not to fix economy on the promise that attending to the former would solve the problems of the latter. Certainly, some stimulus monies were apportioned to infrastructure (though not necessarily spent, as in the case of high-speed rail in Florida, Wisconsin, and Ohio) or to assist in some fraction of underwater mortgages (the Federal Housing Administration mortgage relief program, which was terminated before all of its allocated funds were disbursed).[84] But the government was positioned as an investor of last resort, meaning that public monies were to restore credit liquidity and not to rectify systemic economic problems of growth, unemployment, wealth concentration, mobility, energy or environmental considerations, education, industrial and urban planning, and design. Banks repaid TARP funds from newly robust coffers; hedge funds and derivatives markets rebounded. The economy did not. Finance got on with its business while the economy was headed for another dip in recessionary pools.

This separation of finance and economy was already anticipated by one of the key architects of derivatives pricing, Fischer Black, in his conception of noise. Noise is what prevents knowledge and keeps observations imperfect and expectations arbitrary rather than rational. Financial exchanges rely on trades on noise as if it were information; otherwise, awaiting certainty about what others know would prevent transactions from taking place. Conversely, the presence of traders acting as if they possess information they actually do not have renders prices noisy, increases volume and liquidity, as those with what turns out to be accurate information profit from their relative advantage. Finance is based on those with observable information profiting from the bulk of those lacking it who create an environment of noise. Yet economy is distinguished from finance precisely because its "variables seem generally less observable than financial variables."[85] Black asserts that those economic variables that can be made legible, such as the money stock, are of little practical value for understanding the workings of money in the economy. Economic theory has little purchase on empirical verification and scant capacity for prediction. Rather, models come to have influence because others are persuaded to use them, an approach that has utility for financial trading but not for economic fore-casting, which has no means of rendering uncertainty productive. Econo-mists are unaware that noise clouds their vision while finance profits from the arbitrage opportunities that uncertainty yields. The former therefore will not notice that their explanations account for less and less of what goes on in the world.

Certainly, nostalgia remains for what economy was, and it is difficult to argue with calls from various quarters for more equitable distribution of prosperity and recovery that might be reclaimed from finance's good fortunes. Such backward glances can leave the impression that there is some natural or correct balance between finance and industrial capital and that diminishing the former will restore the sanctity and integrity of the latter. Financialization is most commonly defined as a shift in profits from industrial to financial firms, as if the distinction between productive and nonproductive business sectors held over time, as did the measures of profits as such.[86] A more discerning view of financialization, as Bryan and Rafferty suggest, undercuts this sectoral distinction. Industrial produc-tion and finance are increasingly internal to each other. Factoring inputs from multiple sources precedes manufacture—as, say, when a garment is cut from cloth in Vietnam, stitched together in China, has its buttons sewn on in Haiti, and piece rates for each of these operations are set in advance and pegged to currency exchange rates. The afterlife of the commodity is also extended beyond manufacture by the same firms as credit for pur-chase through financial services divisions of corporations follows the point of sale. Through securitization and derivative instruments, potentials for revenue streams are created all along the way, assets and debts can be taken off-book, and therefore the question of sources and accounts for profits become increasingly complex and multiple.

The prevailing ways to address financialization, nonknowledge, and the derivative would only continue to treat economy as something that might be restored through an external political intervention of regulation and of a reintegration of all—or, at least, most—people within an expansive under-standing of the perquisites of accumulation. Ironically, both those who see government regulation as the source of and those who view it as the obstacle to economic restoration are reporting from the vanishing border that once secured the distinction between the economic and the political. With the effacement of this border, as well, regulation now appears at once excessive and inadequate. This parallax view is not so readily resolved. Reg-ulations have increased in number and increasingly factored in the struc-ture of derivative instruments. What was once seen as self-regulation, of markets operating under their own guidance without government interference, looks in the aftermath of the crisis and bailout like a public-private partnership with a deep and abiding intimacy.

This partnership does not render the state an instrument of capital. Rather, it considers regulatory processes as figuring the particular relation between the two, what was earlier referred to as a kind of disintermediation of the state. Just as banks are no longer the sole sites for issuing credit, the state is not alone as a source of regulation. There is no privileged intermediary to a political or economic transaction. Indeed, derivatives permit parties to create protective security in the face of a specifiable loss for investors much in the way that welfare and entitlements provided a safety net for citizens. As with the notion of speculation, rules appear to be evaded when derivatives fail and made use of when returns are realized. This is evident in the role that portfolio insurance played in the stock market crash of 1987, the derivative positions that nearly bankrupted the Orange County government in 1994, their role in the Long Term Capital Management and Enron implosions. Nouriel Roubini, who concedes that "most derivatives operate without ill effect," nonetheless observes that "derivatives can wreak havoc in other ways as well, hiding liabilities, avoiding taxes, frustrating attempts to restructure debt, and even serving as a means of purposely triggering defaults of banks, firms, and nations."[87]

In each of these instances, havoc wreaking is another way to describe the ill effects of political power after the fact, just as was the case with investment and speculation. Derivatives assume regulatory capacities that had hitherto been the province of governments through their various fiscal operations and policies. Conventional correctives to these issues entail subjecting these various transactions to the scrutiny of regulatory bodies, taking them from the shadows of bilateral contracts to the presumed transparency of a central exchange or clearinghouse. Other measures envision increasing the reserves or margin requirements that parties must hold. These approaches might be taken as means to correct for past abuses while shifting the terms of what would constitute systemic risk as derivative arbitrage proliferates through other avenues. It is not that regulatory schemes are pointless or impossible to reform, but absent a consideration of larger aims and context, the regulatory dynamics of derivatives will continue to be misunderstood and installing new rules will repeat the dull and tragic cyclicality of unintended consequences. Hence, rules that were seen as a source for resolution of conflict from the outside become constituents in a scene rather than neutral supports. Since rules shift the locus of risks in terms of where business costs will fall, how rates and rankings will affect investment decisions, what transaction costs will be incurred, and so on, derivatives become means of regulatory arbitrage that replace transparency with opacity and stability with volatility.

Indeed, as has been noted with respect to finance more broadly, the expansion of guidelines for constructing derivatives and the growth of multiple bodies responsible for regulating them have developed hand in glove. The financial engineer's own handbook increased from seven hundred pages in 1989 under the title *Swap Financing* to the 2006 *The DAS Swaps and Financial Derivatives Library*, at nearly five thousand pages. At the same time, regulatory responsibility is distributed among public and private, state and federal entities, from the separate bank, insurance, and, sometimes, securities commissions across the fifty states to federal offices such as the Securities Exchange Commission, Federal Reserve, Office of the Comptroller of the Currency, and Commodities Futures Trading Commission, and on the private side, the Chambers of Commerce, business advisory groups, member organizations such as the Financial Accounting Standards Board, International Swaps and Derivatives Association, Futures Industry Association, and the like.[88]

Within this variegated and mutually constitutive terrain, both the impetus to reregulate and deregulate, to centralize and decentralize regulatory authority, to apply one-size-fits-all and specialized rubrics (such as capital reserve or liquidity requirements) are likely to thicken the stew of financial innovation and risk management. Increasing capital reserve requirements may increase incentives to take transactions off-book and send the wrong signal to institutions sitting on large cash vaults unwilling to invest or lend. Conversely, providing tax incentives to those firms that do risk investment, even if tied to employment, will only further differentiate the reactions from businesses pursuing any available route to profit maximization. Certainly, many regulatory ideas and principles have been proffered and could be pursued, each with the capacity for significant impact in its own terms, but their shared aim is to enhance general conditions of profitability that they have also had a role in compromising.

If contestation and regulation are both internal to and beyond what is considered productive activity, the efforts to separate good profit from bad—the premise of a financial sector grown too large—will be similarly compromised. As finance and production become inseparable both conceptually and practically, the basic premises of economy—namely, that technological innovation spurs growth that is reinvested in further expansion and consequent prosperity—becomes more difficult to sustain. The combination of a fifty-year high for Americans living in poverty and declining median income over the previous decade points to trends operating beyond the scale of a normal business cycle of recession and recovery.[89] But conventional measures of economic health, such as growth in the GDP, inflation, or stock market indices, focus on things, not people. When it comes to weighing the merits of industrial versus financial products, the good of the goods do not sort so readily along sectoral lines. It is difficult, for example, to delineate the relative ethical value of bombs versus mortgage debt or biofuel futures and deforestation along sectoral lines that presume that the physical commodities are necessarily more beneficial to human development than financial instruments—assuming that the two can, for the moment, be separated. Indeed, the finance-based "new economy" or "great moderation" that purportedly yielded a virtuous cycle of low inflation and sustainable growth without recession was also framed as a productivity-inducing innovation of information technology.[90]

The securitization of mortgages was certainly advanced as a new financial technology in the name of progress to expand home ownership to those who did not have it. The policy lead initiated by the Clinton administration that expanded the brief of Fannie Mae and Freddie Mac and that laid the foundation for subprime national lenders such as Countrywide was framed as a public-private partnership and as a premise of racial equality, democratic participation, and citizenship. Yet for all this promise to bring ownership to the masses, actual home ownership rates would be elevated less than 5 percent, from 65 percent to 69 percent of households in the ten years following 1996.[91] At the same time, the refashioning of homes as sources of liquidity or ATMs effectively leveraged a relatively modest increase in access to a comprehensive expansion of credit at a time that fewer people would see paychecks delivering significant increases. The example illustrates how slippery the very disparate notions of technology are: as particular products, processes of production, media for information and decision, designs for living, modes of governance, means of mutual indebtedness.[92] Housing especially merged construction and credit technologies in a manner that was comprehensively regulatory—from government policy to expand access to new protocols for assigning mortgages to individuals. At the same time, the merging of these technologies through housing was increasingly contestatory—from the meaning of home ownership that ranked credit-worthiness along racial and gender lines as an emblem of democracy to the heightened competition for markets that resulted from disintermediation of credit origination and circulation.

Financialization, far from being a flight from labor by means of technology, emerged from the limits of industrial production to further accumulation when labor costs rose through increasingly militant unionization and, subsequently, wages flat lined and credit was overextended. Although positioned as an obstacle to productivity, the continuous measure and comparison of value is a basis for efficiencies that yield more from the workforce. The assault on labor enabled by the post-bailout obsession with debt limits is not simply an effort to compress paid compensation. The focus on public sector unions is as much concerned with increasing pension and health care costs, which have become the target for worry regarding government's increasing share of GDP. Such future obligations or promissory costs are another dimension of the insinuation of finance in production and the tension between surplus value or revenue from what is done on the job versus the liquidity that may be available from managing these obligations as securitized assets.

The financialization of daily life augurs a kind of second shift for labor wherein the work of personal investment is to be maintained with round the clock vigilance. The contributions to financial funds vary from the free information provided to investment clubs such as Motley Fool to the higher-risk and higher-price debts of those considered more likely to default. The fateful mortgage-backed securities and collateralized debt obligations of subprime fame mix and blend various default scenarios or capacities to sustain debt that hint at far more supportive approaches to inequality of opportunity. But under present circumstances, subprime mortgages yield nonknowledge with asymmetrical consequences for those who can benefit and those faced with eviction or abandonment of their homes. Nonknowledge that arose from generalized risk preyed on those who could not master or benefit from uncertainty. Derivatives accelerated unequal distributions of wealth by concentrating the benefits of arbitrage in the leveraged decisions of fewer market makers.

The Sociality of Derivatives

Without doubt, each of these baleful bailout consequences can be demonstrated and supported with particular kinds of measure and protocols of evidence. All signs may point back to economy without knowing how they all add up or whether the whole can still be deduced from the sum of its parts. Derivatives, too, are made of numbers, but their price eludes consistent quantification. The relation between the worth of a given hedge and the notional value it is attached to is slippery; their aggregate effect, difficult to quantify. Taken together, however, these myriad indicators beg the question of what a social basis or logic of financialization and derivatives might entail. If derivatives are but another occasion for avarice and excess to assert themselves, or for regulation to restore lost order, or for the perils of moral hazard to be reaffirmed, or for the inevitability of crisis or persistence of cyclicality to be confirmed, we have little to learn from recent events and no new questions to ponder.

If, taking a different perspective, the rise of derivatives marks the end of economy—or, at least, the recession of its reign and erosion of its coherence—their explosion in volume and significance cannot be attributed to an internal effect of a coherent whole. Seen as an effect of economy unbound, the larger meaning of a world awash in derivatives needs to be treated as a social principle or process in its own right. Rather than something firmly tethered to economy that then got away, what would it mean to understand the emergence of this dissonant social relation that cuts across the global and the intimate, spheres of production and circulation, future and present, knowledge and nonknowledge? If economy did not simply fall of its own weight, what forces overwhelmed it, entered into its terms and redirected them, reoriented its anchors to value?

Even as economy lies in tatters, its tautology is resurrected as the self-fulfillment of capital requisites that escapes the demands of the very social entailments it had depended on (labor, mass investment, mortgage holders, and so on). Derivatives would simply be a (seemingly) new answer to an old question of how capital delivered its magic of making money from money. Surplus is more of what was and is absorbed directly back into the circuit of accumulation—hence, the tautology of economy as moneymaking and not a means of separating money (through ownership) from the arrays of organized activity on which it depended. But clearly, surplus is not simply more of the same—each turn of exchange also makes something different, something not traded, something remaindered, something unabsorbed. This was certainly the case for labor and relative surplus populations that were formed through enclosure, colonization, and slavery. Surplus assumes yet more forms with industrial production and spheres of domesticity and reproduction, consumption and who and what fits the dreamscape, development and underdevelopment, liberation and subsumption. Knowledge economies further complicate the materialities of surplus in the forms of nonknowledge, the information that never gets reabsorbed, the decisions considered but never taken, the ideas that commerce leaves behind, the appetite for judgment left unsatisfied by expertise.

By the conventions of political economy, surplus is always removed elsewhere, appropriated, secreted away in vaults to be reattached to productive investment by means of private discretion. The derivative presents a different spectacle. Great sums are aggregated and assembled, detached from

concrete application, denied accountability, hidden in plain sight. This is
patently the case for the trillions apportioned to the bailout but also operates more obliquely with the billions lining the pockets of wealthy taxpayers treated as politically impossible to access; the stocks of food combusted
in biofuel; the billions in health care expended in denying care, wasted
diagnostics, remaindered pharmaceuticals. In these last examples, there
is a purported scarcity with a surplus dangling before us, a foreclosure of
the future at the same time that myriad futures are rendered actionable,
a corrosive divisiveness while mutual indebtedness is placed on display.
The frustration that nothing can be done collides with a conviction that
immediate and targeted action can make all the difference, that arbitrage
between observed and desired outcomes and leverage of what can be made
liquid will create a propitious moment for a salutary context.

While financial engineers, Tea Partiers, avatars of extreme sports, do-
it-yourself starters-up, and moshing-up kids are all exemplars of these ways
of being and knowing, none can claim to be originary or sole authors of
them. The skateboarding graffitist and the hedge fund manager take themselves to be masters of their risk universes without imitating one another.
They do not share models even if their models share a logic. Indeed, a certain derivative logic might be said to link these otherwise disparate ways of
being, modes of practice, sites of engagement together. Attributes of giving
and taking risk, seizing something for oneself and acting through others,
attaching a future to a present pass laterally through these myriad expressions in a manner that constitutes a social logic. The derivative here is not
exclusive or exhaustive, singly causal or determinate, precisely because it is
already inside these various expressions and at the same time part of their
animating context. The immanence of so many different attachments and
ramifications to a given body and action comports with the queasy navi-
gation between overconfidence and unknowability. Here is an excess that
is released but never fully absorbed, noise that need not be stilled, a debt
registered yet impossible to repay.

When nonknowledge as the open fields of unabsorbed surplus presses
back on bodies in a circuit of joy or laughter, as Bataille describes, it suddenly becomes apparent that the closed circuit of capital is sliced through
by another, one that is its socializing predicate and residue. Just as Marx's
analysis of those societies where wealth is presented as an immense accumulation of commodities disclosed the commodity that made all the difference—that is to say, labor—as the internal relation of moneymaking,
the self-making sensuous activity, as he elsewhere described it, was also
what preceded and followed from capital. If derivatives do now what com-

modities did in Marx's account, they, too, result from, bear, and release particular social relations and forms. One of the grounds for dismissing the relevance of Marx's analysis in *Capital* to current circumstances is that he is responsible for the determinism and reductive features of economy rather than for the very critique of these same caesuras.[93] Yet if Marx's project in *Capital* is to start with the commodity at the beginning of volume one to arrive at the society of producers as a finding of the internal contradictions of the tendencies of profit to fall that yield social capital or finance in volume three (as Michael Brown has shown), we should ask no less of a critique of the derivative's social logics.[94]

The fundamental logic of the commodity lies in the apparent autonomy of its form. A single unit can stand for the whole wealth of society; it can appear sui generis as means and ends of that wealth and is self-expanding while conserving its basic units of measure. The commodity appears as a thing in itself, bounded, self-enclosed, something individual that can be amassed. The discrete physicality of the commodity underwrites the social imaginary of individual selves and collective masses as the corresponding units of being on which modern society is to be based. Further, both the temporal and spatial aspects of the commodity fit within a Cartesian conception of linear forward movement and unidimensional growth or expansion. Time speeds up and space expands—or is annihilated when accelerating accumulation wipes out what came before. This is the geography of capital that David Harvey formulated so precisely.[95]

While the derivative certainly extends this imaginary of accumulation as the means and end of social life, it also departs from these terms and conditions in significant ways. The binding and blending processes that Bryan and Rafferty describe already speak to an ontology of capital that is not one of boundaries—not only of bodies but also of future and present, of what is near and what is far away—that are significantly eroded but also that leave the putative contents of what was inside and outside these units substantially transformed. Accordingly, derivatives refer not to a fixed relation between part and whole but to a collection of attributes that are assembled together in relation to other discernible features of the bodies, or variables, or environmental conditions they encounter. While derivatives are devised in a language of futures and forwards, of anticipating what is to come in the present so that a significant difference can be acted on, the act of bundling attributes together speaks of a lateral orientation, which is an effect of intercommensurability.

If we were to situate this different geography and state of being in historical terms, we would need to recognize the protocols of finance, risk management, and securitization and derivatives that emerged in the 1980s as the consequence of decades (or really centuries) of struggles around colonization and decolonization. Rather than a sudden rupture or break, a new beginning (of post-Fordism, neoliberalism, New World Order, 9/11, to name but a few such formulations), the social logic of the derivative has been a long time in the making, even if its consolidation proceeded far more rapidly. Colonization is a process of bounding a population, of erasing its content and introducing a binding form delivered forcibly through relations of possession and property. In its most general terms, decolonization violates, displaces, reconfigures that boundary. (It would be naive to suggest a simple freedom from the bounded state.) Considering the critics of colonization, such as Franz Fanon, tearing at the boundary emits hitherto silenced or uncounted voices that now erupt against a civilizing process that hitherto recognized only one speaker.[96] From the perspective of who or what was worth listening to, of what could be claimed as knowledge and what discarded as waste, this decolonizing condition was itself generative of the excess here being called nonknowledge. In the West, these expressions went by the name of identity and multiculturalism. In both cases, an attribute of some self (race, gender, sexuality, bodily ability) was being substituted for a whole of individual person or of a mass, nation, or society.

Against the stability of the order of things and knowledge, the political claims on a variable and multiple identity associated with these various mobilizations (even called new social movements by Chantal Mouffe and Ernesto Laclau, among others) was treated as the cause of political dissensus, cultural chaos, economic underperformance—in a word, volatility.[97] The picture sketched here—of an emergent social logic that precedes and follows from that ascent of finance—should, it should now be apparent, also belong to that of the derivative. The discipline and the discourse of economics have not produced the kind of self-reflection that would allow it to grasp its own limitations; nor can it yield an account of the nonknowledge that envelopes it. This will require a more comprehensive demonstration in terms of contemporary politics and sociality that will lead to a serious consideration of what otherwise is dismissed as a wholly disorienting nonknowledge and an inconsequential realignment of bodies. Realizing this social logic from the ruins of the economic will require a double session that makes both the epistemic and the ontological, the ways of (non)knowing and (other) being that derivative practices beyond the formal relations of finance inscribe in their worlds.

Rather than simply an economic crisis, what has become increasingly apparent in the aftermath of the bailout is the specter of a crisis of economy. No longer able to achieve its constitutive exclusion of the political as a discrete realm and integration of a national population as belonging together, joined in interest through shared applications of knowledge, the field called "economy" is watching its unity and integrity come undone. Derivatives issue from that breach, rendering the political inseparable from wealth creation, and disintegrating the givenness of national populations while opening other prospects for mutual association. Derivatives are now increasingly orienting production and exchange; they are also reorienting how we understand our sense of belonging together and the wealth that issues from our common labors. Economy finessed questions of inequality that were manifestations of social surplus through alignment and division of self-possession and ownership. By virtue of their better decisions, the rich had more, and it belonged to them. Derivatives perform a dispossession of self and of ownership. They re-sort individual entities into bundles of shared attributes and render the present pregnant with the collection of wealth needed to make the world otherwise. Economy promised wealth while it naturalized scarcity. Derivatives pose a wealth already to hand that, with proper investment and sense of return, would render scarcity unnecessary. The money is there, the mutuality exists; the means to make what is desired are to hand. This is the new political imaginary that derivatives potentially augur, subject to what emerges from the tussle with the ways of a decaying economy.

The derivative is a promissory note and a contingent claim. The prevalence of the derivative does not by itself ensure that what replaces the economy will be any more salutary to resuscitating the social from its postbailout drowning. Here it is worth a final comment on what derivative thought might augur for theorizing the present. If the critique of finance has imagined that it might be revealed as false, and used the occasion of crisis as its soapbox, any recovery by conventional standards would suddenly silence the critics. The promise of entering the logic of the derivative to disclose the principles of sociality and wealth that lie there (admittedly a journey likely to induce considerable nausea) lies in divining some other means of valuing the work of criticism itself. This is, after all, what derivative trading claims to do: to look for discrepancies from expectation to discover value and place what was held in reserve into circulation to create liquidity.

Caution must be exercised so as not to collapse the value form, the means of valuation, and the consideration of what to do with the store of value. This is the familiar problem of the multiple dimensions of money.[98] The derivative is a decidedly more complex, elusive, and disbursed entity, a puzzle that delivers commensurability among difference but may never be fully commensurable with itself. While derivatives, by definition, always leave much out (after all, they take only particular attributes and not the whole thing), what they encompass, their object domain, and their consequences are still very much in flux. Marx advised us to enter the hidden abode of production of his day, confident we would find clarity but also complexity there. The derivative is hiding in plain sight, a spectacle we cannot see through, an aggregate of so much that is not transparent. Our approach is to grasp it obliquely, to find the rivulets of movement in its opacity. For these limits to knowledge to be treated as fully productive and not simply the replacement part for a now broken economy, the derivative must be treated not as a financial object that sprang fully formed from a now severed head but as an unknown country that we nonetheless call home.

2

Public Quandary

The public is a quandary. What once seemed uniformly one now turns out to be many. Public had once been thought of as residing within a sphere, an expansive orb of civic participation, a distinctive domain it could call its own. If public expressed the realm inhabited by citizens and their activities, it was equally defined by what it was not. Outside of state and market, it would be a location where difference of opinion could be turned to unity of purpose, where divergence of perspective could find consensus. Whereas economy would traditionally be defined in contradistinction to polity, public would shift cadences from double to triple and stand as a third term that emerged between the boundaries of production and regulation at the same time that it would be contrasted with the private.

Such is the legacy of the double genealogy of "public." In one line, the term descends from the Greek partition between *oikos* (household, the root of economy) and *polis* (generally the city, but more specifically the civic center or marketplace that was the scene for political discourse). A second constitutive duality is the Victorian divide, with its gendered opposition between domesticity (capacities for social reproduction) and the public affairs of governance and moneymaking. Hence, what was contained within notions of public and private came already complicated by this double genealogy— especially as the household was no longer marked through compensated labor. As the center of productive life and sexuality and gender become attributes of an interior moral and cultural formation, the sense that the partition itself was stable and impermeable continued to hold sway and led to the impression that, for all its limitations and exclusions, there could have been a golden age of civic life.[1]

Yet the notion that public refers to a distinct vessel with a determinate content has become increasingly confounded. What was once conceived as the ideally temperate bowl of porridge now seems diminished in capacity and suitability. Getting more that is worth having is posed as coming at the cost of losing what we have. While public had typically been thought in binary opposition to private, in actuality, the two are mutually constitutive and what is referenced by the public is distributed across economy, culture, and polity, respectively, as a kind of good, an expression of popular will, and a problem of critical interest. In each of these dimensions, there has been something expansive that has also proved disruptive to understanding and valuing what the public might be. The nonprofit sector has professionalized charity and formalized volunteerism, yet the growth of this sector has come at the expense of its distinctive identity. The incessant measure of public opinion and assessment of value-added has destabilized the center and increased the leverage of outliers to render the popular ever more volatile. The dissatisfaction with conventional political processes has jostled uneasily with an explosion of critical voices and challenges to conventional expertise. More and more crowds into the space of the public while the evaluation of what transpires there becomes increasingly challenging to discern.

Whereas the ideal of the public that emerged with the Cold War imagined an integrative and unifying national space to advance mass democracy within a market order adjusted for justice and equality, today the public is not a thing in itself but has become in many respects a derivative of private values. Consider just a few consequent examples. Education is treated not as a means of civic participation but an investment in future earnings; government assistance to the disadvantaged is not a universal safety net but impedes people's self-initiative and places them at risk of failure; contribution based on income capacity is no longer the means of building public trust. Rather, cutting taxes is the most direct route to promote the common good. Rather than a level playing field in the game of consensus, the public is a scene of active differentiation around who can play and who is sidelined. And yet the impact of derivative logics on the public does not make the public disappear; it makes it more difficult to locate, evaluate, and trace as an autonomous domain. After all, what is called "private" relies on and crafts all manner of public presence, whether to expand markets, maintain a healthy business climate, or enlist further participation in the glistening malls of subjectivity.

What, then, are the attributes of the public that is not one but that has been dispersed and rendered volatile? Let us consider three attributes that are in common but also contrary use across those operations associated with economy: the concept of public goods; culture, with its grounding in some notion of the people; and polity, which features the idea of democracy. Rather than being a compensation for or alternative to the private, public operates as an expansion and deepening of private perquisites, while the private rests on all manner of debt to public processes, resources, and capacities. The economic category of public goods, was initially conceived of as a kind of demand that was unmet and unmeetable by the market. These were shared resources, knowledge, or collective care that was the material expression of a commons realized through love of people or philanthropy. The potential for profit in selling water or air rights, intellectual property, or social services has now been voiced as a moral imperative that profitability is the measure of whether such goods have been effectively developed and delivered. Yet for all the efforts to generalize social entrepreneurship and venture philanthropy as business solutions to social problems, another social ethos also emerges that re-poses the question of what a public good might be.

With respect to the notion of public as people, a parallel inversion has taken place, with the few standing in for the many; the excellent for the average; the star, celebrity, or outlier as the basis of identification for the common person. Within the protocols of a mass society, the people cannot be known directly, but their voices, views, opinions, or will can be represented through objective means. If public opinion once rested on and located the stable center or central tendency by which populations might be oriented, the voice of the people now has the force of measure at the extremes where volatility reigns. At the same time, incessant measure can open questions as to what values of assessment should be applied and what values escape measure altogether.

Similarly, democracy or critical participation assumed, following its Enlightenment authors, a form of decision making and judgment over values, standards, and policies alienated to government, experts, and critics. Now criticism is positioned as excessive; mass-mobilizations are seen as at once unlikely and incoherent to decision, while the legitimacy and sovereignty of conventional authorities wanes. The public associated with the commons, consensus, and cooperation has been eclipsed by private self-interest, fragmentation, and competition. Whether these shards reflect a broken consensus or an expanded capacity for critical deliberation, articulation of needs, or tactics for crafting political interventions remains a matter for careful conceptual appraisal.

From such comparative perspectives, the public once foundational to society is now lost, and a call for return of what used to be is in order. If, instead, the ways in which the public is currently derived discloses certain social logics—just as had the emergence of the bourgeois public sphere at the moment of consolidation of the capitalist order—then the struggles over what the public can be open to prospects for different futures to emerge from the present and not simply reorientations to a lost (and perhaps never fully present) past. If the public is indeed a derivative expression, the politics it bears will disclose key features of emergent association at the same time that it harkens to forms of communal and mass participation that now seem lost to the aggressive regime of risk-based wealth. The derivative undoes the integrity of part and whole; reassembles attributes into forms of mutual indebtedness, contingency, and commensurability; trades on volatility where small interventions, minor differences, and leveraged investments are felt comprehensively. Thinking publics along these lines may provide some indication of where this critical turn leads beyond nostalgia for what has been lost and recasts an abiding crisis as a moment of decision whose possible consequences can be valued otherwise.

Public Good

The first derivation is perhaps the closest thing to an official notion of public, the neatly tautological notion of that which is not private or made for profit (which more technically becomes a question of whether revenues are designated as profits and then distributed as dividends to owners or investors). These noncommercial or public goods are produced in specific kinds of institutions; individually and together they constitute a site or sector said to be outside of state and market—even if these last are deeply imbricated in each other. Sometimes referred to as a third sector of the economy (the other two being market and government), nonprofits, in narrow terms, are the institutionalization of philanthropic activities, which in turn descend from long-standing practices of charity or caring. Today the range of entities considered part of the nonprofit sector is extensive. To start with, the sector includes any kind of voluntary associations (from trade groups to local membership organizations such as social clubs), charitable trusts (freestanding or embedded in commercial enterprises), tax-exempt and noncharitable nonprofits (the 501[c][3]s, such as educational institutions, and other service providers, such as nonprofit hospitals). In addition, there are some twenty-six other organizational classifications recognized by the Internal Revenue Service (IRS), ranging from trade unions and political parties to cooperatives and mutual benefit societies, religious bodies, and service providers. To make matters more complicated, there is considerable overlap and redundancy between these categories.

Caring for the commons, the root of civil society combines private individuals of means devoting a portion of their wealth to public purposes and giving their time to help others. At the end of the nineteenth century, charity became rationalized as philanthropy and professionalized in nonprofits, assuming what were understood as scientific techniques for diagnosing the root causes of social ills and applying methods of behavioral remediation. More recently, there has been a turn to venture philanthropy, which places the giver not simply as the provider of funds but also at the center of transformative agency and hence as a model for what love of the commons might mean. The wealth of these people not only bears moral sentiment but also reflects a superior capacity for personhood that others can aspire to and emulate. The institutional means of delivery would embody these same precepts of excellence, efficient performance, and measurable gain. While markets might capture goods whose manufacture and distribution was once considered unprofitable, values attached to certain private people would come to embody the making of public goods. The more difficult question would remain what else was made in the bargain.

As a purportedly distinct organizational form that combines product and place, "nonprofit" is a government designation of social purpose that confers benefits of tax-emption on both the giver of funds and the recipient. The conferral of tax-exemption displaces the public-making authority of the state onto a nongovernmental organization (NGO) and a private citizen. For the organization, monies conserved through nonpayment of taxes transfer to all its activities the patina of public benefit while encouraging capital formation in the nonprofit sector. The individual or corporate contributor to the nonprofit assumes a function otherwise reserved for government in judging what public goods are most worthy of support. The proliferation of categories, activities, and entities that make up the nonprofit sphere not only constitutes a kind of privatization of what was once considered the publicly accountable responsibility of government but also disseminates the operations of judgment over what should count as the public good (hitherto monopolized by the state) to private persons and organizations.

The legislative history of tax exemption to support institutionalization begins with the Wilson-Gorman Tariff Act of 1894, which introduced income taxes of 2 percent on corporations and the wealthiest 5 percent of earners. Elimination of tariffs or consumption taxes introduce a measure of progressivity to government revenue collection while also providing a federal reprieve to charitable organizations, mutual banks, and insurers. Whereas Gilded Age inequality prompts ameliorative efforts through tax law, redistributive efforts will be persistently compromised through amendments that free corporate and individual wealth from such encumbrances. Within a year, the U.S. Supreme Court struck down the income tax provision, while the list of organizations exempted from federal tax continued to expand over the next decades to include the literary and the scientific, local community chests, and public health drives that also enlisted mass participation, such as in the fight against tuberculosis. Pursuant to the ratification of the Sixteenth Amendment to the U.S. Constitution in 1913, the federal government was empowered to collect income taxes directly without sharing that revenue with the states. The IRS preserved the structure of charitable and private foundations, and federal collections started out modestly and narrowly—in its first year of operations, given extensive deductions and exemptions, it wound up collecting 1 percent of income form the top 1 percent of earners.[2]

The institutionalization of exemption proceeded through a series of revisions to the tax code over the next hundred years that have generalized charitable activities once attached to church and entrepreneurs to all manner of civic associations. There are two sides of tax exemption. One applies to the organizations themselves, which are forgiven payment of various state, local, and federal charges for such items as income and property purchases. This applies to all nonprofits, even if, like country clubs, they provide benefits only to their own members. The other applies to donors, who can deduct their contributions to organizations that provide charitable services. Such donor exemptions, established by the Sixteenth Amendment and the War Revenue Act of 1917, were subsequently named Section 501(c)(3) by the Internal Revenue Code of 1954. The government recognizes a rationale for such double exemptions that are performing activities in the public interest that otherwise would be procured through appropriation of public funds on behalf of the general welfare.

Tax exemption weds organizational capacity and revenue in the manner that government bodies do, but it also places donors in the position judging what constitutes a worthwhile allocation of resources that makes a claim on what the public interest can be. The donation is an act of will, which, like governance itself, attaches to a general interest and bears a moral authority to do what is right on behalf of all. Yet unlike the state's capacities to exert force or impose law, such contributions are noncompulsory or voluntary—gifts freely given. From this freedom comes the moral positioning of civil society that so excited Alexis de Tocqueville in *Democracy in America* (1835) and subsequent celebrants—namely, that extensive voluntary association was intrinsic to a robust democracy.[3] Freed from the compulsions of the state to maintain order and market to demand work for others to survive, the donation of cash or labor activates the moral authority of common values that, because it issues from a realm of free association, cleanses the giver of the violence associated with profit and rule. What keeps this formulation from devolving into simple tautology—voluntary association confers moral authority because it is freely chosen—is the separation of civil society, or the public sphere, from the powers of state and market. Hence, the circularity shifts from a logical one to a functional one, with the distinct location of the public purportedly accounting for its distinct moral capacities.

Typically, the development of the nonprofit organization is celebrated as evidence of America's classless altruism and widely distributed democratic impulses. But the sector can just as readily be understood as the terrain on which mass and elite clash, where socioeconomic divides are breached and bridged, where the antinomies between pluralism and privilege are contested, and where specific coalitions between public and private sources of funding are forged. President Herbert Hoover, for example, sought to enlist philanthropic capacity to meet the mounting social needs of an approaching depression, applying a formula that had worked during the post–World War I expansion. Franklin Roosevelt reversed this intimate partnership and established a clearer divide between public entitlements and private giving to check the political power of those who might undermine his policy agenda. The postwar mandates of anticommunism invited private foundations to provide cover for what government could not achieve through overt diplomatic channels, which enabled a strengthened political self-concept for private funds such as the Ford Foundation to underwrite area studies or Pew Charitable Trusts to advance a Christian policy agenda. The Great Society programs of the 1960s transferred public monies to private organizations for social service delivery to avert concerns about the poor becoming dependent on government while expanding those very organizations' dependence on state subvention.

But with each of these modulations, the input of private and public was refashioned: the private stands outside, supplements, or covers government action while the public awaits uplift, stands in judgment, or incorporates the perquisites of the private. Hence, calls for a return to the right place of either will be complicated by formations and formulations that look very different today from how they looked in the purported golden age of private initiative or civic engagement. At the same time, the revenues associated with public or private giving ultimately derive from the productive firmament of labor that generates the wealth in the first place and then bears the consequences of which side of the ledger those funds inhabit. Yet when it comes to discussions of transfers between labor and capital, or rich and poor, "ultimately" arrives late, if at all. Strewn across this road is tax policy, in which progressivity is contested by the wealthy, only to be displaced for reclamation by the masses who might come to see reduced payments, exemptions, and returns as their only just recompense for the technical morass in which taxation and inequality reside. If philanthropy begins as the conservation of wealth for the wealthy, a version of this self-preservation is also democratized.

Taking the Rockefellers as her point of reference, Eleanor Brilliant has sketched this history of public and government scrutiny driving the very formation of the nonprofit sector. The Progressive Era's Walsh Commission of 1912 voiced concern that the large foundations launched by Rockefeller and his peers were a means not only of burnishing their good names in God's eyes but also of shielding their profits from taxation. During the Depression, Roosevelt worried that unfettered giving would compromise needed tax revenues—a tension that would be played out in successive amendments to the IRS code. During the Joseph McCarthy era, the Select Committee to Investigate Tax-Exempt Foundations and Comparable Organizations called John D. Rockefeller III to testify in a climate of suspicion toward foundation support for activities considered un–American, such as Alfred Kinsey's research on sexual behavior. Twenty years later, this same Rockefeller was able to get the Treasury Department to co-sponsor commissions that he would fund privately. One was the Commission on Foundations and Private Philanthropy (1969–1970), also known as the Peterson Commission, and the other was the Commission on Private Philanthropy and Public Needs (1973–1977), or the Filer Commission. These commissions sought to unify not only nonprofits large and small, but also progressives who emerged from movements for civil rights and conservatives such as the Kaplan Fund, which had served as a front for the Central Intelligence Agency, into what would be termed the "third sector."

Rockefeller's efforts to integrate the sector were a response to its growth during the postwar period. Early in the 1950s, the IRS considered the 30,000 or so nonprofits too inconsequential to keep detailed statistical information on, but by the mid-1960s, with more than 200,000 registered organizations, it began to track their growth and scope systematically. By the mid-1980s, the categories of the charitable actually outnumbered those of the non-charitable.[4] At issue, as well, was tax reform that eliminated some of the preferences on giving by the wealthy that Rockefeller feared would jeopardize the large foundations' growth and influence. Such was the consequence of the Tax Reform Act of 1969, which formalized accountability by nonprofits to the IRS and sought to incorporate 1960s concerns with inequality and to extend the benefits of charitable contributions to more of the population while providing tax relief for the poor.[5]

While the commissions he convened did not become part of the government as he wished, and Rockefeller himself died in a car accident in 1978, the manufacture of public goods as a distinct economic sector was well on its way to being formalized. Yet this formalization also betrayed a derivative logic. If the ruins of the Bretton Woods agreements recast international monetary affairs in terms of financialization, the crafting of a nonprofit sector was key to the creation of a domestic front for the risk management of what was once organized through the welfare state as a series of entitlements. While nonprofits were formally being rendered as a distinct third sector, the impact of their emergence was to articulate certain aspects of state and market, specifically the regulatory protocols and social service provisions of government with the entrepreneurial and risk-taking aspects of a service-information-knowledge economy.

In 1980, nonprofits become a distinct institutional sector in the National Income Accounts, yet, as Peter Dobkin Hall has observed, the formal separation masked a professionalization, institutionalization, and managerialism that transformed the older voluntary association into something far closer to the rational corporation. He notes that this distinct taxonomy did little to clarify what would differentiate this sector, as the same goods and services provided by nonprofits could also be supplied by business or government. But the expansion of nonprofits as a means of orienting a citizenry toward "leadership education" infused civil society with the values of enterprise in a reworking of public-private partnership. "Once in power," Hall writes, "the New Right discovered that the welfare state against which it had railed for so long was less a vast national bureaucracy built along European lines than a subtly interwoven system of public and private enterprise."[6]

This partnership consisted of melding the rational calculus of tax breaks with the zeal of unleashing the spirit of enterprise. Tax breaks not only served as a means of reversing progressive redistribution of income but also sought to generalize the expansion of price calculation as a way to appraise all social value that was central to the postwar efforts of neoclassical economists to apply their models to all aspects of human behavior, charitable giving and voluntary association included. In 1973, Rockefeller funded Martin Feldstein to study impact of tax exemption on giving, arguing that "transforming the tax-policy debate on charitable organizations into a technical econometric question would effectively depoliticize it, removing it from congressional hearing rooms and placing it in the more rarefied arena of high economic policy."[7] Feldstein, who would become Ronald Reagan's chief economic adviser, wanted to encourage entry-level donors to broaden the sector, and his research found that tax deduction produces more revenues for charity than are lost by government.

Yet by shifting the rationales for giving from civic commitments to a willed ability to deny the government revenue, something enshrined in the Tax Reform Act of 1969, the beginnings of a change in what constituted the public would be affected. Government would reassign authorship and agency over entitlement from services it could take responsibility for providing to an array of calculations and investments. As anxiety over the undeserving poor rose, the share of benefits they received declined. In 1979, the bottom fifth of households received 54 percent of government benefits, whereas by 2007 that share had declined to 36 percent, with increases in spending on Medicare, especially contributing to the allocation of funds higher up on the income scale, as nearly half of U.S. households received government benefits in 2010. These trends are generally not well understood. Despite the popularity of Medicare, barely one in five people in one poll could name it as the source of increased costs, and more thought that programs for the poor were most responsible for increased public expenditures. Still, most respondents thought they would pay out more in taxes than they receive in benefits; 70 percent favored increased taxes generally; and 85 percent support raising taxes on the wealthy.[8] These responses suggest a disconnect between public understanding of how funds are allocated and what the cumulative impact of upwardly redistributive policy has been, on the one hand, and mischaracterization of public sentiment regarding tax increases and revenue progressivity by legislatures, on the other.

The figure of the poor is the visible marker of benefit while the underlying redirection of public revenue away from the poor goes unmarked. At the same time, the shift of expenditures to the middle of the income distribution corresponds to increasing anxiety over the long-term sustainability of that very stability and security of maintaining the status of being in the middle class. Writing on the eve of the financial meltdown, the sociologist Dalton Conley observed, "Driven by a phantom anxiety that something big is going to go wrong, the most successful professional class in the most powerful country in the world lives in fear that its personal house of economic cards is about to collapse."[9] Whether the inability to recognize the sources of insecurity makes for anxiety or the separation between what is acting and what acting on success makes for a phantom agency, the consequence is to conceal outward expression from underlying value.

In this regard, government policy would occlude public agency and result in what Suzanne Mettler calls the "submerged state." The transposition of public goods into private decisions based on tax exemptions generates a huge but largely unacknowledged transfer of public resources into private hands. These programs, in order of magnitude, include the nontaxable nature of health insurance benefits provided by employers; the home mortgage interest deduction; and tax-free retirement benefits provided by employers. Totaling more than $350 billion, these government programs disproportionately benefit those with higher incomes and exceed the costs for food and housing aid that go to the poor. Yet the more lucrative public assistance is less likely to be recognized as such:

> Those who had used a greater number of visible programs were significantly more likely to report that they paid their "fair share" in taxes; other results remained consistent with those in the first model. Thus, individuals' sense of having benefitted from government through visible social programs appears to mitigate their sense of being burdened by it through taxes. Conversely, usage of policies embedded in the submerged state—the types of policies on which [President Barack] Obama's efforts have focused—do not. In short, the expansion of policies in the submerged state, even if they are aimed at low- and moderate-income Americans rather than the more typical affluent recipients, may do little to engender positive attitudes among recipients toward such policies—or, quite likely, toward the political leaders who helped bring them into being. Neither do citizens exhibit much understanding of how policies in the submerged state function nor of the upwardly redistributive bias many of them possess; thus they do not comprehend what is at stake in policy battles surrounding them.[10]

As free-market economists have been wont to point out, the nonprofit economy (roughly a tenth of employment and of gross domestic product) deprives governments of revenue that might be available for public use. Indeed, the Economic Recovery Tax Act of 1981 extended charitable deductions to those who did not itemize their returns and preceded $110 billion that Reagan cut in support to nonprofits between 1981 and 1984. It also allowed foundations to accumulate more for their endowments by lowering the amount they were required to give away and increased tax credits for research and educational organizations.[11] As Olivier Zunz suggests, Reagan's embrace of nonprofits as a means to cut government entitlements was abetted by an unintended convergence between conservative and liberal dispositions around faith-based organizations that were providing social services, an articulation that connected Newt Gingrich's "Contract with America" and Bill Clinton's Welfare Reform Act of 1996. These were supported by a series of Supreme Court decisions that allowed lobbying by 501(c)(4) affiliates, nonprofits that play a role in politics, to become advocacy bodies for the social change they sought to bring about through their programs. Zunz goes on to argue that this shift in orientation toward investment framed the entire understanding of giving:

> Americans have come to think of philanthropy not as a gift only, but also as an investment. Late nineteenth-century Americans who made large fortunes were the first to openly combine the ideas of managing the market and giving in a single mechanism geared for social progress. That money needs to be available before it can be given is obvious; the innovation lay in bridging the gap between a transaction in which you act for profit and a gift, in effect merging in various proportions the two activities. Having inherited a critical distinction between profit-making and giving, inscribed in law and custom, they have made the two behaviors organically dependent rather than outcomes of opposite impulses, as Adam Smith implied.[12]

This series of convergences—between the organizational form of profit and nonprofit; between the use of the sector to advocate for, as well as deliver, particular conceptions of service across ideological divides; and between moral and political economy in which investment becomes the clearest expression of civic commitment—speak to a larger transformation as the outcome of sectoral consolidation. When giving becomes a form of investment, the notion of public good shifts from something that the market cannot provide to a claim on what is good for the public. For giving as investment to apply to rich and poor alike, even as mounting wealth inequality and government entitlements place them farther apart, a tautological but virtuous circle must seem generally accessible. Whatever one gives to is what deserves to be considered good. The procedural regularities of giving allow for a greater dispersion of just what this goodness might entail. In this regard, the third sector amalgamates a call to governance, a type of organizing, and an expression of activism. The public as a derivative of private values does not simply render all goods onto the market. Instead, it infuses civic engagement with expectations of appreciable gain. This is why Smith's normative aspiration for moral economy would need to be realized through participation in a form of exchange that promises a greater return—especially where secular forms of privilege or opportunity such as upward mobility and career promotion may be increasingly foreclosed.

Hence, far from a simple conversion to the market, as suggested by concepts such as privatization, deregulation, and neoliberalism, the philanthropic complex described here is at once regulatory, constitutive of publics, and compatible with a proselytizing conservatism as much as a moralizing liberalism. Returns on investment cannot be left as an article of faith; they need to be measured and demonstrated. The emphasis on accountability not only exacerbates the divide between technical expertise of organizational providers and the local knowledge and understanding of those it serves but also shifts that relationship from one of mutual benefit to measurable outcome that erodes the very civic commitments on which philanthropy is based. Bruce Sievers articulates this conundrum for nonprofit organizations that are forced to trade their commitment to long-term change, uncertainty, and complexity that attach to notions of public good such as education, development, and justice, for the immediacy of measurable gain when their own resources are increasingly directed at accountability:

> There is a growing tendency of both governmental oversight bodies and foundations themselves to interpret accountability not only as procedural responsiveness but also as demonstrated substantive impact on society. What originated as a legitimate public interest in avoiding outright fraud or the misdirection of philanthropic resources toward private benefit has become an unrealistic expectation for philanthropy to yield quid pro quo quanta of social benefits (however these are to be measured) equal to or greater than the costs of tax benefits received. This skewed reinterpretation of the accountability theme stems in part from a third major influence that has shaped the rise of the modern foundation—the effort to apply the commercial success of the business model to philanthropy. This trend originates in the modern tendency to translate the life of society into the language of the market. This language

migrates into philanthropy and is expressed in terms of portions of benefit allocated to financial inputs, providing assurance to donors that their "investments" are producing demonstrable results. While it is not unreasonable to expect that contributions will yield some evidence of beneficial results, the exaggerated emphasis on metrics in the form of substantive accountability is becoming a driving force in the field, creating unrealizable expectations and a distortion of organizational priorities.[13]

Yet if the organizational vessel of the nonprofit allows conservative and liberal projects to advance their causes, both understand this capacity as an affirmation of their general views that call for expansions of social services or market mechanisms. The complexities of the derivative form allow all to see what they seek. The sector may have been organized along the lines of expanded service and entitlement associated with welfare state Great Society perquisites, but its expansion was soon embraced as an entailment of rightist notions of contracting the purview of government and the agency of markets. The links among private charitable giving, economic growth, and general well-being are articulated in a report by the American Enterprise Institute, an exemplar of the advocacy-based conservative nonprofit:

> First, there is evidence that giving makes people happy. A number of studies have concluded that giving affects our brain chemistry. People who give often report feelings of euphoria, which psychologists have referred to as the "Helper's High." They believe that charitable activity induces endorphins that produce a very mild version of the sensations people get from drugs like morphine and heroin.
>
> Second, there is evidence that private giving is implicated in economic growth. Per-capita charity and per-capita GDP in America have moved together over the years. Evidence that the two forces cause each other comes from an analysis of how past values of one variable affect future values of the other. This analysis shows that a 10 percent increase in current GDP per American would lead to a 9 percent rise in charitable giving. At the same time, a 10 percent increase in giving per person would provoke a 3 percent increase in GDP. Given the size of our economy, this means $1 given privately would increase GDP by about $15.
>
> In sum, if we substituted our private charitable giving for government redistributive programs, we would pay a price in terms of

economic growth, personal prosperity, and even happiness. Charitable giving should be seen not just as a nice detail about American life, and even less as a mere tax deduction. It should be seen as
a national priority.[14]

With the exception of recessions, the sheer amount of charitable giving
to nonprofit organizations in the United States has grown steadily, nearly
tripling in the past thirty years. By 2009, it exceeded $300 billion, with
three-quarters of that sum coming from individuals. But if the aspiration
for the third sector, as expressed by policymakers, was that it substitute
for government funds and support, then this increase has fallen far short
of the mark. Indeed, when considered as a percentage of GDP, total giving
today stands at just over 2 percent—what it was in 1969 (although for the
twenty years from 1974 to 1994, the proportion of annual income actually
slid to under 2 percent).[15] Government spending, by contrast, has increased
significantly, from 32.8 percent of GDP in 2000 to 42.2 percent in 2009
(this was up from 7.3 percent in 1870, yet it was still under the average for
wealthy nations, at 47.7 percent).[16] Considering that such expenditure supports nonprofit and for-profits alike through large entitlement programs
such as Medicare and Medicaid, earmarks for district-based programs, and
expanded benefits for pharmaceuticals, the issue may be less the size of the
economy than the purposes and means of application for this social wealth.
Corporate tax rates have been cut over the past forty years—presumably increasing the capacity and discretion over what causes and issues to
support—yet at the same time, private companies have kept their charitable share at 1 percent of pretax profits.[17] Rather than encouraging greater
contributions, reductions in marginal tax rates actually lower the returns
on giving, reducing the economic incentives for charity. For example, a
$1 million gift for a donor taxed at 50 percent yields $150,000 more in
savings than the same donation at current top rates of 35 percent. As with
revenue collection generally, charity is highly concentrated, with half the
total amount provided by those households making $1 million per year or
more. However, while it may be a modest slice of overall wealth, giving is
widespread among households, with some six of ten making a contribution
in any given year. The average contribution per household is $2,000, and
the poorest households give the largest share of their income to charity.[18]
Rather than substituting for government appropriations—the initial rationale for tax exemption to donors— private giving transfers government
authority to personal responsibility without a means to ensure that the

responsibility aligns with capacity or reflects what might be considered common sentiments or needs.

This pattern of extensive participation with a highly concentrated distribution also describes the recipients of giving. As mentioned above, the nonprofit sector has formalized and expanded over the past fifty years as a public-private partnership. From just over 12,000 at the close of World War II, the number of nonprofits grew substantially from 819,000 in 2000 to more than 1.2 million in 2009. At the same time, the largest organizations received more than half the total contributions. No doubt, the same patterns exist in the for-profit realm. Hundreds of thousands of new businesses are started each year, yet three-quarters of these (21 million of 27 million) reflect the self-employed. Fewer than 1 percent of firms with 500 or more employees provide jobs to more than 50 percent of the workforce, while fewer than 1,000 firms employ 32 million of the 120 million total employees.[19] The deeper parallel pertains to what kinds of organizations survive difficult economic times when nonprofits are subject to the kinds of supply and demand expectations and measures of value, outcome, and productivity that apply to the for-profit sector. Holly Sidford reports that the largest organizations (with annual budgets of $5 million or more) make up 2 percent of all arts and culture nonprofits yet receive more than half the funding, while only 10 percent of the funds go to programs for the poor and underserved, despite the crucial role such programs play in sustaining those communities.[20]

In effect, expanding participation has covered the defunding of government coffers through tax cuts while shifting the way in which a public gets constituted from a legislatively defined benefit to what gets framed as an act of individual choice, a personally discretionary contribution. It is not simply that these individuals together add to the public but that their capacity to act on matters of what will create public goods, institutions, and the social economy derive from a qualification and determination made by the state. Their will, in this regard, comes to them not already free but conferred through an accounting of "internal revenue." Indeed, that other salient dimension of the rise of this third sector is volunteerism, in which more than 60 million adults provide some labor without compensation.[21]

Voluntarism might stand simply as unpaid or free labor, but its root in volition, will, or desire bespeaks the capacity to assume the position of decision maker associated with both government expert and private investor. The active participation in what one gives to joins the volunteer and the venture philanthropist, even as the latter claims to represent the motives and benefits of the former. The alignment between the affluent and the humble would take place through the generalization of ownership to apply to personal responsibility that would lift one from poverty—mortgage payments for a home, as opposed to rent, which yields no equity, and micro-finance, which most directly joins the two modes of participation. Giving is intended not merely to alleviate a deficiency but also to effect a change, and its democratization allows rich and poor to imagine themselves as undertaking a shared project. As one manual for such dispositions argues, "Every donor—no matter the level of wealth—has opportunities to go beyond straightforward grantmaking, and become a catalyst that effects systemwide change."[22]

Rather than assuming equality of input or outcome, grant making here is figured as a kind of arbitrage, where concentrating resources on small differences can be leveraged to have an impact on an entire market or environment. The key is to be an early innovator, investor, and adopter to be in a position to move from a discrete enclave to a well-dispersed scale. This does not mean that the investment reaches all as an entitlement might; it means that the initiatives are widely dispersed and well broadcast so that they can be exemplary and influential. Good deeds cannot be left to their own devices. They require effective representation; otherwise, the work of emulation cannot take place. These turn out to be central tenants of venture philanthropy directed at poverty eradication, specifically around the practices of microcredit, in which paid labor is replaced by freely given entrepreneurial activity in parallel to the shift from a defined benefit to a defined contribution.

As developed by Muhammad Yunus through the Grameen Bank in Bangladesh in the 1970s, microcredit fit within the NGO portfolio of nonprofit development. According to this approach, access to credit was defined as a universal human right that was at odds with particularizing profit motives. That right reflected a notion of the human as intrinsically conceived to be a self-helping entrepreneur rather than one whose labor was dependent on opportunities for employment provided by another. Loans for small business startups would be granted largely to women as a means for them to move out of poverty. Bound to the local community by patriarchal obligation, women were seen as more creditworthy than men, who participated in circuits of migrant labor. Microcredit was quickly embraced as a model of global development in rich and poor nations alike—one that could be applied as effectively in hurricane-ravaged New Orleans as it could for recent immigrants and the poor and middle class of Latin America.[23] While it was lauded for evading direct dependence on the state, with its corruption and bureaucracy, microcredit still ran into limitations of scale, since it relied on infusions of aid from public or private sources.[24]

Limits on means of generating sufficient revenue and of gaining access to capital that would provide economies of scale are the twin dilemmas of the third sector. Venture philanthropy's answer has been to show that preference for the poor makes good financial sense because of low default rates and high interest rates, which translate into high rates of return. Not only is the nonprofit model inefficient because it cannot meet demand; it is also insufficiently ethical and unjust because it treats the poor as less self-possessed than the affluent. The condescension that inheres in charity—that giving is based on a divide between property and lack that is preserved through the gift—can be overcome only through the acquisition of property (even if poverty remains intact). This is specifically the argument made by Vikram Akula, who started SKS Microfinance as a nonprofit in 1997 so it could receive donations and shifted the enterprise to a profit basis in 2005 so he could raise capital from private equity funds such as Sequoia. "The notion that it's somehow unethical to enter into a profitable business working with the poor is insulting to the poor," Akula writes. "They are not children who need our protection. They're working women and men who are thriving under a system that allows them to take their economic lives into their own hands. Treating them as anything less is unjust."[25] Akula's SKS Microfinance charges a 28 percent interest rate and boasts a 99.4 percent payback rate. (He borrows at 11 percent, pays his traveling loan officers 12 percent, maintains a 2 percent reserve, and returns 3 percent on the investment.) This interest rate, he notes, is lower than that of other for-profits, such as Compartamos, which can charge 90 percent interest; it is also lower than the costs of government loans, which include bribes and lost income due to travel from country to city. Akula also observes that the high rates of return are due to use of unpaid family labor, the absence of legal fees in the informal economy, no infrastructure costs for cottage or home businesses, and the fact that capital itself is small percentage of input for local production or sales.

Production here relies on the persistence of a peasant economy, and return on investment depends on the aggregations of scale associated with digital information networks. "If a company makes a penny or two on a product it sells to a small number of people, it will never make much money," according to Akula. "But if a company makes a few pennies on each product, and it sells fifteen to twenty products to tens of millions of people—that's when it starts to make real money. This is how Google has become so huge—by having an enormous constituency of 'eyeballs' and making a little bit of money from multiple advertisements targeted to these huge numbers."[26] Akula's network consists of thousands of loan officers who cover the countryside collecting small amounts of repayment. While mobile telephony is digitizing some of these small transactions, the aspiration is to incorporate ever larger shares of the world's population, from the unbankable to the economically active.

In her analysis of global microfinance, Ananya Roy notes that the shift to what Bill Gates calls creative capitalism and eBay's founder, Pierre Omidyar, refers to as demanding capital, in which financial returns and appropriate reward for risk are the priorities, exacerbates the tensions between the financialization of development and the democratization of capital. By 2008, privately funded, investor-driven microfinance boasted more than a hundred funds and total assets of $6.8 billion. Rendering the poor into the bankable draws on their social capital, the integrative trust that binds communities together. She notes that, in practice, social capital is based on an "enforceable trust" in which poor women are held in their places by patriarchal communities. "Such forms of domination and enforcement are of course easily evident in microfinance—from the explicit and subtle patriarchies that make possible the financial discipline of poor women in South Asia to the penal collection apparatus of microfinance in the Middle East," she writes. "The conversion of social capital into economic capital and ultimately into global finance capital is thus underpinned by practices of discipline and punishment. This is the key to poverty capital in the age of millennial development."[27]

This conversion—precisely what Akula effected as he moved his firm from the moral framing he would disdain to the ethically superior circumstance provided by the market—suggests the ways in which the various positionings of the nonprofits themselves become the preconditions for expanding circuits of finance. Activating the hitherto inactive will be achieved by a price mechanism—here, risk as measured by interest rates—despite the very coercive apparatus of purportedly non-market relations that render these particular populations such desirable clients. This tension between opening and closing, enlisting and excluding populations lies at the heart of this new positioning of venture philanthropy, which seeks to benefit from risks that it simultaneously seeks to insure itself against. This double differentiation ties together underserved populations in the developing and rich nations and joins together credit expansions covered by microfinance and subprime lending, which is also aimed at building the morally superior ownership society that itself was tied to conceptions of expanded democratic participation through asset acquisition.

As Roy concludes:

> It is the systematic redlining of particular social groups—defined
> by race, class, and gender—from financial institutions that neces-
> sitates subprime lending. They are now included, but on less than
> equal terms, paying much more than for the same product—a
> loan—than other consumers. This is the peculiar logic of subprime
> credit markets: that they are simultaneously instruments of finan-
> cial inclusion and instances of exploitative, even predatory, lending.
> Such also is the logic of microfinance, for it allows the poor access
> to credit but on terms that are significantly different from those
> enjoyed by "prime" consumers—be they the high interest rates of
> Compartamos or the intimate discipline enacted by the Grameen
> Bank. In other words, the subprime marks the limits of the democ-
> ratization of capital.[28]

That subprime marks that the limit of capital's democratization has become increasingly evident when foreclosure leaves former owners without
home or voice. But if the mere potential for ownership discharges any
obligation for benefit, so, too, has micro-lending pressed on financialization's limits. Self-help is not for everyone; it is for the qualified. It is
not a human right but a standing to achieve. Both in its versions of equal
opportunity and in its need for expansion of markets and externalization
of risks, small business has played a crucial if ultimately limited role in
capital accumulation.

In the four years preceding the global credit meltdown in 2008, the
microfinance industry was growing at an annual rate of more than 40 percent, with an estimated client base of between 100 million and 150 million.[29]
Three years later, the Consultancy Group to Assist the Poor (CGAP), an
interagency consortium linked to the World Bank, had proclaimed saturation in the microfinance market:

> Let's pause for a moment here, because for many people talk of
> market saturation seems odd when most of the low-income popula-
> tion still doesn't have a microloan. This is because there has been
> a tendency to overestimate the actual demand for microcredit,
> sometimes drastically. . . . The reality is that at any given time,
> many low income people simply do not want a microloan, while
> others may want a loan but would be likely to have payment prob-
> lems if they were given one. Still others can't be served viably with

presently available methods. So supply catches up with effective demand sooner than we might think. This was clearly happening in Morocco and Bosnia/Herzegovina, for instance. In a nutshell, one microcredit market after another is entering into a new, uncharted world of credit saturation. In these markets, over-indebtedness will probably pose a major risk for clients, not to mention the lenders.[30]

Granted, this was the group that Roy named as advancing redlining on the unbankable; thus, its later pronouncement of saturation would be consistent with their earlier view of development by exclusion. If nonprofits and NGOs responded to a suspicion toward government's ability to serve the interests of all, the internal displacement of public goods suggested by trust in private lenders might prove still more volatile when that trust is betrayed than what was to be solved separating from the crisis of sovereignty of which governments sought to absolve themselves. In addition to microfinance and venture philanthropy, some investment banks, such as Goldman Sachs, are launching new initiatives that derive profit from reducing the need for public goods; they call these initiatives social impact bonds. If the monies applied up front reduce a social problem such as prison recidivism, then the investors receive a return on the difference between what would have been paid to house prisoners and what was spent on programs to diminish their rate of return to prison.[31]

Framing public goods in terms of investments that maximize returns alleviates them from the burden of being available to all, especially when opportunity trumps equality as a key underlying value. Oversaturation of demand, the way in which subprime and microfinance were understood after the fall, would meet its corollary on the supply side in terms of excess organizational capacity. From this perspective, growth in the number of organizations per se is unwelcome because small, emergent groups lack the capacity for growth sufficient to affect scale. Large, established entities, by contrast, are likely to be wedded to their old ways and incapable of serving as engines of change. Demands for accountability and high costs of fundraising (nonprofits spend more than five times what for-profits do to raise capital, and with administrative costs factored in, fundraising can absorb 20–40 percent of their revenue) further compromise the efficacy and survivability of the small nonprofit.

Steven Goldberg has used these constraints to argue for a stock market–based approach to support of the nonprofit sector, in which midsize organizations best placed to innovate and solve problems would receive funding from an investment pool. His aim is to break the fundraising circle whereby organizations raise what they spend and spend what they raise by separating revenue and capital so that the former covers short-term operating expenses and the latter covers growth capacity. This entails measures of results rather than effort, something that markets do better by aggregating information through price than individual organizations do by apportioning resources to reports and accountability rubrics. The decline of social progress over the past thirty years attests to the inability of nonprofit capital to channel resources where they can do the most good. Prediction markets would establish quantifiable expectations of outcome—say, graduation rates—then compare providers with respect to that measurable outcome based on "meaningful information" through an impact index that draws investors to "growth-ready mid cap social enterprises."[32]

Indexing is an explicit application of the derivative logic, aggregating attributes such as graduation rates to stand for the more uncertain question of what it means to be educated and what education delivers to society. In this example, as well, education, the initial public good, stands as an underlying value from which the index is derived. If philanthro-capital is moving toward organizations and models (such as charter schools), thought initially to be most effective, it could just as readily move on to some other site or symptom of inequality if the initial expression of the underlying structural problem appears to be too intractable to resolve through the available means. The inability of charter schools to make appreciable improvements over public institutions in students' test scores might itself be a case in point, as would the question of what happens when a particular new market for innovation, such as microfinance, becomes saturated. Doubtless, similar questions would be posed for nonprofit financial markets under conditions of market failure that were posed for subprime lenders no longer worthy of attention.

Perhaps more fundamental, uncertainty is being converted into risk as nonknowledge is translated into meaningful information. Rather than closing the gap between effort and results, the social good in question becomes recognizable only through its derivative expression, while the volatility and social disruption become the ungovernable byproducts of the index. Microfinance substitutes the bankable for the economically inactive poor as its aggregated and derived value. The organizational shift from small to mid-cap nonprofits has a parallel impact on the marginalized populations. Once encouraged to self-organize through the formation of nonprofits, those charged with representing the underserved are now abandoned by funding sources in the face of inadequate productivity, which justifies defunding or sacrifice. It is not that social movements were duped into becoming nonprofits, for the opportunity to become sustainable was also an achievement of the push toward cultural equity, even if the perils were long understood.[33] If the autonomy of the organizational form is, in part, what is in crisis, the very fantasy of incorporating as a substitute for mobilizations of other kinds, then the excesses of the nonprofit and its residue of market failure might need to be applied to other principles of aggregation and measure.

The rise of nonprofits has entailed replacing money identified as public with funds marked private, even as they require government sanction. Concomitantly, there has been a shift from democratic accountability through the electoral process to governance through fiduciary boards. By linking together free labor, rational organization, and the capacity to judge how funds should best be allocated for social benefit, nonprofits have also constituted this form of private initiative as a form of public making. While the earlier public sphere had its political economy in the form of what Benedict Anderson called "print capitalism," circulation is now counted in dollars rather than readers, with the capacity to raise funds or expend them its own sign of success.[34] Wealth has long been full of the tidings of its own exceptionalism, with philanthropy proof that exploitation is a form of generosity. Andrew Carnegie's line, "The man who dies thus rich dies disgraced," bears an echo in Warren Buffett's invitation to his peers to give away their wealth. But the robber barons of the late nineteenth century imagined all of mankind their beneficiaries and established their foundations in perpetuity. Buffet's largest gift was to the Bill and Melinda Gates Foundation. Olivier Zunz noted the paradoxically inward turn of the cohort of venture philanthropists from their forebears: "But unlike John D. Rockefeller III in the 1970s, who was active in organizing the nonprofit sector as a whole, Buffett and Gates are talking primarily to their peers."[35]

The sensibility of the venture philanthropist is to inhabit the present with their wealth and to incarnate less a universal will than an investor-based excellence. Rather than acting on behalf of the poor, wealth becomes the exemplification of what personhood should aspire to be. A century of celebrity would intervene between the satiric image of Rockefeller dressed as royalty (from *Puck* magazine in 1901) and the early biopic of Facebook's founder, Mark Zuckerberg (*The Social Network*, 2010). If venture philanthropy moved from the universal to the particular and the public to the insular, its stars would inhabit a time and space of immediacy associated with the popular identification with the singular that is celebrity itself.[36] If wealth claimed to be transient rather than dynastic, this might reflect the more generalized erosion of socioeconomic mobility rather than the opening of opportunity.[37]

The notion that individual contributions were a more authentic reflection of the worth of a civic endeavor than government earmarks or entitlements could be was standard neoliberal fare that positioned charity in the place of state judgment. But it also corresponded to decades of government policy that shifted security and entitlement identified with citizenship to a self-managerial approach to return on risk associated with the role of the investor. The public defined negatively as that which was not distributed for private gain (which nonprofits are prohibited from doing with their revenues as joint stock) comes into conflict with an affirmative notion of public that shares in a common benefit by virtue of being recognized within a given polity. While nonprofits, volunteerism, and philanthropy continue to be locatable on a map of public goods, the very meaning of "public" has shifted in the process. The gestures of Davos Man to address the universe from within the enclave attend to different logics of representation and agency. For those whose wealth has abandoned others after taking what they have, time and place can retain their specificity. But the claim of the new global elite is that their allegiance lies with their own mobility, however long that may last. For this "superclass," mobility can just as easily lead them out of the inner circle as cast them in ever moving encampments of privilege for which the principal commitment is to remaining part of the club.[38] Chrystia Freeland, upon a sojourn to Davos, remarked:

> Our light-speed, globally connected economy has led to the rise of a new super-elite that consists, to a notable degree, of first- and second-generation wealth. Its members are hardworking, highly educated, jet-setting meritocrats who feel they are the deserving winners of a tough, worldwide economic competition—and many of them, as a result, have an ambivalent attitude toward those of us who didn't succeed so spectacularly. Perhaps most noteworthy, they are becoming a transglobal community of peers who have more in common with one another than with their countrymen back home. Whether they maintain primary residences in New York or Hong Kong, Moscow or Mumbai, today's super-rich are increasingly a nation unto themselves.[39]

This dis-identification with the nation certainly makes increased taxation a harder sell, although the history of income tax reminds us that this was early and often suffused with forms of capital flight. What would require greater explanation is how this disposition of the wealthy became a more populist commitment. The move from public entitlement to self-management association, which started with Reagan and continued through subsequent administrations, was also accompanied by what has been called a tax revolt. The catalytic moment was California's Proposition 13, typically taken as a watershed for right-wing populism. Closer scrutiny has made clear, however, that this initiative gained public endorsement in the context of rapidly escalating property values. State revenues were tied to annually adjusted assessments. Professionalization and standardization of tax assessment replaced customary expectations that assessors would undervalue homes and calculate taxes at a lower-than-market rate. Good government reforms meant more accurate pegs of taxes to market fluctuations.

The resulting transparency threatened what Isaac William Martin termed a "hidden welfare state" (fractional assessment was valued at nearly $40 billion at the start of the 1970s, making it the largest single government subsidy in the postwar era), which homeowners sought to preserve rather than dismantle.[40] Low-income and elderly homeowners on fixed incomes sought some insulation from the market, which Proposition 13 promised by limiting the size of tax increases. What was sold through the referendum campaign as protection from market speculation became a basis for it. Those with higher-value homes reaped the bulk of the benefit. A generational divide was opened between existing and future owners that would start to play itself out in other forms of defunding public coffers, and taxation, recently rationalized and subject to bipartisan consensus, became the very stuff of electoral politics.[41] As it did with charitable contributions, mass participation masked regressivity of distributed benefit.

A recent survey of U.S. housing policy notes, "Taxpayers with incomes of $100,000 or more accounted for 16 percent of all tax returns but more than 73 percent of the $66.6 billion in mortgage interest tax deductions taken in fiscal year 2007. On the other hand, taxpayers earning up to $30,000 accounted for 43 percent of all tax returns but less than 1 percent of total mortgage interest tax."[42] The tax revolt stood as a kind of social insurance against market fluctuation at the same time that it rendered taxes themselves a kind of option or claim on future income for a tacit securitization of home ownership. The referendum promised to limit risk, just as a derivative contract would. But the added regressive benefit for those whose homes were more highly valued or who held their homes longer amounted to a kind of disintermediation of entitlement in which one's specific position vis-à-vis the market determined the extent of benefit and how one attributed her or his own privilege as a deserved gain attached to purchase.

These processes of crafting self-initiating, risk-managing, investor-oriented publics that have unfolded over the past thirty years typically go by names such as "privatization," "deregulation," and "neoliberalism." Like other such comprehensive formulations, they hold a compelling appeal to capture a historical conjuncture, an ideological formation, and a political strategy in one elegant turn of phrase. As much as these terms have served as a kind of rallying cry against a particular political project, they can also threaten to overly consolidate the capacity, coherence, and efficacy of a complex of ideas and techniques that lends them more potency than they might otherwise have. The seamless integration of ideas into methods, the assertion of a unitary spirit of the age, and the unmitigated conquest of power project this authority onto what is seen as an inadequate or absent response by oppositional and popular political expressions and exacerbates the woeful declaration that, in Margaret Thatcher's words, "There is no alternative."[43]

More specifically, the sweeping pronouncements of privatization, deregulation, and neoliberalism encourage the view that the public has been "disappeared" by the private; that the two were, and remain, distinctly separate.[44] Instead, public and private are always constituted through a kind of interdependence, and the challenge is to understand what creates their mutual imbrications and differentiation, a problem to which the derivative logic provides some keys. The derivative logic casts these processes in a different and suppler light and enables some of the material pathways and conceptual antinomies to be tracked. The peculiar rise of the nonprofit sector has made evident the fact that privatizing public goods has also socialized and crafted publics. The affirmation of markets, legible in the advent of venture philanthropy, as the self-evident means for valuing human endeavor has required increasing government intervention and regulation. Finally, the freeing of individual initiative, which twins volunteerism and entrepreneurialism, has heightened coercive means of assessing their conformities and policing their transgressions. The sorting of populations into winners and losers, risk-capable and at-risk, as discussed in the previous chapter, is captured not least when the trope of war is used to refer to domestic policy initiatives (the war on crime, war on drugs, culture wars, and, subsequently, the war on terror, in which foreign and domestic regulatory frameworks meet). Privatization, the shift of social goods from government to nongovernment entities, therefore is productive of specific kinds of publics whose actions have a stake in or make a claim to what is most worthy of further funding, even as the differential capacity to provide funding based on a position of privilege is effaced. Private giving is here marked as public investment, an activity that delivers authenticity to the recipient and the authority to decide social worth.

In this respect, privatization is a derivative logic of public making in that it takes a particular bundle of contributions or investments and treats them as standing in for universal access to benefits or entitlements on the basis of citizenship. These affinities of preference allow participants to be aggregated, irrespective of the size of their contributions, at the same time that the scale is tightly linked to control over decisions, just as it would be in the case of stock ownership. This is no doubt the rhetoric of public participation articulated around private funding of public political campaigns, where small contributions provide cover for large and influential ones.

A state voicing flows through these public actions, in no small measure due to the government's disavowal of its capacity to meet social needs, which takes the form of reengineering, ending government as we know it, or, more recently, shorting government—that is, betting that it will fail, which is deployed as a tactic to gain public office. While this idea of a public economy, which putatively self-authorizing practices such as arts, religion, and education, were invited to join, had an ideology, its practical dissemination was as much technical as ideological. Accordingly, giving and raising funds, volunteering and organizing free labor time, and venturing and investing in initiatives occupied a narrowing hierarchy of value, sometimes called excellence, where once were located universal evolutionary terms such as "progress," "development," and "mobility."

Public goods, nonprofit organizations, and the public sector could operate in a space that was derivative of properties once said to be attributes of state and market while disinvesting revenue from the former and providing free labor substitutes for the latter. The ethos of equal access to means of civic participation is traded for the perspective of the investor managing a portfolio of distinctive and value-conferring decisions. While this shift in emphasis helps wealth to concentrate, it also promulgates a populist interest in tax cuts. The shift from citizen-based entitlements to investor-driven redistribution of wealth repositions government actions for fairness and equality through a gift economy of returned taxes that ameliorates (insufficiently) income lost through the past forty years, in which the majority of the population has experienced wage compression or decline and increased working hours per household.

Hence, tax cuts stand as a remodeled kind of public good that, in failing to compensate for what the market cannot provide, presents government as inadequate to its own task. But perhaps the more insidious effect of rendering tax cuts the principal expression of public good is the transposition of what was once lauded for its visibility into something invisible. The edifices of education, health, and welfare constructed through industrializing philanthropy bore the monumentalism of public goods as places all could see and destinations all could reach. When public goods are manufactured through a hidden or submerged state and subject to the disintermediation of the political and the economic that is the hallmark of the derivative, the crisis of visibility, of knowing risk and discerning illiquidity from insolvency, also raises its head. Protection against unwanted exposure becomes indistinguishable from an expected return on that same risk.

Anticipating the impact of others' demands, like the arbitrageur, doubles as a hypersensitivity to their every move and a disavowal of the securitization and sociality that makes self-appreciation possible. Increased revenues through higher taxes are posed as a kind of insolvency rather than a resolution of illiquidity, as sending good money after bad rather than setting things in motion. If the place of the good is no longer visible, then surely it will be difficult to know where to send those revenues or what their returns may look like, other than so many private expressions. If tax exemption, a government action, is charity's proxy, the public will not be able to claim credit for its benefits. As wages fall, labor markets shrink, pensions wither, and security recedes, the reliance on a hidden benefit translates into an insistence that the actual benefactor remains obscure while all manner of proxies can stand for the values being sought.

The value of tax exemption—monies forgone to government coffers—exceeds $1 trillion, more than a quarter of the existing budget and half the funds that now go to entitlement programs. Some 70 percent of the value of these exemptions goes to the top fifth of taxpayers, and households with more than $1 million in pretax income receive nearly half a million dollars in tax breaks.[45] At the same time, what the wealthy retain for personal benefit exceeds what they give in charity, leaving a conception of public good that springs from a particular arc of government policy. From this derivative form of public good we must now move to the dilemma of representing a public as the people that can no longer be seen en masse but are recognizable only through their proxies.

Public Knowledge

While the most pervasive application of "public" is as a kind of good, institutionalized through nonprofits and articulated with the state through tax exemption, the root of the term, from the Latin *pūblicus*, simply means "pertaining to the people" and is linked to *pubes*, or the adult male population. "The people" is an abstract whole assembled out of concrete particulars, where who gets to assemble and what gets gathered together is already partial and selective: adult men as the ones who count, pertaining to the people tacitly delineating that which does apply to all from that which does not. Certainly, there is always a question of representation when discussing "the people" as some delegate who will convey or articulate what all desire (in the sense of parliamentary processes), or some figure or trope that will speak or stand in for the masses (whether a leader as the charismatic face of the people or an individual's story taken to reflect what all experience). Representation, in this regard, would govern the relations between the one and the many, the part and the whole, as one of either substitution or similarity (proxy or portrait, metonym or metaphor).[46] Derivatives neither substitute part for whole nor have a single attribute appear as a picture of the many. Rather, the attributes derivatives gather together are actual features of the particular elements collected and combined to attend to specific circumstances or possibilities. Without doubt, derivatives are subject to all manner of techniques of representation, whether one is pricing them as commodities or reporting on their significance to social life.

The same might be said for the people. While it is indeed the case that their history is one of representation, this does not mean that other principles of association, aggregation, and articulation are not also in play. Without naming it as such, this tension between representation and the derivative was already in evidence with respect to earlier anxieties regarding the unruly crowds that were the impetus for disorder, rebellion, and revolution. Whether gatherings to witness the beheading of the French king or limitations on the number of blacks who could assemble on the streets of apartheid South Africa, authorities feared that some aspect of these bodies would become an incorrigible and volatile force. Even if the people's energies could be quelled by enfranchisement and entitlement, those who would maintain order were always concerned that the actual assemblage of people in public spaces would generate effects in excess of all efforts to contain them. Something kept moving in social movements even after the mobs were broken up.[47]

If the people cannot appear as such but their actual expression rests on an abstraction of certain collected attributes, then this notion of public is always already derivative. Publics are never assembled whole; some attribute that extends throughout that body, however, is manifest in any concrete expression yet also circulates beyond it, whether this takes the form of a measure or a voice. Rather than asking how accurately the part reflects the whole, the derivative logic would ask us to inquire into the features of an entire field that are borne and placed in circulation through some derivative instrument. Modern techniques for making publics tangible would assume a stable inner core of interest or a means of objective conveyance through delegation or representation. Still, the interest and the delegate would be but moments of the public that would stand for the public as such. The edifice of sovereignty and legitimacy would occlude the derivative operations by which part would stand in for whole. Now it would seem that the derivative, far from being a silent partner in bringing the public to notice, is a source of celebration, a means of intervention, and a medium of invention. Far from appearing neutral or independent of what they would measure, the technologies that elevate attributes to circulate as common frames of reference and are worthy of consideration themselves have become the focus of public deliberation. If "the people" was always derivative, the derivative now takes on the mantle of the popular.

The public, which once stood at and for the center of things, is now just as frequently voiced as an outlier, an exception, an excess, be it extreme or excellent. Governed by the mass, the measure of public veered toward the mean, oriented around the center. Now orientations to the margins, the consequent minorities, the derivative publics usurp the homogenizing, stable mass. Arbitrageurs on the hunt for the black swan will be fortunate indeed to land the rare bird. When killings are to be made in the market, by definition few will benefit, as those who can master the derivative's wild ways already possess special access. But because the public comes into being already derived, the terms of access, identification, and participation can be reversed. The many can recognize their values in the movements, decisions, and dispositions of a few.

This is the point at which sampling and celebrity intersect, at which population becomes an effect of its attachments, at which volatility gains appeal over stability. Derivatives provide measures of value before a production process is complete. Public assessments, the quantification of desire, deliver no less. Whereas polls gather together otherwise disbursed attributes, celebrity concentrates a plentitude of value in one place. Abstraction and personification, dispersion and attachment, substitution and origination commingle in a delicate embrace. If the public is most conventionally viewed as a product, a construct or consequence of its measure, identification, or assertion, the labor involved in crafting these assemblages still cannot be overlooked. Nor can the strategies for dealing with cultures of measure and means of instrumentalizing its instruments be ignored. When all is to be measured, many become aware of what is left out. As expertise rests on those who command the means of evaluation, knowledge of judgment is not only doubted but also disseminated. At the same time, if publics are made, they are made not simply from instruments and materials, but from a common capacity to render value that typically goes uncompensated and unnamed. Tracing this arc of public manufacture would move us from the precincts of expertise to the vast expanse of work that people do on the derivative instruments that circulate in their name.

The voice of the people, their opinion, comes, in Jürgen Habermas's famous formulation, from a sphere in which private individuals gather in conversation and, through sustained and uncoerced exchange of views governed by shared norms of communication, achieve consensus. The point is not simply to be heard but to become deliberative by applying reason in the exercise of judgment. Discourse has an ethos that values recognition of others and embraces rules that are formal, that do not discriminate on the basis of content and thereby expand participation. The particularities of this universalizing culture have been widely observed, even as its spread has been embraced.[48] Yet as the institutional and infrastructural capacity for the public sphere has expanded, conventions of punditry and antigovernment rhetoric of politicians have challenged the viability of rules for communication to deliver an expanded deliberative capacity.

In these currents of representation, the people can be made to disappear by invoking their names. Accordingly, the public is drawn as a cultural figure with a single and homogeneous temperament referred to as "the American people." Absent divisions of class, race, gender, sexuality, generation, religion, and politics, Americans can be spoken of uniformly as wanting one thing and not standing for another, of having a free will that they are never free to exercise unmediated by the one who speaks of and for them. Increasingly, this figure of popular will has passed from quality to quantity, portrait to proxy, population to sample. When sampled and surveyed professionally, this will qualifies as what the pioneering pollster George Gallup celebrated (without reflection on his own self-interest for doing so) as "the pulse of democracy."[49]

As an objective technique in the service of the rationalization of its object, public opinion polls and research emerged in the twentieth century through some of the very same pathways as did scientific philanthropy. Rockefeller money underwrote the creation of the Social Science Research Council (SSRC) in 1922 and supported the research of Paul Lazarsfeld's development of market research a decade later. Polling began to have a role in forecasting election outcomes, albeit with mixed results. Roper predicted Roosevelt's 60.7 percent share of the 1936 vote within 1 percentage point, whereas his colleagues Gallup and Crossley had error margins for their samples of nearly 7 percent (more than double what would be considered the industry standard today). The *Literary Digest*, which culled data from its elite subscribers, was off by nearly 20 percent. A dozen years later, the same professional pollsters forecast Thomas E. Dewey's victory over Harry Truman, and newspapers dutifully printed the mistaken headline "Dewy Defeats Truman," which the newly elected president seized on triumphantly. As Amy Fried notes, the pollsters were mocked and ridiculed at the time and agreed to an inquest by the SSRC, which found that the shortcomings of the previous surveys could be corrected only through improved and further polling. Like the military industrial complex that was its postwar kin, the polling industry emerged in earnest at this point to pursue the closure of its own widening gap between credibility and capability, a kindred exercise in creating demand by manufacturing supply.[50]

In addition to popular skepticism, criticism within the social sciences of the very notion of public opinion is long-standing. Even before its pervasive quantification in polls, Walter Lippmann had sounded an alarm in the 1920s about elites' self-serving invocations of the people as directing the course of events, a notion he referred to as the "phantom public."[51] In a critique published in 1924, Floyd Allport cast aspersions on the metaphorization and fictionalization of what he termed the fallacy of the group mind by which an objective interest is given subjective voice.[52] Herbert Blumer, writing in 1948 about the summing of individual responses into a single numerical aggregate, deemed public opinion an "untenable fiction."[53] Thirty years later, Pierre Bourdieu voiced concern about the decontextualizing and passifying precepts of polling in which respondents are isolated and choices are pre-given: "In real situations opinions are forces and relations of opinions are conflicts of forces."[54] For these critics, public opinion is an artifact of the slippage between sign and reference, between a representational marker and the never fully representable phenomenon to which it refers. Yet despite the criticism over the course of the twentieth century, survey research would shift from the margins to the center of the social-science enterprise as policy and social engineering was required to become ever more evidence-based. The institutionalization of information as a domain, in which the public would be constituted as a long march that leads to the Elysian Fields of big data, implies a shift not simply where public views are represented, but where the bits and pieces of what publics stir up are to be mined.

The default position of the field that has expanded and solidified its methods and claims despite long-standing doubt is to treat polls and public opinion as one and the same thing. Twenty-five years ago, political scientists could declare victory over a "captive public": "Poll results and public opinion polls are terms that are used almost synonymously."[55] As another observer recently put it, "Polls not only derive their legitimacy from the expectation that they are expressions of public will, they also legitimize the idea that such a will exists."[56] Technically, such legitimacy rests on the confidence that those who participate in the poll, the sample, accurately reflect the range of views that can be discerned in the population. If mail is the most common way to distribute polls (which remain unopened as junk mail) or the most direct way to reach people is by a land-line telephone, then those who lack access to mailboxes and phone lines or who remain skeptical of those who would want to measure their views will be under-represented. If calls are made when the young are not at home, when households with children are engaged in childrearing, or calls are being screened, then each respective demographic will be inaccurately counted. Samples may be adjusted or weighted to compensate for these sampling challenges, but those who do wind up responding may not turn out to be representative of the group to which they are said to belong. Generalizing from samples so compromised is called nonresponse bias, an increasing problem given the rising number of people who do not respond to polls.[57]

Declining response rates are one feature of polling saturation, where the incursions of public measure into private lives produces a heightened awareness of surveillance and scrutiny. The measure is often privately financed while the compromised privacy and attendant reticence becomes the raw material from which publics get aggregated. This, in turn, engenders the internal corollary of the refusal to be seen as objects of public opinion or to provide the free labor by which it can be attested, for those who do respond are seen as doing so in the context of their perceptions of the authority of those who seek their views. This awareness of expected answers or language regarding matters of race, gender, or personal or political preference are treated as a further distortion in accurate findings for actual opinions—a deformation known as response bias.

While the history of polling has produced more polls and increasing densities of measure, the question of whether the foundational distinction between privately held beliefs and publicly constructed opinions can still be upheld remains largely unexamined. Whether respondents are still trying to please those in authority—the concern with obedience to authority made famous in Stanley Milgram's experiments—or see themselves as making a public presentation when answering questions, both the occasion and the setting of the poll bear on a broader cultural sensibility that pollsters treat as capable of a merely technical correction.[58] Klaus Krippendorff notes that the professional field of public opinion has not produced any consensus on what the term means, but it does generate recursive effects to which it remains indifferent. "Polling literally creates a social situation whose effects it records," he writes. "Pollsters seem blind, not realizing that the power relationships that operate during interviews become inscribed in the data being generated: complying with instructions, being paid for participation, communicating with detached or anonymous interviewers, and prevented from talking about what really matters to them."[59] Hence, while polls may be instruments in the propagation of a culture of measure, they, like the market protocols of price that are their kin, rely on an unknowable excess for their continued work, to which they remain indifferent.

For those engaged in the enterprise, a certain pragmatic has emerged that attends to problems of measurement through improved instruments of measure. Given that the wording, ordering, and framing of questions can alter the responses and that respondents may hold inarticulate, weak commitments or contradictory sentiments toward the views being solicited, all manner of reforms have been devised to sort, filter, probe, and qualify respondents' responses.[60] Yet it is not simply that the instrument and the object of public opinion are difficult to prize apart; so, too, is the relation between message and messenger, which generates constant slippage and imbrication between public opinion and mass media. Susan Herbst studied political activists and staff members to understand their use of polling culture as a means of mobilizing and not simply measuring public views, a finding that counters the more common sentiment that publics are insufficiently informed to provide meaningful responses.[61] Rather, the field imagined by public opinion is not a naturally occurring array of discrete and settled objects to be constructed by measure but a self-constituting assertion that makes a claim on what is meant by the public as such. If public opinion is constructed, the building materials lie all around in both the myriad tools and the labor that are applied. As a construction site, public opinion is messy, indeed, with more material than can be applied to the edifice and a shortage of blueprints that would direct where everything is to go. Still, the project continues; people toil on, working and being worked over by these materials. Skepticism does not make measure stop; it does not keep people from making use of their own capacities for assessment; and it does not collapse sign and referent.

The concern with the decline of the public sphere that could be inferred from the resistance to formal polling therefore would need to be tempered by the shifting of polling practices from the imagined space of opinion formation to the applications of polling in a long march through the institutions of work and social reproduction. The refusal to be polled would seem to suggest a public that has escaped from the captivity of measure, yet the modes of assessment that are the current obligations of the work-place—schooling, service delivery, consumption and debt ratings, social entrepreneurialism, and art—all point to a deeper insinuation of derivative logics in the place of the public. If the derivative prices value before production is complete, it also subjects all production to norms of productivity as a global standard, as Bryan and Rafferty note. The operations of risk management are, after all, an effort to derive value from risk through a managerial regime. Doubtless, the rationalization of public opinion that emerged with Taylorist principles of scientific management in the early twentieth century came from, but never really left, market pressures on labor for increased productivity. But this movement between spheres also rests on a partition between public and private within each. Individual and mass had its corollary in the interior mystery of the worker's body that needed to be disciplined by an all-seeing managerial eye. The derivative violates both these boundaries. Not only is the public constructed through techniques of market measure, but the interior movement of the body, the quintessence of the private, divulges its secrets in bits and pieces, short answers, and scaled preferences while making its affective dimensions—satisfaction, performance, position, preference—the very attributes of the public of which it would be in the service.

What began as a means to aggregate publics is now a medium for market niches and public differentiation. The technologies of review, assessment, rating, and ranking weave work and leisure, consumption and commerce, into continuous flows of information acquisition, analysis, comparison, and recalibration. Human resources management touts the 360-degree review in which everyone is to rate the performance of all co-workers, whether they are superiors or subordinates.[62] The inductive algorithms that break students' learning into continuous applications of skill capture along multiple dimensions displace end-of-term grades, and students learn to manage their time in response to the weighting of the evaluations.[63] The micro-preferences recorded by Facebook exchanges or the real-time credit ratings based on constant purchase feeds seek to merge real-time attention to the ecstasies of communication with value-adding information that converts lateral exchanges into hierarchical preferences.[64] The public may once have been a phantom, but it haunted the ideal of a mass, a collected body with common dreams and shared dispositions, interests, and means of delegation. If lower returns and less reliable findings stimulate the political economy of polling at the expense of a depleted sense of public capacities, the migration of polling technology from evidence of a will to voluntary response to an obligation of all manner of activity disperses the sites where an assertion of public can be detected. Whether in the form of test scores, presidential leadership, or indicators of consumer confidence taken from differences between credit card debt and returned merchandise, a derivative logic is in evidence. Slicing and dicing public attributes and reaggregating them as measures of public value will yield volatility for their underlying attachments and their own representations of value, as they do in the stock market.

If mass public opinion is made by experts out of unpaid work or voluntary input that participants are asked to provide, derivative publics are no less replete with agency and the consequence of action taken. The notion that the mass public was a passive object whose collected voice was activated by measure was an enabling fiction of the polling industry. When polling is integrated into the fabric of an ongoing and obligatory assessment, expertise is still required, but legitimacy and authority shift into the realm of uncertainty. No one knows what the public thinks, what performances are worth, what politics opinions enact, yet all are compelled to search for value and to act on the differences they perceive. Taking information from noise, acting on minor differences, concentrating resources on leverage points—these are the entailments of arbitrage. Derivative publics insinuate this work of arbitrage widely, even as rewards get concentrated. Self-assessment is all-pervasive; the public is miasmic, while gain accrues to the few.

This is where concepts of social capital—the relative position or proximity of individuals in a network—privilege notions of scale. Ronald Burt's ideas regarding structural holes, brokerage, and neighbor networks deploy a language of face-to-face encounter of rational actors seeking advantage through decision that comes from market models to suggest that certain behavioral patterns can operate in the same manner, whether at small scale or large.[65] Recall that this was the claim for Mandelbrot's fractals, the natural recurrence of the same pattern of mathematical relations at different scales. The mathematical basis of these claims, as in behavioral finance, is meant to assuage doubts about the recurrent and essentialist group mind fallacy that Allport saw at the root of public opinion with a pure referentiality of the fact. This would also be the fantasy of the machine basis of the market: If all behavior is indeed mathematical, then all phenomena, large and small, human and non-human, would be most directly expressed quantitatively, not simply represented by such models. Sampling is a version of this confidence in scaling, as is arbitrage. Whereas the logic of the rich in relation to the mass was of kind, not degree, arbitrage reverses this polarity and treats market makers as having more of what all are trying to get, of getting there first in a common race, of seeing what others miss when all eyes are scanning for value.

But derivatives are not simply about counting, they are not simply a way of knowing. They also engender intensities of feeling and invite a way of being. To cut into the mass and disaggregate it so that attributes can be ordered, or to focus on intimacies so that attachments can be formed, shifts not only the relation between the part and the whole but also the relation of the many to the few. Poised between noise and information, between non-knowledge and knowledge, derivatives emerge from the space between the measurable and the immeasurable—not simply making a quanta actionable but charging the medium in which they move with certain qualities. Rather than hewing to the image of a world free from quantification or measure, the seemingly independent attribute continues to bristle with reference, to suggest comprehensive connection, to compel consideration of what makes value contingent. Hence, there is no simple route from measure to the thing as such, no unmediated sociality, no available return to the halcyon days of pure quality. If these pictures of public are in decline, then more will be gained by redrawing the terms and conditions under which publics operate. As has been done with the larger scrutiny of construction, it is time to move from the debunking observation that the world is made to the more difficult (self-insinuating) investigation of what the constructs themselves are made from and what they do. This process is aided by a materialist account of the derivative and the politics of quantification.

Gone, then, is the normative drive toward central tendency, an orienting middle for which a return is always available. It is not that randomization disappears or statistical evidentiary protocols have ground to a halt. Rather, they must turn from the consideration of the increasingly hostile land-scape they make evident—in this case, the volatile and disruptive ground of what is termed "public opinion." There is a curious tension between the widespread identification of the U.S. electorate as moderate and the persistence of concentrated intensities of partisan affiliation by which the agenda for the multitude are presumably set. Here, the bipartisanship by which government is to represent both sides—liberal and conservative—is complicated by the fact that at about 40 percent of the electorate, more voters consider themselves independents than see themselves as Democrats or Republicans. It is also complicated by the fact that, while the nearly two-thirds of citizens are registered, the majority did not vote in the 2010 election, in which the majority in the House of Representatives switched to Republicans, despite an electorate with larger Democratic leanings.[66]

While elites and party functionaries are increasingly polarized along the lines of the parties that they increasingly rule, partisanship functions more as an interpretive heuristic for an increasingly complex world.[67] James

A. Stimson distinguishes between operational and symbolic ideology to account for, what he terms, "conflicted conservatives" or those who identify as conservatives but support bigger government. (He notes that a majority endorse more spending even as they diverge on how it should be allocated.) This tension makes the center of the political spectrum anything but placid or stable. "The conflicted conservatives are the interesting group," he writes. "Large enough to swing all elections one way or the other, their votes are potentially available to both parties. They want liberal policies and respond to specific Democratic appeals to do more and spend more on various domestic priorities. They think of themselves as conservatives and respond to Republican identification with conservatism. Which has the stronger appeal, liberal policies or conservative symbols, is a close call and so varies with the times."[68] Rather, what needs further attention is how quantified measure generates a tacit or underlying quality or value that looks to be at odds with its own finding. Particularly salient to these discussions would be measures of recognized tensions between rich and poor—which have reported to be exacerbated in the years since the financial crisis—wealth is still portrayed as an achievement of effort, education, and ability.

Larry Bartels has carefully examined public opinion pertaining to measures of economic and political inequality since 1980; these measures reverse trends toward well-dispersed political influence and widely distributed economic gains of the 1950s, when the ideals of American pluralism based on small-town life were crafted by political scientists. There is a notion that Americans have become more tolerant of inequality and that the lower income strata have become more conservative in a betrayal of their interests, which was popularized in Thomas Frank's *What's the Matter with Kansas?*[69] In contrast, Bartels finds that, with the exception of the South, where whites' aversion to the Republican Party ended with Reagan, low-income whites generally in United States have become more Democratic. Yet Democrats, like Republicans, have shifted to the right, a move that has been driven by and translated into representation defined by contribution rather than by the defined benefit of citizenship that was the basis for what was termed "pluralism." Based on an examination of whose views get translated into action, elected officials have become "utterly unresponsive to the policy preferences of millions of low-income citizens, leaving their political interests to be served or ignored as the ideological whims of incumbent elites may dictate."[70]

Rather, Republican presidential victories correlate with gains in very recent economic performance, growth in high-income wealth, and campaign spending. Yet when examining public responses to tax policy, Bartels finds public response to President George Bush's comprehensive tax cuts of 2001 and 2003 to be contradictory and confusing as to the implementation and effects, whereas there was wide support to repeal the estate tax based in large measure on a mistaken belief that it would apply beyond the tiny fraction of beneficiaries. Conversely, wide public support for raising the minimum wage did not translate into policy, while poor relief translated to the Earned Income Tax Credit, despite limited support among non-recipients. In sum, he finds that elite control of policy, information, and the terms of technical sophistication for implementation trump what would turn out to be public preferences if they were readily discernible and translatable into the minutiae of legislation:

> I believe it is a mistake to suppose *any* specific package could be said to represent "popular wishes" or "majority views" regarding such a complex matter of public policy. For one thing, detailed probing would almost certainly reveal a good deal of ambivalence, uncertainty, and outright contradiction in the views of various citizens regarding the various provisions of any specific plan. What is more, even if individual citizens were splendidly clear and consistent, "majority views" would not be; political theorists have demonstrated that for policy issues of any real complexity, there is generally *no* specific policy outcome that could not be defeated by some other proposal in a majority vote. Thus, the appealing-seeming notion of popular sovereignty is both psychologically unrealistic and logically incoherent.[71]

People took tax cuts as applying to them even when they did not; opposed inequality even as they imagined that they might someday be the beneficiaries of it; and felt that the rich did not contribute their fair share, even as they endorsed what they took to be the still widely available means to become wealthy. The doubt regarding the notion of popular sovereignty treats it as a strictly empirical phenomenon, where interest can be transparently conveyed into policy through some technology of representation. If the people do not resemble the sovereigns in this dimension of power, then it may be the conception of popular sovereignty that needs to be rethought. Needless to say, Bartels's study, published on the eve of the financial crisis did not take into account the financial bailout, although it might help explain why politicians could seem immune to raising taxes.

Still, the tolerance for the rich as a category of person remained largely what it had been before the bailout until a social movement articulated a compelling counter-narrative for concentration of wealth. In a poll taken at the end of 2011 by the Pew Research Center, two-thirds of respondents believed there are strong conflicts between rich and poor in the United States, up from 47 percent in 2009 and including a majority of Republicans and the largest increase among those identified as independents. While 46 percent report that wealth results from unearned privilege, 43 percent say that it results from hard work, ambition, or education, a figure unchanged from 2008.[72] The polls display a gap between recognition of increasing inequality as a problem and a shift in analytic frameworks to account for the perception, leaving open the question of how that gap might be filled. Yet if recognition of inequality corresponds to its increasing measure (the concentration of wealth), this does not necessarily disrupt attachment to the ideal of the personage of the wealthy, the prospect that an attachment could be formed that would continue to compensate in some fashion for the increasingly obvious deficit.

This culture of attachment to the exceptional, the outlier, the outperformer forms the basis of the celebrity complex. While stardom is certainly an effect of mass media and emerges from theatrical audiences in the nineteenth century and their fidelity to transnational ballet dancers, opera singers, and actors, the one served as a screen for the desires of the many. Contemporary celebrity is infused with a different sort of intimacy, where the inner details of daily life; access to the actuality of the person, not the persona; persistent tracings of their every move operates as a kind of derivative possession of the celebrity body. Performance has crossed the transom and moved into daily life, not simply for attention to the star, but for access to stardom out of quotidian experience, the hyperactive spread of reality television and Internet genres in which any utterance can suddenly go viral and receive excessive attention or anybody can garner sufficient support to win the race.[73] Spectatorship here is not a matter of distance between a passive audience and what is taken to be active onscreen or onstage. It constitutes its own forms of arbitrage, where viewers' participation rests on a kind of hedge, an attachment to one of many minor differences among players to bet on the desired outcome.[74] The attachment to inequality is not the same as a tolerance for it. Fans feel the betrayal and disappointment much as the rich are loathed while the means to obtain wealth are endorsed. Mass arbitrage meets the arbitrage of the masses. The middle cannot speak when voice is found only at the extremes, as an outlier or a forecast of failure and impossibility.

Since the whole of the American people can be only a speculative ideal, its concrete, if transitory, manifestations can be known only by bundling some attributes, artifacts of measure whose expectations to fix public opinion contribute to its volatility. The culture of measure is not lost on its objects. The people so procured do not sit still or bristle at being mistaken for their attributes, even as a world is delivered according to these expectations of fit between what people want and what they get. If the public good depends on a kind of site or place and the nonprofit is where it is produced, polls are a technical device that stands in for an authentic voice that yields a perspective from which the people can be known. As with the nonprofit economy, this culture of measure may translate public inclinations into a number, a static object, even something that for a moment could be priced, but it also set the public to work by providing a continuously dynamic view of it. If polls transcribe the public into something normative, measure is also deployed to achieve certain outcomes, to direct performance, to enhance productivity. Approval ratings, consumer confidence, and happiness indices assert themselves to be in the very midst of where the people actually are as a function of their statistical aggregation around what is referred to as a central tendency.

Yet much of what occupies public attentions, counts as news, accumulates as celebrity lies not in the middle but at the extremes of distributed behavior. When a norm is oriented to an outlier, when common attentions are focused on the extremes, when stars make the fields we lie in, upward pressure is placed on the midpoint. The center holds less not because it is impossible to quantify but because it remains in motion, at the heart of volatility, throbbing, shifting away from the prospect that it can anchor the effluvial masses. Nor can the center serve as a phantom norm, a repository of security or an expansive distribution of equanimity. Being average is not good enough, productivity is continuously referenced to the exemplary, and assessments must be ongoing to anticipate slips in performance. No, the center does not hold; nor does it contain a stable majority. This orienting and model-making work is now done at the outskirts. Financial institutions are thrilled that their best managers are seven times more productive than the average because the firm reaps the rewards and because expectations for output are raised for all. Academic deans can say no less of the coveted star hires whose field-making contributions raise the profile of the entire institution. This, too, is the derivative at work, the arbitrage by which the many are set in motion by the volatility unleashed by the one. The stability of the public is undone by its very operations. Mobilization is understood to pivot on small numbers leveraged to significant gain rather than toward construction of a capacious and centering consensus of the mass. Such was the tactical mastery of a Karl Rove but also the social media savvy of the first Obama campaign.[75] Those who master micro-polling, wedge issues, or triangulation keenly appreciate how effective this mobilization of a volatile public can be, and once the measure is taken and benefit is gleaned, they need not concern themselves with the aftermath.

Public Gathering

The public is a kind of good made in a certain place: the nonprofit sector. It is a perspective on the people that situates a way of knowing all through the measure of a few (either at the volatile center or the shifting outlier). In both instances, "public" turns out to derive from private values that divert from one conception of public to build up the banks of another. This, again, is the etymological root of "derive" as the redirection of a flow of water, as in the bank of river (*rive* in French)—a redirection that results in some kind of accumulation, surplus, or excess. What was once in the middle, safely secured between two sides, does not stay there. Yet not everything escapes, just what could not be contained, this active third force. The derivative reorients the boundaries of economy and of the cultural—in this case, the sense of what it means to be a people together. But the public is a complex concept that courses through all societal domains, diverting from some presumably private matter to what pertains to all. Such was the case for two of the three foundational domains of society's holy trinity. That leaves the question of the political. The derivative logic undoes the partition of public and private. A flood of the political ensues.

Politics, too, can be thought along the lines of a derivative, whether as the consensus taken away from a process of deliberation, as the delegation of the authority of the many to their representatives, or as the antagonism and conflict that are the residue of an active encounter of difference or an unmasterable excess.[76] Consensus and delegation have been key to maintaining the boundaries of the political; dissensus, by contrast, threatens to undo the legitimate processes and decisions that delimit what counts as the political. This latter perspective emerges as a critique of the former in the work of Chantal Mouffe:

> I contend that the belief in the possibility of a universal rational consensus has put democratic thinking on the wrong track. Instead of trying to design the institutions which, through supposedly "impartial" procedures, would reconcile all conflicting interests and values, the task for democratic theorists and politicians should be to envisage the creation of a vibrant "agonistic" public sphere of con-

testation where different hegemonic political projects can be confronted. This is, in my view, the *sine qua non* for an effective exercise of democracy. There is much talk today of "dialogue" and "deliberation" but what is the meaning of such words in the political field, if no real choice is at hand and if the participants in the discussion are not able to decide between clearly differentiated alternatives?[77]

Whether conceived as a moment of settlement or disruption, of incorporation or refusal, politics in this regard is the effect or consequence of some mobilization, activity, engagement, or gathering. Accordingly, politics would belong to the formal domain of decision, while the political would refer to the firmament or assembly of differences. While these might be distinguished as formal and informal, bounded and unbounded, fixed and in motion, the relation between them could well be described as derivative. Deliberation and choice, as the means and ends of politics, assume that interests come already attached to the mass of the body politic and that alternative futures are already inscribed in the different directions that can come from present direction of forces. "Democracy" would be the name given to this intersection of normative dispositions and operational processes, of values to be achieved through particular means of participation that can be distinguished from the other two societal domains of economy and culture.

Certainly, there is much in the institutional arrangements and means of assessing politics that would bear out this apparent separation between the production of political interests and their realization through some circulation of deliberative decision. The concern that democracy has fallen would pertain to the sense that the range of possibilities (choices and alternatives) had been narrowed and circumscribed. Yet this narrowing of the choices that get attended to and presented in the formal arena of parliamentary decision has come up against a vast proliferation of issues, affects, and means for articulating and voicing what counts as political. Rather than being able to speak of a class, a people, or a group with a fixed interest, the dimensions of political consideration are multiple within and across individuals in ways that suggest an active circulation of attributes that can be aggregated and leveraged in all manner of ways. Without doubt, the domain of what can count as a recognizable object of contention has expanded greatly since the inauguration of mass democracy. With the revolutions against monarchy, capital, and colonialism of the past 250 years, the universe of political subjects, of who can be recognized as eligible and entitled to the exercise of rights, has expanded enormously. So, too, the means to mobilize political sentiment, articulate political sensibility, and occupy a space so it is marked as political now exceeds the legitimate authority to sanction politics and channel it into legislative form. The expansion of rights conferred by states or others and the self-assignment of capacities to empower, differentiate, invent, or express a means of participation may not await or be oriented toward official recognition, legitimation, or consignment.

Politics overflows its banks; regulatory capacities are disintermediated; political value is assembled from shared attributes that come from far and near; affiliation is rendered volatile; the face value of the political exceeds the underlying means of representation and formal channels of participation; sentiments are judged in anticipation of their completion as consequences. These features of the derivative begin to illuminate a political economy that otherwise appears incoherent, excessive, ungovernable, and indeterminate. This inchoate, affective, and effective materialization of political forces is here understood to be an excess criticality. Disbursed in and outside of what formally counts as the political, what appears and forms its visible sensibilities are other kinds of calculus, different ways to be in touch, to make manifest what will come to have political value.[78]

Two sensibilities of surplus or excess become legible. One would be marked by an expansion of rights, resources, distribution of goods, or allocation of capacities. This is a demand of more of what is, either because public goods, services, and spaces have been cut, curtailed, or assaulted and devalued or because more are able to assert expectations and demands to share in what would be considered the vast and total store of social wealth and capability. Health and education should be universal; jobs and housing should be available to all; freedoms and protections should be applied to people irrespective of their claims on or access to property. This is the conception of expanding equality that underwrites the democratic trajectory. The other conception of excess or surplus generates the basis for what cannot be readily absorbed, for expanding the horizon of desire and possibility beyond what currently exists, for an ability to grasp current affairs comprehensively and to critique them fundamentally. Here critical capacities do not readily translate into demands that can be met. Instead, they leave a residue that creates the need and desire for more of what is not here (at least not yet). Self-expanding and self-directed critique does not dissipate when goods or rights are allocated. It continues beyond itself, producing an excess, an excess criticality.

We have seen, in the case of economies (profit or nonprofit) and for the cultural means through which the public is represented, that the instruments devised to manage risk themselves produced an excess, a surplus, an ungovernable uncertainty, and a pervasive volatility. Such would certainly seem to be the case for politics. Politics treated as a realm where conflict is resolved, interests are articulated, consensus is achieved, and decisions are taken—all against the threat of a generalized disorder and breakdown if resolution does not happen—confounds the persistence of what resists or refuses settlement. "Pluralism" was the name given to the way in which difference of interest, opinion, or affiliation, said to characterize a democratic polity such as the United States, congealed into a mass. Each part could be balanced against the other through an expert process of representation, which would resolve the spread of views into a single outcome through a polling of politicians in the legislative process.

Democracy in this regard hewed closely to the Hayekian market, with all information taken in, weighed for its value and assigned a single true price incorporating all difference. Conflicts are normative in that they reinforce the supra-individual mechanism from which the many become one. Under pluralism, this friction might be conceived as the minorities insufficiently attended to or a decision ineffectively crafted in consideration of various constituencies. Such notions assume that people are bearers of interests that can be readily dissociated from them and parsed or combined like the patches on a quilt. Further, people bear these interests silently until given voice in an occasion for decision, such as an election or a legislative vote. In this Jeffersonian ideal, people do not suffer the alienation of their inalienable rights; rather, they achieve happiness because the pursuit of their interests is not detoured by a political process, even if this last mimics the operations of the market itself.[79]

From this perspective, politics is scarce among a population that otherwise lacks the time, desire, intelligence, information, or disposition to effectively grasp and execute political action. Yet whatever this American ideal of pluralism—one ironically dependent on all manner of exclusion from the political process by those populations within and beyond the nation-state, whose differences might exceed what procedural forms could accommodate—something in the mix between the felicitous inclusion and exclusion has broken down, even in the eyes of those who would continue to defend the pluralist project. The increasingly technical, expert-based, elite-driven character of politics opens a chasm of increasing disaffection from politicians, parties, policies, and institutions. In some kind of nefarious feedback loop, politicians themselves run for office against the claim that government can do good and position themselves as outsiders ready to purge the machinery of once disinterested representation from its slide into the grip of special interest.

The rift between aspirations and satisfaction makes for what Pippa Norris, a leading scholar in the field, calls a "democratic deficit," which "arises from some combination of growing public expectations, negative news, and/or failing government performance."[80] While pluralism adhered to a market metaphor, so, curiously, does its demise. What was once a source of an expanding horizon of credit is now perceived as a problem of overexpenditure, a deficit that will never be repaid. On what she calls the demand side, increased literacy, education, and cognitive skills lead to emancipative values (or, conversely, a collapse of trust), whereas on the supply side would be government underperformance, with an amplifying role of these deficiencies performed by the media, all of which ultimately could jeopardize the legitimacy of democratization itself.

Critical citizens as Norris understands them require grounding in trust, tolerance, and adherence to the rule of law if the disequilibrium between supply and demand is not to lead to a collapse of democratic value. To be critical in this regard is to be circumspect about the limits to criticism, which means being willing to subordinate a desire for comprehensive change to the need to uphold the regulatory framework that holds the citizenry together. The state is hereby culturalized as the tacit agreement to stay within its bounds of dissent or to risk its delegitimation and therefore the loss of democracy altogether. Once again, these are the stabilizing cultural foundations of modernization that form the basis of social capital as the required dispositions of a citizenship to achieve a democratic polity.

Yet despite the faith in the explanatory power of the market metaphor, of social capital that maintains equilibrium between the demand for political performance and what can be delivered, an excess of criticality can seep out in the gap between critical citizens who must tolerate the democratic deficit and those forms of civic engagement that bear their own kinds of debt. Streets can fill. Demands go unmet, or antagonisms do not get translated into what the formal realm recognizes as politics. Whether the deficit is to be reduced by lowered expectations and a reinvestment of trust in the instruments of representation or the gap feeds its own expansion and excess as people exercise critical capacities that escape the containment of delegation or regulation poses a pressing juncture for the relation between the people and politics as such. The concerns that a "culture of complaint" would undermine American values was a conservative rendering of the problem of deficit, wherein the expansion of democratization had met its limits not from corruption by elites but by overextension to a racial or otherwise insufficiently educated mass.[81]

Naming this political constraint with the presumably nonpolitical concept of culture made it easier to assign blame for failure and reinstate earlier terms of exclusion from democratic participation. Democracy was perfectly rational, but many who would aspire to be part of it were not. In this, what came in the late 1980s and early 1990s to be called the culture wars name a larger dilemma of decolonization that provoked anxiety that democratization would be the enemy of democracy. Identity, here meaning non–European in origin, non–male and heterosexual in orientation, and non–urban and industrial in address would escape from the private sphere of domesticity and reproduction to press into the political field—expanding it, yes, but also straining its ability to be recognized. In less guarded moments, those rattling the gates of civilization would be dubbed primitives—humans closer to nature, where nature, too, would be figured beyond the ken of deliberative demand and contestation. Too many would demand too much, and somehow the recent arrivals at the table of rights would spoil things for those who had been quietly enjoying their meal. Hence, the notion that those who named racism, sexism, or other ills were "un–American" in form and content betrayed an uneasiness regarding the delimitation between populations inside and outside the United States who were crowding out what pluralist visions of progress once promised, exacerbating tensions around borders insufficiently policed and immigrants with undeserved claims to rights or protections.[82]

More generally, thinking of democracy in the context of colonial mimicry, by which capitalism with a particular trajectory was to be generalized around the world, promised self-determination and participation on condition of extracting the energy needed to drive the process of development as such. If excessive differences could be curbed and a common civilizational disposition embraced, short-term loss of particular identities could be traded for long-term prosperity. This would require recognizing the place from which such future freedom would emanate as the source of a sovereignty to be gained and not lost. Positing an ideal or original model of democracy from which there is a gap or deficit fits with a political program whereby development looks like an imitation of the West by the rest, or internally of the elite by the mass. Surely for such copying to maintain credibility, it must also seem achievable; there must be a sense that space exists if not now, at least in the future, that would render the democratically deficient into full participants. Yet time and again, those promised but yet to receive the fruits of democratic or market-based emancipation have been refused in their demands or turned away at the door.

This compulsive modeling in which the ideals of democracy are sacrificed to the thwarted actualization of democratization is what Tim Mitchell, whose earlier work was discussed in Chapter 1, refers to, in a sly double entendre that also articulates the apparatus of energy with that of politics, as "carbon democracy." Responding specifically to the arguments counseling that cultural predispositions must be acquired (and others lost) if democracy is to be attained, he scans the horizon and observes:

> Yet there is no reliable evidence, as far as I am aware, that the presence of a civic culture—attitudes of trust, tolerance, mutual respect and other liberal virtues—facilitates the emergence of democracy. There is, in fact, no shortage of historical evidence to suggest the opposite. Once can find repeated examples in the history of democratic struggles in the West of tolerant, educated, liberal political classes who were opponents of democratization, fighting to prevent the extension of effective political rights to those who did not own property, to religious and racial minorities, to women, and to colonial subjects. In many cases, the civic virtues that dominant political classes possessed provided the grounds on which to oppose democratizations. Their own civility and reasonableness, they often claimed, qualified them to act as spokespersons for the interests of those who were not yet ready to speak for themselves. Once democratic rights have been achieved, their exercise may encourage the development of virtuous civic attitudes, at least among members of the expanded political class—virtues whose inculcation and practice become a mode through which people subject themselves to democratic authority. Democratisation, on the other hand, has often been a battle against those attitudes. It has required a more intransigent set of engagements and practices.[83]

Here, Mitchell is referring to a particular socio-technical process by which what is below the surface is made manifest on the ground as an expressive political economy. His carbon democracy is about the process of colonial mimesis whereby the extraction of oil that fuels global development is articulated as consistent with the support of spreading democracy. His scrupulous attention to the contradictions that inhere in the rendering of this natural resource into a political arrangement hinges on producing its own kind of knowledge deficit between that which can be represented and that which cannot. What he says about oil as the framing of a particular nexus between nature and culture might readily be taken back to understand the problem of the people and the lack or excess of democracy considered here: "This gap between the declining quantity of known oil and the expanding quantity of unknown, yet-to-be-discovered oil creates a (new) space: a space to be governed by economic calculation. For it is economists who claim to have mastered the methods of representation."[84]

It is this same method of calculation, of an insertion into a gap meant to stabilize the relationship between a source and an outcome, that is to anchor the relation between democratic values and techniques of democratization. The politics of knowledge open when the mechanisms of calculation falter and the place that a particular expertise issues from becomes destabilized. The prevailing version of neoclassical economics translated into oil extraction around the price system, which mediated between a naturally occurring supply and a rationally structured demand. Technology and information would make oil permanently abundant, even if it meant shifting to sources such as shale and tar sands, while political power—whether military intervention, human rights, or spreading democracy—would secure future reserves.

This knowledge regime is being contested by the return of the institutional economics repressed not only by the rise of neoclassical price technologies undone through derivatives trading (as discussed in the previous chapter) but also by the popular responses to political arrangements of democratic development that had been put in place. The institutional school has now contested the neoclassical rule through the notions of peak oil based on rates of flow rather than movements of price. Accordingly, rates of flow have a history that can peak at a certain point (although this peak first forecast in the 1950s to arrive in the 1970s itself has been a shifting target), focusing attention not on price but on the whole social arrangements and consequences of reliance on a particular kind of energy flow.

The relation of energy to democracy is not metaphorical but materially linked to shared logics of representation, expertise, and growth or progress. The promise of mass democracy was that ever higher attainments of education would multiply expertise, which in turn bears mechanisms of self-rule that are generalized to civic participation. But if the formal realms of democracy are shrinking as representation accommodates less and less of the population and of what are articulated as popular needs, demands and aspirations, critical citizenship will turn into a mobilizing excess. As with economy, it would seem that democracy too no longer presents itself as an expansive space that can accommodate all who make a claim for inclusion. Rather, the work of the public would be to sort which critical dispositions can gain a voice that translates into policy—that is, to regulate flows when a future without scarcity is no longer on the horizon but there is still a need to make decisions taken appear as the consequence of an objective process of measure. If nonprofit organizations and polling are two such technologies not only for putting a price on public input but also for regulating its flows, how might we best grasp the dynamics of this energic flow known as the people? If the developmentalist strategy of democratization was thwarted by the failure of the means of delivery of democratic ideas, how are we to understand the political flows that issue from mobilizing populations?

Democratization has been fueled by certain flows of energy that may have peaked. One potential solution would be to change the definition of what counts as the people from the deep, inexhaustible wells of the masses to more viscous and opaque substrates that require more active processing. Like oil, the people would need to be derived from sites and materials where they were previously thought to be inaccessible. Accordingly, costs of access would rise and those best positioned to take the risks of exploration, and development would need to be given a wide berth to ensure continued supply. Lobbyists, consultants, pollsters, staff members, super–PACs (the political action committees empowered after the U.S. Supreme Court ruled in 2010, in *Citizens United*, to remove limits on spending to advertise political views), and massive infusions of advertising monies would need to be applied to keep the machineries of democracy humming. Costs would rise, the wealthy would enjoy disproportionate influence, politicians would need to be more responsive to those constituencies with greatest leverage, but the people who really counted would continue to be heard and their will acted on. The din of discontent could be dismissed as so much noise, incapable of converting itself from vague protest to focused action.

The logic of flows is not only that there are many but also that the ebb of one may take attention away from the emergence of others. In the case of the commodification of energy, changing from coal to oil can break the strength of labor unions to apply choke points on distribution as much as the shift to biofuel can exacerbate hunger by raising food prices—if the emerging technologies do nothing to disturb the concentrations of ownership and control of these vast stores of wealth. So, too, referenda and digital technologies, micro-fundraising, and networked swarms do not necessarily rupture corporate pipelines to power or breach elite walls of exclusion. Still, there is the prospect that what looks to be the exhaustion of one flow of democratization could turn out to augur the emergence of a radically different flow. Detecting the basis for this shift would entail examining the various gaps that have been opened in the flows of public making discussed thus far and to see how this applies to the critical capacities of a people no longer conceived, like nature itself, as a mute and undeveloped mass—a resource to be discovered, purposed, and rendered productive.

The gaps opened by nonprofit organizations and public opinion are tangible; those from which the excess criticality of the people issues seems far less so. How is this concept any different from the move from informal to formal on which representation is based or the translation of intangible to tangible that property rights regulate? Financial derivatives are, of course, interparty contracts that mediate a concrete price and an underlying value. In what media is excess criticality inscribed? What differences does it mediate? What materiality does it assume? With nonprofits we saw that charitable giving bears a kind of state agency, both the capacity to judge what deserves public attention and the transfer of funds via tax exemption from public coffers to private hands. Because the public good is derived from a privatizing circuit, the very dependence on the state for public benefit gets denied. This not only covers the inequality of who gets to decide what gets valued as a public good (through the magnitude of the gift). It also disavows the transfer of the distribution of public benefits away from the poor. Government is left in a double bind. Its legitimacy rests on denying its agency, while its efficacy in distributing social wealth to those with more of it goes unmarked. A gap opens between what the state can do and what needs doing. Derivative logics manufacture risk in the name of managing it.

So is the case with the volatility in measures of the public that accompany the disequilibrium of sanctioned public processes. Polling disaggregates some actionable collective will into individual responses that it then re-collects as measures of central tendency. At the same time that rating, ranking, and surveying that become deeply imbricated in every aspect of thoroughly managed lives and satisfaction must be gauged before the result is delivered, the outlier, the exception, the star or celebrity become the point of orientation for public dispositions and expressions of what is most valued. This gap between the obsessively measured and the excessively immeasurable departs in salient ways from the public quandary of mass society. In that case, the disenchanted masses, made indistinguishable through sheer number, could project a re-enchanting attachment to the charismatic leader, in the now classic Weberian formulation.[85]

The force of representation of the many incorporated in the one lent creditability to the office or station that the dear one inhabited. Now, it would seem, celebrity is a far more fragile affair, where one is only as good as his or her last film, his or her most recent quarterly earnings, speech, or game. In the realm of politics itself, charisma can attach much more readily to candidates than to incumbents, a cooling of coolness that President Obama had to confront, where the audacity of hope could remain promissory and imagistic. If results are the thing, productivity is the measure, and performance is the imperative, then attachments are likely to be fleeting and their foundations insufficient to provide stability. When such attachment is lost, or the prospect of attaining some measure of what the privileged have is removed, then the presence of this gap between a dwindling mean and a soaring outlier will seem unbearable to more. This yawning breach between democracy and democratization may open a failure to accept the austerity of expectations that deficits demand. Instead of a scarcity of public goods or distributed rights, the rift between political demands and politics' supply does not extinguish criticality but becomes its condition of possibility and elaboration.

None of these gaps ensure a particular political mobilization or tendency; nor do they ensure a given outcome. What seems more reasonable to say is that the terms of evaluation of the political, the means of recognizing how polity might flow and what it might be, require substantial adjustment. All that has been said so far about the public as a derivative of private values makes it difficult to see how the standard formulation of civil society as a realm of interconnection, cooperation, and association outside of state or market is still viable in concept or in practice. An NGO may differ from government, but it is hardly outside or independent of state processes. Rather, it takes on certain aspects and effects without assuming the place of the whole. Similarly, public opinion is scarcely independent of the market but is an expression of particular marketing devices that are entwined within disequilibrating flows of capital and wealth. Those excluded from circuits of decision may be portrayed as merely complaining, lacking coherent demands, or bereft of the intellectual or rhetorical capacities to make coherent criticisms, but they are nonetheless produced by effects of state that it cannot absorb.

Certainly, this is the case for the expansion of institutions of higher education, as for the professionalization of expertise where knowledge is to serve as a form of rule. As suggested in Chapter 1, the knowledge failure or limitation augured by the financial crisis and subsequent bailout made prominent the derailment of the professional managerial class's expansion as a technocratic channeling of enlarged critical capacities. If the conception of a shrinking middle class pertains to diminished capacities for consumption as a means of mobility—whether homeownership, consumer goods, health care, education, or retirement (to name the largest categories that are now managed so imperfectly by private insurance, contribution schemes, mortgages, student loans, and credit card debt)—it is devoid of a critical conception of its relation to growth. The link among personal prosperity, social progress, and increased GDP is axiomatic. There is no occasion for a critical interrogation of its terms. The pretensions to autonomy and self-governance of the professional managerial class suggest a different trajectory and itinerary.

The occupational girth of the professional managerial class continues to expand, driven by managerialism, intellectual property, industrialization of culture, and the like—making it the largest of all occupational categories and more than six times the number employed in manufacturing.[86] But its basis of association and its internal logic of association are to be decomposed and reformed from autonomous control of expert domains to highly specialized and technical knowledge that is subject to managerial requisites rather than self-rule (exemplified by the rise of managed care in medicine). This is not the only circuit of excess criticality; certainly, it is joined by other formations that are being broken up and reconfigured—pertaining to manufacturing employment, whiteness, heterosexuality and patriarchy, religious authority, immigrant assimilation—all of which nonetheless have been affected by the forces unleashed through the decomposition of the professional managerial class. It is instructive, for example, that there is increasing support for Republicans in those states that spend more in federal benefits than they collect in tax revenues, whereas the reverse is true in states with greater support for Democrats.[87] Where farm subsidies, deindustrialization, veterans' benefits, and other transfers articulate with decaying life ways, the criticism of government as a generic concept that stands in for lost autonomy is not the same as a critique of particular revenue flows that underwrite personal security through a social economy. The unequal distribution of population and representation that the system of states establishes (most explicitly through the equal apportioning of senators, irrespective of population) would make such a contradiction structural to the political geography of the United States.

The point here is not to dismiss all of the various mobilizations that are grouped under the names of civic participation, grassroots democracy, cultures of protest, or conceptions of political engagement grounded in generational cohorts or technological innovations. Yet taken together, these various frameworks might seem to be insufficiently comprehensive, coherent, or sustainable to serve as a source of alternative political energy.

Indeed, the very proliferation of categories of the political might augur a return to the concerns with fragmentation and failures of unity that were part of an earlier critique of radical democracy, new social movements, and identity politics.[88] For both the earlier and the more recent mobilizations, whatever their self-designation or inflection, the question remains how to value their emergence as part of a larger social process without reducing their significance or omitting their specificity. Once again, this is precisely what a derivative logic provides—namely, the capacity to see how aspects, attributes, or particular variants can both be associated together and placed in broader circulation; how they attain leverage; and how seemingly small or local volatilities can ripple elsewhere.

To make these circuits of excess criticality legible and to ground the term itself, it is worth applying to some of the aforementioned conceptual frameworks, vocabularies, and grammars of emergent, alternative, or inchoate political processes. If the value of these various political expressions can be affiliated without being reduced to some singular body or form, then what looks like deficit, deficiency, or scarcity of the political may itself be recalibrated in different terms. Notions of identity and new social movements may have seemed at the time to be fragmentations of an otherwise unifying political process, yet they shared the form of being movement with a determinant identity as their content. If anything, political matters have become more complex as protests and movements, networks and organizations, policy and public opinion, democracy and democratization, or other couplets that describe structure and agency, formal and informal dimensions, seem to bear very different approaches for how to understand what counts as the means for producing the political. Just as nonknowledge was the generalized excess of economic relations oriented toward knowledge making, excess criticality would stand as a parallel kind of phenomenon for grasping what makes the field of the political expansive. Hence, it is the dimensions of this field, as well as the conditions for its ongoing expansion, that need to be accounted for if the political is to move from a calculus of scarcity to a valuing of abundance from which generative possibility springs.

Let us begin with the notions of civic participation so firmly rooted in Tocquevillian traditions of American democracy and move to networked forms that reference other bases for association and engagement. In a narrative that is key to the very formulation of modernization, the intimacy and integrative ties grounded in face-to-face community are shielded from the loss of value orientation that mass or industrial society brings through the florescence of civil society. The march of progress would embrace market rationalization while casting an eye back toward precapitalist kinship, sustaining nostalgia for a past where terms of association would have been involuntary for many. Civic participation is said to spring from the twin motivations of self-interest (or Madisonian liberal individualism) and civic duty (or Jeffersonian republican communitarianism). The anxiety of those who champion civic participation is that self-interest has colonized even voluntary associations and compensatory institutions such as family, school, and media, thereby undermining the capacity for trust and tolerance of difference.

Consider a few of the secular trends that might suggest a disintegrating civil society. Voter turnout peaked at 80 percent in the late nineteenth century (when most people living in the United States were ineligible to vote) but had fallen to 49 percent by 1996 (before rising to 59 percent in 2008, fueled by effective voter registration drives). Voluntary associations such as 4-H clubs and the American Legion peaked in the middle of the twentieth century, replaced by professionally managed citizens' associations and advocacy groups. Church attendance follows a similar pattern, peaking at nearly half the population in the mid-1950s before falling by a fifth, to 38 percent, at the end of the century. Interest in public affairs (as conventionally understood) has declined from a high of more than one-third of the population in the 1970s to less than one-quarter forty years later.[89] As we have seen, a common response to the communitarian critique that social capital is being lost is to shift focus from civic participation as an expanding mass base to civic or social entrepreneurialism as a mark of those most capable of seizing opportunity and therefore deserving of the rewards they reap. This might be taken as a gambit that a return to business models, especially for a new generation said to eschew conventional partisan lines and ideological divides, will reinvigorate public purposes through private means.

Another line of argument is based more explicitly on claims to generational shifts. Rather than political disfranchisement, recent college graduates are found to value community over jobs and to be more active politically.[90] These emergent sensibilities have been cast in generational terms wherein certain prevailing archetypes based on how young people are reared engender a particular disposition to the world, be it idealist, reactive, civic, or adaptive. These generational traits are viewed in cyclical terms, with the current rising cohort the largest and most diverse, with nearly one hundred million Americans born between 1982 and 2003 and 40 percent of them nonwhite. According to this literature, this age group is reared in a similarly protective manner, with strong social norms and group bonds.

In electoral terms, this age cohort, said to be more civically oriented, stably partisan, and optimistic in outlook, constituted one in five voters who supported Obama by a margin of two to one over John McCain and delivered 80 percent of the 8.5 million vote margin.[91] The cyclical formulation of generationally based change fits with a conception of crisis as an oscillation between disequilibrium and resolution encountered in the narratives of the financial bailout, but in this case the outcome is a reinstatement of a new political norm.

These generational claims constituted a kind of applied social science and were clearly central to Obama's campaign strategy. Democratic advisers have been quick to understand his victory in these terms to affix demographic trends with their own political future in a manner they hope to be self-fulfilling. In one synthetic popular account, Morley Winograd and Michael D. Hais, both Democratic Party media consultants, adapt their view of the millennial era from William Strauss and Jeff Howe, who examine generationally marked political cycles of eighty years (four generations) starting with the American Revolution and continuing to the Civil War, the Great Depression, and the financial crisis. In a kind of trans-historical prehistory of the public before polling, contemporary trends are read backward to explain changing patterns and outcomes. Traumatic historical episodes become generic turning points that reset demographic tendencies. Each of these crisis events becomes the basis for a regeneration or reenergizing of civic life toward a climax of heightened fear, uncertainty, doubt, with attendant polarization and conflict that eventuates in a resolution that unfolds in the twenty-year aftermath of the critical turn. The cyclical analysis renders credible forecasting claims that direct campaign strategies and applications of resources to realize a particular expression of popular will.

Millennials were more likely to prefer activist government than the rest of the population (58 percent versus 52 percent), with nearly two-thirds coming from households in which someone was unemployed and themselves experiencing unemployment at rates two to three times that of the rest of the population. Millennials also have been found to be more tolerant of religious, ethnic, and sexual difference than older generations.[92] Public service is now a standard feature of college-bound teenagers' experience, with more than four-fifths considering it an effective way to solve national problems. In 2009, volunteering hit an all-time high of more than 63 million, with all of that increase coming from the 1.3 million Millennials who offered an additional one billion hours of their time.[93] This version of local engagement leveraged to national aspiration for change is evident in the centrality of digital platforms and social media that permit customization and issue-driven participation. What serves as a means of cultural participation through leisure activities is also enfolded in realms of commerce and of civic engagement. Without doubt, this type of survey-driven argumentation is speculative in a manner that aspires to be predictive by convincing both political leaders and potential constituents to find their common cause in each other. Certainly, the ongoing prospect is there, as well, for the particular confluence of attentions to become unmoored and for what was mobilized toward electoral ends to be redirected to other kinds of activism. This would describe another route to the production of excess criticality.

Even in this very cursory account of generational explanation, the recurrent cyclical terms are in tension with some kind of unique crisis event (here, those of 2008) and of some unforeseen sociocultural change (the advent of social media). From this perspective, it is less clear whether the increase in voluntary activity represents the return to a moment of civic engagement in an earlier cycle or some array of developments whose etiologies are far more complex. Gabriella Coleman has cautioned about homogenizing either generationally based uses of new media or the political temperaments of so-called hactivists any more than one could collapse the anarchist and Tea Party moments of libertarianism.[94] If college-bound students are taken as the measure, unpaid labor in nonprofit community organizations is both part of that professionalized economy and replete with tacit and explicit compulsions to build résumés, be well-rounded, fulfill graduation requirements, and the like. This is not to deny that teenagers (or anyone else) have dispositions toward helping others. It means only that it would be difficult to isolate such attitudes as variables independent of the larger processes by which free time is captured by circuits of nonprofit activity. Such complexity would argue for the continued relevance of some kind of derivative logic where civic and public spheres are permeated with market instrumentalities while still affiliating and associating people through scalable, rankable, and targeted aspects of their social activity.

That some technological innovation itself is fundamental to the emergence of new social and political expressions is another key *explanandum* that suggests a different way to grasp excess criticality. A well-established affirmative position now exists that the Internet is inherently democratic because it replaces hierarchical structures with person-to-person interactions. Crowdsourcing enhances access to and from those in power; allows for direct real-time conveyance of popular views, needs, and solutions; and allows for rapid mobilization of large numbers of people on behalf of a particular problem. Typically, these perspectives articulate closely with a cultural, generationally based shift (although the average age of Facebook users is thirty-eight).[95] Among these commentators, Clay Shirky has identified a cognitive surplus, more socially developmental than generational per se, in which he argues that excessive television watching, like excessive drinking in England in the eighteenth century, is turning from passive consumption to active forms of participation that engender emergent forms of civic space (then, public houses for debate; now, the Internet) and engagement. A cognitive surplus results from people who are interconnected donating a portion of their free time to create something at a larger scale (such as Wikipedia).[96]

Yet whether digital democracy flattens hierarchies or supports them; connects the base and the leadership or opens a gap between them; serves as a medium of disclosure or surveillance, consensus or contestation, inclusion or partition is subject to considerable debate. Elizabeth Losh has focused on "how computer technology creates secondary purposes and secondary audiences never imagined by the original senders of an official message or the architects of a given system of state-sanctioned communication."[97] She traces the ways in which government websites and online campaigns get hacked, repurposed, appropriated, and parodied, which in turn heightens the anxieties of legislatures, especially in the context of the war on terror around the dissemination of means for making videogames, blogs, PowerPoint presentations, and the like. Fantasies of more fully participatory modes of citizenship and open source access clash with proprietary and security concerns around piracy and leaks (although Losh's book was published before the WikiLeaks imbroglio). The subversion of channels and suffusion of communication challenge rational notions of decision making, responsibility, and accountability.

These are concerns not only of contemporary politicians but also of the founders of information science, such as Norbert Wiener, Claude Shannon, and Vannevar Bush.[98] In their models they sought to rescue objective information signals and transfers from the noisy environments that would render them incoherent. They also, through both scientific communities and public policy in what is now recognized as the Cold War partition of pure and applied research, would align professional expertise with lay interests. The risks of unintended consequences, abundant and divertible means of communications, confusions of value and message, and ungoverned conflict all compel more active professional and amateur attention to digital platforms not as neutral tools but as media for political agendas in which rights and responsibilities get worked through. Anna McCarthy has perceptively documented the corporate engagement with norms of civic engagement in the development of public service television during the 1950s that meets counterpoints in the form of labor-produced broadcasts. What was initially imagined as a solution to the potential unruliness of mass democracy through expert design protocols of communication generates a whole field of excess.[99]

That regulation generates not only anxieties of what rules cannot fix, but also re- and de-channeling of information flows, the threat of noise, and the founding intersection in cybernetics of the ideas that would shape both digital and pricing technologies, suggests the salience of the discussions of financial disintermediation to consideration of political processes. Under both circumstances, the regulatory apparatus does less to contain what are legitimate terms of exchange than to amplify forms of circulation that overflow the banks of established channels. Hence, if civic participation and citizenship could be conceived of as a particular type of exchange between government and people that would establish who gets to be involved and what gets to be the object of deliberation, the expanded field of the political would be populated by many genres of alternative and new media practice.

Leah Lievrouw charts an array of these genres that operate along dimensions of scope or magnitude of participation, from small collectives to multitudes; of stance or tone of critique, such as serious, parodic, ironic, satiric, and so forth; and of agency or orientation to action, whether interventionist, illicit, reconfigurative, or remediative. The relations of and among technological channels and social intercession she understands as mediation. Culture jamming transpires in the social domain of popular culture, mainstream media, and corporate advertising. It appropriates images, sound, and text from popular culture toward ends of cultural critique and political and economic commentary. Alternative computing resident in both hardware and software focuses on hacking, open source system design, and file sharing in the name of open access to and use of information technology. Participatory journalism operates through reporting, news commentary, and public opinion through online services, blogs, and independent media to cover what typically is under-reported or not investigated.

Mediated mobilization works through social movements and identity and cultural politics to get people onto the streets by means of social media, mobs, virtual worlds and blogs toward activist mobilization, and exemplification of alternative lifestyles. Finally, common knowledge operates through professional disciplinary expertise and socially sanctioned knowledge that takes the forms of tagging, bookmarking, wikis, and crowdsourcing to mobilize outsiders' amateur knowledge and archiving of divergent or arcane ways of knowing to expand from proprietary and expert circuits to consider who, what, where, when, and why knowledge is generated.[100] Certainly, this proliferation of voicings does not begin with social media. Looking back at the formation of the industrial proletariat, for example, Jacques Rancière has suggested, "To insist on the overly broad words of people, worker and proletarian is to insist on their inherent difference, on the space of dissenting invention that this difference offers."[101]

Among students of social movements, a distinction is made between civic participation, which ranges from voting to membership in churches or sports clubs, and contentious political activity, which includes participation in social movement organizations, protests, marches, and direct action.[102] In one recent study, nearly two-thirds of a nationally representative sample had been part of a contentious political event of this kind, although only about a fifth of these have sustained or organizationally core relations to such movements, and two-fifths more move from one to another. While organizational affiliation has declined over time, participation itself has actually increased, with the one-year rate standing at 15.2 percent of the population in 1965 and rising to 21.7 percent in 1997.[103] Participation in social movements and activism can follow multiple trajectories and is conceived as persistence (when individuals remain with the same movement over time); transfer (when they join another grouping); abeyance (when they leave and return at a later point); and disengagement (when they stop engaging in collective action).[104]

This fluidity within an increasing level of participation is at odds with a narrative of decline in political interest and a zero-sum notion that digital engagements have replaced more traditional assemblies of political activity. Young and old people remain the most likely participants in political protest, also at odds with the notion that the young are uniformly disaffected or uninterested. Such trajectories of mobilization suggest what might be understood as a movement internal to social movements. If over some expanded duration the majority of the population lends itself to some kind of direct involvement, the ebbs and flows through these circuits of contestation cannot simply be treated as a fragility or instability in sustaining presence in the realm of political activism. That many leave only to return indicates that underlying issues that generate mobilization do not go away. Instead, dispositions are carried through a medium and over time in a way that is not conventionally recognized or captured. This larger body would be the referent of polity or the people when treated not simply as a potential but as a reservoir from which activity continues to spring.

None of this specifies what this politics does, what its engagements consist of, what its ideas or orientations augur for the direction of society. The social science literature that this work draws on is formalistic by design, treating dynamics that engender political participation rather than claiming normative judgments as to the nature of the politics involved. Yet they certainly retain a normative dimension of social capital, participation as its own ends for a democratic polity, and the value of contention where social change becomes a cognate of progress without necessarily sharing this last's prescriptive directionality. To consider these various phenomena within the framework of excess criticality points to a different kind of problem—namely, that of an abundance of the political, of unabsorbable participation, of lines of affiliation and association that are not fixed by conventional means of representation and policy formation. For such institutional powers, excess criticality poses the problem of containment the same way communism once did, but now as an internal feature of its own lack of interest in expansion. If representational means are capturing less of the popular imagination as they become increasingly oriented to voters who count, and the field of what counts as the political continues to expand, the fateful difference poses a larger dilemma for the mechanisms of democratic measure. Further, if excess is no longer simply the fat tails or outliers as exceptional and self-deserving conditions, then the mobilizations that persist do not fit within the confines of distribution but move in multiple directions.

This greater means of producing critical excess realigns expert and self-knowledge and challenges the unidimensional distributional structure of inequality by which those with less must bide their time until they can receive more. Equality in this regard assumed a linear path to the future. Not only has this future been cast in doubt as no longer a guarantee of greater good and goods, but the shift, especially in the language of Republicans, to equality of opportunity rather than outcome emphasizes support of investment capacity rather than collective means. What appear as formal criteria of civic engagement or political participation may in this regard name a more substantive basis for politics than they otherwise suggest. The excess generated is not a politics frustrated that becomes dissipated but a capacity to enlarge the scope and scale of production that various modes of private ownership hitherto disallowed. Tolerance for difference is the individualized and negative expression of an expansive affection for sociality. That the sources of this affiliation were once associated with the private—sexuality, cultural, racial, and religious difference—and now spill over to the public points to what the effacement of the partition between these realms does to refigure the notion of privatization as such.

While it is clearly the case that the public has lost many of the entailments that distinguished it from the private and that its goods and its institutional and managerial forms are in many ways derivative, this derivation moves in both directions. Politics has become riskier, more volatile, more subject to the leverage effects of locally applied difference in myriad ways that elude the standard calculus and valuation of the political, just as they did with respect to the economic. In political terms, the derivative bears difference elsewhere, sustains its potent volatility, expands what is taken to be its horizons. That politics does not reside in a single sphere, filled by some volute of a popular mass whose energies can be assimilated and co-opted, shifts dramatically the very conception of mobilization as an aggregate of individual decisions taken. Rather, excess criticality occupies the kind of epistemic and ontic state of the dark pools, shadow banks, and arbitrage conditions by which new currencies of political value are generated.

In this respect, publics would be valued not simply for the speech acts they generate, but as an assertion of themselves. Here, a value would need to be given to the means for gathering or mobilizing and to this occupation or constitution of public space out of sites not recognized for their input as bearing a capacity for critique. While mass protests of the nineteenth century and twentieth century were tied to anxieties of an irrational mob or directionless crowd, the occupations featured in the various movements called Arab Spring, Occupy Wall Street, or simply Occupy, bore an unexpected suspension and duration, as if the impossible persistence of a physical presence switched silence, ephemerality, and marginality toward the opening of the political space as such.

As with the notion of the people and their opinions, interest has been seen as something stable, a translation of need into want derived from objective circumstances or actual position in life. Within this tautology, polities could be rule-governed or democratic because publics were rational. A well-governed polity would gather the public and yield consensus. Decision would transmit into rule. Surely, such a fable is at odds with the exclusionary practices of citizenship, the maldistributions that attach to consumption, and the unclaimed surplus built into the structuring of labor. But here, too, the public was to be compensatory, to promise access even if the delivery would be long deferred. Confidence in a democracy to come would translate immediate mobility into a compact for justice. Conviction in such a future is possible as long as each knows his or her place, so that what is seen as missing now, gathered through public criticism, could be accurately represented and interests could be acted on through the rule of experts.

Yet where managerialism is generalized, where all claim expertise and credentialing education endorses it, where incessant judgment becomes a feature of the national popular, an excess of criticality results. Far from a culture of complaint, narcissism generated when traditional values cannot temper desire, this excess of critique points to the limits of knowledge to govern. The unknown unknowns, the outside of what can be managed, would present public gatherings, protests, and mobilizations as energy wasted rather than as a capacity displayed. Somewhere in the disappointment over public institutions, such as the university, stands a statement of its efficacy, a frustration about its limits to the very access that it had helped make possible to begin with. The presentism of "We want it all" belongs not just to a few activists, subprime swindled, occupied, displaced, or downsized. Futurity is also made part of the present when all claim critical capacities that leave their own delivery out. The sense of temporality where the future is brought into the present, where a conceivable outcome can be appraised and acted on, where doing so fractures the futures in myriad decisions taken and expectations unfulfilled, also belongs to the social logic of the derivative.

3

De-centered
Social Kinesthetics

Finance works through flows. It moves production inside of circulation. It is a kind of compulsory movement that mandates going forward. Even after crisis, we must keep going at all costs. The price paid for this compulsion is that finance claims to see everything but has no knowledge of how it moves, or has no language for its own movement. When it stops, all is crisis and ruin. When it lurches forward again, all is forgotten, and the dance resumes. When used in this way, dance is always suspect. In conventional politics, to characterize something as a dance is to see it as evasive, afield of authenticity, swirling around its object, somehow caught out of time and unable to effect the progress it seeks. According to the *Oxford English Dictionary*, this figurative invocation of dance suggests, "*to lead*, rarely *give* (*a person*) *a dance*; *fig.* to lead (him) in a wearying, perplexing, or disappointing course; to cause him to undergo exertion or worry with no adequate result." A casual scan across the digital horizon would yield such phrases as "The Reconciliation Dance" (on politics and crime), "Wild Finance: Where Money and Politics Dance" (on the financial bailout), and "The Dance of the Apologists" (on the persistence of racism in response to Barack Obama's election).[1] Dance, in these examples, is a prelude to real decisions taken—more, it is a distraction, side-stepping what really needs to get done if only a more muscular encounter could plant antagonists firmly before each other. The political stage is already set; its props are familiar; the characteristics, motives, and methods of its dramatis personae are already known. The actors take their places, ready to make history once the music stops and the distracting dance comes to an end.

In this moralistic dismissal of the salience of dance to life, we can detect echoes of finance portrayed as mindless movement or cunning jockeying for position, aimless revelry, or a subterfuge that distracts from what is really moving and shaking the world. In this, dance and finance could be analogized as equally ephemeral, diversionary, epiphenomenal to what is really real, what actually matters and should be cared about. It is time to break the tyranny of metaphor, for dance and finance share more than rhyme; they move in consonant rhythm. The relation is not mimetic, not of an origin that starts in one place and emanates outward or proceeds through a trail of anxious influence. Rather, the relationship of movement practices across disparate sites that share certain kinesthetic attributes is derivative in character. The founding fables of finance are that the originary ideas on which all is modeled sprang fully grown from the mind of an Irving Fisher or Messieurs Black and Scholes, yet in actuality, the genealogies, contexts, and vectors of determination are far more diffuse and multilayered, as we saw in the previous two chapters. The rhythms and cadences of bodies in motion and the manner in which value circulates through society share mutually constitutive principles of association whose language is poorly articulated and more readily explained as a succession of ideas from exalted individuals. The turn to dance here is meant to make this language of social movement audible, perceptible, sensible, and legible.

Dance, of course has a specific history, populated casts of venerated characters, and moments of expansive possibility and disciplining submission, but it also provides a scene for the production of knowledge, and its limits that can inform how movement happens in other domains. To learn from dance is not the same as insisting that all learn to dance; it is not a claim that dance could be the privileged practice that leads us all to the Promised Land, any more than the claim of finance to lead us to wealth and happiness should be taken at face value. To privilege dance analytically, as a critical method, invites thought from within its own conditions of movement, from the means through which bodies are assembled and not by the terms through which their impact is brought to an end. To find ourselves in dance is to locate our repertoires of engagement as already in motion. These self-making bodies move variously, interdependently; they multiply. Even in unison, difference is legible. Choreography discloses multiplicity under an artistic signature. What seems to issue from one body rests on the coordinated and interdependent effort of so many and brings about a self-expansive sociality. Dance is an ensemble of ensembles, an accomplishment of its own surplus that bequeaths a fateful remainder, an unabsorbable promise to all in attendance. In these respects, dance comports with the generalized excess associated with nonknowledge.

Dance was a key site for the cultivation of the body where confidence lay in a civilizing mission that could effectively colonize nature—human and geophysical. Culture (*colere*) braided these two enclosures, or colonizations, of the primitive drives, desires, will that would transform human bodies into sources of labor and nature as the wild and untamed raw materials—both of which were in need of disciplined and directed mastery. Civilization in this respect was always an incomplete project, both for the barbarous means it deployed to achieve its ends and for the unceasing resistance to subordination that fueled rebellion and revolution, as well as invention and creativity. Culture in this sense would pertain to making bodies fit, but it would also apply to bodies remaking what fits, ordering and reordering, colonizing and decolonizing. Decolonization in this most general sense entails breaking from enclosing rule but also making something different out of what is broken, an emancipation from restricted movement and through an opening and transformative mobilization.

Politics today suffers a crisis of evaluation. Millions the world around have taken to the streets to depose governments, gathered from one state of precarity to enact another. But the tendencies of those on the ground, the dispositions of those who assumed positions of authority, the conditions of the institutions issuing debt and demanding ransom have not been so easy to figure out. The political appears at once as a problem of too much and too little. No aspect of human endeavor or expression is beyond deliberate contestation, yet each spirited intervention can leave the sense that not enough was done. Movement everywhere, crescendos of volatility, vertiginous shifts in direction leave an impression of being out of time or adrift in space. The ensuing disequilibrium has proved disorienting to thought and made it difficult to discern direction amid a thicket of practices moving this way and that. General assemblies and mass occupations are posited as lacking demands or orienting ideas; mobilization is posed as the enemy of representation.

But surely, moving through disequilibrium, divining ways through spaces made for infinite possibility, is what dance does best. Dance, at least in its Western modernist formulation, is conventionally considered movement for itself.[2] Yet such hard-won autonomy has not always secured it a place in the world. Precarity, ephemerality, and instability are frequently voiced as lamentations. Dancers, too, struggle to make a living; presentation venues strain against diminished support; audiences contend with escalating ticket prices. For dance to move the political beyond arrested development, its knowledge of how bodies are assembled, of how space and time are configured, of how interconnections are valued must be made legible beyond the ends of choreographic endeavor. Foregrounding the analytics of movement so redolent in dance can make for a richer evaluation of what is generated through political mobilization. For a politics that is abundant and undervalued, the question becomes: How can dance be mobilized to think through the present?[3] No doubt, the present itself is not one thing but many. Indeed, politics is the pathway forged through possibility, the realization of purpose in a contentious field of movement. What moves us beyond existing conditions and constraints usually consists of finding a way between obdurate oppositions that threaten to subsume the imagination of generative and fluid socialities.

The ethereal, sylph-like presence that is perhaps the most conventional casting of dancers, especially women, has been applied to dance itself at great cost to the ways in which it has been valued and supported in a kind of impossible economic anorexia. At the same time, dancers are prized for their creativity, flexibility, absence of material needs—they can work in spare rooms with nothing more than their bodies, often unshod, can purportedly subsist on few calories, and even among performing artists they deliver more for less by garnering the most meager wages.[4] Their love of art subsidizes their pursuit of perfection—making them the ideal laborers in an idealized creative economy.[5] Dance is caught between the disavowal of the corporeality of laboring bodies and acting as a model of work without strife, complaint, or much by way of recompense. Rather than accepting this nefarious dichotomy between the real and the fictitious said to distinguish industrial production from financial monetary circulation as separate sectors of the economy, dance might be taken as a key site to grasp the ways in which bodies in movement make value. In the old conception, the factory floor is a fixed locale where bodies sweat and toil, commodities are made. Subsequently, those things are alienated from their makers, move or circulate far and wide through representations of their worth manifest as instruments of credit and debt. Finally, they wind up at some moment of reception or consumption, where they are purchased and put to use. Dance could be said to describe a different condition where circulation is fully inside of production, where bodies sweat in place and move through space, where use transpires in exchange through a moment of performance. Credit for a creation collectively tendered, and debt among bodies of performer and audience entangled for a particular duration, assembles attention to a transient value, fills a void, and leverages that moment to some promise of further exchange.

Dance might, at first blush, be embarrassed to take on the mantle of the derivative. Modernist pride would dictate an/the embrace of originality, innovation, autonomy as what makes dance capable of ruling its roost and securing its treasures. If, however, that confidence belongs to conditions of dance making that no longer prevail, other principles of sovereignty will need to be divined if dance (and other performative practices, for that matter) is to realize its esthetic and political value. The point of departure here is that the derivative, when treated as a social logic and not only as a financial instrument, discloses what these altered conditions of sovereignty entail. The derivative brings to notice the potential impact that issues from seemingly minor variations and how agency is incorporated and dispersed so that the capacities to direct the flows of life that might have appeared scarce, broken-down, and useless are reappraised as a kind of abun-dance. Seeing how a derivative logic operates in dance holds the double promise of giving notice to what dance generalizes as social life beyond the underlying activity of dancing and what sustainable principles and creative practices may already lie to hand in what otherwise appears from the perspective of crisis as a world in ruins.

Further, the focus on the ways in which small movements can be lever-aged to larger gains, the practice of arbitrage is specifically the key subject position of the derivatives trader. By aggregating these interventions, the idea is not to capture the whole person but to set identity in motion, to deliver what momentarily will stand as a public interest in which so many brief site visits and moments of attention or hits add up to a hit with sig-nificant impact. One hopes that this account of the derivative is begin-ning to get a bit more physical, to inscribe the ephemeral in some tangible corporeal animation. Finance is indeed all about compulsory movement, the obligation to keep going at all costs, to go forward into the future unencumbered by historical claims. But while finance spreads movement everywhere, it generates no language of movement, no sensibility regarding how we are disposed to go one way and not another, no logic by which we might grasp how the imperative to move rules us, how we are oriented by it, through it, against it toward some realization of how else we might be moved and by what we might rule together. This silence and stillness at the heart of finance stages the turn to dance, a jubilee of practices that sing the praises of bodily indebtedness and provide flight patterns by which friendly skies might be known.

The point finally is not to generalize from dance to other practices or to offer it as a model of behavior that should be imitated elsewhere. Rather, it is to privilege it analytically as making legible the kinesthetic dimensions of a social logic that operates as movement but does not provide its own language of account from the perspective of bodies in motion. In dance terms, we can expose the derivative logics that course between network and organization through the concepts of mobilization and the social kinesthetic. Mobilization pertains to the medium generating consequences of movement that render tangible the otherwise ephemeral entailments of time and space. Dancing mobilizes in one place time and space making capacities that draw from wider sensibilities and are dispersed through aspects of many movement practices by which bodies move together. To inquire into what dance is made of and what it makes besides itself is to refer to questions of context or conjuncture—to cultivate a sensibility that slices through as it conjoins or cleaves bodily attentions and orientations— in parallel fashion to the manner in which the ascent of finance has itself been understood.[6]

Like the ideas that come from various cultural studies of a structure of feeling, a pre-political disposition, tacit or virtual socialities, it is possible to imagine the material surround of corporal activity before it crystallizes as a specific practical expression.[7] A social kinesthetic can be understood as the orientation, sensibility, or predisposition that informs approaches to movement, the historically specific microphysics that generates and governs motional force fields. From within mobilization all is networked, and from the perspective of a social kinesthetic, an organizational rule or logic can be discerned. Neither term is originary; both are derivative. Mobilizations coalesce in one place from what has been made and will wind up elsewhere. Social kinesthetics are multiple and simultaneous, a polyphony of forces and flows. They impose not a genealogy of influence but a series of lateral connections where disparate practices are joined through some (but not all) of what organizes them. This vocabulary is as abstract as that of financial derivatives. It needs to be grounded in a few practices that will make tangible the operation of a derivative logic in dance and that allow us to see the ways in which dance fleshes out what a derivative might do beyond the halls of finance.

Toward Conjuncture

For those who follow the rule of money, the early 1970s are remembered for the collapse of the international financial architecture. These arrangements for integrating the noncommunist world through currency exchange established at the close of World War II anchored the value of all money to the U.S. dollar, or what is termed "currency sovereignty." This grand

design, which included the creation of the International Monetary Fund
and the World Bank to help mend and stitch together national economies
wrecked by war, depression, and colonial depletion, was worked out by John
Maynard Keynes and other prominent economists and came to be known
as Bretton Woods, after the New Hampshire ski resort where the meetings
took place. The exchange rates of all currencies would be pegged to the
dollar, which in turn would be guaranteed through reserves of gold bullion,
thereby providing a physical heart and soul that would align nations into a
world body and ensure trust and security to propel the integration of global
economies. As Europe recovered and oil-producing economies rose, dollar-
denominated holdings outside the United States (variously referred to as
euro-dollars and petro-dollars) made dollar sovereignty unsustainable. The
center did not hold, and between 1971 and 1973, the edifice was dismantled,
opening the door to a new era of financial intermediaries. At first, just dust
rose as recession and inflation tore into American economic expansion, but
eventually, towering derivatives would emerge from the ruins.[8]

Within the precincts of architecture itself, a no less significant moment
occurred for prevailing principles of esthetic and design sovereignty, or
what had been understood as modernism. On March 16, 1972, shortly
after 3:00 P.M., plumes of white smoke rose from the base of the first of
thirty-three buildings to be demolished in the sprawling Pruitt-Igoe housing complex. Carefully planned for months by state and federal officials,
the implosion effectively collapsed the building onto its base. After the
trial run proved successful, the destruction of the second tower was filmed
and widely televised. Designed in the early 1950s by Minoru Yamasaki
and completed several years later, the eleven-story rectangular structures
replaced the then decrepit tenements of DeSoto-Carr, an African American
community in St. Louis, Missouri. With its parks and open green spaces,
light-venting fenestration, off-street parking, and elegantly symmetrical
master plan, Pruitt-Igoe stood for the promise of better living through
design even as it designed in existing inequalities of shoddy construction
for housing the poor and racially segregated buildings. The initial short-
cuts, coupled with inadequate maintenance, soon compromised the liv-
ability of the dwellings, and the whites fled the Igoe buildings that were
reserved for them.

By 1971, most of the African American households encouraged by federal housing authorities to leave the disintegrating warrens followed suit,
and only six hundred residents remained in a development designed for ten
thousand. The demise of the complex was taken by critics at the time as the
eclipse of architectural modernism per se—namely, the notion that uni-

versal design principles could be applied to craft abstract geometries that could deliver the orderly machinery of enlightened existence.[9] We might also detect the echoes of this 1971 real estate implosion with the subprime meltdown nearly forty years on. Urban blight and blemished credit share a racialized victimology of the undeserved poor receiving more generous housing than they could sustain and visiting a contagion on the markets that brought valuable housing tumbling down.[10]

But Yamasaki's own work was reaching ever greater heights. The spring after Pruitt-Igoe went down, the ribbon was cut (April 4, 1973) on the World Trade Towers, into which tenants had been moving since 1970. The surrounding landfill (constructed from more than a million tons of dirt and rock excavated from the towers' site) would come to be another expansive planned community, Battery Park City. Initially, this expansion of Manhattan Island was mandated for housing low- and middle-income families. But as costs escalated, these goals were deemed economically unfeasible, and the project was repurposed by state and local officials, and by the banking-governor brothers David and Nelson Rockefeller, to become the village of new finance. Subsequent promises were made to divert funds for poor housing in Harlem and the Bronx, but these monies rarely made their way uptown before being absorbed in New York City's general operating expenses.[11] Beside the heavily contested forced evictions from the Radio Row area that would be razed for the new construction, the towers attracted similar disdain for their modernist hubris of scale that overwhelmed interpersonal conviviality from urbanists such as Lewis Mumford, who referred to their "purposeless giantism and technological exhibitionism," and from a range of voices within the architectural profession.[12] That criticism itself was largely erased from memory with the destruction of the buildings by nongovernmental authorities on September 11, 2001.

But long before the World Trade Towers were reduced to ruin in what now looks like the run-up to the larger implosion of financial architectures, a less destructive but no less audacious repurposing of the towers took place. On August 7, 1974, Philippe Petit, who with a small band of conspirators had secreted himself in the South Tower's crown the night before, walked a tightrope between the two buildings. What would be called the "artistic crime of the century" was six years in the making, with Petit working from models of the towers and accounting for their sway. He snuck into the towers at night to test security and went up in a helicopter with the photographer Jim Moore to take surveillance images. Using a bow and arrow to rig a 450 pound steel cable across the 200 feet that separated the twin towers, Petit embarked on a forty-five minute high-wire act. When he was spotted by crowds gathering below, Port Authority police gathered at the roof, and Petit left his aerie under arrest. Petit's walk was filmed at the time by the cinematographer Sandi Sissel and made into a documentary by James Marsh more than three decades later (*Man on Wire*, 2008). Perhaps the most searing image of the feat is a long shot of Petit, balanced in the space between, with the nose of a jet plane seeming to close in on the South Tower.[13] After being given a psychiatric evaluation and taken before a judge, Petit was released to a sentence of community service, performing in New York public parks. His crime and its publicity were soon enlisted to ameliorate the bad press of the trade center, and he was bestowed with a lifetime pass to the rooftop observatory and invited to place his signature on a steel beam. Petit came to embody a certain civic memorialization, with risk turned to a benign poetic pride. He walked for the opening of the Superdome in New Orleans and the Cathedral of St. John the Divine in New York, the bicentennial of the French Republic at the Eiffel Tower for an audience of 250,000 in 1989, and the twelve-hundredth anniversary of the city of Frankfurt for an audience of 500,000 in 1994.

The life-threatening risk he had taken for his art was quickly reincorporated into a civic cultural program hungry to soften the effects of its own urban woes. As with Pruitt-Igoe, the World Trade Center could not stanch the ills of urban political economy. New York City was on the road to fiscal crisis and a real estate implosion that would see landlords abandon a million properties and employ arson for insurance as a substitute for rent and taxes. The twin towers of financialization would entangle risk that emanates from investment and from art. Like Yamasaki's architectural icons, rise and fall, implosion and expansion, would share a constitutive moment. Sealed together would be real estate ruin and eroded currency sovereignty, with a risk-driven passage toward the instrumentalization of culture itself as a rescue operation for urban woes. Petit's celebrity, renewed with the accomplishments of each performance, was nonetheless part of a larger landscape of risk-infused movement that took a moment of ruin and disclosed what else might arise across the city's face.

As with the bailout of economy, too much and too little can be made of a moment. Doubtless, the ruin in the cities, the collapse of architectures financial and otherwise, as well as risk-based movement were all years in the making. Yet, as with the quandary posed by the public as an increasingly volatile basis for the political, the unity and autonomy of the domain known as the cultural was coming undone. Culture, the source of all that is common and shared, might seem least likely to become infused with social logics of the derivative. More likely, associations would have roots, origins, and the deep lineages of heritage. Despite the earliest line of humans descending from nomadic circumstances, the long walk seems to have stopped with culture. As Raymond Williams famously alerted us, the term "culture" came into usage as a derivative of agriculture, from the Latin *colere*—to tend or cultivate, precisely where folks put down roots and stuck their seeds in the soil.[14] That humans might be distinguished from one another by race was certainly of a piece with the colonial trick, but also an extension of this very etymology of roots (*raiz*).[15] At the same time, nothing would spring from the soil without proper attention—hence, cultivation—and therefore engender the doubling in culture of noun and verb, naming and doing. Culture in the West would come to be central to colonialism's civilizing mission. An anthropological humanism would recognize among the newly colonized an equivalent complexity manifest in language, customs, and norms that would make it possible for a universal appreciation of those subject to external rule by those claiming possession of it.

Culture in this respect was the horizon of human diversity and fit with the impulse to collect, classify, and display that Tony Bennett termed the "exhibitionary complex."[16] The confident taxonomy that underwrote the impulse to differentiate humanity along the lines of cultural specificity operated in not only a horizontal but also a vertical dimension. Matthew Arnold's assertion that culture pertained to the best that had been thought and known rotated the classificatory schema on its axis and yielded a vertical hierarchy of what was the best and who was in a position to know.[17] Just as the anthropological affirmation of culture sprang from a progressive impulse to salvage and preserve what conquest would readily destroy, Arnoldian excellence was a brief for universal education and elevation of those unwashed classes, hitherto deemed unworthy or ineligible to reap civilization's benefits.

In both cases, culture was a field on which the contradictions between modernity and modernism, between the advance of social welfare through technological progress and the forward movements of style through esthetic innovation, would be played out. Growth, evolution, and the expression of creativity would require that the past or prior state of affairs give way, be destroyed, or demonstrated to be inferior. Whereas modernism was to embrace the new, excellence was to be established for those artifacts that could withstand the test of time. While efficiency and rationality would drive developments forward, distinct spaces of pleasure and leisure, special venues from which to gaze on all that humanity achieved or could be, would become organizing principles not simply for the elite but for populations at a mass scale. Museums, exhibitions, popular amusements,

sports arenas, and concert halls would constitute the institutional archi-
pelago of a distinctive cultural realm. Older, residual forms—churches and
festivals, weddings and funerals—persisted, of course, but now as separate
from state, on the one hand, and economy, on the other. Culture had rooms
of its own.

The career of an autonomous culture, like other inventions of modernity such as economy and the public as the engine of the political, proved
enormously productive. The palaces of culture would assemble a mass audience that would fuel the emergence of vast networks of popular entertainments. These centers of broadcast and cinema would follow the pathways
of industrialization with vertical integration of production and tightly
concentrated hold over distribution. The separation of culture from what
belonged to the world of work and politics opened a new consumer frontier
by which capital accumulation could stake a claim—both through expansion of what could be brought to market and of how commodities that could
not be paid for with monthly wages might be financed over time. That is
to say, consumerism from the get-go was entangled with the expansion of
finance, and both imbricated more deeply the lives of particular households with the general *oikos*. Culture was a realm of fantasy not only of ever
expanding acquisition of a good life that came to be called a(n American)
dream but also of the ability to do heavy lifting to compensate for all that
capitalist modernity disrupted, sullied, and destroyed.

Mass culture was to integrate common values among those populations
who gave up their own cultural moorings to assimilate to a new land of
opportunity, according to Talcott Parsons's classical sociological formulation of the mid-twentieth century.[18] Cultural inputs of middle-class utopia
may have been mass-produced—the television sets, automobiles, and suburban homes—but the output was to be a secured, private, and individu-
ated existence in which choice would reign and time would be one's own.
The cultural contradictions of capitalism, about which Daniel Bell would
write after the 1960s, would sound a theme of cultural permissiveness erod-
ing the social fabric from which market expansion would maintain stability.[19] Such concerns of cultural conservatives and economic modernizers
were already decades before an anxiety for Joseph Schumpeter, who did
not think that capitalism would survive its own "creative destruction" as it
became indifferent to the very "mentalities" that had spawned it and who
resituated culture as the scene of disintegration and decay.[20]

For those populations excluded from the dream from the get-go, or
those eligible for its rewards but unwilling to submit to its discipline, normal life was confronted by a counterculture. These counter-tendencies

operated along two fronts, effectively reversing the colonial logics by which culture had been rendered in the hundred years up to that point (the mid-nineteenth century to the mid-twentieth century). Fredric Jameson has understood the colonial processes in the developing world, or Third World, and the industrial First World as a means of incorporation or enclosure of nature and the unconscious, respectively.[21] The Third World, a realm of raw materials and cheap labor, would enter development, with economic growth enabling the childlike primitives to develop into the adulthood that characterized their masters. The land grabs that late nineteenth-century imperialism and the subsequent decades of war visited on the bulk of the world's peoples figured as a massive colonization of nature, the state in which the discoverers found their charges. First World consumerism, by contrast, rested on a colonization of the Arnoldian sublime, where excellence would be transvalued as acquisition of cultural commodities. Driving desire to market would be a no less forceful endeavor, requiring the sciences of persuasion and communication to do their work of publicity and ultimately colonizing the unconscious.

In Jameson's elegant formulation, the break with these twinned colonizing processes of modernity, of anthropological nature and esthetic unconscious that align with the two meanings of culture rehearsed above, usher a broader decolonization that he understands to be constitutive of the postmodern. For the Third World, decolonization would be figured in terms of national liberation, both a freedom to form a nation-state independently in the image of the colonial fathers and a freedom from the bond of *natio* (birth) or geopolitical boundary that colonialism had imposed. As Margaret Kohn and Keally McBride put it succinctly, decolonization is "the dream of self-rule" that emerges from the divide of colonial subjects who both internalized and resist their subordination. Self-determination remains a horizon, and "decolonization is unrealized, but not necessarily unrealizable."[22] This relation between an interior and exterior, a desire to rule and to be ruled, a formalization and informality of what makes for popular sovereignty have been features of decolonization since it became a part of the brief of the United Nations with the establishment of the Special Committee on Decolonization in 1961. Fifty years later, eighty former colonies containing 750 million people have achieved formal self-rule, while there are still sixteen entities designated "non–self-governing territories."[23] Formal recognition has jostled with what remains unrecognizable, as capacities for rule do not neatly align with the conferral of the rights to self-representation. In broader cultural terms, these movements opened to what Ngũgĩ wa Thiong'o referred to as "decolonizing the mind," whereupon imperialism acted as a "cultural bomb" that compelled Africans to view their own past and traditions as a "wasteland" from which they must flee.[24]

Needless to say, these emancipations of decolonization have been full of promise and peril, of peoples who could assert their voices and movements on the world stage and who would just as often receive not applause but the cruel slap of states still in the grip of neocolonial authority. Concomitantly, decolonizing the unconscious, making legible and audible the secreted spheres of domesticity and the private—hence, a politics of race, gender, sexuality, consumption, and other entailments of the cultural—would proliferate under the banner of new social movements. Yet these, too, now look to be subject to a tragic divide, relinquishing an older strategy of universal power based on class, political economy, and the state, to the particularizing and fragmenting appeals to identity. In both cases, radical impulses were said to be recaptured or reincorporated, either into the authoritarian apparatus of nominally independent states or into a lifestyle, intellectual property, and financialized late cultural capitalism. Yet as was the case with economy and polity, what might appear to be a failure of contemporary response to the magnitude of crisis may turn out to be more a crisis of evaluation, of the integrity of older concepts, and of the means to make sense of what is in our midst than of the present circumstances as such. If culture also has lost its autonomy, how do we understand cultural processes in the present conjuncture? Here, as well, the derivative may prove to be of some value. Further, if decolonization threatens to reinscribe the colonial boundaries it was meant to efface, with culture figured as either a recidivist fundamentalism or an ineffective diversion, we may need to take a different approach to what gets opened, how processes are set into motion, and, hence, whether the body also might be a candidate for decolonization.

The road that leads back to the autonomy of culture may already be closed, while the approaches to articulate it more closely with economy are also freighted. Culture has suffered analytically from being a mere superstructural reflection of an economic base in radical political economy, just as it has been devalued as peripheral to the fundamental industries that index collective social well-being in neoclassical conceptions. Modernity, for all its differentiated spheres, was an escape from these primitive mysteries of the cultural. The postmodern would seem to augur a certain return, an intimacy of representational and material value, an entanglement of cultural and economic form. This conceptual opening appeared despite the influential formulations from Jean-François Lyotard, Fredric Jameson, and David Harvey that reiterated a base-superstructure relation while, at least for Jameson and Harvey, referencing the economic cycles that Ernest Mandel had deployed to describe the movements of capitalism itself. Lyotard's postmodernism followed from the advent of a knowledge economy; Harvey's reflected fragmentation in capitalism more broadly; and Jameson's followed the third major economic cycle or stage in capitalist development that Mandel had outlined: the competitive (from the eighteenth century to the mid-nineteenth century) monopoly capitalism that held sway until World War II and the postwar boom period of late capitalism that foregrounded finance and generalized industrialization.[25] While postmodernism is taken to be the cultural dominant of late capitalism, the cycles are out of phase and the cultural itself would seem to be belated, coming in the aftermath of what Mandel would term the second slump of the mid-1970s. Perhaps more germane than whether culture aptly reflects certain arrangements of capital accumulation is whether cultural processes are best understood cyclically or in terms of periodization.

Recall that crisis in the formulation by economists—even by those of a critical cast, such as Nouriel Roubini—is an enactment of the business cycle at a larger scale. Here, economics is to establish its bona fides by showing that its own movements follow natural laws. What goes up must come down. The materiality of a cycle is a nettlesome problem. (What, after all, are cycles made of? What makes for their regularities? Why do cycles close and repeat?) Yet that of a cultural style drawn into a period would seem more so, as the movement of time would seem just as inexplicably to produce changes in expression and affiliation rather than inquiring into the ways in which certain principles of movement are formed and how these, in turn, might circulate in and transform their world. The point here is not to lose sight of the relation between the cultural and other social relations and processes or to jettison the historical dimensions of particular sensibilities. On the contrary, if these relations are not predetermined by a given resemblance or reflection or by a pre-established duration or cycle, then the burden of explanation falls on the credibility of connections that can be drawn. To suggest, therefore, that a derivative logic is present across cultural and financial practices is not to assign particular places in an architectural order (which was what the idea of structure was based on), but to identify principles of movement that associate an array of activities, and flows of people, without forcing them to conform to a singular idea.

Seen from the perspective of the aftermath of Bretton Woods's fall, the derivative as a financial instrument that colonizes cultural experience as the economic reasserts epistemological priority even as it is undone as an autonomous realm. Yet if we are in a condition after economy, the predicates of this situation need to be located not only in the internal limitations of market mechanisms but also in a wider array of social processes through which people craft various associations and entanglements from which capital continues to seek emancipation. The move here is to treat the social logic of the derivative as a consequence of these various decolonizations, an undoing of imposed unities and alignments of people and places meant to gather wealth for others and subordinate interdependence as a sociality in its own right to a dependence on forces of subordination. Decolonization is about the unmaking of the naturalness of dominating principles of rule, of an unconscious embrace of terms of exchange that are uneven and unequal, where desire is traded for a depreciating debt. Decolonization is a movement away from these encapsulating forms of nation, selfhood, mass that pose as terms of autonomy and freedom but alienate these very concepts of liberation to an impregnable authority. This movement away, therefore, is not simply an escape from some intolerable power, but a capacity of assembly, affinity, and association—a value giving circulation that capital in general and finance in particular always claims as its own.

Financial risk is concerned with the departure from an expected magnitude of return, but it cannot trace its own path of how it achieved this appreciation. The inability to discern illiquidity from insolvency speaks to the paucity of understanding of how to evaluate financial risk's own internal movement and, therefore, to being condemned to persistent crisis when the movement and the music stop and to the feigned shock that it has happened again. This indifference to what circulation creates, to what moves value and what values movement, cannot be divined from finance; it requires exploring the principle of association for itself. This is why is it important to grasp the historical process of decolonization as reorienting the principles of sovereignty by which people might rule their own movements and of how to value these associations from within, on their own terms. This bundling of attributes to generate value can now be applied to the scene of the cultural, where sense is of made of the world, where value shifts between what gets made for others and what is constitutive of selves. The derivative operates on these dispersed and distributed moments of ways that people have learned to move together, to act on certain sensibilities and interdependencies. The derivative references that movement because it abstracts only those attributes that can flow together, entangles them in relations that operate beyond their local manifestations, allows us to notice the rhythms that animate seemingly separate domains while still recognizing how differences continue to course through our social veins.

Cultural scenes are made from people in movement. They come and go, etch pathways, leave traces, inhabit and abandon, deposit and withdraw their treasures. The action of population, to populate (*populare*), bears this double meaning to fill spaces with people and leave them to ruin. Such movements have been described as starting and stopping (as in a historical period), rising and falling (as in a cycle), or ebbing and flowing (as in a tide). Yet there is more to movement than presence or absence: Certain qualities, orientations, dispositions, and organizing principles may reign under particular circumstances. Kinesthetics are the ways in which movements incorporate sensibilities among some aggregate of bodies. These particular sensibilities toward movement, prior to or more general than any specific stylistic manifestation, constitute what can be considered a social kinesthetic. If an episteme describes a way of knowing that frames what will count, will be valued, and will direct the trajectory of further knowledge, social kinesthetics form kinesthemes, or embodied forms of sovereignty or rule.

Whereas an episteme is an array of rules by which knowledge is validated, or of regularities within which it is produced, a kinestheme is the regularization of bodily practices, the moment of power by and through which bodies are called—and devise responses—to move in particular ways. Epistemic movement has been thought in terms of temporal succession of spatially delineated way of knowing, what Michel Foucault famously described as an archaeology, an order of things from which the very category of the human would be derived. The classical episteme articulates all that is knowable in representational taxonomies. It is followed by the modern, where abstraction ascends as language and is emancipated from representation. The postmodern, which Foucault anticipates but does not name, is the rupture from these universalizing ideological schemas.[26] While kinesthemes also have a history, they generate and occupy more of a spatial configuration. As such, various social kinesthetics can exist at the same time or even in the same place.

Clearly, this is a very abstract and general claim. Just as contemporary financial instruments make legible various means through which derivative value is realized, dance makes tangible these means of moving together, the larger social kinesthetic of which a concrete performance is the particularization. Dance conventions of a particular period would typically be approached as sharing a given style, grouping them together by appearance and influence. The gain of these formalistic approaches, evident in the seminal works of dance history and criticism such as those of John Martin, is that dance ascends to its own language and interrogates the possibilities of movement for its own sake.[27] This perspective replaces more universalizing dance ethnology, such as that of Kurt Sachs, which views dance as expressing underlying impulses expressive of a shared human nature.[28]

Here, scholarly approaches to dance would recapitulate the tropes of reflection of an underlying natural reality, or formal autonomy, that characterized the discussion of culture more broadly according to the anthropological and esthetic conceptions of the term. Rather than treating dance as a reflex from natural dictates or in a formal world of its own, starting with a social kinesthetic makes it possible to inquire into the ways in which the materialities of movement's orientations in the social world are made legible in and through dance. It is not that style becomes irrelevant or longer continuities of movement orientation become incoherent. Rather, it becomes possible to look at the kinesthetic resonances between practices that are generated with very different stylistic attributes and cultural scenes and circumstances. The bundling of cognate movement attributes from disparate sources would make sense of a derivative in kinesthetic terms, disclosing its logic as a social relation.

A logic is not a law but a tendency toward rationalization of what is in force. A logic is not necessarily complete or successful. The accumulation of capital forever oversteps its bounds, fails to realize that the value it has assembled betrays its interests, undoes its purported unity. The social logic of the derivative is no less certain or secure. Treated here as a principle of association, interdependence, and mobilization, dance is being deployed to articulate the inner movement that finance rests on but cannot speak. Dance, no more than any other cultural practice, is not simply produced by following rules. Training, for sure, is a form of discipline, but no one dances by discipline alone; nor does a kinestheme arrest what can be made of principles for moving together. Dance makes legible a means of embodied sensibility that allows for a valuing of mobilization of bodies in circulation that produce conditions and occasions for further assembly. Dancing and attending to dance—each engenders the desire for more. While the cash nexus, opportunities for performance, career duration, and durability of the body all link dance to scarcity, each instance of performed movement opens to what is beyond it and what cannot be absorbed in the moment of performance.

These ephemeral moments whereby the bodies of dancers and audience encounter one another are the media through which pass the distributed links and mutual debts that may be paid for but can never be repaid.[29] There is no direct and contained exchange between what dancers impart in performance and what audiences take with them when they leave the scene. Mark Franko insists that for dance, "Metakinetic 'exchange'—the transfer of expression and interpellation to its audience—was its labor" and "dance is also political because of the ways in which its models proliferated throughout the social world."[30] What is engendered in performance is an embodied empathy, which, as Susan Foster describes it, "demonstrate[s] the many ways in which the dancing body in its kinesthetic specificity formulates an appeal to views to be apprehended and felt, encouraging them to participate collectively in discovering the communal basis of their experience."[31] The desire on both parts to return to this scene, to further dancing, is the basis for the accursed share in dance, its own version of unabsorbable excess that was discussed in Chapter 1 with respect to Bataille's notion of nonknowledge. Recall that this surfeit of sociality comes back to the body, overwhelms the senses, hits it as laughter or some other affect. Dance would be one node to observe this boomerang effect in reverse, a site of accumulated kinesthetic value that discloses what happens to all this excess. The dreaded figure of contagion, of an alien force that rapidly spreads through a population, becomes palpable in the dispersion of movement sensibilities.

Dances emerge from a larger field that is their social kinesthetic, yet the rules and powers of this scene are not legible as such. There are, of course, textbooks on finance and manuals for choreographic composition, but there is no legend that maps the social kinesthetic. Its contours need to be derived from concrete instances. For each of the three kinesthemes, an exemplary choreographic instance is selected. These are meant to be neither typical nor archetypal. There is no fixed relation between the concrete particular and the abstract general. Rather, the dances in question are trolled for their kinesthetic undercurrents in ways that begin to assemble other aspects of the cultural scene that they illuminate. These three instances fit a rather restricted conception of dance that takes place on a Western proscenium stage. The question of what rules is a process of selection and sorting of what kinds of practices can make a legitimate claim to authority or sovereignty. Sovereignty in this regard applies to bodily practices as much as it does to forms of currency—in both cases, much is in circulation while what ascends to the status of a practical universal, what is embraced for exchange everywhere, can be rather circumscribed. Indeed, it might be observed that the sovereignty linked to a given kinestheme is regulatory of what can pass as dance, in the same way that financial instruments for risk management are regulatory of what counts as value. Beginning with this restricted economy allows us to see what has come undone and what has been opened up when one form of sovereignty yields to another.

If kinesthemes describe the general architecture through which bodily practices are valued, the dispositions that orient movement in relation to certain forces of authority, the way that stages are peopled by dancers, gestures toward the occupation and ruination of a particular scene. The risks taken at these precarious moments do not simply bring movement to an end.

They can also shift how we move together, what we value of those debts, and what can rise from the ruins. Sovereignties of currency, of political authority, of cultural scenography can profitably be articulated together and through these kinesthetic means. The co-presence of these various kines-themes discloses a capacity to sustain various bodily sovereignties at once, a spatial multiplicity. It also points to the ways in which domains separated from one another by boundaries overflow their banks, a flood that ush-ers in another pathway by which movement transpires. Once this has been accomplished for dance in the restricted sense, a world of movement can be opened up to emergent sensibilities. The scenographic closures where dance takes place can be decolonized, and with it, the social kinesthetic can be de-centered along the lines of the derivative, a flow that exceeds its boundary.

Classical Kinestheme

La Sylphide is the iconic romantic story ballet. First choreographed in 1832 by Filippo Taglioni for his daughter Marie, the piece was a showcase for an international star, though the surviving version is by August Bournonville in 1836. Ballet is dance for heavenly bodies, its long lines and elevations of divine descent presented as an ideal spectacle. Yet the dance inserts the bodies of the common folk in the position of royalty and in its own way realizes the bourgeois ambition to assume the sovereign seat of power, at least insofar as a theatrical excursion would allow. *La Sylphide* is a retelling of older tales of courtly love, of tragic endings for those who would deviate from marriage vows, and especially for women who dwell in the ethereal realm of desire. The story is about the Scottish farmer James Ruben who, while asleep on the eve of his wedding, is enchanted by a forest sprite who falls for him when she sees him through the window. A witch, Madge, comes into the house as Effie, the fiancée, and her bridesmaids gather. Madge foretells James's betrayal of his commitment to marriage, and James ejects her from the house. But when the wedding commences, the Sylphide returns, snatches the ring from James's hand, and runs into the forest, with him in hot pursuit. James catches up to the Sylphide and her com-panions and is entranced. Gurn, James's best man, proposes to the forlorn Effie, and she accepts. Madge provides James with a magic scarf to bind the Sylphide's wings so she cannot fly away. When he does so, the sylph dies in his arms. The wedding procession of Gurn and Effie crosses the stage, and the Sylphide ascends above it. Madge directs James's attention upward. When he realizes that he has lost what he once thought was his of spirit and flesh, he perishes as well.[32]

The story of human foibles, frailty, and failures is here counterpoised to the extreme accomplishment and confidence of step that is ballet. The witch Madge, while disdained for her powers, scarcely gets off the ground. The principal dancer, whose character is ethereal and who is positioned to pursue her desire but without agency over it, still stands out for her strength, clarity of line, elevation, and expressive projection. Yet while the story brings the ballet to a tragic close, the virtuosity that organizes the scopic economy of the performance begins long before and transcends the nightly demise of the character. Ballet bodies are formed from an early age and, for most, exit too soon, leaving a longer life in the balance. Similarly, the dance vocabulary from which the choreography is composed exists prior to a particular dance and is largely unaffected by the specific composition. This sense that movement comes from without—that it is independent of the moment of performance but it achieves transcendence only through a moment of sublime embodiment—is indeed the constitutive paradox of the classical kinestheme.

Ballet itself is many years in the making, a wide-ranging incorporation of folk dances from the Italian and French countryside into the corresponding courts of the sixteenth and seventeenth centuries. Yet there is a compelling fable of ballet's origins that revolves around a sovereign's dilemma.[33] Accordingly, King Louis XIV, himself an accomplished dancer, had a problem. His minions were having difficulty accepting their place in his dominion. Feudal absolutism, which had rescued the order through political centralization in the king's throne, was straining and, as we know, ready to break asunder. The king summoned them all to Versailles to dance, but not just as they pleased. They would move according to a vocabulary over which he had command, following his steps, imitating his positions. He would insert himself in the place of God, and in this place he would insert a mirror whereby they would appear in his and His image. All of this synchronization would align itself on a grand vertical axis, one that extended from the feet in relevé, in a long extension through the upwardly held torso and infinitely out from the top of the head. Grace would be defined as a defiance of gravity, an engagement with the heavens, a great leap into the realms of faith. Mortals would derive their sovereignty from putting themselves in the place of God, of perfecting their performance in the place of that appearance, where form and convention are given beforehand but the singular achievement is to be transcendent.

The worldly bodies could assume their position, but only in performance could sovereignty be achieved. The corps, the synchronized field of performers, held its line so that the principal could assert a place of singularity. This references the other genealogy of ballet: coordinating battle-field movements to achieve effective command and control in the theater of war.[34] Command was limited by field of vision, and the generals needed to assume high ground, sit astride a horse, ascend to a tower, or deploy a device to magnify their view. The science of optics, like that of munitions, extended the range of power.[35] The ballet theater, like the one where *La Sylphide* was performed, was an architecture of these visual hierarchies. Sightlines could be perfected for the privileged, while the plebeians would need to crane their necks. The stage machinery could be hidden from view so that the final elevation offstage could appear as an illusion of the dancer's ethereality and of the choreographic logic itself.[36] What was presented as out of reach onstage was returned to its carnal materiality backstage in the sexual relations that men of privilege availed themselves of after the performance concluded.[37]

As with the ballet, classical sovereignty was continuously meeting its undoing, insisting on holding the place between spirit and flesh, reflection and the body, imagined and achieved verticality. The line that ran from the mirrored studio to the mimetic performance to command of the many as one in the theater of war could at any point be broken or broken down. Still, representation was burdened and bequeathed with a state authority that in turn descended from an unbroken vertical axis. Immanuel Kant's two moments of the sublime—the mathematical and the dynamic—are negotiated artfully in ballet.[38] Greatness beyond imitation, without measure, awe-inspiring, is given a place by five fundamental positions of the body, by movements on a count of three or four, by rigorous synchronicity and precise musical accompaniment. The authority of the sovereign is always prior to its exercise, given by office, which bestows force on the utterance in a performative transference to the speaker. Just as *La Sylphide* persists in many a contemporary ballet company's repertoire, the classical kinestheme is more than a passing jubilee. It is a persistent call to occupy a place in a long line of authority and to see what can be performed there.

Modern Kinestheme

A sociological convention to describe the advent of modernity is the shift in how status is denominated from ascribed to achieved. The former is written on the body while the latter is crafted from within; the classical self is given, the modern is self-made. One is born into peasantry or royalty and the life course is marked accordingly. Sovereignty would name not only the one who rules but also the larger process of regulation by which bodies are assigned their trajectory. Surely such ascriptions remain long after the rule of royals has ebbed. Social divisions are maintained not by edict but by failing schools; inadequate credit scores; elevated body mass index; and other quanta of racial, class, or other social divides. The modern kinestheme is less a succession of the classical than an overlay, one where achievement through mobility constitutes its own demands on bodies that are commanded to stay in their place. In dance, these contending demands on the body are explicit; most dance schools will instruct students in ballet and modern dance—even as this master grammar holds all manner of styles and as the modern is supplemented by other genres, such as jazz, tap, ballroom, or hip-hop. Such bodies can disclose the fissures between contending sovereignties in the ways that they are able to shift between movement regimes. Interestingly, such contemporary promiscuity is at odds with the ideologies of the development of dance techniques, which claim a fidelity to a particular choreographic authority. Despite the emergence of these techniques through the appropriation of others' movements, they derive their originality from a disavowal of their dependence and appropriation of these disparate sources.

The Sun King had claimed authorship of ballet in God's name, even as others would be scribes of its codification. In modern dance, Martha Graham would come closest to being in a position of equivalent hegemony. Graham codified her technique over the better part of the twentieth century and at the time of her death, in 1991, it was being taught around the world. As Mark Franko has shown, Graham achieved an unparalleled renown as a public figure beyond the dance world at mid-century, when American modernism was in full flower and professional studios emerged (in the case of George Balanchine's School of American Ballet as well) to feed and support careers in dance companies.[39] Graham was joined by Hanya Holm, Doris Humphrey, and Charles Weidman as the "big four" of modern dance who constituted the core faculty at the American Dance Festival held at Bennington College in the 1930s and, subsequently, at Connecticut College. Alwin Nikolais, Merce Cunningham, Erick Hawkins, Paul Taylor, and others who had studied with these modern masters launched their own studio schools in the 1950s, to be followed in the 1960s by the creation of increasing numbers of dance departments at colleges and universities.[40]

Graham herself stopped performing in 1969, but her technique both emerged from and transcended her body. The relationship between choreography and technique was an active dialectic. Dance classes developed not only a particular capacity but also the oblique angles and spatial geometries that were the signature of her work. At the core of both dances and training was the contraction, an internal spiral that emanated from the tip of the tail bone, the tilting of the pelvis that then curved the rest of the spine like a whip and left the neck open and exposed with face pressed upward. At once a move of strength and vulnerability, the contraction begins with an initial impulse and then deepens into its coil, before releasing to the next movement. Profoundly influenced by the work of Karl Jung, Graham assimilated the lexicon of archetypes and the twinned figures of anima and animas, masculine and feminine forces, into her choreographic works. While Graham underwent her own stylistic developments, mining tropes of American iconography and Greek mythology with equal fluency, a sense of connecting a highly personalized approach to movement with universal themes and expressions was prevalent throughout her work.[41]

In her near-century of life, Graham created nearly one hundred works, none perhaps more renowned than *Appalachian Spring* (1944).[42] This was in many ways the blockbuster of modern dance. Aaron Copland composed the Pulitzer Prize–winning score, itself incorporating a theme from the Quaker hymn "Simple Gifts." The sculptor Isamu Noguchi provided the sparse set whose angularities picked up those of the dancers bodies. More character- and scenographically driven than narrative per se, the dance is set in the nineteenth-century Pennsylvania of Graham's birth, after a barn has been raised, a couple has wed, and a preacher has convened his revival. Premiered not in a conventional theater but at the nation's repository of knowledge, the Library of Congress, Graham is the soloist. Her closing gesture is an extension of her arm, a reach that seems to pierce the horizon and move beyond, an implacable figure wedded to the future.

There are no children onstage (or in Graham's life), but the ballet is full of her choreographic progeny. She places herself at the intersection of a dance and a nation's creation, although certainly in both cases there are precedents in her own formation at Denishawn and for all the other American genealogies. At the height of war, in the nation's capital, in the heart of urban industrialization, Graham parses an industrialization of the body from the sparsest elements of self-construction. Denishawn was replete with the Orientalism that fascinated many a turn-of-the-century modernist, and Graham added to these appropriations those of African and Native American dance, which she took to be the two primary sources for an American dance.[43] For her, however, the markings of these cultural references had to be erased so that she could create her own originary scene. Graham is most typically associated with other great geniuses of modernism: Frank Lloyd Wright, Pablo Picasso, Igor Stravinsky—exemplary individuals whose own ceaseless creativity drove emulation that never matched its influence. That such greatness sprang from the depths of self-inventiveness is specifically what the Graham contraction enacts. Depth is the cognate axis for the modern kinestheme that the vertical performs for the classical. Influence is not simply borne through the singularity of the mother body but instituted through siring the institutions that would make the dance world. "Institution" has as its etymology "to take steps or set in motion," in contrast to its association with immovable buildings and staid bureaucracies. In genius resides uncontainable creativity, an urge constantly to move beyond oneself that speaks to the obligatory forward movement that ties finance to the modern. The modernist dancer goes forward at all costs, surpassing each achievement with the next. Clearly, this trajectory is at odds with the actualities of reputation and output. Few of Graham's dances achieved the prominence of *Appalachian Spring*, even as the economy of maintaining a professional dance company required choreographing something new for each season. The premiere and the repertoire balance a program that must integrate the ascription of genius with its ongoing achievement. Modern dance does not eschew verticality, but it does open fields of depth. The contraction and spiral are the basis for the rapid or sustained fall to the ground that characterizes not only Graham's work but also that of other modernists, such as Humphrey and Holm, who explore the momentum of swinging limbs as they carry dancers to the ground.[44] But where verticality is a property of a Cartesian spatial perspective that the body must assume, depth speaks of an interior discovery, a mining of what others can only partially achieve, which justifies and explicates a hierarchical ordering of people on the basis of talent. Such claims to self-making, purely on the basis of individual endowments and not structural circumstances, are what make modern artists the poster children of capitalism. Anyone, but not everyone, can make it, although all are obliged to try. Genius is there to be discovered but can be found only by diligent and persistent training. Genius is disclosed through a self-mastery manifest as technique that disciplines others to locate their prospects and limitations and accept the extent of their achievement as no one's responsibility as their own. The modern kinestheme helps to negotiate the contradictions of an ethos of mobility that lets few pass but promises passage to all so that each body is enlisted in the journey.

Postmodern Kinestheme

Movement for its own sake, modern dance's credo, would nonetheless pose the problem of where to go that lurks in the imperative to move forward.[45] The succession of styles and genealogies of dancers borne in the depths of the maternal pelvis might exhaust itself or come to question the myth of origins, of perpetual cycles of birth, death, and rebirth by which cultural modernism attended to the contradictions of social modernity. After all, an older work could always be restaged, but mass destruction through war or genocide or colonial conquest or nuclear annihilation scarred the otherwise hopefully forward-looking landscape. The turn against the exalted body of the creator was not long in coming to modern dance, even though the sovereignty of the individual as a free creator required centuries of struggle with classical rule.

The postmodern in dance is most commonly figured as a turn to the pedestrian, away from rarefied movement that only geniuses can create and only great critics can validate.[46] Susan Foster has provided an elegant delineation of the genealogies of choreography that align with three kinesthemes described here. Choreography initially referred to the readers and writers of dance notation, such as King Louis XIV's dance master Pierre Beauchamp, who codified the court's steps, and Raoul Auger Feuillet, who inscribed and published this vocabulary. Choreography was a map for movement; it allowed a view from above that maintained orienting directional coordinates that could incorporate all movement in a universal abstract geometry that disavowed the sources and effort of dancing. "Choreography" as a term recedes in the eighteenth and nineteenth centuries as romantic ballets such as *La Sylphide* feature performance of stories by Marie Taglioni and other stars. The logic of sovereignty retains its classical features but is transferred from the body of the king to that nascent form of bourgeois personhood, celebrity. With modern dance, choreography makes a return as a kind of authorship that aligns an individual vocabulary with a universal expression. The postmodern turn in choreography returns the disclosure of labor and location that the classical formulation had repressed and that modern dance figured as authorial self-expression. Foster underscores the difference of this emerging choreographic operation:

> The terms "making-dances" and "making new work" came to signify a daily decision to enter the studio and construct movement or to sequence phrases of existing movement, thus signaling a redefinition of the arts as labourer and collaborator who worked with the materiality of movement. Feuillet notation had secured a substantiality for movement, but as an event that could be documented through a lexicon of established principles that were then symbolized on the printed page. Modern dance had imparted a sense of its materiality to movement by articulating a pedagogy of composition

and showing its possibilities for repetition, variation and reiteration. For modern choreographers, movement was always placed in the service of the artist, who transformed it into psychological and universal expression. In contrast, the artist as maker of dances assembled movement from diverse sources and arranged it, not as personal expression, but as a statement about movement itself. This imbued the dance with a significance separate from that of its maker's intent, and at the same time, it reinforced the dance as a made event distinct from its execution. The choreography, now allied with the process through which a performance was made rather than the feeling or desires of its maker, became increasingly separated from both the choreographer and the dance.[47]

Here choreography begins to resemble a process without a subject, the inversion of authorial capacity that transferred sovereignty from the king to the artist, to now be the disclosure of how bodies move in the world, what labor must be assembled to accomplish this, and what kinds of material inscription and value are engendered when making work is the means and ends of dancing.

In historical terms, the postmodern is well within modernism, despite the association of coming after. It, too, is typically narrated as having an originary place and time—the early 1960s at Judson Church in Greenwich Village, New York, even if it was undoubtedly a collective creation.[48] What was called Judson Dance Theater gave a series of concerts at the church between 1962 and 1964. Just as Louis Horst had a seminal impact teaching music composition to the Bennington crowd in the 1930s, the Judson group emerged from workshops offered by Robert Dunn, a musician who had studied with Merce Cunningham's partner and composer John Cage. Cunningham, who had also danced with Martha Graham, is considered the avatar of modernist formal movement as a thing in itself. Like Graham, he developed a distinct technique and vocabulary, but he eschewed narrative and musical accompaniment for sound and movement environments that had an aleatory relationship to one another. Rather than character-driven archetypes, Cunningham was interested in intricate movement sequences that were sometimes ordered not by intentional design but by randomly generated cues. If Graham's conception of universalism relied on assuming the archetype of the other, Cunningham abstracted modernist Orientalism as a distancing from Western conception of the ego-driven moving subject. Cunningham's work was full of references to natural forces and processes, and some of this sensibility came to inform the early Judson work.[49]

The use of scores was a principle pedagogical device in the Dunn workshops and consisted of written directions for movement based on objects or
relations found in the environment that could serve as cues. One dancer,
Ruth Emerson, who had graduated from Radcliffe College with a degree
in mathematics, used number sequences that could be found in the environment to generate movement. In one score created in the early 1960s,
she referenced a traffic signal that was visible outside the studio's window.
Dancers were distributed in front of the various windows. When the signal flashed "Don't Walk," the dancers would inhale, count that number of
flashes, then proceed to move for half that number of counts. The score
would assign various dancers in front of different studio windows to rotate
this activity, generating a larger pattern of movement. Dancers would then
randomly select pieces of paper that named sounds or actions. The sounds
could be phrases at different pitches and actions, such as carrying another
person, collapsing on the floor, or moving the head and stamping the feet.
These activities were sampled from the movement vocabulary of nonviolent
resistance, including dancers' taking turns issuing orders and following
them, and the score was written on the back of a flyer soliciting participation in nonviolent direct action and discussion groups.

Trisha Brown, Meredith Monk, Lucinda Childs, and other dancers
involved in the Dunn workshops and initial Judson performances became
influential over the next four decades of contemporary dance. The first concert, held on July 6, 1962, offered work by Steve Paxton, Fred Herko, David
Gordon, Alex and Deborah Hay, Yvonne Rainer, Elaine Summers, William Davis, and Ruth Emerson. Thought of as its own internal repertory
company, this collectivity would not so much produce a signature work,
such as *La Sylphide* or *Appalachian Spring*, as sort professionally between
those who would ascend to the scale of the large proscenium theater and
international tours (such as Brown, Monk, and Childs, who choreographed
Philip Glass's magnum opus *Einstein on the Beach*) and those, such as Paxton
and Rainer, who contributed mightily to reworking the movement sensibility of dance and hewed more closely to the venues of the experimentalists.
Indeed, two years after the Judson formed, this differentiation was generating strains—for instance, when Judith Dunn and Paxton were asked
by Judson's director, Al Carmines, to form a company that could sustain
work, or when some members were invited to tour outside New York and
leave others behind. While innovating with movement sources and logics
of composition and improvisation, postmodern dance was in many respects
contemporary with the modern and consistent with the succession of dancers to emerge from those who had been their mentors and choreographers.

The twenty-three dances by fourteen choreographers of the first Judson concert were offered free and meandered over several hours. Against the hierarchy of the eponymous dance company and technique, this was a cooperative in which dancers and choreographers changed places from work to work and methods of generating movement were prominently featured as elements of the dances. Emerson performed a solo called "Timepiece," generated by a chart whose fields had various directives for percussive or sustained movement quality; six speeds, from very slow to very fast; and other variables for duration and use of space, including facing, level, and shape. Herko performed "Once or Twice a Week I Put on Sneakers to Go Uptown," a piece with an explicit pedestrian reference that featured him doing a version of the Twist, barefoot (contrary to the title), in a semicircle in a multicolored bathrobe. Paxton sampled ballet, pedestrian movement, and the walking through the steps during a rehearsal that dancers call "marking" in a piece entitled "Transit" and dissected the movement by repeating it over and over again at different temporal and spatial scales. Summers used large, numbered Styrofoam blocks as cues for randomized movement sequences activated by dancers throwing the props on stage, like giant dice, in "Instant Chance."

In her meticulous documentation of these performances, Sally Banes observes:

> The first Judson concert had incorporated choreographic techniques and human values that reflected and commented on both the smaller dance and art world and the larger social world the dancers inhabited. Through chance, collage, free association, cooperative choice-making, slow meditation, repetition, lists, handling objects, playing games, and solving tasks, the dancers and the dances described a world: a world very much like an innocent American dream pocked with intimations of anxiety; a world of physicality, bold action, free choice, plurality, democracy, spontaneity, imagination, love, fun, and adventure. A world where traditions existed to be freely sampled or ridiculed. But also, a world where that very freedom was interwoven with the experience of a shattered, fragmented universe.[50]

While claiming a democratization of the body, Judson was, after all, a church, a sanctuary from the madding crowds of the street and the palace alike. While modern dance companies were beginning to professionalize, to tour internationally, and to assume the proscenium scale of the grandest ballets, postmodern dance, at least initially, was a practice of and for other dancers and artists, a reinscription of avant-garde demographics at a moment when modern forms where achieving a measure of popularity. The postmodern kinestheme therefore could not stand as a straightforward liberation of the body from its other demands but would insinuate itself among these contending directions as to how movement should be oriented. The classical kinestheme is a gesture of bringing all power to the center, of rendering sovereign the model that others would imitate, the light that would be reflected in the mirror. The modern kinestheme embodies the interior depth of the centered sovereign subject, the command of an infinitely expansive space that places the uniquely self-fashioning individual at the center of a universe of accumulation. Progress and development demand ever expanding spaces, but the body of the great creator centers this form generating ability within a mastery that rules itself for itself, that can claim to live for nothing other than pursuit of artistic excellence.

While these two compelling centripetal forces remain in dance and in society, the counter-tendency—centrifugal, spinning out of movement—is also in effect. This is less a break in time, a succession of styles, as fissures that obtain simultaneously and whose effects are increasingly legible. To associate the postmodern with a movement away from the center is not to dismiss forces of centralization, to assert that all is fragmentary, because some sovereignties remain too concentrated to make such claims credible. Instead, the persistent decolonization of what had contained the body and placed it at the center of some universe requires explanation and articulation. As soon as the movement away from the center becomes legible, the notion that the center is all there can no longer hold. Dance here provides the language for that legibility. It provides form for what otherwise might seem inchoate and unregistered logics of moving together. Judson is an especially rich site within the genealogy of Western concert dance, itself taken to be a realm of specialization of movement practice.

If the postmodern referenced a shift from centered to de-centered movement sensibilities, this would need to be understood along several dimensions. The first is a break with the vertical, transcendental lines from which all movement worthy of value descended. Many in the Judson collective started out within the master-apprentice model. They either studied dance at college or were convened through the Cunningham studio, where Robert Dunn assumed the role that Louis Horst had for the modernist cohort in the decades before. Music provided the shorthand for dance's sovereignty, one that carried principles of order, harmony, and arrangement in space that dance notation relegated to the descriptive. Hence, scoring for the Judson dancers acted as a kind of decolonization internal to the compositional method. Improvisation did not mean doing anything or being without means of articulating and associating bodies together. Rather, it was a realm of discretion that was being distributed to the performers by means of the scoring device. Movement was neither divine nor sublime. It was transmitted through simple algorithms on scraps of paper or props. While the epistemological status of chance was not interrogated, the interest in randomization was of a piece with a larger move in information, organization, and systems theory taking place at the same time. Postmodern dances and the statistical models that would inform cybernetics and finance were equally designed processes. Emerson was experimenting with random walking at the same time that Eugene Fama was using the exact same term to describe the "behavior" of prices on Wall Street. Fama's paper "The Random Character of Stock Market Prices" was published in 1965, and Burton Malkiel's book *A Random Walk down Wall Street* (1975) popularized the term.[51] While Judson dance is full of naturalistic tropes, they could also be understood as having the effect of replacing God with gravity, of crafting a choreographic physics that governed the movement of bodies in space according to logics that could be disclosed and acted on.

Second, Judson was concerned with the refusal of the interior opacity of creative depth associated with genius. Genius, like centering forms of sovereignty, is about clearly demarcated distance from others, a gap achieved through both the architecture of the proscenium stage and the affective demeanor of the performer. The passions of romantic ballet make for amplified and mask-like facial expressions, eyes wide and mouth agape. With modernist focus on movement as such, facial expression was less burdened with narrative obligation, but the dancer's gaze still betrayed a kind of fixity that placed him or her in the other world of art for itself. The eyes projected a depth of focus that polished the windows to the soul. Judson performers often made a self-conscious effort to alter this performance demeanor, taking drama out of gesture, making eye contact with the audience whose space they shared and acknowledging this connection. Reciprocity was to replace opacity as the performers made themselves available to the audience rather than removing themselves as a distinct kind of otherworldly being, whether sylph or dancer. The pedestrian therefore was not simply a source of movement but a reach across the divide of the proscenium, even where this last was already absent.

The third dimension would be the emphasis on collectivity over individuality in the process of generating movement. Judson, no less than Graham or Cunningham, produced a refined technique for movement innovation by assembling and concentrating dancerly energies within a rehearsal studio and performance venue. But the technical approaches to movement that would emerge from Judson and its contemporaries—especially release technique and contact improvisation—were, to state the obvious, named after principles of motion and not after people. Published in 1937, Mabel Todd's *The Thinking Body: A Study of the Balancing Forces of Dynamic Man* circulated the notion of ideokinesis, which combined the use of mental images and the structural alignment of the skeleton.[52] Along with other early twentieth-century explorations of bodily technique that saw themselves as closer to actual movement processes, such as that of F. Matthias Alexander and the movement systems of François Delsarte and Rudolf Laban, *The Thinking Body* would become a key source work for contemporary dance technique.[53]

Rather than descending from the line of God through the body of the sovereign or from deep within the creator's body, postmodern technique emphasizes the spaces in between the bodies of dancers or the spatial and kinesthetic relations that obtain between dancers and their environment. Release technique is grounded in what bodies would (or should) do if movement emanated from the relation between physiological principles of skeletal and muscular structures, relations and processes, and in where movement would go if the consolidated and singular self were opened to the weight, flexibility, amplitude, and qualitative properties of the body and its physical surroundings. More than simply letting go of ego or de-centering creativity, postmodern techniques pursue a bodily intelligence set in motion through dance. This is the basic principle of contact improvisation—that a point of contact between two bodies is what moves the particular dancers rather than the dancers beginning with intent, an idea that is translated into a gesture, form, or fixed movement vocabulary.

While these de-centered and de-centering techniques that distributed bodily sovereignty as an ensemble or collectivity would emerge and be refined over the next several decades, many of the foundations for these subsequent explorations could be detected in Judson Dance Theater's work. So, too, Judson's dance concerts were collaborative and distributed credit rather than concentrating the source of its art in a bodily archetype of the contraction, as was the case for Graham. Even as postmodern dance companies gained notoriety, it was common for programs to acknowledge the dancers' collaborative role in the creative process. Common as well was the formation of dance collectives such as Grand Union, initiated by Yvonne Rainer in 1970, or MoMing, which started in the 1970s and continued for more than twenty years, and Pilobolus, founded in 1971, which continues to enjoy widespread attention.[54] Instead of concentrating the relation between technique and choreography in the name of the sovereign or the artist, these are disbursed in the collective in terms of a theory of what dances does and a method of how dances are composed.

Fourth, the scrambling of styles—one of the key markers of what I refer to as pastiche—is also evident in Judson's work. Style in dance is the result of years of technical training. A ballet dancer might move from corps to principal to character dancer to rehearsal master or choreographer over the course of a career but would remain within the realm of physical regimen; of daily classes, rehearsals, and performances through which style is produced. Graham herself may have broken from her training with Ruth St. Denis and Ted Shawn to develop her own movement signature, as others such as Hawkins and Cunningham would break with her in modernist succession, but many dancers, including Yuriko, Bertram Ross, and David Wood, remained Graham dancers for their entire careers and continued to teach the technique in professional studios and university settings. Paxton's mix of ballet, rehearsal marking, and modern and pedestrian movement could be taken as a break with this linear anxiety of influence that characterized the modernist compulsion to stylistic innovation. It could also be seen as shifting dance from a craft and studio apprentice-based model of stylistic production to an industrial, mediated creation of an entire discursive and kinesthetic field.

To be postmodern in this sense was certainly not to eschew a commitment to exploring movement innovation—indeed, Judson introduces a rubric of experimental dance where the Renaissance workshop is exchanged for the analogy with the scientific laboratory. Foster has observed that this shift from singular to multiple styles accompanies a move of dance to the market, where bodies are prepared for hire and dance labor is abstracted as a commodity. Depersonalizing training in this respect could ultimately undo the prevalence of choreographic style and shift the emphasis on stylistics in performance to the ways in which dancers combine the various competencies in which they are schooled and to which they are exposed. As dance is made academic as part of higher education, the mixture of styles that would make it a discipline rather than simply a training is institutionalized in the curricular mix between required ballet and modern dance technique classes. All of this is to say that stylistic heterogeneity is far from a liberating, unalloyed good. Rather, it shifts the relations of rule between the sovereign individual who is the dancer's master and a distributed sourcing of movement information that is reinscribed as a form of research. Indeed, the dance organization that has taken up the legacy of

Judson Dance Theater and continues to produce events at Judson Church is called Movement Research—a network of dancers and choreographers programming and performing together.

Fifth, Judson suggests a shift in the way in which dance makes reference to what lies outside the specialized movement space. Certainly, ballet scenography and the apparatus that allows a sylph to ascend into the wings with a fly system, or technical rigging used to hoist people and things into the heavens, portray the continuation of a world or another world altogether. The performance space onstage is subtended by an imaginary space offstage that, while concealed by curtains, contains the machinery that produces the scenographic movement that makes possible the transportation onstage from one imagined place to another. Whether modern dance takes place in a proscenium theater or not, and however much it abstracts from scenographic representation (from Noguchi's spare sculptural lines that suggest allegorical settings to Robert Rauschenberg's abstract objects for Cunningham's early works), the perspectival conventions and economies of the gaze are largely continuous with ballet. Much postmodern dance would come to share these staging conventions, but Judson did admit some intriguing openings to the closed representational world of its theatrical forebears.

The mirror is both a training device and a performance trope in ballet and modern dance. If perfection lies in imitation of the ideal or the originary source of movement, then placing oneself in the outline of this reflection and repeating this placement daily becomes a key training device. The dancer needs to see himself or herself making movement for how others will see it and for how the dancer will fit in the overall choreographic design and schema. The proscenium frames an entrance into another world, but it also relies on the conventions of the mirror in which the audience can identify with and reflect back on themselves the action that is taking place onstage. Performers who train before a mirror are inserted into sight lines that fix the scene and the terms of identification with the characters on stage. An idealization of world and body meet at the transecting lines of performer and audience gaze, substituting mutual reflection for a meeting of the eyes. This, at least, might be taken as the closed circuit that the postmodern turn brings into relief.

Taking a flashing traffic light outside the studio as the metronome for movement within constitutes a literalization of external reference meant to elude the centering closure of the proscenium form. Direct verbal address to the audience, breaking the muteness of the dancer's body by conversation among performers, casual glances, and direct visual engagement with those seated in the room are readily reinscribed within performance conventions and contained within an artistic community yet figure an access to reference that will redirect what that community takes as its own productive orientation. The move away from the center, the crack in the mirror of representation, the refiguration of how dancers appear to others remain inside a particular community of movers but reorient how they draw on and reference their world.

Sixth, social and political citation within formal movement certainly does not begin and end with Judson but is modified in some intriguing ways. King Louis XIV command to his vassals to assemble in his chambers and follow his every movement is an explicitly political act that aligns governance of bodies and of state. Ballet never matched that degree of instrumentality, although there are certainly many instances of court dance around the world that freight movement with the necessities of rule in equally direct ways. That Isadora Duncan and Loie Fuller displayed avowedly feminist politics and a cultural critique of the U.S. imperium guided many expatriate artists to take their talents abroad. Graham refused an invitation to dance in Hitler's Olympiad and created *Tragedy* and *Deep Song* in 1937 in response to the Spanish Civil War. The Worker's Dance League of the 1930s was an explicit part of the United Front, as was the work of Anna Sokolow, Helen Tamaris, Jane Dudley, and Sophie Maslow. As Franko has shown, this work not only thematized the politics of the moment but also resonated in specific ways with a politically oriented audience.[55]

Judson proposed a different relation of the politics in dance, its internal kinesthetic operations, with the politics of dance, its ways of engaging its world. If all dance rests on an appropriation of some other movement, Judson is concerned with avoiding the disavowal that renders the movement of others into that of the sovereign body. The vocabulary of direct action and sit-ins is treated as a found object that can be brought onstage, with the dancer serving as a go-between for the social referent and the kinesthetic material, as in the instance of the score that Emerson wrote on the back of a pamphlet. Rather than representing political movements, their kinesthetic aspects were let into the studio, pushing the dance away from its own histories and toward an affinity with a space outside. The opening of dance movement to its outside constituted the decolonization that Judson effected for what had been the lineages of dance modernism. The dancers were not originators of this movement but placed it in a moment of adjudication between what might be considered valuable of their own training and heritage in dance and what could be valued of the universe of movement beyond it.

Dancing this space in between was Judson's own moment of arbitrage, its capacity to recognize the apparent difference between movement taken to be equivalent from distinct domains and the immediate action or intervention in that shuttling activity. In this regard, the hinge between inside and outside, between the politics that dancing assembles and that it references, is at least partially undone through Judson. The partiality is tied to Judson's location within a formal dance world and the limits to what can be opened from within. Nonetheless, the ways in which Judson opens dance to its kinesthetic outside ushers in a world to which dance itself can attribute valuation but cannot govern. This predicament is familiar in the derivative forms of polity and economy examined earlier in this book. By refusing limits on what movement can count as dance, dance is also placed at its limits to know itself, to contain how and where it is valued, to rule its domains of circulation. At this point, the social kinesthetic takes us outside the conventional sites of production of movement and provides an opportunity to recognize the kinds of association of bodies that are available in this expanded realm.

Moving Derivatives

Until the postmodern turn in dance, everything is on the up and up, as ascent is grounded in genealogical descent. The classical and the modern combine the Age of Discovery with the Age of Empire. In many ways, the new financial order breaks up these very sovereign claims to bodies the world round, something made legible in the play between centered and de-centering social kinesthetics in dance. This takes place under the aegis of a very partial multilateralism whereby some will be included and enclosed and others will be reconstructed and excessed at the same time that new lines appear of liberation, affiliation, and organization (from national revolutions and the coalition known as the Third World, to the Organization of Petroleum Exporting Countries). Together, these shifts will spell the formal demise of this vertically integrated colonial reach, to be displaced by a lateral, asymmetrical, horizontal contest between neocolonialism and decolonization. This rupture, self-interestedly dubbed "Pax Americana," takes a course in dance from the pedestrian elaborations of Judson Church to the risk-taking pyrotechnics of contact improvisation, along the way upending conventional locations of figure and ground, superstructure and base, culture and economy.[56]

In terms of a social kinesthetic, this break figures a shift from the vertical to the horizontal, a promissory decolonization of the body that suddenly brings to notice troves of movement riches once consigned to the periphery.[57] Certainly, the desires for the innocence of nature and the exoticism of the Orient had been worthy fodder for the classical and modern kinesthemes. Now choreographic appropriation would have to contend with a cacophony of bodily practices that erupted in this dispersed and lateral topography. Just as Third World liberation movements were delivering forms of national sovereignty that jostled against colonial claims to have the word, the bodily mobilizations that issued from the ruins of financial sovereignty bore their own demands of what debt should deliver. These practices turn out to be more generatively derivative in their expressions, more assertive about what can rise from the ruins of progress, able to deal with alacrity when confronted by indifference and enclosure.

As discussed earlier in this chapter, what is now called "financialization" emerges from the ruins of the Bretton Woods agreements in which the postwar sovereignty of the dollar is undone. What begins to be ruined in this moment, as well, is the very dreamscape by which America can be imagined. Innovations such as mortgage-backed-securities respond to a real estate market gone south. More broadly, the breakup of that enclosure around the privacy of the home pointed to what a house could no longer hold. What was released was taken to the streets. Such is the setting for the movement examples here, each figuring a capitalist promise of utopia that subsequently is abandoned. Liquidating these grounds is the basis for lateral mobility that suffuses a de-centered social kinesthetic and for derivative mobilizations that do not require unity to move together. While ruins in general, to say nothing of the pronouncement regarding the postmodern itself, tend to emphasize disorienting fragmentation that results in political importunity, a closer look at the socialities carried by derivative forms opens the blockage between a seemingly declining sphere of production and a hyperactive domain of circulation.

The movement practices that help specify a de-centered social kinesthetic where decolonized bodies assert other modalities of risk are themselves derivative forms that share not so much esthetic influence as attributes that are features of their self-production. In addition to postmodern dance, we can look at hip-hop and boarding culture as practices that share kinesthetic attributes and principles of mobilization that enable us to grasp political potentialities for valuing the mobilizations that suffuse our world but otherwise go unrecognized and that inhere in the social logic of the derivative. The *fin* that lies at the root of finance pertains to the process of bringing transactions to an end, but this closure refers to a process of life as well. Bringing a transaction to a close is the condition for initiating another, even as much that was initially seen to be of value is left behind or not enclosed to begin with. Against the indifference to how movement is made and where it might lead us, the ruination that the compulsory drive of finance leaves in its wake, we can look carefully at those ruins to see what else arises from them.

Trisha Brown Retakes Soho

By the end of the 1960s, walking in strange places had captured public attention. On July 21, 1969, Neil Armstrong took his own small step on the moon and leveraged it to a "giant leap for mankind." The footprint he left on the pristine lunar surface signaled conquest of the final frontier, a race to space won by the side that planted the flag first. Granted, all was not going as weightlessly back on earth. The Tet Offensive at the start of 1968 pealed a death knoll for forthright colonial expansion. White flight, a predicate of the Pruitt-Igoe implosion, was linked to the lunar walk as the ultimate abandonment of inner cities in Gil Scott-Heron's stinging rap precursor, "Whitey on the Moon" (1970).[58]

On April 18, 1970, Joseph Schlichter stepped from off of the roof and went down the side of a building at 80 Wooster Street in New York City's Soho neighborhood. A terrestrial being and not a sylph, he did not fall but walked deliberately down the face of the building, altering the rate but not the weight of gravity's force. The building face is not smooth. It is full of architectural detail: Large metal shutters—some open, and others shut—beckon like so many craters, while a fire escape suggest a road down not taken. Awaiting Schlichter at the bottom is a small band of onlookers who clap and cheer when he touches earth. The premiere is filmed, the descent captured in a grainy, textured, black-and-white long shot from below that describes what appears to be his gradual approach from the horizon of the building's edge. As they had for Armstrong and Petit, all manner of devices made Schlichter's unusual stroll possible. He was strapped inside a harness and assisted in his descent by accomplices on the roof and ground with pulleys and ropes. Unlike the romantic ballet machineries that conceal the artifice of defying gravity, the harness and cords appear as a kind of mobile spider's web, prominently displayed as he labors in and with them, submitting to capture in order to brave the wall. Each footfall seems carefully placed, making the effort of relinquishing his mass to gravity apparent with each step.

He was performing a choreographic work by Trisha Brown, then his wife and a Judson alum, titled "Man Walking down the Side of a Building." The three-minute premiere, which was filmed, remains part of the Trisha Brown Company repertoire.[59] Brown herself performed a similar piece walking down the ladder of a water tower on the rooftop of a neighborhood building around the corner at 130 Greene Street (1973), and created other works, such as "Roof Piece" (1971), that arrayed dancers across the tops of several Soho buildings, increasing the scale and blending body and cityscape.[60] Forty years later, "Man Walking down the Side of a Building" was performed by Liz Streb, a self-described "extreme action choreographer," on the side of the Whitney Museum.[61] Streb, who maintains a company and school that includes trapeze instruction in Williamsburg, Brooklyn (the urban cognate of Soho several decades later), described the sensation of grappling with gravity and with architectural and mechanical elements to accomplish the performance: "The first time I walked down, my balance was so precarious that I was on the head of a pin and everything I did dislodged that balance. . . . I feel like each walk that I took there was nothing that became familiar."[62]

This spectacle of de-familiarization, of taken-for-granted movement reoriented to render it remarkable, points to a special treatment of the pedestrian. The walk down the wall is at once utterly utilitarian, determined by the necessity of circumstances, and transformative, denying the ordinariness of everyday movement while still making the extraordinary possible. The dangers seem to be an insistence of the harnessed body but still require the assistance of others. The precarity relies on a double capture in harness and on film, with an eye toward witnesses present and absent, which are the conditions for placing this body at risk. Needless to say, the risk proves productive and is here featured in its zero degree. The expectation is of falling and harm, and the dance defers this outcome while relying on it. The performance records a debt to its accomplices and to its memorialization, to the apparatuses that would momentarily capture and release its value and place this unlikely activity, and repurposing basic elements that are the choreographer's ambient circumstances—walking, a residence, a husband, some friends with equipment, and no place else to perform but one's own backyard—as performance.

Brown recalled some of her impulses for this work in an interview conducted in 1993 by Charles Reinhart, longtime producer of the American Dance Festival. Brown had studied Graham's technique at Mills College in Oakland, California, in the 1950s, including composition with Louis Horst. She would later work with Anna Halprin in Marin County before coming east at the suggestion of Simone Forti to take the Robert Dunn workshops that led to her participation in Judson. She observed that in Judson, someone was always contesting whether a particular activity, such as crying, could be considered a dance. As a student, she created a piece called "Trillium" that caused her mentors to take umbrage; Bessie Schoenberg was asked to persuade Brown to leave out the score, and Brown recalls being told, "You can't just take things and put them together in any order—like this pepper shaker and this pencil—well actually, this is looking rather nice."[63]

Just a few blocks south of Judson Church, Brown, Schlichter, and their son were residing illegally at 80 Wooster, where "Man Walking down the Side of a Building" was performed. Brown found "Soho some kind of a ghost town, desolate beautifully so." Her dance interests were "in collaboration with architecture and equipment," and she acquired the mountain-climbing rigging from climbers who taught her how to use it. In 1970, she decided to "make a formal organization and develop a language of movement." She saw herself as excluded from the proscenium, given the absence of venues for choreographers younger than thirty-five; the reasons were "economic and by invitation and there were no invitations." Given these economic limitations and her parental responsibilities, she said, "I worked at my pace as I could and couldn't go on doing dangerous dances without support." Her work with Judson and with music, sculpture, and other visual arts amounted to an "intense bath in contemporary art." She views her work as a series of cycles and advises that "you have to take me in parts" with "permission to take from whatever part of my body I want in making choreography." The cycles of work she described began with the equipment-based work of the early 1970s; mathematically based systems of accumulation; unstable molecular structures, elusive structures of movement joined by choreography; interruptions to non-fluid collages; and working with the unconscious.

Brown is grateful that she never joined a major dance company such as Cunningham's (to which she had initially aspired when she moved to New York in the 1950s). This modern apprenticeship with a master through repetitive daily technique classes "molds you into the body of the other person," she says. She does not consider a Trisha Brown technique to exist; her own study of release technique and the work of Susan Klein and "muscles closest to the bones" led to "an amalgam of many things that have worked." Klein has trained many in the postmodern scene, including Stephen Petronio and Wally Cardona, but is not a choreographer. Rather, she is following in the tradition of women's alternative health practices from the early twentieth century, such as Mabel Todd's, which sought a holistic approach to the body with the safe space of a private practice. This marks a kind of rupture between the unity of technique and choreography that characterized the modern kinesthemic formulation. Klein herself has developed a school and private physical therapy practice over the past forty years that she has trademarked and described in the following terms:

> Klein Technique™ is a process through which the body is analyzed and understood to improve and to further movement potential. It is intellectual in that it uses anatomical realities. It is corporeal in that we strive for an internal knowing, an understanding which is integrated into the body. It is a movement education and re-education, that can be an underpinning for all movement styles, improvisations, athletics, and for the general health of the body in everyday movement. It is a technique that honors the individual. Klein Technique™ works at the level of the bones, to align the bones using the muscles of deep postural support: the psoas, the hamstrings, the external rotators, and the pelvic floor. We don't work to exercise these muscles but rather to wake them up, to become conscious of their role in the support and movement of the body. We work for the body to become elastic, responsive, and open to choices and expression. Although Klein Technique™ was developed by a dancer for dancers, it is a technique that works for everybody, from the virtuosic dancer to the non-dancer. When the bones are aligned we become connected, we become powerful and we become strong. The body becomes efficient and alive, and injuries often heal.[64]

Klein Technique claims an approach to moving that is for dance but not exclusively for dancers; it is concerned with the relation between anatomical structure, the bones that conduct energy, and the deeper layers of muscles beneath that hold shape and gesture. She is, in effect, undoing the juxtaposition between structure and agency by treating the density of the bones as a means to avert the resistances to movement that might be applied from excess force. The avoidance of injury, the protection from risk of harm, is what engenders the risk capacities of the dancers trained in this approach. It asserts itself as at once more scientific—a more efficient use of what bodies can do—and allowing a greater subjective expression, "open to choice." The language of sovereignty is of bodies moving according to their own physics, their own structural properties, and not commanded by what external authorities, cultural referents, or archetypes might demand. The consequence is a capacity to generate movement that comes from a derivation of movement principles said to be prior to any particular expression, an abstraction into movement that articulates a derivative logic.

As she has aged, Brown has turned over teaching to her company members who "share concepts" and "internalize an information process through the body which comes out through exercises they design." If release technique describes a de-centralized intelligence in the body, it also pertains to the distributed authority for cultivating dance knowledge. Brown's company in the 1980s included Irene Hultman, Eva Karczag, Diane Madden, Stephen Petronio, Vicky Shick, Randy Warshaw, Lance Gries, Nicole Juralewicz, Gregory Lara, Carolyn Lucas, Lisa Schmidt, Shelley Senter, Wil Swanson, and David Thomson. While Robert Dunn's workshops assembled dancers in one place to experiment together, Brown gave company members the opportunity to prepare privately and arrive at rehearsal to share what they had discovered.[65] Gries, who joined the company in 1985 and continues to teach release technique internationally, observed, "You the dancer are creating the system, and you are articulating your thought process." This prepares each dancer so that "body and thought are working in multi-directions."[66] Teaching and composition would parallel this process of putting information into a room for all to work with, on the model of research. This distribution of authority for generating movement follows the interior logic of multiple sources within the body for initiating movement impulses. Gries notes, "The initiation, or the key to a sensation of release, can start in many different places, and it is different for different people."[67] Rather than fixing the image of ideal movement in the reflection of the external source (whether the mirror, the teacher/choreographer, or a notational scheme), this interior investigation focuses on generating conditions of "flow" that "unblock energy to use in new ways."[68] Release could therefore be considered the arbitrage moment of movement, where the path between equivalents in different spaces is blocked and an initiating impulse needs to be introduced to bring about the circulation that creates equilibrium. In release technique, this moment of pure interaction with other bodies in motion is termed "presence," which describes the maximum openness to influence by the information that is available in the environment. Rather than being taut and vigilant to respond accurately to an external movement command from an upright position, much release technique training begins with the body lying with the back on the floor and the knees bent and feet gently placed on the floor, a posture known as constructive rest. It is not simply a mode of relaxation in opposition to taut vigilance, but an alert receptivity that enhances the capacity to respond to information coming from all around. Modern dance technique honed the swing of the limbs and fall to the floor centered in a potent pelvic core. But release technique reverses the polarities of up and down. Starting on the floor, the movement problem is not gravity but levity, or how to move up from the base.

The formalism of release technique resonates with other technical practices such as the mathematical modeling of derivatives. The expansion of research capacity, the dissemination of arbitrage as an orientation to a field of difference, the scanning and rapid processing of information, and the search for means to generate flow constitute a kinesthetic alignment between dancers and financiers. So, too, do the exploration of the relation between risk and uncertainty and the seizing of moment of stability whose consequence is a generative instability or volatility that becomes productive of further instruments of value. The vocabulary of dance may indeed go further in articulating how these associations are crafted:

> Stability/instability has been an area of interest in modern, later also in contemporary dance, since Doris Humphrey. Trisha Brown was interested in specific variations during the middle phase of her creative work in the 1980s, for example in Set and Reset, in which, along with falling principles, appear tossing (throwing individual body parts into space), dropping (letting individual body parts fall), breaking (allowing a shape to explode outwards with its energy), and organizing (bringing individual body parts into stable organization, aligned on top of one another). In those years, execution always focused on what is "real": with Gries tossing does not lead to a fully executed and perfected swing, nor does a breaking arm hold back its energy. It is necessary to really and truly hit the middle: execute simply and clearly the real energy expenditure of a tossing motion originating from the joint.[69]

Here, as with finance, we get the sense that properly applied technique accurately distills all available information, models it effectively in a decision (a sale that is also executed as a move or action), and that to "truly hit the middle" is to catch that very moment where value is made and therefore to capture a fragile alignment between the technical device and the "execution always focused on what is 'real.'" One of the closest observers of derivative traders, Donald MacKenzie, recognizes the affinity between the inner processes of dance and finance: "Perhaps the modelling of derivatives in investment banking always has an aspect of what one of our interviewees memorably called a 'ballet,' in which highly paid quants are needed not just to try to capture the way the world is, but also to secure co-ordinated action. Perhaps the quant is actually a dancer, and the dance succeeds when the dancers co-ordinate."[70]

This career narrative of invitations from others that never arrive or are deferred (to have her work accepted, to join dance companies, to be produced in dance venues), drive Brown to generate the internal organizational infrastructure, occasions, and materials that will generate her body of work. Neither that body nor the work turns out to be one, and her interest in examining her own body in pieces and her work in cycles yields movement that follows the circuits of the body through elegant yet disjointed and unexpected articulations. While her movement is a careful exploration of what bodies can do when unleashed from their own kinesthetic conventions, her creative process is constantly de-centering that capacity from her own body, incurring debts to her dancers and passing on the means of training to them. Assembling attributes that do not initially appear together—walk and wall, pencil and pepper shaker—she provides other modalities by which their value assembles attributes that they appear to use to magnify the effects and the attentions of what bodies can achieve. In this she was not alone. Petit also dared to walk between the towers of urban purpose, to commit to a seemingly impossible arbitrage that placed him between two equivalents and disclosed a value differential. The "post" in postmodern did not stand upright, demarcating an absolute difference or break. It opened spaces that seemed uninhabitable or from which others would only have fallen to a deliberate transit along a dangerous path. Petit and Brown were not simply conquering new spaces for performances; after all, what they claimed for their art was not theirs to keep. More provocatively, they can be seen as decolonizing the places and conditions under which their art was made. Brown's ways of working certainly relied on the unsanctioned space that Petit championed, but also displaced, albeit without removing the figure of mastery at the center of choreographic organization. These bodies would constantly be slipping away from themselves, finding movement in the spaces—large and small—between the mimetic unities of self and world.

Hip-Hop City

Buildings fall where once they stood, but urban ruins continually displace. The implosion of public housing and the funneling of public monies to monumental centers of trade was not simply a moment internal to a marquee architect's career. It came to figure prominently in the ruination of one path of urban development and the emergence of another. Artists like Brown who repurposed jettisoned industrial spaces would find themselves unwitting hinges of gentrification as much as they were articulating the movement that would make such shifts possible.[71] That art itself might be bound up with world trade would probably have surprised Brown as much as Petit in the 1970s, even as they become international icons of the very project of creative cities in which artists would figure as economic drivers.[72] Hip-hop stars would shine still more brightly in this reconstellated urban galaxy, even as they embodied a deepening paradox of racial divides in the United States—revering the celebrities of popular culture while denigrating the culture of the popular. Some keys to this paradox can be found in the roots of hip-hop in the abandonment of social housing that the demolition of Pruitt-Igoe represented. For far more poor urban youths of color, the projects remained home even as they could not house them. Rather than new buildings, they got theories of broken windows.[73] Rather than an industrial labor policy for economic development, they would come to be measured at risk, and their schools would be converted into factories of test-driven productivity.[74] The streets had long served as urban playgrounds, but now they would become workshops in cultural production that would transit around the city and then around the world. In New York City, it was not a single housing complex that was exploded. A massive destruction of housing stock took place—some one million units concentrated in the Bronx, Brooklyn, and Harlem and on Manhattan's Lower East Side—that constituted the urban ruins from which hip-hop emerged. Landlords' abandonment of properties that were depreciating in value was one source for the amalgamation of finance, insurance, and real estate (or FIRE) that would come to rule the city.[75] Fire was also an instrument of destruction employed by these same absent owners to collect insurance in lieu of rent. Against this derivation of housing stock for other values that was a kind of predicate for securitization, hip-hop engaged its own forms of spreading other currencies of rule and territorial logic across the face of the city. Tagging was not confined to the sides of buildings but took mass transit, the principle means of connecting work and home, as its canvas in a context where that link was being severed through the kind of deindustrialization that had made Soho possible. Just as postmodern dance came from an immersive bath in the whole sea of the arts at a time that their disciplinary differentiation was a hallmark of modernist professionalization, hip-hop culture was distributed across music, visual art, and dance and the corollary self-organization of youth into their own forms of collectives, whether they were named gangs, posses, or crews.

The movement of hip-hop was no less derived than the pedestrian sources and environmental inputs of the postmodern. It, too, featured a reorientation of the body in relation to the forces of gravity, the vertical orientation of the body, the capacities for lateral movement, and the processes of collaborative invention. Breakdancing itself is a consummate iterative and citational derivative practice, with each boast of betterment referencing its sources and rivals and grabbing hold of the tight place that differentiates it from what others might value very much in the manner of arbitrage. The first breakdancing to emerge in the Bronx in the early 1970s was an upright form that was inspired by a television broadcast in 1972 of James Brown's "Get on the Good Foot." Brown's quick lateral shuffles and spins, combined with sudden vertical drops to the knees and down to the floor in splits, displayed the juxtaposition between elaborate upright stepping and dropping down to dramatic low positions that would characterize b-boying. "Toprock" was the term for the precision rhythmic stepping that a dancer took into the circle and was composed of distinctive combinations and remixes of steps familiar to all in attendance but that showed the mastery and ingenuity of the dancer. To this was added up uprock, the wide-stance horizontal steps, and downrock, the drops to the floor and held freeze positions that demonstrated athletic agility and dangerous movement. The floor-oriented movement required the ability to displace the base of movement from feet to the head, shoulders, or back, freeing the legs to twist and torque to generate the force of momentum with these other parts of the body on the ground that a James Brown might create on his feet.

As Juan Flores and others have noted, breakdancing relied on a practical multiculturalism that drew on Latino forms such as Bomba, with its released hips and percussive footwork that generate a capacity to quickly shift directions, an embodiment of the rapid decision making entailed in going short and long.[76] In the late 1970s, Puerto Rican breakers such as Richard "Crazy Legs" Colon and the Rock Steady Crew generated an elaborate floor movement vocabulary. Crazy Legs is credited with the continuous backspin with legs in the air known as the windmill. Spinning on the hands with the rest of the body horizontal and low to the ground was based on a gymnastic move on the pommel horse and was called a "flare."[77] Dropping from toprock to downrock by a backflip or chest dive could invite injury, and such power moves required constant practice. As Bryan Bower, a dancer known as "Slink," remarked, "I take a lot of risks and have to practice them daily to make sure I have it perfected."[78]

While the breakdance groups or crews would perform in competitively framed knockdowns or slams, with each group trying to outdo the other in its kinesthetic accomplishment, as judged by the audience members who would attend the performances, movement was developed iteratively within the ensemble, much as it would be for a postmodern collective. By 1981, Rock Steady and Dynamic Rockers had held a faceoff, or Apache Line, produced by Lincoln Center. The Rock Steady Crew claimed for itself a large number of distinct moves. Many of them involved reorienting the axis of the body and the process of locomotion from the movement of the feet to spinning on the top of the head or twisting the pelvis and quickly uncorking this spiral to generate a rotation on the back, or leaping on the hands, or supporting the rest of the bodily weight with them. The mobility of this movement, the ease with which a performing platform made from a flattened cardboard box could be installed in any playground or street corner, constituted its own version of taking opportunity without invitation. The musical sources—large boom boxes that broadcast outsize portability—became the instrument of choice at a moment when New York City's public schools had abandoned their instrumental music programs through fiscally induced budget cuts.

Movement and music shared a highly interactive sensibility of sampling, where bits and pieces of each would be assembled from the whole field of the popular forms and traditions that were available to them. Hip-hop was in effect an amalgamation of major variations in 1960s popular music in the United States: electric boogie, funk, breakdancing, and locking. Locking and its inverted form, popping, isolated parts of the body so that the joints were stuck while a part of the body was free, such as the robot, where the forearm spins at the elbow or moved mime-like, with one segment moving while the rest of the body stayed in place. Rap had developed over the 1970s from the liberationist African American voices of Gil Scott-Heron and the Last Poets and quickly took on a commercial inflection with the first hit single, "Rapper's Delight," by the Sugar Hill Gang in 1978 and Run DMC's cover of Aerosmith's "Walk This Way" a decade later. In the interim, intellectual property would become a leading edge of economic development in a knowledge economy but would find particular challenges in a music industry whose hold on these very properties and, in turn, the pathways of commodification as dissemination were coming undone. Aram Sinnreich refers to the shift from origination to the mash up as a culture of configurability.[79] While in musical terms "derivative" may still signal the inauthentic and inferior, sampling nonetheless generalized a derivative ethos for the production, dissemination, and representation of music. The composer was displaced by the DJ or producer who assembled cuts or smaller sound loops out of a vast range of stylistic possibilities.

The space of the break turns out to be a shared kinesthetic crafted between hip-hop music and dance, an opening created by cutting into a continuous flow of sound or movement, where a departure or risk will be displayed. If the bridge in jazz improvisation and from the famous James Brown song "Take It to the Bridge" was an invitation for improvised bravura, the break exploded the closure of the song as a discrete unit of value and enabled the manipulation of recordings to extend the mutual entanglement of music and dancing indefinitely. This latter reference goes back to 1969 when a Jamaican immigrant, Clive Campbell, known as DJ Kool Herc, isolated the beats from the melody by using two turntables and two copies of the same record. One was rotated counter-clockwise and the other played continuously. The repetition prolonged the song, and he would enjoin the dancers to keep moving, calling out that those who danced most fiercely and creatively were "breaking loose on the dance floor." A few years later, Joseph Saddler, another West Indian immigrant known as Grandmaster Flash, used headphones to pre-cue beats and stitch them together from two turnstiles, thereby pinpointing the break in the music. The break, from this perspective, could be considered a space of arbitrage, a place where a manufactured difference between two sources becomes a generative realization of some value. The spinning of the body in isolation and off-center in dance and the manipulation of spin of disks with hands rendered the movement of music and dance isomorphic with each other and the ensuing break mutually constituted by what DJs and b-boys and b-girls were seizing of their own ongoing space and time on the club floor. The competitive aspects of DJing and breaking organized participation also enabled a certain antiessentialism. A winning dance could be assembled from any combination of elements, just as beats could be abstracted and extracted from any music source. For some DJs, such as Afrika Bambaataa, slipping in music that dancers might disdain, such as the white bubble gum rock group the Monkees, was a claim on the openness of sourcing for what could move a room.

Music sharing and downloading became means of self-dissemination or distribution through Internet startups rather than recording companies, with their vertical integration of musicians, recording studios, and record labels. Sampling in this respect was a form of decolonization, not simply of musical relations of production, but of stylistic and generic boundaries by which musical value could be created and conserved. While copy left and creative commons initiatives did not escape commerce, the lateral distributions complicated the neat divides between what could be considered public domain and what was private intellectual property—even as the latter was increasingly defined through global protocols like the TRIPS and TRIMS of the General Agreement on Tariff and Trade and subsequent cultural diplomacy over matters of piracy.[80]

The circle or cipher is a basic way in which hip-hop is arrayed in space. According to the choreographer Rennie Harris, the circle can be understood as a form of protection and support, with dancers facing one another, absent hierarchy, a momentary enclosure that sustains the ground for individual stylistic differences to emerge. The circle and the genealogy of hip-hop itself, as Moncell Durden documents, are contested in its origins and influences, and although it is widely disseminated, it generates ongoing debates as to whether the term is a transliteration of the Wolof *xippi* (being aware) or from early twentieth-century popular dance references to hep cats in the know.[81] This politics of authenticity, of untraceable origins, of indeterminate links, but also of widespread appropriation that effaces sources and influences, stages hip-hop on derivative ground without certainty of underlying value yet consistently released to circuits of innovation and dispersion that affiliate while complicating lines of affiliation. Hip-hop is at once the circulation of black identity as an attribute of popular culture the world around and a medium for rendering that identification volatile, mobile, and in transit.

The consternation at homophobia and misogyny in hip-hop both treats it as an exceptional instance and worries over contagion from exposure, a contradiction that comes to define poor, black young people, which Tricia Rose has exposed with great clarity. Rose nonetheless regards hip-hop, despite its commercial success, as in "a terrible crisis" and the scene of a polarized divide between defenders and detractors that she likens to a "war."[82] As Joseph Schloss observes, this mixing between what might be approved and what disapproved renders hip-hop itself an arena of ongoing critical evaluation, which is part of the cultural resource that makes it significant:

> Hip Hop is a problem. It is the cultural embodiment of violence, degradation, and materialism. Hip-hop is rappers exploiting women in videos and shooting each other in front of radio stations. Hip-hop is parties on $20 million yachts and Cam'ron claiming that he would never "snitch" to the police, even if he knew that a serial killer was living next door. It is a multibillion-dollar industry based on debauchery, disrespect and self-destruction.
>
> Yet, when I think of hip-hop, I think of shipping for rare funk records on a Saturday afternoon. I think of a 12-year-old girl defeat-

ing two older boys in a dance battle as her mother proudly video-
tapes her. I think of people from all over the world popping and
locking in Manhattan's Union Square as the sun sets on a hot summer evening. I think of Zulu Nation founder and deejay pioneer
Afrika Bambaataa wandering around a jam, happily taking pictures
of random strangers—including me—as if we were his nieces and
nephews.

That, to me, is hip-hop.

So why is the hip-hop I've been experiencing so different from
the hip-hop that I see on television and read about in books? After
all, it's not as if the hip-hip portrayed in the media doesn't really
exist; it does. But hip-hop, as both a community and an art form, is
far more heterogeneous than it is given credit for. Should that make
its more troubling aspects immune to criticism? Not at all. If anything, hip-hop's conceptual diversity actually *encourages* criticism:
that's what battling is all about. And just as it would be an insult to
refuse to battle someone, it would be an insult to refuse to critique
them. It would mean that you didn't take them—or their point of
view—seriously. When it comes right down to it, the most sincere,
most effective, most passionate critic of hip-hop has always been
hip-hop itself.[83]

The diversity of hip-hop pertains not only to this critical ambivalence,
but also to the references to the dance of the 1970s, the rap music of the
1980s, and the demographics of the 1990s. Schloss cautions that the tendency to treat hip-hop as a single phenomenon has led to its dismissal or
romanticization, and he wants to maintain its ambivalence, which he traces
not only to its simultaneously affirmative and baleful aspects but also to
the dance being unmediated and uncommodifiable, an "advertisement with
no product,"[84] whereas even alternative and underground rap becomes a
commercial object that can be estranged from its cultural context. The
subsequent emergence of a hip-hop generation starting in the 1990s would
underscore the complex class and racial crossings who respond to the
appeal of these various forms. That the value of hip-hop is continuously
under scrutiny, that a battle is an internal means of assessment that can go
either way, aligns the critical disposition of hip-hop with hedging and the
ongoing appraisal of minor differences with a kind of arbitrage. As with
other dance forms, Schloss notes the challenges to translating movement
into revenue streams for those who make it. Still, hip-hop dance moves
are thoroughly mediated at their point of derivation, especially from other

dance moves, and through their dissemination. Television, boom boxes, turntables, and other devices of mediated reproducible audio and visual images were prime tools for assembling the vast array of inputs that would continually be mixed and remixed to craft the form. The dance party elongated the space and time of musical reception, but the creation of the short form music video became just as crucial in the dissemination and innovation that sustained hip-hop, as well as in temporarily reinvigorating a flagging commercial recording sector.[85]

Hip-hop circles with individual dancers jumping into the center to a take turn before being replaced by another featured mover were reminiscent of African-derived slave movement and singing practices. Most recognizable among these was the Ring Shout, where people moved counterclockwise in a circle and engaged in call-and-response exchanges, foot stomps, and body slaps as a kind of corporal drumming. Thought to have come from the Congo and widely dispersed by slaves through the Caribbean and the United States, the Ring Shout was practiced in black churches. It was also practiced as a form of fugitivity, as among free settlements of the Carolina Gullahs, and among slaves taking refuge in the woods and claiming the night as their own in an exhausting dance 'til dawn. House parties, or Jooks, of the 1940s incorporated not only some of these elements of physical ardor, self-production, and reclamation of space, but also the relinquishing of the body to gravity's pull that characterizes dances celebrating deities located in the ground rather than in the heavens. Rock-and-roll in the pelvic gyrations of a Chuck Berry or Little Richard maintained a debt to these Africanist roots as it recapitulated the migration of attention from black to white audiences that is a persistent topoi of popular culture in the United States going back to minstrelsy and tap dance. Soul of the 1960s, Motown, and rhythm and blues continued to unleash the pelvic girdle, and the addition of the televisual, as in the pioneering show *Soul Train*, allowed the host, Don Cornelius, to spotlight and call on one couple after another in this oscillation between the soloist and the ensemble.[86]

Its own embrace of released pelvis, reversed polarities of hands and feet, flying low to the ground, risk as ,reward and the posse or ensemble that sustains it organizationally bear overtones of what will become contact improvisation in a parallel development over this same period. Breaking describes a body disarticulated from its normal posture and isolated into parts, as most evident in the percussive explosions from the neck, shoulders, and pelvis called popping. This is a literal de-centering of the impetus or locomotion for movement, with a muscle-torqued release of energy in a wave that moves from right to left fingertips or through the length of the body. Breakdancing also goes global in the same conjuncture as the other slave-derived movement practice, capoeira, and the two practices came to inform each other without merging together. Capoeira is also a circular dance form that emerged from martial arts in which Brazilian slaves, with feet bound by chains, moved cartwheel-like on their hands and kept knives between their toes.[87] The weapons gone, capoeira remains part of the Candomblé religious convenings, but is also spread throughout the world in quasi-secularized studios. For youthful practitioners, the urban environs would join these movements' risk profiles. Flips, somersaults, head spins, and walkovers are all more dangerous and potentially deleterious when concrete or pavement is the surface.

At the same time that Crazy Legs is considered the original b-boy and Africa Bambaataa is considered the coiner of hip-hop, the diffusion of the form through all manner of popular dance and aerobics classes— and, therefore, its crossing between leisure and fitness—have amplified the derivative manifestations and effects that get aggregated together under the same name without being codified or regulated. While locking and popping were emerging as East Coast styles, more funk-based West Coast expressions such as roboting, bopping, hitting, locking, bustin', popping, electric boogaloo, strutting, sac-ing, and dime-stopping were being developed at the same time. Terfing, jerkin', and krumping are more recent derivative styles. Not a specific art form or fixed underlying value, hip-hop would come to name an ever morphing affiliation with certain movement practices, such as the four bounces (deep bounce, boxer's bounce, march bounce, and step bounce) that keep the body in motion and provide an underlying motor from which all manner of explosive actions can occur.

It would be tempting to think about this proliferation along the lines of a model of diffusion. Hip-hop began in the Bronx in the early 1970s. It was discovered by captains of media industries, broadcast globally, especially through the short form of the music video, and imitated widely. While this narrative of media commercialization captures one direction of the flow and is a theme within many a hip-hop anthem about individuals' escape from poverty, bypassing the middle class and landing straight in the rarefied precincts of celebrity, the vectors of fantasy also need to be read in the other direction. The ruins that appeared on the margins of urban life in the 1970s—the canceled movement toward central tendency and centered kinesthetic sovereignty that modernism had promised to all—were increasingly applying to ever expanding swaths of the population. The partial capture of some excessively upward flows did not cancel the far more pervasive lateral mobility that hip-hop embodied and provided the means to move through.

The desire named hip-hop could not be reduced to an escape fantasy but was also a claim on a global abundance of movement, an entangled dance visible everywhere that provided no single vantage point from which all could see what they had together. Drilling down into the Earth, torquing and twisting the body to release it into an accelerating spiral, and isolating movements that might emanate from anywhere provided a rich firmament for creative expansion of a sociality for its own sake, and not for the measures by which it would be taken. That it provoked all manner of affiliations, weak and strong, also aided its movement, crafting the uneven landscape, the jagged frontiers on which it would continue to circle and spin.

Boarding Culture

That the projects would become but a partial reprieve from the sordid conditions of the tenement slum inspired the fantasy of the urban getaway, like the waterfront pleasure zones of Coney Island and Rye Playland. The notion that a pastoral realm of leisure and consumption could become the organizing principle for laboring masses who left their workplaces behind was no small inspiration for the suburbs.[88] With water diverted from agriculture, Southern California real estate developers of the 1950s wanted to make a strong run on this dreamscape, although the mass entertainments of the West Coast had a longer history. The tobacco magnate Abbot Kinney opened Venice of America on July 4, 1905, on canal-drained swampland, and within five years the miniature railroad, gondolas, and amusement ride-laden piers drew more than 100,000 people.

Annexed by the city of Los Angeles twenty years after it opened, the area had grown beyond its infrastructure. Some canals were paved over, and others were polluted with oil that had been discovered in the area in 1929 and extracted by hundreds of rigs until the 1970s. African Americans who worked the oil fields settled in Oakwood through a racially segregated real estate covenant characteristic of the time. After the tourists departed and the piers burned and were shut down in the 1940s, Venice, with its cheap oceanfront bungalows and edgy clubs, including the Gas House, Venice West, and, later, the Cheetah Club, became a magnet for Beat poets of the 1950s and Jim Morrison, who would form the Doors in the 1970s. The Venice Shoreline Crips and Latino Venice 13, African American and Latino gangs, became potent neighborhood forces at this time.[89]

The seaside precincts of Santa Monica and Venice would be augmented by the fantastical Pacific Ocean Park (POP; 1958–1967), which, perched atop what had been the old Lick and Ocean Park pier, could serve as a port of call for suburban bliss. What started as a drive by a joint venture of CBS and horseracing Santa Anita Park to compete with Disneyland quickly became ensnared in Santa Monica's program of urban renewal in 1965, which closed the streets that led into the park and prevented access. The pier itself fell to ruin over the next ten years. Its rides were sold off; its buildings burned; its pieces fell into the sea until it was finally finished off by demolition early in 1975. The main ride of the park, the Sea Serpent rollercoaster, took passengers on a rising and falling wave, where speed and sudden turns, near-death experiences shared with others, were to be the source of great delight. Such staples of modernist mass pleasure celebrated the machinery of speed redolent of Filippo Tommaso Marinetti's Futurist Manifesto of 1909:

We declare that the splendor of the world has been enriched by a new beauty: the beauty of speed. . . . We will sing of the great crowds agitated by work, pleasure and revolt; the multi-colored and polyphonic surf of revolutions in modern capitals: the nocturnal vibration of the arsenals and the workshops beneath their violent electric moons: the gluttonous railway stations devouring smoking serpents; factories suspended from the clouds by the thread of their smoke; bridges with the leap of gymnasts flung across the diabolic cutlery of sunny rivers: adventurous steamers sniffing the horizon; great-breasted locomotives, puffing on the rails like enormous steel horses with long tubes for bridle, and the gliding flight of aeroplanes whose propeller sounds like the flapping of a flag and the applause of enthusiastic crowds.[90]

Sixty years later, Marinetti's engines were sputtering—the massive machinery falling from the skies, the wells dry, the hulking factories empty of labor, the masses de-agglutinated, their brawny frame agile, angry, and precarious. Certainly, the will to thrill was still there, and the rides would rise again not with their gaze fixed on the future but with a wink to the past. The steel horses would be replaced by fiberglass, the smooth chrome by geometric graffiti, and the enthusiastic crowds by ensembles of outcasts. Once again, the mysterious blight that descended on this paradise issued from a toxic mix of real estate market collapse, development-induced drought, and deindustrializing job loss. The futurist vision relied on a secure place for spectacle, a gap that would enable the crowd to witness what was to come.

The collective fantasy of a flight to the future was propelled by its opposite number, a fear of falling into the past. The mass witness of the one who might defy the downward pull, what Garrett Soden calls the gravity hero—a rebel who rises from the masses to confront the pulls of nature and sovereign authority—has captivated public attention for more than two hundred years. Soden describes the shift from mass spectacle to participation. The spectacle of falling has non–Western and church traditions but enters commerce with the first parachute jump in 1797 by André-Jacques Garnerin in Paris, who sold hundreds of tickets, was reported in newspapers, and ridiculed as an absurdity. Gravity feats certainly persist, but the terms of spectatorship and sponsorship have changed from local theatrical productions to globally mediated corporate campaigns. Emblematic is Felix Baumgartner's supersonic parachute jump from a helium balloon–lofted capsule twenty-four miles in the air over Roswell, New Mexico, on October 13, 2012, which was viewed by an estimated eight million people via video stream, courtesy of a sponsor, the energy drink Red Bull.[91] The apotheosis of commercial mass spectacle might be pegged to the tragic final fall of Karl Wallenda. The patriarch of a clan of tightrope walkers, Wallenda met his demise before a clutch of spectators in 1978 at age seventy-three attempting to walk between ten-story hotel towers in Puerto Rico. In the span of time between, the vertical drops provided by the likes of Niagara Falls, which attracted numerous barrel riders, and grand bridges that connected cities, such as the Brooklyn Bridge and the Golden Gate Bridge, which by the mid-twentieth century had become the two most popular places to commit suicide, the gap separating participants and spectators was being closed. "By the time Karl Wallenda died in 1978," Soden writes, "the old world that had admired his kind of gravity heroics was long gone. In its place was a youth culture that admired antiheroes and saw gravity not as a fearful threat but as a convenient plaything."[92] The board that slid across water, land, and ice would transcribe gravity's pull into a wave form and rotate falling from vertical sheer to horizontal face (even where heights were still being scaled). Allowing the rider to stay close to the surface, whatever the orientation, rendered the board "the wheel of gravity play."[93]

The passage from the spectacle of risk as a theater where the singular feat of the lone individual would be played against the perils of an overwhelming natural or social world to participation in a world where danger was made to intimate a crumbling edifice of the future wound its way through multiple sites and circumstances. The conjuncture of risk and ruin was a cauldron for cultural creativity. Certainly, this was the case for the decaying seaside pleasure arenas. As the Santa Monica pier itself fell into ruin, it drew the attentions of surfers. Surfing itself had suffered a fall from grace. It had emerged and migrated over hundreds of years from New

Guinea, Easter Island, New Zealand, the Solomon Islands, the Western Carolines, the Vanuatu Islands, Fiji, Samoa, and Tahiti to Hawaii, where it became a sovereign right. Attacking surfing became a proxy for the assault on native sovereignty, as Calvinists missionaries, who arrived in 1820, condemned surfing and converted King Kamehameha's widow, Queen Kaahumanu, to Christianity. She, in turn, joined in the rejection of the practice. By 1900, few people surfed, and most of the skill of standing up and riding waves was lost. Surfing itself was professionalized and resurrected as an activity suitable for tourists and the leisure-capable by athletes such as George Freeth, an Irish Hawaiian teenager credited with reviving stand-up surfing and attracting popularity to it at surf clubs and demonstrations in Hawaii and Southern California. But by the time the POP closed, the innocence of Gidget and the Beach Boys had given way to a more marginal outlook for surfing. Like towers in sudden need of fording and brick walls demanding a languid pedestrian descent, the jagged pilings of the old pier provoked the breakers to swell their amplitude and beckoned the boarders to cluster together and catch them just at the right moment with room for but one at a time.[94]

While danger, heroism, individualism, and nonconformity are frequent tropes to describe the values of boarding culture, the collectivism, ensemble, and cooperation are crucial features of the practice that complicate the common narratives of loners and outcasts. Whereas the waves were caught alone, someone was usually there to witness the feat, an accomplice who might take the next wave, still sitting on her or his board to take the measure of success. There were no mirrors here, but all movement was closely observed. The basic moves of sweeping low off-center, gathering lateral momentum, and customizing equipment with neighborhood tags propelled the migration of oceangoing boards to landed planks on wheels and, eventually, to other platforms, such as snowboards. To speak of boarding culture, then, is a reference to a movement across various kinds of landscape but with a shared disposition. As one commentator said of snowboarding, it is "an expansion of surfing and skateboarding, a way to explore different terrain with the same mind-set."[95]

Skateboarding is attributed with multiple origins and with a pattern of fluorescence and disappearance that has been described as a "concrete wave." [96] The skateboard appeared on the national scene as an innocent novelty item initially developed by surfers in the 1950s who put roller-skate wheels on wooden planks; it was then marketed to wholesome white youth in the 1960s by companies such as Jack's, Hobie, and Makaha. The boards were ridden down hilly streets or along slaloms, and the riders remained upright like ice skaters or ballet dancers gliding along a frictionless surface. By 1965, the advertising exuberance of the skateboarding craze, fueled by media attention, competitions, and stars such as Torger Johnson, Woody Woodward, and Danny Berrer, had dissipated and, along with hula hoops and pogo sticks, went the way of the POP. But what, from a commercial perspective, could be considered a fad did not go quietly. The notion that the pleasures of youthful movement could be dangerous to childhood led to the banning of skateboarding in some twenty cities, along with the association of sidewalk surfing as a public nuisance to others who might claim pedestrian spaces. The association of youthful transgressions as a causeless rebellion certainly appeared quaint and unsustainable in relation to more explicit antiestablishment challenges of student and counterculture social movements of the time.

During the 1970s, skating was re-concentrated among the precincts of beach subculture, and its practitioners returned to its do-it-yourself roots, with riders crafting their own boards from clay wheels of roller skates and scavenged parts from other discarded boards. Amid the subcultural engagement was a decided entrepreneurial impulse that ranged from magazines and movies to product lines for equipment and fashion, skate parks, and commercial contests. But if the skate parks were a sign that the activity was coming into its own, they also displayed the fragility of growth, as increasing numbers of accidents in a more litigious climate pushed insurance rates up and shut many of the parks down. A similar waxing and waning occurred at the end of the 1980s, when skating hooked up with a punk revival and grunge expansion that extended from music to fashion that, in turn, saw its moment pass.

The volatility in skateboarding's popularity would continue until a broad enough demographic was generated across age, socioeconomic, gender, and racial lines, and the activity was distributed among categories of formalized sport and informal play. In one axis of this development, the migration of boarding across various terrains would get reconsolidated under the moniker of extreme sports, which has come to include rollerblading, windsurfing, skydiving, bicycle motocross (or BMX), mountain biking, eco-challenge, kayaking, climbing, surfing, skateboarding, extreme skiing, and snowboarding. The institutionalization and professionalization of extreme sports were marked most significantly by the first X-Games, held in Rhode Island in 1995. The cable sports network ESPN has made the event an annual franchise, with summer and winter competitions and a stunt vocabulary of flips and turns, such as Tony Hawk's 900-degree rotations (two and a half 360-degree spins), Anthony Napolitan's double front flip on a BMX bike, and Heath Frisby's front flip on a snowmobile. Aside from staging novelty, broadcasting the games has served to demonstrate the translatability of certain risky moves across a range of platforms, some of which further hybridize vehicle and environment, such as street luge, downhill skateboarding, skysurfing, and ultracross—a relay race that pairs skiers and snowboarders. Yet while these events are certainly spectacular, their professionalization exists in relation to a base of extensive participation that diverges from prior incarnations of gravity spectacle. Commerce still relies on a more extensive impetus to engage in the risk activity partitioned as extreme. Writing about the larger and frequently amateur appeal of these activities, Patrick Laviolette observes:

> This cultural turn of physical performativity, in societies that have themselves become obsessed with risk . . . , is interesting because such games come to mean more, signify more, carry more weight than they did in the early colonial period. Adventure sports are indeed becoming more serious while war and political strife become ever more strategic—more game like, as it were. And so, because they are dangerous, take players to the limit, hazardous sports harbour a certain connection to peacekeeping and violence. For instance, many are used for law enforcement and military train-ing purposes. In an increasingly pacifist context in the 'western world,' where most violent conflict is carried out in liminal cultural areas by professionals, citizens are converted into spectators—war itself has become a bloodless spectator sport. Meanwhile dangerous sports amongst citizenry have become more serious than the play between life and death. This is one reason that their seriousness is being sought. . . . That what they offer in their anomalous character is becoming a social quest to find something significant, a device to signify the newness of social action that is more game-like than it used to be and yet just as serious.[97]

Skateboarding was also characterized by persistent introduction of new instruments in the boards and stylistic approaches to riding. The polyure-thane wheels created by Frank Nasworthy that were introduced in 1972 provided more lateral control and allowed skaters to expand the surfaces, angles, and tricks they undertook. Backyard swimming pools, the icons of suburban success, were left as fetid waters when residents were mandated to leave their pools empty in response to water conservation measures. The artifice of unsustainable water and land use rendered these concrete holes the equivalent of broken windows and abandoned walls of urban streets. The curving surfaces of the kidney-shape pools emulated the ocean waves' geometries but arrested the motion of the sea.

Teams of skateboarders, most notoriously the Zephyr Boys (Z-Boys), drained the pools and rode the undulating surfaces of concrete. From the lip of the pool, Tony Alva would drop in and re-create the wave form of the aquatic cognate, deriving the same off-center movement, speed, and balance on the land-based platforms. Rather than standing upright as in 1960s freestyle, these skaters would crouch low and touch the pavement in a move called a Burt that they took from the surfer Larry Burtleman, who would let his hand ride on the surface of the wave. Jeff Ho, Skip Engblom, and Craig Stecyk opened Zephyr Surfboard Productions in 1972 in the area between the Santa Monica Pier and Venice known as Dogtown. Ho hand-shaped the boards, and Stecyk appropriated local graffiti iconography into the designs and started the eponymous surf team that soon became a band of skateboarders that included Stacy Peralta, Tony Alva, Wentzl Ruml, a number of other young men, and one women, Peggy Oki. The Z-Boys represented a generation who were the children of manufacture and whose future would be canceled by the flight of oil, tire, automobile, and, finally, aerospace industries out of the state.

The Z-Boys bore the image of the deindustrialized white precariat. Their days were their own, and schools were less sites to mine their intellectual depths than expanded playgrounds to provide the surfaces for their kinesthetic explorations. The local elementary schools in the precincts around Dogtown were all built into hills with asphalt slopes. The Z-Boys' local surround, filled with broken promises for upward movement in work or home, was recast as an expansive arbitrage opportunity. The daily regimen was to take to the streets to compare sites—pools, playgrounds, hills—to see which might be most advantageous for riding. Some research was required to ascertain whether anyone was on-site to chase them off or whether they could get a few rides in before police came and shut them down. The team required not only a scout for sites but also a lookout for the police. The inward gaze was matched by an outward imagination. Peralta brought his Super 8 movie camera to the pool parties and captured the footage that would be the core of *Dogtown and Z-Boys*, the 2004 documentary he produced with the shoe manufacturer Vans.[98] Stecyk's photos and early articles, such as "Aspects of the Downward Slide," published in 1975, increased the group's fame, which was crystallized in the competition the Z-Boys won at Del Mar, California, that year.

As with other forms of arbitrage, this one suffered the volatility it relied on, and the team, like Judson Dance Theater and the Rock Steady Crew, met its undoing on the shores of excessive attention to those who would be stars. Commerce had never been outside these art forms—boarding culture especially. But commercial attention just as quickly abandoned the boarders, and new waves jettisoned such attention. As with arbitrage, getting to the salient difference first drives the race to innovation, but it also makes that difference unsustainable. The ruins of one ensemble released energy for other creative innovations. Alan Gelfand, nicknamed "Ollie," is credited with creating a move in 1978 that came to bear his name and distributing skateboarding from its designated haunts in pools and skate parks to a wide range of sites. An ollie begins with the rider's foot stomping on the back of the board to send both body and platform into the air, then sliding the front foot forward to reorient the board's movement to a forward horizontal plane, then landing both feet down on the moving surface, allowing the board itself to simulate the effects of the wave form and launch the rider into low lateral flight.

The ollie is skateboarding's version of flying low, but it also opened the various surfaces of the city—a park bench, a stair railing, a retaining wall—to repurposing as a means for exploring movement and treating those surfaces as a sketchbook on which lines of urban flight might be inscribed. These etchings were as much sonic as visual, the rhythms of wheels, trucks, or axles and boards grinding against metal and concrete, echoing and reverberating into one another. As Iain Borden suggested, "Skateboarding, I propose, is a critical practice, challenging of both the form and political mechanics of urban life, and so in its own small way is part of this birth of differential space. Through an everyday practice—neither a conscious theorization nor a codified political programme—skateboarding suggests that pleasure rather than work, use values rather than exchange values, activity rather than passivity are potential components of the future, as yet unknown city."[99]

While skateboarding was certainly legitimized as professional sport, its framing as a professional activity does not exhaust the various dimensions of the cultural practice. Jeff Howe, for example, keeps open the resonance between skateboarding and dance:

> Dance, to return to that, speaks in a language codified through centuries of usage. The conventions of this language have seeped into our culture to such a degree that we can't help but register its voice, even if the components of its speech are nonverbal. Like dance, skating is a form of nonverbal expression, but unlike dance,

skateboarding has very little of the history helpful for building an agreed-upon vocabulary—a set of meanings. Also unlike dance, no attempt is made to 'read' its language. Yet I don't believe this means a skater can't express the range of ideas and emotions that a dancer can. Skating can be mournful, or playful, or as with my friend Sean, ferociously angry. Or like much dance, it can simply express the sheer exuberance of living in three dimensions, a celebration of the physical body in play. . . . Skateboarding offers a way out, a path of opposition. A board is more than a slab of wood; it is a lifestyle of abdication, a silent vote for freedom without fame, glory without glamour, entertainment without consumption. Even if skateboarding doesn't need us, we need skateboarding because we need to know what we aren't in order to understand what we are.[100]

As with postmodern dance and hip-hop, boarding culture engages a population deemed at risk of disappearance with activity considered to be extreme. Unlike the Owl of Minerva, these black swans do not wait for midnight to take flight but depart at all hours. All three will make for themselves a kind of global audience and long cast of participants who move between scenes and glean value in the lateral spaces that make up their respective domains of arbitrage. Each claims a certain specialization and combination and refers to cultural practices that maintain volatility now as a condition of risk-based sustainability. In hip-hop, that larger sensibility is sampling, and for boarding culture, the context from which it draws is that of extreme sports. Here, too, a kind of derivation takes place that effectively decolonizes the extreme sports of the 1950s—big game hunting, sports car racing, mountain climbing—from the precincts of the very rich to the quotidian spheres of a populace faced with creating movement through its own ruins. Being impaled by a rhino, freezing in the Himalayas, or crashing on the track were all considered honorable ways for the truly blue-blooded to depart the planet. Without doubt, such activities continue, but extreme sports are now niche marketed directly to "high net worth individuals" as a pitch to fly down to the Bahamas to kite surf or shark dive as "offering an adrenalin rush unmatched by the stock market."[101] The local streets are dangerous enough for those who cannot afford to travel far as extreme sport has cultivated its mass base.

Financial and kinesthetic risk are here transvalued as embodied activities through which membership gets earned one run at a time. Kite surfing and volcano boarding (riding a special flame-resistant composite board down a soft spill of volcanic ash) up the ante on costs of equipment and access as they maintain a derivative relation to the grit and danger of their street-based forebears. The older gentlemanly extreme sports revolved around journeys of conquest of some beast, natural formation, or racetrack. Peril could result from placing the body in harm's way in an environment distinct from the staid executive suites where wealth was summoned and commanded. Now the body is being asked to move in such a way, to execute a stunt or trick, to achieve a level of speed with minimal machinery or assistance (like the Sherpas and carriers on the treks and hunts) to effect an unmediated relation to the sources of risk. If the adrenaline rush was a displacement of employment for precarious youth, it was an extension and intensification of workplace kinesthetics for masters of the financial universe.

The logic of appropriation is complicated from the unidirectional incorporation that was evident in ballet's use of folk idioms or Graham's and other modernists' Orientalist, African, and Native American sources. De-centering both distributes and disburses kinesthetic practices of risk; it also yields its concentrations at the extremes. One measure of this would be the costs of entry and access, as in the equipment- and transport-laden forays for the wealthy. But the drive to exceed the performance of others, to locate value that others have overlooked or missed, does not simply drive the creation of new platforms for novel environments (like the volcano), but reaches back to pre-existing practices and transforms them as well. Nowhere is this reconfiguring of extant boarding practices more apparent than in extreme surfing.

If a drought was the condition for vertical dropping to mimic the ocean waves, climate change in the other direction has yielded globally disbursed waves of hitherto unimaginable and unrideable scale. With increased purses for competitions, and corporate sponsorship, surfing has now produced its own elite athletes capable of traveling around the world on the report of gigantic swells. While they have long been part of seafaring lore, hundred-foot waves, like other black swan events, required conditions "so far beyond rare as to virtually never happen."[102] Laird Hamilton, Raimana Van Bastolaer, Garrett McNamara, Justen Allport, Brad Gerlach, Mike Parsons, and other surfers were crisscrossing the globe, from Hawaii to California, South Africa to South America, on the wings of satellite weather reports and forecasting. They were riding shortened boards with greater maneuverability inspired by windsurfing and snowboarding and were dropped in by helicopter or towed on jet skis to access hundred-foot swells.

Susan Casey, a writer for *Sports Illustrated*, followed both the surfers and the scientists to examine the interaction between climate change as an

ambient risk condition that creates those once rare giant wave conditions
and the culture of surfing that pursues these risk opportunities:

> As the waters heat up, wind velocity increases; storm tracks become
> more volatile; polar ice and glaciers melt, causing sea levels to rise.
> As a result of all of the above and likely, other factors no one's aware
> of yet, average wave heights have also been rising steadily, by more
> than 25 percent between the 1960s and the 1990s. Planetary waves,
> massive subsurface ocean waves that play a key role in creating the
> climate, are speeding up as well. The details about what a warmer
> planet will look like are still coming into focus, but there is one thing
> our environmental future will clearly hold: a lot of restless water.[103]

Tsunamis also are linked to this planetary volatility, and surfers, no less
than postmodern dancers and breakdancers, pursue the movement made
possible by these ruins.

The perils of discarded youth making what they can of what they have
are more typically treated with condescension, unless fame comes to the
rescue. The proletarianization of risk practice may turn out to be the return
of the repressed that accompanies the financialization that descends from
the fallen utopias of the 1970s and 1980s dreamscapes and eventually winds
up in the big bang of 2008. Through boarding cultures' multiple expressions and locations, much risk is sorted. Populations at risk, those at the
margins of a degenerative whiteness, those whose own privileged race no
longer retained its purchase on privilege, shared a practice that nonetheless
shuffled their fates with a few who would rocket to stardom for mastering
the arts of risk, while many more would negotiate lateral mobility, social
and kinesthetic, that kept them close to their own mean streets. Boarding may have emerged as a lost or last bastion of an increasingly incapable
masculinity, but it moved beyond such fixities of identity. In the 1970s,
Peggy Oki may have been the only woman to break the homosociality of
the Zephyr Boys. Now more women, including Alex White and Cara Beth
Burnside, who has been a professional snowboarder as well as a skater, have
begun to complicate the gender unicity of the sport. At the same time, the
class, racial, and gender dimensions are more complex than the prevailing
images of white male teenagers would allow. Recently, the California African American Museum in Los Angeles mounted an exhibit documenting
the forty-year history of skateboarding in the African American community, featuring a number of professional skaters.[104] Emily Chivers Yochim
has gone a long way in complicating the form of masculinity in play. She

notes that "skateboarding culture, which is steeped in consumption, is also a space of citizenship in which young men produce a politics of identity" and "adopt a type of willful otherness."[105]

For all of this, the de-centered kinesthetic practices emerge at the point at which some upward mobility is blocked, and where some scene of ruin has been repurposed for its promises of risk-based creativity. Urban ruins, conventionally figured as a kind of trap, an enclosure from which racialized poverty has no escape, are, by means of these practices, restaged as a ground to rupture enclosure while trans-valuing areas abandoned or of depreciating worth. This rupture of various spaces of enclosure signals precisely the shift from the disciplinary societies described by Michel Foucault to what Gilles Deleuze terms societies of control based on coding and surfing:

> The numerical language of control is made of codes that mark access to information, or reject it. We no longer find ourselves dealing with the mass/individual pair. Individuals have become "dividuals," and masses, samples, data, markets, or "banks." Perhaps it is money that expresses the distinction between the two societies best, since discipline always referred back to minted money that locks gold as a numerical standard, while control relates to floating rates of exchange, modulated according to a rate established by a set of standard currencies. The old monetary mole is the animal of the space of enclosure, but the serpent is that of the societies of control. We have passed from one animal to the other, from the mole to the serpent, in the system under which we live, but also in our manner of living and in our relations with others. The disciplinary man was a discontinuous producer of energy, but the man of control is undulatory, in orbit, in a continuous network. Everywhere surfing has already replaced the older sports.[106]

Just as Foucauldian bodies were not only docile but also resistant, encoding of control is met with a continuous decoding and recoding of lateral, de-centered, and distributed mobilizations. The wave, the undulation, unfolds and circulates through an array of sense-making, affiliative, and intercommensurable practices. Yet these movements never converge, they may be used variously, but they are never taken over; something is always spilling out; more bodies move in take the generative place of what was left behind. Through the gaps in the ruins, the tears in the urban fabric, small spaces are opened from which larger volatilities emerge.

Generative Risk

It has become common to narrate this migration between ruin and mobility as one of commercialization and even recuperation of resistant impulses.[107] In this narrative, the free spaces and alternative practices of the street and the avant-garde lose their autonomy to the voracious appetite of the market, and their own critical bite is blunted. Surely these instances of upward mobility are evident in postmodern dance and hip-hop, but the intriguing feature of derivative logics is what they leave behind—which turns out to be most of the networked and organized sociality, the precarious materiality crafted and created by the practitioners engaged in these forms. For better and for ill, the derivative flows from decolonization and takes the undoing of what was whole, the unbounding of what was enclosed, the bundling of what was scattered and shred as its conditions of possibility.

For finance, the case is seemingly clear, even where commerce is cloaked as a public good. For popular culture and artistic practices, derivative efficacies are far less so. Claiming such narrow parameters of commercial success or making it to stardom trades a selective outcome for a reductive account of intentionality that begs the question of why so many people spend so much time doing an activity that they claim for themselves. Mobility is the climb up a narrowing ladder. Those who fall off along the way are forgotten and must accept their fate. The apparatus of financialization sorts the risk-capable from the at-risk in a neat, if unstable, calculus of winners and losers. But the risks engaged through decolonizing movement deposit value and engender debt among precarious, at-risk populations that enhance their capacity to make what they love, say why they do, and let the world know.

These clouds rising from the ruins, so many particles giving form to one another, reveal the kinesthetic forces of a derivative social logic. While some are spirited away to the upper reaches of celebrity, what remains closer to the ground alerts us to what comes after economy, polity, and culture have ended their terms of confinement. Unleashed are partial yet pervasive affinities to move together and multiply. From the ruins of economy we now see self-production—a de-centered, disbursed, and distributed means not only for moving but also for creating movement. From the breakup of the public, we can hear a polyphony of critical voices staking their claims for self-representation. From the decolonization of culture, seeds are spread everywhere and sources are released and captured, sampled and posted, through expansive webs of self-dissemination. Dance and other specialized movement practices bring these derivative socialities to notice, open the paths of assembly of what can be valued socially, point to ways in and out of our current predicaments, shift the principles by which our bodies are ruled.

A de-centered social kinesthetic runs on sentience in a world marked by spectacle. Yet the very conception of a society of the spectacle was articulated by Guy Debord in the 1960s as a colonization of public attention by means of a saturation of daily life by a unidirectional broadcast of radio, television, cinema, advertising, mass sporting events, and the like.[108] Spectacle is here seen as a suspension of critical attention as viewers are rendered passive and live variously through the action of others. This chasm between performance and audience is both violated and bridged in these decolonizing movement practices, which in turn elicit and amplify various modes of participation. Spectacle would stand as an esthetic reduction, a collapse of the senses onto a flat screen of the visual, a loss of the ability to make sense of and for oneself.

The risky movements of postmodern dance, hip-hop, and boarding culture do not fit in the same image or descend from the same line. They all de-center bodies' relation to their surroundings, reorienting what is up and down, prize flying low and moving laterally, shifting suddenly, in the midst of a dangerous situation in which one has placed oneself. A gap, a break, an opening allows the body to move otherwise, to seize a moment in which a minor difference prevails and accelerate through, cleaving what had once been safely apart. Releasing, dropping, verticality—moments of danger for each of these practices—suspend the mover as arbitrageur, between spaces of value, cutting into that space to leave it stitched anew with a residue of value behind. The value is both the accomplishment and the desire, the expanded sense of what is possible.

The iterative process of rehearsal, of taking turns doing movement for one another, amounts to a continuous shuttling between viewer and actor to render the spectacular internal to performance. Watching does not substitute for, but it does enable, doing. Nor is the rest of the ensemble merely watching. The crew, posse, team, company are a first audience bearing witness as much as they are baring their bodies' inventive means to come up with next moves. They are securing the space; documenting the event; serving as critics and publicists, showing, comparing, appropriating what others are doing. The long-interview form that Trisha Brown undertakes throughout her career and the insider accounts of Stacy Peralta for boarding or Afrika Bambaataa for bombing rest on intimacy with creation of the form that undoes the separation between critical utterance and creative activity that choreography initiated in the classical kinestheme. Recall that choreography initially referred to those who could read and write dance notation and therefore represent dancing in its absence. The modern kinestheme deploys notation as document, whereas Judson postmodernists write their own scores to generate movement. But contemporary stages and streets are now noisy with the boasts, ruminations, accompaniments, and critical appraisals of practitioners, who have claimed the representational prowess of choreography as their own.

Hip-hop, boarding culture, and postmodern dance have made their way around the world, carried through all manner of commerce circuits, from contests to cinema, from concerts with pricey tickets to broadcast, print, and other mass media. The sampling techniques that have been so integral to the composition of these forms has also been a key factor in their dissemination. Without doubt, the modern kinestheme relied on capture technologies, the quintessential example arguably being Dziga Vertov's *Man with a Movie Camera*, with the camera fixed to its tripod serving as a recurrent trope of the kino-eye, the machine for seeing the movement of the masses.[109] Capture technologies for the de-centered kinesthetic are hand-held—from the Super 8 movie camera to the video camcorder and the smartphone. These eyes do not aggregate the masses in one place but disperse bundles of attention through media of distribution—the social in social media. Granted, YouTube and Vimeo are commercial sites that were purchased in 2006 by Google and IAC/InterActiveCorp, respectively; by 2011, they could boast nearly half a billion worldwide visitors to their sites.[110]

As with investors clubs and other digital fantasies of open access, much of what is free is the labor and content that participants provide to the revenue streams of these large corporations.[111] But what is neglected in such considerations is the widespread capacity for composing and editing these materials, for positioning them and for commenting and reflecting on their significance. The surfeit of memory storage, of archives placed in repertories of reception, of file sharing, practical expertise in placement, indicates a different array of capacities for engagement from that pictured in the mollified masses of earlier spectacles. Like the movement itself, much of this reception cannot be absorbed to specific instrumental use; rather, it serves as a kind of medium of circulation through which cultural values are engendered.

The emphasis in these three movement practices on flying low, off-center release to gravity, reversing position and purpose of hands and feet (for mobility and balance) all serve to reorient the motional drive of the body from vertical lift to horizontal propulsion. These kinesthetic conditions do not form a stylistic unity but could be said to express the lateral mobility by which derivative logics themselves become so prominent a feature of movement. The underlying sources of pedestrian, slave, and indigenous bodily practices are decolonized from their initial terms and settings to refigure those who, by tradition, would be assigned to the populations at risk into crafting corporal economies where risk counts as its own reward. A risky move is granted immediate value by the creative ensemble; it need not await final delivery precisely in the manner that a derivative provides a price for a good or service that has not yet been made or come due. Derivatives promise continuous and real-time assessment of value that moves the constant calibration of the market into the hitherto hidden abode of production. The streets, pools, walls on which these decolonizing bodies move are exposed already to the prospects of evaluative surveillance (whether cops chasing out boarders and taggers from illicit grounds or cameras capturing the deed itself for further distribution). The question of who owns a given move may certainly be an object of spirited contention, but the insinuation of these lateral, risk-making maneuvers across so many ruinous sites eclipses the proprietary claims of possessive individualism by which celebrity may be measured, replacing it with a distributed possession by which participation in these practices multiplies. The measure of these taken risks is to reappraise which attributes will get bundled together, given excess capacity.

The capacity to revalue lateral mobility collectively that these movement practices demonstrate also speaks to the demographic shift away from opportunities for upward mobility that will characterize the prospects for so many young people, artists, and communities of color that the risk-shifting 1970s and 1980s yielded. The disinvestment in infrastructure and social services, flattening of wages and mounting consumer debts, and repositioning of government from a guarantor of security through a bundle of defined benefits to an investor based citizenship based on contribution all converge here to darken the screen of the American dreamscape and spread a dissolute precarity. The supposedly iconic figure of the yuppie, the hyper-affluent precocity of effective self-investment, effaces the much broader trend of diminished opportunities and rewards for those who would follow the postwar boomer generation.

While the ranks of the professional managerial class continued to swell, the autonomy by which these knowing selves would achieve sovereignty was increasingly diminished. While public funding for the arts may have been under attack from the 1980s forward, the notion that artists could serve as models for the revitalization of what financial ascent had left in ruins led to a litany of privatizing public works by which creativity would raise all boats—be they depleted cities or deplenished middle classes. Canceled entitlements and shredded public goods would be compensated for by a growing self-help industry through which companies would profit from risk-induced anxieties once ameliorated by the social security of government, labor unions, and professional associations. At the same time, youth culture taken as both a marketing opportunity and an achievement of self-organization and production was reoriented around a do-it-yourself ethos in which precarity might seem a virtue.[112] The moral panic directed by reenergized conservatives at idle (but really idled) youth would cast a broad net of guilt over errant culture—whether that is onscreen or stage, digital monomania, or excessive street life.[113] But we could see in these de-centered movement practices derivative cousins of moshing, mashing, and mixing, as well as in alternate artistic practices of collectives and collaboratories, images for self-production, self-representation, and self-dissemination.[114]

The past forty years in which finance emerged from one ruined ground to plough through yet another have reoriented some senses by which what can be done, what is available for doing, and what wealth exists for have been subject to particular regimes of evaluation. It is no doubt easier to trace what formed this conjuncture than to entertain what might follow its undoing. The year 2008 has been taken as the ruination of a larger dreamscape: an abandonment of security toward the generalization of precarity; a cancellation of a promised future by diminishing access to higher education and professional occupations; of home ownership that appreciates over time; of similarly financed retirement accounts that sustain the end of life; and of health care that would make lives per se sustainable. How the affiliated sensibilities of a de-centered social kinesthetic activate the capacities for life making from movement is by no means a straightforward or assured path to pursue. But what is now apparent is that the proclamations of scarcity that structure the prevailing schemes of valuation and mandate deficit reduction and budget cuts—that is, wars against cultures and populations whose riskiness is unbearable—must confront a super-abundance of capacity to move together, to assemble riches, to decide what to do next, to find uses for the creative endowments of others, to place ourselves in positions of mutual indebtedness. These emergent sovereignties animate and sustain the pleasure in danger, the openness to where the known meets what is not, that begins to cross from creative to social and political mobilization.

Derivatives came to stand for vast aggregates of wealth unmoored from any particular purpose. The imperial power that historically has underwritten financial sovereignty has also morphed into a kind of discretionary intervention—it is easy to enter but difficult to sustain justification for. Yet what is also clear is that among these imperatives to be driven by risk, other sensibilities of what it means to make more or other out of what we have are also to hand (and foot). Sensing dance from the perspective of the derivative, between the fluid ephemerality of networks that vanish without a trace and the static durability of organizations that lurch from crisis to crisis, replicating their structures, opens approaches to embodied ensembles that assemble attributes to leverage further movement and value.[115] If the polarity between network and organization into which precarious movements themselves have been cast has proved to be a trap that promised escape but leads back to the starting point, the derivative logic as presented here plays inside and outside these dance practices, allowing them to shuttle between the ground they inhabit and the world through which they ripple. Difference is realized immediately in the risk well taken and deferred to other connections that remain promissory notes—a lateral move teetering on a wing and a prayer. The derivative logic might also help dance out of its own trap of ephemerality and location. Performances are, after all, derived from many other times—of rehearsal, of training, of touring—and they gather together movements from myriad locales, experiences, and sources and recalibrate and recompose them for a given intervention. Seen from this expanded field, dance is already everywhere. Rather than appearing merely fleeting and ephemeral in performance, dance is the concatenation of varying durations, of reaches near and far that nestle among the moving bodies.

Conversely, finance has touted vast abundance that leaves scarcity for others in its wake. But like the hands and feet of de-centered movement practices, the polarities of value can readily be reversed, and the extremes of movement possibility can be mined to point to what else we might be and do together. Lateral mobility lives with what it has. If capital has jettisoned its own utopian promises, emerging social logics of the derivative point us in different directions. Utopia is an end we touch through our own means of intervention. The ruins left are not sources of poverty, depletion, and shame but the very roots of what could make population assemble for its own sake, to establish its own terms of tenancy, to value its ensemble capacities as creative choreographies. "Populate" (from the classical Latin *populāre*), like "precarity," has a double and internally antagonistic etymology in the action of laying waste or ruin of the country and to people or inhabit a domain.

Valuing the ways in which we are linked together without being one, that we share certain sensibilities of moving together without needing to model or imitate someone, opens conceptions of sovereignty as self-production that just might serve as a momentary realization of the future in the present. The much vaunted and readily dismissed ephemerality of dance (and finance) would thereby assume a generative durability, an elaboration of times and spaces in which collectivity itself would gain and circulate its own currency. This self-conferred tenancy would claim a different ground from which the uncertain movement of precarity might circulate its politics. Precarity bears its own undoing. It teeters between prayer (*precor*) and debt (*precarius*), between a wish tendered on a promise and a claim to inhabit a space or tenancy held at the pleasure of others. This uncertain movement casts bodies into a state of vulnerability and risk that may prove depleting or sustaining, a marginalizing call to bondage, or a realization of value yet to receive their just rewards. Precarity poses a transformation of one kind of encumbrance into another, an embrace of debt for some other expression of mutuality.[116]

Getting to such possibilities, however, might entail traveling a rather tortured road. The power to forgive a sin or an unpayable bill might have allowed the otherwise dispossessed to work or occupy common holdings, but it also affirmed the authority of those in the church or state that held the underlying right, even if, as now, the legitimacy of that power was being contested. The figure of margins implicates some normative conception and potential assimilation to the center. Further, if precarity descends from some foundational meaning, geopolitical ground, or historical point of reference, the salient global differences between, say, displaced urban professionals and expropriated subsistence farmers—to say nothing of how noncapitalist formations persist in or depart from the present—may not be adequately addressed.

For precarity to yield some form of debt that is generative of an expansive sociality and not simply be all subsuming or consuming—as the recent financial debacle threatens—attention must be paid to what is made in movement together. A politics of precarity would need to dance between a ceiling of debt that has become punitive and a floor of forgiveness that does not interrogate what we want to be liable for; it will need to move off-center, fly low, and gather its forces laterally, to animate the coincident rhythms of dance and finance. Fleshing out how dance moves in and makes a world entails breaking from the weak links of metaphor that confine arts politics to questions of reflection in order to grasp the powers of incorporation and interdependence that finance bears but does not disclose.

Conclusion

Derivative Knowledge

What has become of the social? What is its limit? How might we know it? What is its logic? From what is it derived? Finance seems to have overtaken our basis for being together, canceled the future and replaced visions of what could be with an imperative to move forward at all costs. All of our hard work is to go into making finance viable, but so saved, these riches take flight. Yet if finance has appropriated the social as the means and ends of our mutual entanglements, it is itself derived from a determinate sociality, from our debts to one another. Indeed, finance persistently cuts into the social fabric, sundering connections and dividing populations and resources unequally. But it also reassembles, bundles, and imposes interdependence and shared predicaments among what were once disparate situations and circumstances. Finance is its own antagonym, a single word with opposite meanings, the most salient here being "to cleave," to cut and to connect. In this respect, finance suffers and thrives through its own antagonism. Risk management is its cure-all and its poison, its way of knowing whose investment in measurement of all variation is its means of mastery, but also the portal through which flows the queasy, vertiginous excess of uncertainty, the anxieties and the absurdities of the immeasurabilities of nonknowledge.

Finance also marks an antagonism of the social, the logics it unleashes on the world, and the worldly movements that make such logics possible. Finance resides and flourishes in the volatility it mines and engenders as it straddles the measures of social surplus; the abundance of wealth by which inequality is addressed; and the proliferation of difference, variation, and dissemination by which the terms and terrain of the social are expanded beyond measure. Both of these conditions of the social figure in arrangements of debt (the debt to those creditors who claim property as their own) and convert time and memory into units of repayment (the debts we assemble in making life together, which expand but never get repaid). If finance names an antagonism of its technical operations (risk management) and its sociality (mutual indebtedness), it also articulates a historical process of self-formation, a rupture or break, that still rests on all that came before.

Recall that the root of finance, from the French for ending, *fin*, suggests the act not only of bringing a transaction to a close, but also of pursuing the opportunity that ending opens up. *After*, the temporal disposition of finance, is in this respect both a movement beyond and a pursuit into the present; it assembles disparate time frames past and brings aspects of what has taken place to bear on what can be done in the present. That finance comes after also captures a future, a claim on what could be that is converted into a decision that can be made in the present. "After," in this regard, references the acceleration of past and future into the present. Taken in a different way, "after" is another name for the derivative as such, that which comes from something else, takes after it, adopts aspects of it, pursues it, and does not replace what was with what is newly original but carries forward the elements of what has been in a different arrangement. So again, the point is not that what once made up "economy" has disappeared overnight but that the unity that the term took for granted, the integrity that it rested on, is no longer available as a means to ensure a home or resting place that would anchor the concept. Pursuing where the derivative leads across varied and scarred landscapes provides routes and means of moving between those landscapes but clearly is not the only thing of which they are composed. The derivative journey does not tell a completely different story. It is not a new master narrative, but it does allow us to sense and value the ways in which we are linked together.

This derivative "after" displays both a spatial and a temporal dimension. It complicates linear temporal succession—that of one state of affairs coming to an end and another starting up anew. It upends the spatial order, as well, as it unleashes the complexity of forces, factors, and forms thought to operate at separate scales of small and large, far and near. Ruins are a trope of what has fallen but remains with us, the bricolage that we sift through, the obstacles on the course that we duck and dodge as we chart our routes. That local movements—or mortgage rates—can be abstracted from their points of origination and circulate globally does not cancel the local but makes the local come after the global as a response to and a continuation of what is swirling around the world, whether it is the risky moves of a low-flying fall or the blizzard of measure in relation to international standards that places schoolchildren in a particular inner-city school district at risk.

It is not simply that the big and the small, the durable and the transient, can trade places, that minor difference can be leveraged to large effects, as is evident in the excess criticality of contemporary mobilizations—the small or temporary clusters of bodies that gather in the streets captivating public attentions. The order of scaling itself seems to be upended as well. What is known as postmodern dance engages thousands of performers and attendees; boarding can count millions among its participants; hip-hop, the most culturally diffuse array of practices and sensibilities (from a dance step to a sampled beat and a generation) might be said to touch billions. The decolonizing kinesthesia that these forms share suggests more a fractal reiteration of movement patterns and values than an ordering by influence or origin. The decolonizing movements from which the derivative issues courses through many places and makes itself felt in myriad ways, with affinities and affiliations that are sometimes close and intensive and at other moments are dispersed and widely mediated.

Each of these derivative operations—the technical, the social, and the historical—cuts through the fields in which it moves, leaving an uneven terrain that appears to be sliced in two but also is subject to the conceptual confusion of any dualistic schema. When antagonism takes the form of two parts that confront each other, action, activity, and engagement are presented as a matter of mutually exclusive choices, of a dilemma of either–or, that reinscribes the very terms of the possible to what is and foreshortens the imagination of what could be. Here, the derivative logic may aid in opening this conceptual blockage but discloses what moves among the parts, what reassembles the shards and remains, what provides multidirectional pathways. Whereas the cleavage cuts in two, a derivative logic also unfolds in three. This third pulse that moves against the two sides is evident in the etymological root of the derivative. Recall again, the French word *derive*, meaning to overflow the banks, as in a river or channel. The *derive* bears the force of what cuts away from the established channel and overflows the banks on both sides, the binary structure, that had previously contained that movement.

In terms of rhythm, a triplet—an oscillation of two beats that move through the space of three—is the basis of a waltz, of swing, and especially, when the two are brought together, of the uneven emphasis of beats or syncopations that animate jazz. A rhythmic figure, such as a swung triplet, is at once abstract and concrete—an approach to any musical composition and a specifying grounding in a decolonizing move. Abstracting the movement of finance at this level, something that derivatives facilitate and make legible, leads us to the point where the rhythms of dance and finance meet. The lateral steps, flying low, release, dropping, verticalism, in the de-centered kinesthetic define a movement vocabulary that flows between the ruins and entangles bodies in this sensibility of moving with others one cannot see. The derivative adds the critique of mobilization, of how and why we move together, to the critique of representation, of how form is invested with significance, which has been the basis for much contemporary philosophical energy.

The critique of mobilization entails an interruption of the taken-for-grantedness of obligatory movement, of endless circulation and accumulation, of going forward at all costs. What is one is divided into many; a single beat becomes a layered polyrhythm. The move of two against three is at the root of the derivative: what is flowing between the banks; what separates two sides; what is taken as the passive and invisible boundary between one way and another, changes course, exceeds what contains it, carries it off to the side and forges a different path. If we stay with rivers and their beds, the metaphor quickly becomes strained, as the banks, after all, are formed by the movement of the river, which is constantly changing, and even with a flood or crisis, banks are overrun and flows are redirected, but some binary of rivers and sides is reestablished. But if the attention to the three over the two allows us to bring to notice the flow and the internal properties and principles of redirecting movement, of forging communication between what was separate and connecting masses that were distinct, then derivatives provide a language for and means of valuing that which is in motion, the production internal to circulation.

Derivatives in this respect follow a logos, a line of reason, a means of rationalization. Such a logic does not fix what happens, what is done with and against it. This is where arbitrage, as the labor of the derivative, the agency and manner of being that takes the line of reason somewhere, does something to it, alters it somehow along the way. The anthropomorphizing of finance under the guise of a market that speaks, acts, or displays affect is at once a way to name the sociality of finance—that it is taken as a call to which we respond—but also, this alleged personification of what is not a person, or prosopopoeia, is a symptom of agency that does not name itself.[1] Arbitrage may be an occupation and preoccupation of finance, but it is also a means of discerning how movement takes place in the spaces in between, among the ruins; how intensities are applied. Bodies suddenly exceed what were thought to be their capacities; they are linked in flight to where others have been but no one has gone. Arbitrage is the derivative's double, the intensity or extremity of action that disappears into its own activity, leaving no trace of its efforts, despite self-evident gain, but the desire to go again. Recall that for the financial arbitrageur, the discovery of a different valuation between two markets for the same good puts money in the pocket "risk-free" but also reestablishes the "one true price" that reconciles the heretofore unrecognized difference into one. The de-centered and distributed movers pocket the pleasure of the risk taken, of the movement executed, which then allows that move to circulate in the world in a disbursed and multidirectional appropriation.

At this point, it might be apparent that this oscillation between a double and triple rhythm describes what the derivative does in the world but also maps the form that this book takes in its own presentation and movement of argument. It echoes with the footsteps of twos against threes, a present condition in which the financial bailout brings to fruition what is after economy in the displacing operations of the derivative undoing the boundary between polity and economy—a public quandary that undoes the binary between public and private; renders the public derivative of private values; and lends the public a triple inflection of economy (as in public good), culture (as in representations of the people), and politics (as in excess criticality). Culture, once anchored between nature and the unconscious, is increasingly animated by an expansive decolonization. If finance absents an account of its own movement, fixed as it is on results, the turn to dance as embodied practices that stage the critique of mobilization takes the form of two triplets (the classical, modern, and postmodern kinesthemes) and the differently scaled, globally distributed derivative movement practices (release, hip-hop, and boarding culture).

The three main chapters that constitute this book pursue the derivative to its limit in the production of nonknowledge variously understood in terms of financial uncertainty, excess criticality, a de-centered social kinesthetic that, it may now seem apparent, is the overflow of the conventionally unthought embankments through which knowledge of the social world had been set to flow. The grand trinity of economy, polity, and culture does not neatly align with the disciplines of liberal arts, with their own trinity of humanities, natural sciences, and social sciences. History is variously located within the humanities or the social sciences. Even within the social sciences, the largest field, psychology, attends to the animating dynamics of the self in a manner that scrutinizes what of this belongs to culture and what to nature (human or otherwise) and inscribes its own binary between self and society. Equally large in scope and each explicitly encompassing the grand trinity itself, anthropology tracks the range of what can be considered human, and geography operates across the manifold registers of space; both vary widely in their methods and objects of inquiry. Rather, we might observe that economy, polity, and culture assumed their holiness as a trinity or master grammar by which the social would be thought. The larger claim that a formation of knowledge has reached a limit is therefore that the autonomy of these three terms, the sense that they separated the social order into distinct domains, each with its own dynamics and determinations, is what has come undone.

Certainly, the persistent anxiety of the moment is that the world as we once knew it has been lost. The spatial and temporal ordering that traded in the past through a unity of the present so that it could deliver a more highly developed, progressively better future—what typically goes by the name "modernity"—now looks to be at an end, broken and in crisis. Even the established alternatives—socialism, communism, religious fundamentalism—are said (often by those who continue to battle them as concepts and practices) to belong to a past that is no longer available or relevant to us. The deeper irony is that these alternatives derived from prevailing social frameworks such as capitalism and Christianity, and it is likely that they still do. Rather than drawing strength from the sense that the old order is exhausted, we are told that the present must be consumed by paying off the debts of this past, of living the future as a reduction in present deficits—in short, of making do with less. From many environmental perspectives, this would certainly make sense, although the question of what it would mean to make more that is renewable, sustainable, and invigorating is still begged when ecology is analogized as a machine with fixed capacity or a distribution of zero sum.

On closer inspection, this world of ours was never one. The social has always been an uneven landscape, where invoking a "we" that goes by the name of humanity was always a partial and contested claim. At the same time, these histories that have forced populations together have yielded a circumstance in which is it possible to ask what all have made together, what resources can be drawn on, what common wealth and creative capacity can be accessed. What the universal is—what it covers and excludes— still needs to be worked out by taking stock of how difference is sustained, how parts are aligned without being subsumed to a homogenizing whole, what is owed and what remains unpayable. Perhaps the concept of humanity can finally be placed in consideration when there is in actuality the productive and distributive capacity for all to have what they need and the critical faculties to figure out what kinds of indebtedness such shared human and material wealth would entail. An unprecedented social surplus would reckon with an effusive surplus of the social. If such possibilities are already immanent in present circumstances, how might they best be approached?

Against these dreary and deadening pronouncements of scarcity, knowledge was meant to be something different. Using knowledge did not use it up; rather, it made more of it, and many could make use of it at once. These properties distinguished knowledge from other material commodities and made it amenable to being made freely available as a public good. But specialized expertise and intellectual property appeared to challenge this cornucopian view with their own visions of scarcity. Few, after all, could truly be excellent; gates toward what was most worth knowing would need sentinels; and the very finest knowledge available would definitely fetch a handsome price. Such would describe a knowledge economy in which finance stands at the pinnacle, in which capital masters knowing but is indifferent to the knowledge on which it rests.

The generalized condition of this limit to knowledge is now upon us. If the decolonizing forces of the derivative have brought us to this state of affairs, these dissembling and reconstituting currents and flows have also delivered us to an aftermath. Against the confidence in self-regulating and auto-correcting markets, financial crisis is treated by conventional observers as coming out of the blue, springing de novo and without warning. But derivatives did not originate within finance, even if financial services profited from their dissemination and patented some of their proliferating flows. Derivatives sprang from longer-standing movements of decolonization, of unbounding what was enclosed, whether within financial relations or around them. It is unlikely that all was once solid and whole and now has gone derivative. Social life has careered from ruin to ruin, rebuilding, reinventing, and reaffiliating along the way.

The conception of the social generated over the past century and a half, upon which have arisen the edifices of knowledge, each with their distinct disciplinary and methodological address, was holistic. At its most general, society was itself thought of as a whole, as an integrated system, an imaginary machine in which each part sits in the right place and serves the larger purpose. The social whole was itself parsed into units and partitioned into shapes with internal volumes called spheres. The single unit of society would be people who possess roles, identities, selves that are individual or incapable of being further divided. The vessel that held all these lovely orbs has crashed—its engines in overdrive, its moorings lost, its warning devices unable to protect it—spilling its contents every which way. In the aftermath, the concern that no one has seen the ship veering toward the iceberg is ultimately a claim about how knowledge steers society based on moving from a stable present to a predictable future. The crisis this time is not a matter of who is in the watchtower but of a whole way of seeing, sensing, knowing, and moving accordingly. The question is less how we avoid the ruins than how we give value to what rises from them. That problem itself can be broken down into several more. How do we think ourselves across what were once treated as distinct epistemic domains of economy, polity, and culture? How do we notice the value of these other accounts as they move among the knowledge ruins? What does it mean to know by means of the derivative?

The grand trinity of the social is a hallmark of modernity. The abandonment of this universal motif is an insignia of the postmodern. The critique of the presumptive claim to know all through the perspective of one translated into a pronouncement that all was fragmented, dispersed, particularized. As a critical dialogue, postmodernism also foundered on this dilemma—the critique of universalism was itself universalizing; at the same time, a world sundered into so many fragments and broken shards had no way for the parts to relate to one another. But if what was once taken as whole has been disassembled, it is no less interconnected. The world we live in is more interdependent than ever, even if the contributions of many considered too poor, marginal, or difficult are disavowed and denied a claim to available resources. Further, our world is saturated with languages of mutual indebtedness to an unprecedented degree so that what might be proclaimed a dissociated fragment is, by means of that very attention, asserting the impact of a minor variation on an entire field. This leverage or amplification is a feature of arbitrage, and this is what features in so much contemporary political activity, whether it is called terror, occupation, shorting government (such as the Tea Party), or going long (like a millenarian movement). In the tripartite scheme of knowledge production, each sphere absorbed its own surplus.

More knowledge of the economy at once created more wealth and more economics. Knowledge of power was power and generated a demand for further advice, consultation, modeling, polling, and measurement of public opinion and other entailments of political expertise. Cultural knowledge was culture as it made culture; academics and critics could pursue legitimating interpretations while to the best producers of cultural artifacts, expressions, and properties went the spoils. Clearly, there was already trouble in this conception even before expertise began to lose its purchase on a monopoly of legitimate knowledge. If knowledge is seen as intellectual labor, much of this is organized into professional fields that are larger than any conventional academic discipline. Business is the largest undergraduate major in the United States. Medicine is the largest business. These fields are not simply applied economics or practical science. They are far more complex braids of cultural, political, and economic endeavors. As they emerged out of the nineteenth century, academic disciplines colonized other existing fields. The professional training that emerged in the twentieth century, however, was already engaged in a kind of decolonization, of disassembling and repacking practical and conceptual approaches from a whole range of disciplines.

But aside from the mounting skepticism toward modernist specialism that swelled at the end of the twentieth century, there were two attendant but contradictory tendencies. One was the continued professionalization and formalization of knowledge practice that drove increased participation in postsecondary education. Mass access to higher education in turn animated the dissemination of managerial protocols of measurable assessment and performance outcomes, translated into calculable risks of exceeding expectations or failing to meet standards. The other tendency was the do-it-yourself movements that combined several currents. One was foreclosure of professional opportunities for employment. A second was dissemination of techniques and technologies for capture, sampling, creation, and distribution of what one made. A third was social entrepreneurialism that translates an incessant invitation to judge into a self-confidence to know what might make a situation better. Professionalization of knowledge engendered its own relative surplus population—not simply in the sense of those who earned credentials but never gained secure and stable positions in their chosen fields (casualized and precarious academics, attorneys, artists, for example). More pervasively, the enormous capacity to generate knowledge—professional and otherwise—could not be absorbed through formal circuits, the cash nexus, or the labor market. More creative endeavor and understanding of how to do things moves in the world than could ever be contained through commodity relations, even as these activities make use of and sometimes become commodities in their own right.

Within the terms of expertise, we could say that the disciplines have lost sovereignty over their object domains. This does not mean that the experts themselves have changed their stripes or become extinct—even as more of their career habitats and familiar professional haunts are endangered. Still, most well-appointed economists and political scientists have persisted in their methods for telling their truths about the world, and the spectrum of punditry on mainstay media hardly seems to have expanded. Meanwhile, back at the banks and in the back offices, in the aftermath of the bailout, the volume of derivative trading has reached unprecedented levels. As Jamie Dimon of JPMorgan or Jon Corzine, former governor of New Jersey and a principal at Goldman Sachs, can attest, huge amounts of money can be made and lost hedging risks.[2] Grasping the technical aspects of these models, understanding financial-speak and risk assumptions, is important, even if the field itself produces no consensus about how it does or does not work (witness Andrew Lo's recent survey of twenty-one accounts of the crisis from commentators fluent in the various dialects of finance).[3]

But it is far from clear what constitutes adequate technical knowledge to gain critical insight. Too little leads most commonly to moral pronouncements as to the evil intent of financial actors and the need to banish these deviants from the stage; too much seems to absorb the pursuit of inquiry into the very technical processes themselves. Hence, that a model or a step in the process failed to work as it should leads back to consideration of what might make that detail functional again. The analysis effectively resembles the thing it looks at but cannot generate an agenda of its own. However, amid all the crisis talk is a plethora of information about how finance operates that quickly makes apparent its own knowledge limits. Read from the perspective of these limits, rather than as a seamless and self-replicating narrative of what caused the machine to break, openings can be found to insert and assert other values. Here the social and conjunctural analyses of finance become especially valuable.

If finance engenders a sociality but cannot do so sui generis, then understanding finance relies on an account of what social relations constitute finance and what exceed its horizon. Bataille's work discussed in Chapter 1 is certainly exemplary here. It is also intriguing as contemporary with the intellectual foundations from which finance was generalized and operationalized in the 1930s and 1940s. Bataille, of course was not a professional economist (or an appointed academic, for that matter), but he might stand as an individual figure of the accursed share, general economy, and nonknowledge that has now been collectivized and socialized among so many. Whether of the financialized multitudes who must manage their own portfolios and absorb the risks of doing so or of the arbitrageurs of the street who place themselves at risk to occupy a time and space denied to them, an abundance of knowledge is afoot. At the same time, there is a scarcity of ways to enter the edifice of finance itself and explore what it might mean to reoccupy the scheme of credit and debt that it has produced.

It might be tempting in the absence of such popular claims to simply eradicate the machineries of credit and refuse the entanglements of debt. From alternative currency Local Exchange Trading Schemes (LETS) such as Ithaca dollars that have developed over the past several decades to the Student Debt Refusal campaign that emerged from the Occupy Wall Street movement, there have been varied and creative responses. Such cries have been effective in garnering widespread attention to the dimensions of power and inequality. But the more difficult path may lie in what needs to be known to craft modes of credit that provide genuine access to societal resources on favorable terms of those who generate them and forms of debt that ensure we take one another into account in ways that add to the store of our sociality and enhance our ability to move among one another creatively and expansively. The social logic of the derivative is a mutable discourse of such multifarious currencies of credit and debt.

Finally, we might observe that finance is historical but cannot take account of the history of its own concepts. In this respect, the notion of a cycle, whether a normal waxing and waning of fortunes during a regular business cycle or an aberrantly large swing away from expected growth and gain that defines a crisis, is an abdication of historical reflection. The conceptual consequence is to be bruited about between continuity and rupture, stasis and change, an untouchable past and an unpredictable future. A conjuncture is the intersection of many surfaces, an array of different scales that slices through the present, some of which have been going on for a very long time and others of which are just getting going, like the form of the derivative itself. While the crisis did little to reorient established habits of thought, this, perhaps, is not the most useful way to put the problem. To see what it means for one conjuncture to yield to another, for a different horizon of possibility to open from the ruins of the present, entails thinking from the perspective of the disruption, of being displaced from the norm, of moving laterally across the fractured but still fertile approaches to understanding.

Once, this movement in between fields was called interdisciplinarity. Now we can pay more attention to the ground that is opened up when bits and pieces from various locations and learning places are assembled together. Interdisciplinarity is now widely institutionalized as a means for combining different domains of expertise and advancing innovation. It is also commonly under-resourced and marginalized. Doubtless the derivative is another way of thinking interdisciplinarity, one that draws attention to the epistemic arbitrage undertaken by those who operate between fields. The derivative might remind us of other analytic endeavors to take stock of what was left out of conventions of representation, of what might lie between a simple opposition or binary relation of categories. Poststructuralism generally, and deconstruction in particular, promised precisely this openness to the disruptive attentions at the limits of authorized knowledge.

These intellectual movements that have constituted the contemporary critique of representation themselves emerged in alignment with movements of decolonization, not only of the Third World but also of the private sphere, of the unconscious and desire associated especially with queer studies. It is interesting that the thinker who has perhaps gone the furthest in articulating deconstruction with postcolonial critique, Gayatri Spivak, has recently turned to an earlier formulation of what it means to dwell in the space in between—namely, Gregory Bateson's concept of the double bind.[4] Bateson had developed this concept at Stanford in the 1950s when working with collaborators in the field of psychology on the problem of schizophrenia. Bateson and his colleagues observe that for the man they have in mind, the double bind emerges "in a situation where he must respond, where he is faced with contradictory messages, and when he is unable to comment on the contradictions."[5]

The derivative, which redirects us toward a critique of mobilization, seems to be more of a sensibility and a figure for reassessing value than a unitary method for how to move otherwise. It is a means of aggregating difference and a way to get to and move through a difficult place in between. The obligation to respond without being able to comment on the predicament one is in forces a person to remain and act in that place in between. But while the double bind directs us to suspend comment, the derivative works to amplify what the contradictions might yield. The derivative in this respect could be considered a double unbind: a disassembly of the terms of contradiction, of the internal unity of contrary movement, and of a release through some space in between toward some larger domain where the actions, comments, and contradictions of others are aggregated. Against the dilemma, persistently present in efforts to act to effect enabling change, that whichever way one goes will be dangerous, derivative logics reassign risk as an amplifying movement, acceleration through a difficult moment. In both cases, critical embodiments of debt and desire find themselves not on the precipice of worldly intervention trying to figure out how to enter but already falling, in the midst, and needing to make sense out of what is to hand. What is upon us are vast capacities for being together, for using what we have made together without ever using ourselves up.

Notes

CHAPTER 1

1. Andrew Ross Sorkin, Diana B. Henriques, Edmund Andrews, and Joe Nocera, "The Reckoning: As Credit Crisis Spiraled, Alarm Led to Action," *New York Times*, October 1, 2008, available at http://www.nytimes.com, accessed June 30, 2011.

2. Nouriel Roubini and Stephen Mihm, *Crisis Economics: A Crash Course in the Future of Finance* (New York: Penguin, 2010), 15. Roubini casts himself as one who did see it all coming.

3. "Text of Draft Proposal for Bailout Plan," *New York Times*, September 20, 2008, available at http://www.nytimes.com, accessed June 30, 2011.

4. Testimony by Secretary Henry M. Paulson Jr. before the Senate Banking Committee, September 23, 2008, available at http://www.banking.senate.gov, accessed June 30, 2011.

5. Brian Wingfield and Josh Zumbrun, "The Paulson Plan: Bad News for the Bailout," Forbes.com, September 23, 2008, available at http://www.forbes.com, accessed June 30, 2011.

6. U.S. House of Representatives, "Emergency Economic Stabilization Act of 2008," HR 1424, 3, available at http://www.c-span.org/pdf/hr1424_100108.pdf, accessed July 6, 2011.

7. "The Final Report of the Congressional Oversight Panel," March 16, 2011, 155–156, available at http://www.gpo.gov/fdsys/pkg/CHRG-112shrg64832/pdf/CHRG-112shrg64832.pdf, accessed March 16, 2011.

8. U.S. Congressional Budget Office, "Report on the Troubled Asset Relief Program," March 11, 2011, available at http://www.cbo.gov/doc.cfm?index=12118, accessed July 6, 2011.

9. Board of Governors of the Federal Reserve System, "Aggregate Reserves of Depository Institutions and the Monetary Base," Statistical Release H.3, June 30, 2011, available at http://www.federalreserve.gov/releases/h3/current, accessed June 30, 2012.

10. For a time series of the changes in reserves, including their precipitous disappearance in 2008, see ibid., table 1.

11. Andrew Pierce, "The Queen Asks Why No One Saw the Credit Crunch Coming," *The Telegraph*, November 6, 2008, available at http://www.telegraph.co.uk, accessed November 6, 2008. The queen was at the London School of Economics to dedicate a new building. She had lost a quarter of the value of her personal portfolio of £100 million in the crash.

12. Greenspan's comment was in response to the question "Were you wrong?" by Democratic Representative Henry Waxman of California in testimony before Congress on October 23, 2008, as reported by Judy Woodruff on *PBS Newshour* that evening: transcript, available at http://www.pbs.org/newshour/bb/business/july-dec08/crisishearing_10-23.html, accessed October 23, 2008.

13. Joe Nocera, "Sheila Bair's Bank Shot," *New York Times Magazine*, July 10, 2011, 29.

14. Neil King Jr. and Scott Greenberg, "Poll Shows Budget Cut Dilemma," *Wall Street Journal Online*, March 3, 2011, available at http://online.wsj.com, accessed March 23, 2011.

15. See, e.g., Paul Mason, *Meltdown: The End of the Age of Greed*, 2d ed. (London: Verso, 2010); Bethany McClean and Joe Nocera, *All the Devils Are Here: The Hidden History of the Financial Crisis* (New York: Portfolio, 2010); Michael Lewis, *The Big Short: Inside the Doomsday Machine* (New York: W. W. Norton, 2010); Michael Hudson, *The Monster: How a Gang of Predator Lenders and Wall Street Bankers Fleeced America and Spawned a Global Crisis* (New York: Times Books, 2010); Mike Gearhardt and Will Gates, *The Financial Tsunami: Will It Drown Us in a Wave of Debt?* (Bloomington, IN: AuthorHouse, 2010); Gretchen Morgenson and Joshua Rosner, *Reckless Endangerment: How Outsized Ambition, Greed, and Corruption Created the Worst Financial Crisis of Our Time* (New York: St. Martin's Press, 2011); Gillian Tett, *Fool's Gold: The Inside Story of J. P. Morgan and How Wall Street Greed Corrupted Its Bold Dream and Created a Financial Catastrophe* (New York: Free Press, 2010).

16. See, e.g., Niall Ferguson, *Empire: The Rise and Demise of the British World Order and the Lessons for Global Power* (New York: Basic Books, 2004); Niall Ferguson, *Colossus: The Rise and Fall of the American Empire* (New York: Penguin, 2005); Carmen M. Reinhardt and Kenneth Rogoff, *This Time Is Different: Eight Centuries of Financial Folly* (Princeton, NJ: Princeton University Press, 2009); Roubini and Mihm, *Crisis Economics*; Robert Brenner, *The Boom and the Bubble: The U.S. in the World Economy* (London: Verso, 2003); Doug Henwood, *After the New Economy: The Binge and the Headache That Won't Go Away* (London: Verso, 2005).

17. F. A. Hayek, "The Use of Knowledge in Society," *American Economic Review* 35, no. 4 (September 1945): 519–553.

18. Ibid., 520.

19. Ibid., 525.

20. Philip Mirowski, "Why There Is (as Yet) No Such Thing as an Economics of Knowledge," in *The Oxford Handbook of Philosophy of Economics*, ed. Don Ross and Harold Kincaid (New York: Oxford University Press, 2009), 101.

21. Philip Mirowski, *Science Mart: Privatizing American Science* (Cambridge, MA: Harvard University Press, 2011), 325–326.

22. See Hersh Shefrin, *Beyond Greed and Fear: Understanding Behavioral Finance and the Psychology of Investing* (New York: Oxford University Press, 1999).

23. Here as well, Mirowski's analysis of the internal inconsistencies of neoclas-

sical economics has proved invaluable. For a discussion of the inability to abide the frightful image of nature that issues from the blurring of the boundary between order and chaos, and the challenge that Mandelbrot provided to economic theory, see Philip Mirowski, *The Effortless Economy of Science?* (Durham, NC: Duke University Press, 2004), chaps. 11–12.

24. Frank H. Knight, "The Limitations of the Scientific Method in Economics" (1924), in *Selected Essays by Frank H. Knight, Volume 1: "What Is Truth" in Economics?* ed. Ross B. Emmett (Chicago: University of Chicago Press, 1999).

25. Frank H. Knight, *Risk, Uncertainty and Profit* (Boston: Houghton Mifflin, 1921), 313.

26. Joe Nocera, *A Piece of the Action: How the Middle Class Joined the Money Class* (New York: Simon and Shuster, 1994); Joe Nocera, *Good Guys and Bad Guys: Behind the Scenes with the Saints and Scoundrels of American Business (and Everything in Between)* (New York: Portfolio, 2008).

27. Derivatives contracts are constructed directly between firms or over the counter (OTC) and traded on exchanges. The Bank for International Settlements (BIS) maintains statistics on the notional or face value of both, including time series that track their precipitous rise over the past twenty years. The quadrillion-dollar figure comes from adding up the two kinds of derivatives for June 2008 ($672 billion for OTC and $428 billion for exchange-based): see BIS, "Exchange-Traded Derivatives Statistics," available at http://www.bis.org/statistics/extderiv.htm; BIS, "Derivatives Statistics," available at http://www.bis.org/statistics/derstats.htm, accessed June 25, 2013.

28. Joe Nocera, "Risk Mismanagement: Were the Measures Used to Evaluate Wall Street Flawed? Or Was the Mistake Ignoring Them?" *New York Times Magazine*, January 4, 2009, 27.

29. Ibid., 29.

30. Elie Ayache, *The Blank Swan: The End of Probability* (Chichester, UK: John Wiley, 2010), 167.

31. "Banks Keep Bailout Spending Secret: Banks Unable or Unwilling to Disclose How They're Spending Billions in Aid," MSNBC.com, available at http://www.msnbc.msn.com, accessed July 19, 2011.

32. Peter Burke, *A Social History of Knowledge: From Gutenberg to Diderot* (Cambridge: Polity, 2000).

33. Especially relevant here are Christopher Newfield, *Ivy and Industry: Business and the Making of the American University* (Durham, NC: Duke University Press, 2003); Christopher Newfield, *Unmaking the Public University: The Forty-Year Assault on the Middle Class* (Cambridge, MA: Harvard University Press, 2010).

34. For an influential formulation of the antinomies of the professional managerial class, see Barbara Ehrenreich and John Ehrenreich, "The Professional-Managerial Class," *Radical America* 11 (March–April 1977): 7–31; Barbara Ehrenreich and John Ehrenreich, "The New Left: A Case Study in Professional-Managerial Radicalism," *Radical America* 11 (May–June 1977): 7–22. My analysis of this problem of lost autonomy for expertise in the context of higher education is in Randy Martin, *Under New Management: Universities, Administrative Labor and the Professional Turn* (Philadelphia: Temple University Press, 2011).

35. Douglas Keay, *Woman's Own*, interview with Margaret Thatcher, London, September 23, 1987, archived at http://www.margaretthatcher.org/speeches/display document.asp?docid=106689, accessed June 1, 2010.

36. Bethany McClean and Peter Elkind, *The Smartest Guys in the Room: The Amazing Rise and Scandalous Demise of Enron* (New York: Penguin, 2003). Closer still to the failed models of the Nobel Prize–winning economists Robert Merton and Myron Scholes was the Long-Term Capital Management hedge fund collapse in 1998 chronicled in Roger Lowenstein, *When Genius Failed: The Rise and Fall of Long Term Capital Management* (New York: Random House, 2000).

37. Karl Marx, *The Eighteenth Brumaire of Louis Napoleon* (New York: Norton, 1978), 608.

38. Ibid., 614.

39. Metaphors of disaster aside, the analysis of proximate causes and narratives for the Deepwater Horizon and Fukushima Daiichi Nuclear Power Plant incidents bear remarkable resemblance to the financial crisis, with compromised regulatory oversight, reliance on risk models that generates undo risk, difficultly in measuring and disclosing the extent of damage, and uncertainty as to adequate remedy: see, e.g., U.S. Coast Guard, "Report on the Investigation into the Circumstances Surrounding the Explosion, Fire, Sinking and Loss of Eleven Crew Members aboard the Mobile Offshore Drilling Unit Deepwater Horizon, April 20–22, 2010," available at http://media.nola.com/2010_gulf_oil_spill/other/FINAL%20REDACTED%20VERSION%20DWH.pdf, accessed April 22, 2010; Great East Japan Earthquake Expert Mission, "IAEA International Fact Finding Expert Mission of the Fukushima Dai-ichi NPP Accident following the Great Easy Japan Earthquake and Tsunami," May 24–June 2, 2011, available at http://www-pub.iaea.org/MTCD/meetings/PDF plus/2011/cn200/documentation/cn200_Final-Fukushima-Mission_Report.pdf, accessed June 2, 2011.

40. Karl Polanyi, *The Great Transformation: The Political and Economic Origins of Our Time* (1944; repr., Boston: Beacon, 2001), 3. Fred Bloch's introduction stresses these themes.

41. It should be noted that the literature on middle-class decline goes back decades. While it looms large in the imaginary of the American dreamscape, the conceptual basis for orienting an understanding of contemporary life in the United States around a putative center is problematic. My thoughts on this are in Randy Martin, "Dead Center? Rethinking the Middle for a Different Left," in *On Your Marx: Relinking Socialism and the Left* (Minneapolis: University of Minnesota Press, 2002), 159–184. For a recent installment of the declinist literature, see Arianna Huffington, *Third World America: How Our Politicians Are Abandoning the Middle Class and Betraying the American Dream* (New York: Broadway, 2011).

42. Michel Foucault, *The Order of Things: An Archaeology of the Human Sciences* (New York: Random House, 1970), 387.

43. Michel Callon, "Introduction: The Embeddedness of Economic Markets in Economics" in *The Laws of the Markets*, ed. Michael Callon (Oxford: Blackwell, 1998), 2.

44. Timothy Mitchell, *Rule of Experts: Egypt, Techno-Politics, Modernity* (Berkeley: University of California Press, 2002), 291–292.

45. Donald MacKenzie, *An Engine, Not a Camera: How Financial Models Shape Markets* (Cambridge, MA: MIT Press, 2006). MacKenzie's careful study of the devices that construct financial transactions provides a critique of standard economic accounts in which theory merely reflects the world as it is. MacKenzie relies on a partial reading of Austin's notion of performativity—namely, the illocutionary effects of an utterance to enact what it says. He subsequently added a concept of counter-per-

formativity to include the perlocutionary or unintended effects of those statements to account for the misshaping of markets. See Donald MacKenzie, Fabian Muniesa, and Lucia Siu, "Introduction," in *Do Economists Make Markets? On the Performativity of Economics*, ed. Donald MacKenzie, Fabian Muniesa, and Lucia Siu (Princeton, NJ: Princeton University Press, 2007), 1–20.

46. Binyamin Appelbaum, "Politicians Can't Agree on Debt? Well, Neither Can Economists," *New York Times*, July 17, 2011, available at http://www.nytimes.com, accessed July 17, 2011.

47. Standard and Poor's, "United States of America Long-Term Rating Lowered to 'AA+' due to Political Risks, Rising Debt Burden; Outlook Negative," August 5, 2011, available at http://www.standardandpoors.com, accessed August 5, 2011. The U.S. Treasury responded by asserting that the downgrade had been reached in error because of an overstatement by $2 trillion in long-term debt. Standard and Poor's acknowledged the error and countered that the political disarray that ensued from the downgrade justified its decision, which did not lead to an immediate run on Treasury bonds, an investment that is still seen as more stable than others, despite the lowered grade.

48. Henry Petroski, *Success through Failure: The Paradox of Design* (Princeton, NJ: Princeton University Press, 2006).

49. Russell Stannard, *The End of Discovery* (New York: Oxford, 2010), 220, 222.

50. U.S. Secretary of Defense Donald Rumsfeld, press conference at North Atlantic Treaty Organization (NATO) headquarters, Brussels, June 6, 2002, available at http://www.nato.int/docu/speech/2002/s020606g.htm, accessed February 2006.

51. Peter Bergen and Paul Cruickshank, "The Iraq Effect: War Has Increased Terrorism Sevenfold Worldwide," *Mother Jones*, March 2007, available at http://mother jones.com, accessed March 2007.

52. Mahmood Mamdani, *Saviors and Survivors: Darfur, Politics, and the War on Terror* (New York: Doubleday, 2010).

53. For an elaboration of these arguments with respect to the war on terror, see Randy Martin, *An Empire of Indifference: American War and the Financial Logic of Risk Management* (Durham, NC: Duke University Press, 2007).

54. Ulrich Beck, *World at Risk* (Cambridge: Polity, 2009), 53.

55. Ibid., 115.

56. Georges Bataille, *The Accursed Share: An Essay on General Economy, Volume 1: Consumption* (New York: Zone, 1988), 10.

57. Georges Bataille, "Nonknowledge, Laughter, and Tears" (1953), in *The Unfinished System of Nonknowledge* (Minneapolis: University of Minnesota Press, 2001), 140.

58. Ibid., 133.

59. Ibid., 135–136.

60. Robert Proctor, "Agnotology: A Missing Term to Describe the Cultural Production of Ignorance and Its Study," in *Agnotology: The Making and Unmaking of Ignorance*, ed. Robert Proctor and Londa Schiebinger (Stanford, CA: Stanford University Press, 2008), 26.

61. Taking a longer historical view on the existence of derivatives poses its own problems, especially if this is meant to naturalize them as part of universal human traits. While describing the historical and cultural antecedents of derivatives, this larger issue is in evidence among the contributions to William N. Goetzmann and K.

Geert Rouwenhorst, eds., *The Origins of Value: The Financial Innovations That Created Modern Capital Markets* (New York: Oxford University Press, 2005).

62. For a list of these definitions, see *Oxford English Dictionary Online*, November 2010, s.v. "derivative [*adj.* and *n.*]," available at http://www.oed.com, accessed November 2010.

63. The BIS maintains records on aggregate derivative transactions by type and over time. McKinsey and Company maintains statistics on global financial markets, including derivatives transactions: see McKinsey and Company, "Mapping Global Capital Markets, 2011," McKinsey Global Institute report, available at http://www.mckinsey.com, accessed August 15, 2012; BIS, "Derivative Statistics," 2012, available at http://www.bis.org/statistics/derstats.htm, accessed August 15, 2012.

64. Philip Mirowski *More Heat than Light: Economics as Social Physics, Physics as Nature's Economics* (Cambridge: Cambridge University Press, 1989).

65. Charlotte Hess and Elinor Ostrom, "Introduction," in *Understanding Knowledge as a Commons: From Theory to Practice*, ed. Charlotte Hess and Elinor Ostrom (Cambridge, MA: MIT Press, 2006).

66. For a critique of cap and trade market logics and the implications of economists in them, see Philip Mirowski and Edward Nik-Shah, "Markets Made Flesh: Performativity and a Problem in Science Studies, Augmented with Consideration of the FCC Auctions," in MacKenzie, Muniesa, and Siu, *Do Economists Make Markets?* 190–224.

67. For an elegant statement of the ongoing utility of neoliberalism, with a core definition of unregulated markets free from state intervention, as a means of orienting resistance by providing a coherent political narrative, see Stuart Hall, "The Neoliberal Revolution," *Soundings*, no. 48 (Summer 2011): 9–27. Jodi Dean has queried the underlying attachment of critics of neoliberalism to its homogenizing efficacy: see Jodi Dean, *Democracy and Other Neoliberal Fantasies: Communicative Capitalism and Left Politics* (Durham, NC: Duke University Press, 2009).

68. Key texts that naturalize market rationality as what individuals would choose—and hence argue that capitalism is the best expression of human want—are Milton Friedman, *Essays in Positive Economics* (Chicago: University of Chicago Press, 1953) and Gary S. Becker, *The Economic Approach to Human Behavior* (Chicago: University of Chicago Press, 1976). While the claims of rational choice are that it can be verified empirically, the record on this front has been rather weak. Duncan Foley provides a comprehensive critique of this line of argument, with its unexamined assumptions, tracing it back to Adam Smith: see Duncan Foley, *Adam's Fallacy: A Guide to Economic Theology* (Cambridge, MA: Harvard University Press, 2006).

69. These numbers are drawn from a report by the Heritage Foundation that bemoans regulatory bloat: James Gattuso, "Red Tape Rising: Regulatory Trends in the Bush Years," Heritage Foundation, March 25, 2008, available at http://www.heritage.org, accessed March 25, 2008.

70. The notion that regulation is intrinsic to capital accumulation expressed as a particular logic of rule or regime is developed in Michel Aglietta, *A Theory of Capitalist Regulation: The U.S. Experience* (London: Verso, 1979). For measures of increasing regulatory density, see Brian Goff, *Regulation and Macroeconomic Performance* (Boston: Kluwer Academic, 1996).

71. For accounts of the sectoral shift from industrial production to finance, see Gerald Epstein, ed., *Financialization and the World Economy* (Northampton,

MA: Edward Elgar, 2005); Özgür Orhangazi, *Financialization and the U.S. Economy* (Northampton, MA: Edward Elgar, 2008); William K. Tabb, *The Restructuring of Capitalism in Our Time* (New York: Columbia University Press, 2012). On domestic policy and the risk shift, see Jacob Hacker, *The Great Risk Shift: The Assault on American Jobs, Families, Health Care, and Retirement and How You Can Fight Back* (New York: Oxford University Press, 2006).

72. "OTC Derivatives Market Activity in the Second Half of 2010," BIS, Monetary and Economic Department, May 1, 2011, available at http://www.bis.org/publ/otc_hy1105.pdf.

73. Shyam Sunder, "Held to Account," in *ICGN Yearbook 2010* (London: International Corporate Governance Network, 2010), 27.

74. Emile Grunberg and Franco Modigliani, "The Predictability of Social Events," *Journal of Political Economy* 62, no. 6 (December 1954): 475.

75. Alan Greenspan, "The Role of Capital in Optimal Banking Supervision and Regulation," *Federal Reserve Bank of New York Economic Policy Review*, October 1998, 163–168.

76. Roubini and Mihm, *Crisis Economics*, 80. Roubini sees the financial crisis as resulting from the conversion of risk into uncertainty, which could be righted by appropriate regulation that anticipated and ameliorated otherwise inevitable crises, rendering these last something like business cycles writ large.

77. Dick Bryan and Mike Rafferty, *Capitalism with Derivatives: A Political Economy of Financial Derivatives, Capital, and Class* (Basingstoke, UK: Palgrave Macmillan, 2006), 37.

78. The newly negotiated contract did lead to workers' picketing their union offices over the two-tiered wage rates that the United Automobile Workers negotiated for the industry: see Jane Slaughter, "Unequal Pay for Equal Work," May 17, 2011, available at http://labornotes.org, accessed May 17, 2011.

79. See, e.g., Ralph Milliband, *Divided Societies: Class Struggle in Contemporary Capitalism* (Oxford: Oxford University Press, 1989).

80. See Robert Shiller, *Market Volatility* (Cambridge: Cambridge University Press, 1991); Lawrence Summers, "Does the Stock Market Rationally Reflect Fundamental Values?" *Journal of Finance* 41, no. 3 (1991): 591–601.

81. Bryan and Rafferty. *Capitalism with Derivatives*, 206.

82. This is the notion that individuals are the sole proprietors of their life chances and abilities, which they bring to market without any debt to society: see C. B. Macpherson, *The Political Theory of Possessive Individualism: Hobbes to Locke* (Oxford: Clarendon, 1962).

83. Daniel Beunza and David Stark, "Looking Out, Locking In: Financial Models and the Social Dynamics of Arbitrage Disasters," Institute for Public Knowledge, New York University, 2010, 59–60, available at http://www.thesenseofdissonance.com/media/paper_looking_out_locking_in.pdf, accessed June 2010.

84. Timothy Williams, "Florida Governor Rejects High Speed Rail Line, Fearing Cost to Taxpayers," *New York Times*, February 16, 2011. Florida's Governor Rick Scott had estimated that the $3 billion in cost overruns would exceed the $2 billion in federal stimulus money. He and his colleagues were also able to show that by rejecting such funds at the state level, a national rail network or infrastructure plan was also doomed to fail, effectively wagering their promised return against the aggregate outcome in a manner consistent with political arbitrage. Similarly, in March 2011,

the Republican-led Congress terminated the mortgage relief program that was part of the original TARP and apportioned the unspent monies from the original $8 billion allocation to pay down the debt: Emily Miller, "House GOP Shuts Down Failed TARP Mortgage Programs," *Human Events*, March 10, 2011, available at http://humanevents.com, accessed March 10, 2011.

85. Fischer Black, "Noise," *Journal of Finance* 41, no. 3 (July 1986): 536.

86. The most thorough conception along these lines is Greta Krippner, *Capitalizing on the Crisis: The Political Origins of the Rise of Finance* (Cambridge, MA: Harvard University Press, 2011). Krippner defines financialization as "growing importance of financial activities as a source of profits in the economy" and notes that such profits, which had ranged from 10 percent to 15 percent in the 1950s and 1960s, had grown to 40 percent by 2001 (ibid., 27–28). But her argument is that this was not a product of economic evolution; it was a failure of political will:

> The chapters in this book chronicle how state officials managed over several decades to avoid difficult political choices by turning to financial markets, but critically, these strategies deferred rather than resolved the underlying social and political tensions that gave rise to them. Now that financialization appears to be failing as a model of economic development, these tensions appear to be coming to the fore once again. In particular, in the context of the current financial crisis, questions regarding the allocation of scarce resources are now unavoidable in U.S. society. Yet the experience of financialization has not prepared us particularly well to answer these questions. For several decades, Financialization has largely eclipsed concerns with distribution, eroding collective capacities to confront issues of economic justice. (Ibid., 26)

87. Roubini and Mihm, *Crisis Economics*, 200.

88. Ibid., 214–215.

89. Sabrina Tavernise, "Poverty Rate Soars to Highest Level since 1993," *New York Times*, September 14, 2011, 1, 21. On the basis of figures from the U.S. Census Bureau, 46.2 million people living in poverty was the highest number recorded in the fifty-two years the bureau had been publishing these data. The poverty line is an amount adjusted for household size: $11,344 per year for a single person and $22,314 per year for a family of four. More of the population fell into "deep poverty," defined as half the poverty line; 22 percent of children live in poverty; and poverty rates are roughly twice that for African Americans and Latinos as for non–Hispanic whites. Median income, the midpoint in the distribution of households, declined from an inflation-adjusted $53,252 in 1999 to $49,445 in 2010.

90. See Henwood, *After the New Economy*.

91. Morgenson and Rosner, *Reckless Endangerment*.

92. For an exploration of this more expansive sense of technology as a productive and regulatory apparatus, see Andrew Barry, *Political Machines: Governing a Technological Society* (New York: Athlone, 2001).

93. For my efforts to reread Marx against the grain of the most common means of dismissing him, see Martin, *On Your Marx*.

94. See Michael E. Brown, *The Production of Society: A Marxian Foundation for Social Theory* (Totowa, NJ: Rowman and Littlefield, 1986).

95. David Harvey, *The Limits to Capital*, 2d ed. (London: Verso, 2006).

96. Franz Fanon, *The Wretched of the Earth* (1961; repr., New York: Grove Press, 2004).

97. See Ernesto Laclau and Chantal Mouffe, *Hegemony and Socialist Strategy* (London: Verso, 1985). For views from the left that these emerging movements were a sign of lost opportunity for progressive change, see Todd Gitlin, *The Twilight of Common Dreams: Why America Is Wracked by the Culture Wars* (New York: Henry Holt, 1996); Russell Jacoby, *The End of Utopia: Politics and Culture in an Age of Apathy* (New York: Basic, 2000).

98. See Viviana Zelizer, *The Social Meaning of Money* (Princeton, NJ: Princeton University Press, 1997).

CHAPTER 2

1. For an overview of some of the various conceptions of public and private going back to Aristotle, see Gürcan Koçan, "Models of Public Sphere in Political Philosophy," Eurosphere Working Paper no. 2, 2008, available at http://eurospheres .org/files/2010/08/Eurosphere_Working_Paper_2_Kocan.pdf, accessed August 2010. On the gender divide in particular, see Jean Bethke Elshtain, *Public Man, Private Woman: Women in Social and Political Thought* (Princeton, NJ: Princeton University Press, 1981).

2. Steven R. Weisman, *The Great Tax Wars: Lincoln—Teddy Roosevelt—Wilson How the Income Tax Transformed America* (New York: Simon and Shuster, 2004).

3. Alexis de Tocqueville, *Democracy in America* (New York: Alfred A. Knopf, 1945). Scores of books have been written about Tocquevillian conceptions of democracy, and Tocqueville's ideas are central to current notions of civil society and social capital.

4. Peter Dobkin Hall and Colin B. Burke, "Historical Statistics of the United States Chapter on Voluntary, Nonprofit, and Religious Entities and Activities: Underlying Concepts, Concerns, and Opportunities," Working Paper no. 14, November 2012, Hauser Center for Nonprofit Organizations and Kennedy School of Government, Harvard University, Cambridge, MA, 4, available at http://www.hks .harvard.edu, accessed November 14, 2012. As the authors note:

> Perhaps the most important factor shaping the organizational demography of nonprofits in the postwar decades has been legislators' and policy makers' increasingly expansive definition of charity. Originally freighted with the notion, inherited from English law, that charity involved relief of the needy—dependent, disabled, ignorant, or distressed people—through religious, educational, or charitable interventions, modern tax writers defined charity far more broadly, in terms of nondistribution of surpluses and absence of private benefit, As the definition of charity has broadened, the range of entities that could qualify for the coveted 501(c)(3) charitable tax exempt status expanded to include publishers of books and periodicals (like *The Nation, Ms.*, and *National Geographic*), radio and television broadcasters, and, if appropriate educational programs were initiated, trade associations. The impact of this policy shift was dramatic: in 1967, there were twice as many noncharitables as charitable among the exempt organizations registered with the IRS; by 1986, the number of charitables had surpassed non-charitables. Many of the new charitables were noncharitables that had taken advantage

of the IRS's increasingly permissive definition of charity and the tax benefits associated with charitable tax exempt status. (Ibid., 4)

5. Eleanor L. Brilliant, *Private Charity and Public Inquiry: A History of the Filer and Peterson Commissions* (Bloomington: Indiana University Press, 2000).

6. Peter Dobkin Hall, *Inventing the Nonprofit Sector and Other Essays on Philanthropy, Voluntarism and Nonprofit Organization* (Baltimore: Johns Hopkins University Press, 1992), 7.

7. Ibid., 76.

8. These figures are from Binyamin Appelbaum and Robert Gebeloff, "Even Critics of Safety Net Increasingly Depend on It," New York Times, February 12, 2012, A1, and the accompanying poll report by Allison Kopicki, "Most Expect to Give More than They Receive, Poll Finds," *New York Times*, February 12, 2012, A25.

9. Dalton Conley, Elsewhere, USA: *How We Got from the Company Man, Family Dinners, and the Affluent Society to the Home Office, BlackBerry Moms, and Economic Anxiety* (New York: Pantheon, 2009), 16.

10. Suzanne Mettler, "Reconstituting the Submerged State: The Challenges of Social Policy Reform in the Obama Era," *Perspectives on Politics* 8 (2010): 809. See also Suzanne Mettler, *The Submerged State: How Invisible Government Policies Undermine American Democracy* (Chicago: University of Chicago Press, 2011).

11. Interestingly, the literature on nonprofits registers anxiety over their drift toward for-profit models of both organizational means and ends: see esp. Burton J. Weisbrod, *To Profit or Not to Profit: The Commercial Transformation of the Non-profit Sector* (Cambridge: Cambridge University Press, 1998). Weisbrod argues that rising tuition might also be a cause of reduced government grants as "legislators come to see that the university will sustain itself financially with less funding" (ibid., 59). While the Reagan years were seen as encouraging giving to nonprofits through tax cuts, lower marginal rates for those in the top brackets also render giving relatively more expensive and reduce nonprofits' ability to take over government services, a point that Weisbrod also makes in *The Non-profit Economy* (Cambridge: Cambridge University Press 1988). Figures for the impact of the Economic Recovery Act of 1981 are in Gary N. Scrivner, "A Brief History of Tax Policy Changes Affecting Charitable Organizations," in *The Nature of the Nonprofit Sector*, ed. J. Steven Ott (Boulder, CO: Westview Press, 2001), 126–142. For further discussion of the tax implications of charitable giving, see Susan Rose-Ackerman, *The Economics of Nonprofit Institutions: Studies in Structure and Policy* (New York: Oxford University Press, 1986).

12. Olivier Zunz, *Philanthropy in America: A History* (Princeton, NJ: Princeton University Press, 2012), 295. In chapter 8, Zunz discusses the convergence between conservative and liberal nonprofits and the shared juridical and operational strategy that emerged during the 1960s.

13. Bruce R. Sievers, *Civil Society, Philanthropy, and the Fate of the Commons* (Boston: Tufts University Press, 2010), 146.

14. Arthur C. Brooks, "A Nation of Givers," *The American*, March–April 2008, available at http://www.american.com, accessed April 2008.

15. During the recent recession, total individual contributions held steady while foundation grantmaking and charitable bequests declined (by 8.9 percent and 23.9 percent, respectively). In a decade, the number of 501(c)(3) organizations increased by some 50 percent, from 819,008 in 2000 to 1,238,391 in 2009. Religious organiza-

tions are the largest recipients of contributions, followed by educational institutions ($100 billion and $40 billion, respectively), but campuses have increased giving at a higher rate: see Giving USA Foundation and Center on Philanthropy, Indiana University, Giving USA 2010: *The Annual Report on Philanthropy for the Year 2009*, 4, 6, 21–22, available at www.pursuantmedia.com/givingusa/0510, accessed May 2010. The National Philanthropic Trust offers higher numbers for nonprofit growth. It states that the number of nonprofits doubled from 2000 to 2005 and levels of volunteerism grew at a rate of 55 percent, to 83.9 million (with an equivalent value of $239 billion). The trust estimates that in 2006, nearly 90 percent of households participated in charitable giving, up from 70 percent in 1998, and that wealthy donors were more likely to give to education (80 percent) than to religious organizations (72 percent) or to health organizations (70 percent): see National Philanthropic Trust, "Philanthropy Statistics 2007," available at http://www.nptrust.org/philanthrophy/philanthrophy_stats.asp. For additional measures, see http://generousgiving.org.

16. John Micklethwait, "A Special Report on the Future of the State: Taming Leviathan," *The Economist*, March 15, 2011, available at http://www.economist.com, accessed March 15, 2011.

17. Giving USA Foundation and Center on Philanthropy, Indiana University, *Giving USA* 2010, 32.

18. "Majority of U.S. Households Give to Charity, Study Finds," *Philanthropy News Digest*, December 6, 2007, available at http://foundationcenter.org, accessed December 6, 2007.

19. "Statistics about Business Size (including Small Business) from the U.S. Census Bureau," 2007, available at http://www.census.gov, accessed December 6, 2007.

20. Holly Sidford, "Fusing Arts, Culture and Social Change: High Impact Strategies for Philanthropy," National Committee for Responsive Philanthropy 2011, available at http://heliconcollab.net/files/Fusing-Arts-Culture-and-Social-Change.pdf, accessed December 1, 2011.

21. For a breakdown of volunteerism by activity, see U.S. Bureau of Labor Statistics, "Table 5: Main Volunteer Activity for Main Organization for which Activities Were Performed and Selected Characteristics," available at http://www.bls.gov, accessed December 1, 2011.

22. Leslie R. Crutchfield, John V. Kania, and Mark R. Kramer, *Do More than Give: The Six Practices of Donors Who Change the World* (San Francisco: Jossey-Bass, 2011), 17.

23. Caroline Moser, ed., *Reducing Global Poverty: The Case for Asset Accumulation* (Washington, DC: Brookings Institution Press, 2007).

24. Aminur Rahman, *Women and Microcredit in Rural Bangladesh: Anthropological Study of the Rhetoric and Realities of Grameen Bank Lending* (Boulder, CO: Westview,1999); Nabiha Syed, *Replicating Dreams: A Comparative Study of Grameen Bank and Its Replication, Kashf Foundation, Pakistan* (New York: Oxford University Press, 2009); Susan Holcombe, *Managing to Empower: The Grameen Bank's Experience of Poverty Alleviation* (Atlantic Highlands, NJ: Zed, 1995).

25. Vikram Akula, *A Fistful of Rice: My Unexpected Quest to End Poverty through Profitability* (Cambridge: Harvard Business Press, 2011), 153.

26. Ibid., 156.

27. Ananya Roy, *Poverty Capital: Microfinance and the Making of Development* (Florence, KY: Routledge, 2010), 68.

28. Ibid., 218.

29. Alexia Latortue, "Microfinance in 2010," May 17, 2010, available at http://microfinance.cgap.org/2010/05/17/microfinance-in-2010.

30. Richard Rosenberg, "Is Microcredit Over-indebtedness a Worldwide Problem?" November 7, 2011, available at http://microfinance.cgap.org, accessed July 7, 2011.

31. Jessica Toonkel, "Analysis: Wall Street Sees Social-Impact Bonds as Way to Do Good and Do Well," Reuters, November 12, 2013, available at http://www.reuters.com, accessed November 12, 2013.

32. Steven H. Goldberg, *Billions of Drops in Millions of Buckets: Why Philanthropy Doesn't Advance Social Progress* (New York: John Wiley, 2009), p 8.

33. For critical appraisals of the relation between social justice movements and organizational form from within communities of color, see Cheryll Y. Greene and Marta Moreno Vega, *Voices from the Battlefront: Achieving Cultural Equity* (Trenton, NJ: Africa World Press, 1993); Incite! Women of Color against Violence, eds., *The Revolution Will Not Be Funded: Beyond the Non-profit Industrial Complex* (Cambridge, MA: South End Press, 2007).

34. Benedict Anderson, *Imagined Communities: Reflections on the Origin and Spread of Nationalism* (London: Verso, 1991).

35. Zunz, *Philanthropy in America*, 298.

36. See Ernest Cashmore, *Celebrity/Culture* (London: Routledge, 2006); *Richard Dyer, Heavenly Bodies: Film Stars and Society* (New York: St. Martin's Press, 1986).

37. That the United States now lags behind other wealthy nations on scales of mobility has become an item of concern for conservatives who, like venture philanthropists of the present, stress opportunity over equality: see Jason de Parle, "Harder for Americans to Rise from Lower Rungs," *New York Times*, January 5, 2012, A1.

38. This is the point made in David Rothkopf, *Superclass: The Global Power Elite and the World They Are Making* (New York: Farrar, Straus and Giroux, 2008).

39. Chrystia Freeland, "The Rise of the New Global Elite," *Atlantic Magazine*, January–February 2011, available at http://www.theatlantic.com, accessed February 15, 2011.

40. Isaac William Martin, *The Permanent Tax Revolt: How the Property Tax Transformed American Politics* (Stanford, CA: Stanford University Press 2008), 9–22.

41. See also David O. Sears and Jack Citrin, *Tax Revolt: Something for Nothing in California* (Cambridge, MA: Harvard University Press, 1985); Arthur Sullivan, Terri A. Sexton, and Steven M. Sheffrin, *Property Taxes and Tax Revolts: The Legacy of Proposition 13* (Cambridge: Cambridge University Press, 1995).

42. Alex F. Schwartz, *Housing Policy in the United States*, 2d ed. (New York: Routledge, 2010), 92.

43. The dilemma of a critique of neoliberalism becoming an unwitting functionalist account is evident in perhaps its most elegant, sweeping, and influential narrative: Naomi Klein's *The Shock Doctrine: The Rise of Disaster Capitalism* (New York: Metropolitan Books, 2007). Shock, for Klein, is at once a trope and a structure of domination that operates similarly on individual and national bodies to de-pattern critical capacities and promote passive submission. Like a plague of locusts, political hope returns when the clouds of misery depart and new shoots of alternative practices spring from the grassroots, a naturalizing gesture that can minimize recognition of ongoing contradictions and opportunities for contestation and generative change.

44. While the bailout certainly spread the view that the era of neoliberalism had come to a close, the requiem asserted a revisionist history that the triumph of markets rested on state intervention in the economy. For a range of views, see Kean Birch and Vlad Mykhnenko, *The Rise and Fall of Neoliberalism: The Collapse of an Economic Order?* (London: Zed, 2010).

45. Eduardo Porter "Economic Scene: A Nation with Too Many Tax Breaks," *New York Times*, March 14, 2012, B1, B7. The data are from Eric Toder and Daniel Baneman, "Distributional Effects of Individual Income Tax Expenditures: An Update," Urban-Brookings Tax Policy Center, February 2, 2012, available at http://www.taxpolicycenter.org/UploadedPDF/412495-Distribution-of-Tax-Expenditures.pdf, accessed February 2, 2012.

46. For a deep articulation of how this double session of representation is constituted and what limits and confusion it bears, see Gaytri Chakravorty Spivak, "Can the Subaltern Speak?" in *Marxism and the Interpretation of Culture*, ed. Cary Nelson and Lawrence Grossberg (Urbana: University of Illinois Press, 1988), 271–313.

47. The instability of regicide was made famous in the opening account in Michel Foucault, *Discipline and Punish: The Birth of the Prison* (New York: Pantheon, 1995). The gathering of crowds creates a potential for unstable consequences, such as riots and insurrections: see Gustave Le Bon, *The Crowd: A Study of the Popular Mind* (London: T. F. Unwin, 1897); George Rudé, *The Crowd in History: A Study of Popular Disturbances in France and England, 1730–1848* (New York: John Wiley and Sons, 1964); E. P. Thompson, *The Making of the English Working Class* (New York: Vintage, 1963). For a critical appraisal of this literature as it generates the notion of the people, see Michael E. Brown, "History and History's Problem," *Social Text*, no. 16 (1986–1987): 136–161.

48. For his initial formulation of the public sphere, see Jürgen Habermas, *The Structural Transformation of the Public Sphere: An Inquiry into a Category of Bourgeois Society* (Cambridge, MA: MIT Press, 1989). On discourse ethics, see Jürgen Habermas, *The Theory of Communicative Action*, vols. 1–2 (Boston: Beacon, 1984–1987). For recent criticisms, see Nick Crossley and John Roberts, *After Habermas: New Perspectives on the Public Sphere* (Oxford: Blackwell, 2004); Pauline Johnson, *Habermas: Rescuing the Public Sphere* (London: Routledge, 2006); Pieter Duvenage, *Habermas and Esthetics: The Limits of Communicative Reason* (Cambridge: Polity, 2003); Gayatri Chakravorty Spivak, *A Critique of Postcolonial Reason: Toward a History of the Vanishing Present* (Cambridge, MA: Harvard University Press, 1999).

49. George Gallup and Saul F. Rae, *The Pulse of Democracy* (New York: Simon and Schuster, 1940).

50. Amy Fried, *Pathways to Polling: Crisis Cooperation and the Making of Public Opinion Professions* (New York: Routledge, 2012). Fried provides a synthetic account of the emergence of the field in the decades before the war and its consolidation thereafter, as well as a detailed examination of the election forecast of 1948. The figures on the 1936 poll are on page 30.

51. Walter Lippmann, *The Phantom Public* (New York: Harcourt Brace, 1925).

52. Floyd H. Allport, "The Group Fallacy in Relation to Social Science," *American Journal of Sociology* 29, no. 6 (May 1924): 688–706.

53. Herbert Blumer, "Public Opinion and Public Opinion Polling," *American Sociological Review* 13 no. 5 (October 1948): 542–549.

54. Pierre Bourdieu, "Public Opinion Does Not Exist," in *Communication and*

Class Struggle, Volume 1: Capitalism, Imperialism, ed. Armand Mattelart and Seth Sieglaub (New York: International General, 1979), 128.

55. Benjamin Ginsberg, *The Captive Public: How Mass Opinion Promotes State Power* (New York: Basic, 1986), 60.

56. Lisbeth Lipari, "Polling as Ritual," *Journal of Communication* 49 (1999): 83–102.

57. For the response to this recognition in the field, see Eleanor Singer, "Introduction: Nonresponse Bias in Household Surveys," *PublicOpinion Quarterly* 70, no. 5 (2006): 637–645.

58. Stanley Milgram, *Obedience to Authority: An Experimental View* (New York: Harper and Row, 1974).

59. Klaus Krippendorff, "The Social Construction of Public Opinion," in *Kommunikation über Kommunikation. Theorie, Methoden und Praxis. Festschrift für Klaus Merten*, ed. Edith Wienand, Joachim Westerbarkey, and Armin Scholl (Wiesbaden, Germany: VS-Verlag, 2005), 138.

60. See George F. Bishop, *The Illusion of Public Opinion: Fact and Artifact in American Public Opinion Polls* (Lanham, MD: Rowman and Littlefield, 2004). Bishop provides a synthetic review of the skeptical literature on which I have drawn, as well as an inventory of various techniques for clarifying the reliability and validity of questions and responses.

61. Susan Herbst, *Reading Public Opinion: How Political Actors View the Democratic Process* (Chicago: University of Chicago Press, 1998).

62. Robert Bacal, *Managers' Guide to Performance Reviews* (New York: McGraw-Hill, 2004).

63. Grading software such as JumpRope (see http://www.jumpro.pe) allows teachers and students to record daily progress for "true mastery tracking": see Richard J. Stiggins, *Student-Involved Assessment for Learning* (New York: Pearson Merrill Prentice Hall, 2005).

64. For a treatment of the various socialities of Facebook from an anthropological perspective, see Daniel Miller, *Tales from Facebook* (Cambridge: Polity, 2011).

65. See Ronald S. Burt, *Structural Holes: The Social Structure of Competition* (Cambridge, MA: Harvard University Press, 1992); Ronald S. Burt, *Brokerage and Closure: An Introduction to Social Capital* (Oxford: Oxford University Press, 2005); Ronald S. Burt, *Neighbor Networks: Competitive Advantage Local and Personal* (Oxford: Oxford University Press, 2010).

66. Gallup maintains running poll data on party affiliation, which show independents at a low of 32 percent on the eve of the 2008 presidential election and reaching 45 percent in December 2011. Republican affiliation reached a low of 21 percent in September 2011 and a high of 33 percent in October 2008. Despite the Republican Party's electoral gains in 2010, 26 percent reported Republican affiliation as opposed to 31 percent for Democrats, making the politics of voter turnout and districting all the more important. On turnout, see U.S. Bureau of the Census, "Table 401: Reported Voting and Registration among Native and Naturalized Citizens by Race and Hispanic Origin: 2010," 2012, available at http://www.census.gov/compendia/statab/2012/tables/12s0400.pdf, accessed December 2012.

67. This argument is made by Marc Hetherington based on his reading of trends over the past few decades in partisanship and polarization among different strata of the electorate: see Marc Hetherington, "Partisanship and Polarization," in *New Directions in Public Opinion, ed. Adam J. Berinsky* (New York: Routledge, 2011), 101–118.

68. James A. Stimson, *Tides of Consent: How Public Opinion Shapes American Politics* (Cambridge: Cambridge University Press, 2004), 93–94.

69. Thomas Frank, *What's the Matter with Kansas? How Conservatives Won the Heart of America* (New York: Metropolitan, 2004).

70. Larry M. Bartels, *Unequal Democracy: The Political Economy of the New Gilded Age* (Princeton, NJ: Princeton University Press, 2008), 2.

71. Ibid., 175.

72. Sabrina Tavernise, "Survey Finds Rising Perception of Class Tension: Friction between the Rich and Poor Is the Greatest Source of Tension in American Society, according to a New Survey," *New York Times*, January 12, 2012, A1.

73. See Susan Murray and Laurie Ouellette, *Reality TV: Remaking Television Culture* (New York: New York University Press, 2009); Laurie Ouellette and James Hay, *Better Living through Reality TV: Television and Post-Welfare Citizenship* (Malden, MA: Blackwell, 2008).

74. This would be a turn away from the kind of distancing between spectator and spectacle imagined in Guy Debord, *Society of the Spectacle* (1967; repr., New York: Zone, 1994).

75. James Moore and Wayne Slater, *The Architect: Karl Rove and the Master Plan for Absolute Power* (New York: Crown, 2006); Rahaf Harfoush, *Yes We Did: An Inside Look at How Social Media Built the Obama Brand* (Berkeley, CA: New Riders, 2009).

76. For a discussion of the politics that issues from the people as an irreducible heterogeneity and unmasterable excess, see Ernesto Laclau, *On Populist Reason* (London: Verso, 2005), 223.

77. Chantal Mouffe, *On the Political* (New York: Routledge, 2005), 3.

78. The conception of the political as the production of the sensibility—of what is allowed to appear and be recognized within a determinate realm—has the tremendous benefit of focusing attention on how a political space and sensibility is constituted even as it relies on certain conventions of visibility and representation, scarcity and legitimation, singularity of interest and expression. Such has been the sustained contribution of Jacques Rancière's exploration of the relations between sense making or esthetics and the space of the political: see Jacques Rancière, *The Politics of Aesthetics: The Distribution of the Sensible* (London: Continuum, 2004).

79. See Robert Dahl, *Pluralist Democracy in the United States: Conflict and Consent* (New York: Rand McNally, 1967); Robert Dahl, *Who Governs? Democracy and Power in an American City* (New Haven, CT: Yale University Press, 1965).

80. Pippa Norris, *Democratic Deficit: Critical Citizens Revisited* (Cambridge: Cambridge University Press, 2011), 5.

81. See Robert Hughes, *The Culture of Complaint: The Fraying of America* (New York: Oxford University Press, 1993).

82. A sign, perhaps, of their canonization as an interpretive trope, the Culture Wars have now become literally an encyclopedia of contested sites, even as the empirical basis for polarization continues to be challenged on evidentiary grounds: see Roger Chapman, *Culture Wars: An Encyclopedia of Issues, Viewpoints and Voices* (Armonk, NY: M. E. Sharpe, 2010); Morris P. Fiorina, Samuel J. Abrams, and Jeremy Pope, *Culture War? The Myth of a Polarized America* (New York: Pearson Longman, 2006).

83. Timothy Mitchell, *Carbon Democracy: Political Power in the Age of Oil* (London: Verso 2011), 4.

84. Ibid., 251.

85. See S. N. Eisenstadt, ed., *Max Weber on Charisma and Institution Building: Selected Papers* (Chicago: University of Chicago Press, 1968).

86. It should be noted that there are many ways to determine who is in the professional managerial class. A rather blunt measure is the U.S. Bureau of Labor Statistics, "Household Data Annual Averages, 10: Employed Persons by Occupation, Race, Hispanic or Latino Ethnicity, and Sex," available at http://www.bls.gov/cps/cpsaat10.pdf, accessed December 1, 2011. For 2011, it counts 37.6 million in "managerial, professional and related occupations" and 5.8 million in production occupations.

87. This finding of disproportionate revenue flows structured as a retention of resources is one way to understand the Republican project more generally. It is based on research by Dean P. Lacy as quoted in Appelbaum and Gebeloff, "Even Critics of Safety Net." The freedom to hold onto capital, rather than risking it in expenditure, backed by the state is foundational to the longer history of austerity that is the current common sense of governmental discipline. For an account of this history, see Mark Blyth, *Austerity: The History of a Dangerous Idea* (Oxford: Oxford University Press, 2013).

88. For a thoughtful reflection on the history of these debates, see Linda Nicholson, *Identity before Identity Politics* (Cambridge: Cambridge University Press, 2008).

89. Quentin Kidd, *Civic Participation in America* (New York: Palgrave Macmillan, 2011), 12–28.

90. Morley Winograd and Michael D. Hais, *Millennial Momentum: How a New Generation Is Remaking America* (New Brunswick, NJ: Rutgers University Press, 2011), 27.

91. Ibid., 1–4.

92. Ibid., 34–35, 208.

93. Ibid., 266.

94. Coleman notes, "Digital media have certainly played a crucial role in establishing mechanisms for communication, shifting social relationships, and cultivating collective political interests, but in less tectonic ways than often assumed by the term *digital* generation": Gabriela Coleman, "Hacker Politics and Publics," *Public Culture* 23, no. 3 (2011): 512. See also her study of the emergence of debian as an open source participatory network: Gabriela Coleman, *Coding Freedom: The Ethics and Aesthetics of Hacking* (Princeton, NJ: Princeton University Press, 2012).

95. For data on the "graying" of Facebook users, see Pew Research Center's Internet and American Life Project, 2011, available at http://www.pewinternet.org, accessed December 1, 2011. For key articulations of network culture and politics, see Yochai Benkler, *The Wealth of Networks: How Social Production Transforms Markets and Freedom* (New Haven, CT: Yale University Press, 2006); Howard Rheingold, *Smart Mobs: The Next Social Revolution* (Cambridge, MA: Perseus, 2002); Clay Shirkey, *Here Comes Everybody: The Power of Organizing without Organizations* (New York: Penguin, 2009).

96. Clay Shirky, *Cognitive Surplus: Creativity and Generosity in a Connected Age* (New York: Penguin, 2010).

97. Elizabeth Losh, *Virtualpolitik: An Electronic History of Government Media-Making in a Time of War, Scandal, Disaster, Miscommunication, and Mistakes* (Cambridge, MA: MIT Press, 2009), 4.

98. Dorothy Lilley and Donald Trice, *A History of Information Science, 1945–1985* (San Diego, CA: Academic Press, 1989).

99. Anna McCarthy, *The Citizen Machine: Governing by Television in 1950s America* (New York: New Press, 2010).

100. Leah Lievrouw, *Alternative and Activist New Media* (Cambridge: Polity, 2011), 23, table 1.1.

101. Jacques Rancière, *Staging The People: The Proletarian and His Double* (London: Verso, 2011), 18.

102. Long a student of social change and mobilization, Charles Tilly has come to focus on the performative aspects of activism: see Charles Tilly, *Contentious Performances* (New York: Cambridge University Press, 2008). See also Sidney Tarrow, *Power in Movement: Social Movements and Contentious Politics* (New York: Cambridge University Press, 1998).

103. Catherine Corrigall-Brown, *Patterns of Protest: Trajectories of Participation in Social Movements* (Stanford, CA: Stanford University Press, 2012), 135.

104. Ibid., 37.

CHAPTER 3

1. For representative examples after the financial bailout, see William Irwin Thompson "Wild Finance: Where Money and Politics Dance," *Wild River Review* November 5, 2008, available at http://integral-options.blogspot.com, accessed November 5, 2008; Big Tent Democrat, "The Reconciliation Dance," Talk Left: The Politics of Crime (blog), December 1, 2009, available at http://www.talkleft.com, accessed December 1, 2009; Carl M. Cannon, "Joe Wilson, Obama and the Clintons: The Dance of the Apologists," *HuffPost Politics Daily*, December 9, 2009, available at http://www.politicsdaily.com, accessed July 11, 2012.

2. Of course, this tension between dance's particularity and its universalism runs through the historical and ethnological impulses that had constituted the conventional approaches to the study of dance until dance studies undertook a more philosophical and theoretical turn: see, e.g., John Martin, *The Modern Dance* (1933; repr., Brooklyn: Dance Horizons, 1965); Judith Lynne Hanna, *To Dance Is Human: A Theory of Non-verbal Communication* (Chicago: University of Chicago Press, 1987). For the text of the break that initiated the distinctive domain called dance studies, see Susan Leigh Foster, *Reading Dancing: Bodies and Subjects in Contemporary American Dancing* (Berkeley: University of California Press, 1986). For a recent instance of the philosophical turn in European dance studies, see Petra Sabisch, *Choreographing Relations: Practical Philosophy and Contemporary Choreography in the Works of Antonia Baehr, Gilles Deleuze, Juan Dominguez, Félix Guattari, Xavier Le Roy and Eszter Salamon* (Munich: Epodium, 2011). For a recent compilation that reflects this turn, see Gabriele Klein and Sandra Noeth, eds., *Emerging Bodies: The Performance of Worldmaking in Dance and Choreography* (Bielefield, Germany: Transcript, 2011).

3. This question has informed my previous work on dance: see Randy Martin, *Performance as Political Act: The Embodied Self* (South Hadley, MA: Bergin and Garvey, 1990); Randy Martin, *Critical Moves: Dance Studies in Theory and Politics* (Durham, NC: Duke University Press, 1998).

4. At fewer than 25,000, dancers in the United States are the fewest in number of the listed arts occupations and average $27,392 in annual salary, as opposed to $27,558 for musicians and $30,254 for actors: National Endowment for the Arts, "Artists and Arts Workers in the United States Findings from the American Community

Survey (2005–2009) and the Quarterly Census of Employment and Wages (2010)," 2011 Research Note no. 105, available at http://www.nea.gov/research/Notes/105.pdf .2011, accessed December 1, 2011).

5. This effective subsidy of artistic labor is what Andrew Ross has called the "cultural discount": Andrew Ross, "The Mental Labor Problem," *Social Text* 63 (Summer 2000): 1–32. For a trenchant critique of creative class appeals, see Matteo Pasquinelli, "Creative Sabotage in the Factory of Culture: Art, Gentrification and the Metropolis," in *Animal Spirits: A Bestiary of the Commons* (Rotterdam: Netherlands Architectural Institute Press, 2009).

6. Here we would want to refer to those frameworks in the tradition of Marxist historical analysis that rely on differently scaled temporal cycles or waves. The notion of long and short cycles as a way to understand historical movement and transformation through crisis was developed by Fernand Braudel and his peers in the Annales School based on the work of the Russian economist Nikolai Kondratieff. This work was furthered by Ernest Mandel, on whom Frederic Jameson based his periodization scheme for postmodernism, as well as the World Systems Analysis of Immanuel Wallerstein. The most accomplished articulation of these schemas for finance in particular is in Giovanni Arrighi, *The Long Twentieth Century: Money, Power and the Origins of Our Times* (London: Verso, 1994). While all of these analyses continue the focus on what Braudel calls material civilization, the figure of the wave or cycle is strangely metaphysical—that is, it is not clear what the cycle itself is composed of, what generates its movement as movement, besides the notion that certain phases last for a particular duration. Here my efforts are to use dance itself to ground what is otherwise discussed metaphorically in large-scale historical treatments of societal transformation and change. See Fernand Braudel, *Civilization and Capitalism, 15th–18th Century*, 3 vols. (Berkeley: University of California Press, 1992); Ernest Mandel, *Late Capitalism* (London: Verso, 1970); Immanuel Wallerstein, *The Modern World System*, 4 vols. (Berkeley: University of California Press, 2011).

7. "Structure of feeling" is a term from Raymond Williams, *Marxism and Literature* (New York: Oxford University Press, 1977). "The pre-political" describes the emergent sensibilities of the working class in E. P. Thompson, *The Making of the English Working Class* (New York: Vintage, 1963). The idea of the virtual as tacit norms that govern activity is developed in Erving Goffman, *Stigma: Notes on the Management of Spoiled Identity* (Englewood Cliffs, NJ: Prentice Hall, 1963).

8. For an account of this transition, see Robert Elson, *Governing Global Finance: The Evolution and Reform of the International Financial Architecture* (New York: Palgrave Macmillan, 2011).

9. The demolition of Pruitt-Igoe was taken as the signal event for architectural postmodernism, which was promulgated before the term assumed its broader cultural usage: see Charles Jencks, *The Language of Post-Modern Architecture* (New York: Rizzoli, 1977).

10. Yamasaki's account of his work is in Minoru Yamasaki, *A Life in Architecture* (New York: Weatherhill, 1979). Resources on Pruitt-Igoe are in *Pruitt-Igoe: An Annotated Bibliography* (Chicago: Council of Planning Librarians, 1987); Chad Freidrichs, dir., *The Pruitt-Igoe Myth*, documentary film, Unicorn Stencil, Columbia, MO, 2011.

11. See David L. A. Gordon, *Battery Park City: Politics and Planning on the New York Waterfront* (Amsterdam: Gordon and Breach, 1997).

12. Lewis Mumford, "Chapter 20 Homage to Giantism," in *The Pentagon of*

Power: The Myth of the Machine, vol. 2 (New York: Harcourt Brace Jovanovich, 1970). For an overview, see Eric Darton, *Divided We Stand: A Biography of New York City's World Trade Towers* (New York: Basic, 2001).

13. James Marsh, dir., *Man on Wire*, documentary film, Magnolia Entertainment, Los Angeles, 2008. For Petit's testimony, see Philippe Petit, *To Reach the Clouds: My High Wire Walk between the Twin Towers* (New York: North Point, 2002).

14. Raymond Williams, *Keywords* (New York: Oxford University Press, 1983), 87–93.

15. See Robert Young, *Postcolonialism* (New York: Oxford University Press, 2003); Bill Ashcroft, Gareth Griffins, and Helen Tiffin, *Post-Colonial Studies: The Key Concepts* (London: Routledge, 2000).

16. Tony Bennett, *The Birth of the Museum: History, Theory, Politics* (New York: Routledge, 1995).

17. Matthew Arnold, *Culture and Anarchy* (1867; repr., Cambridge: Cambridge University Press, 1948).

18. Talcott Parsons, *The Social System* (New York: Free Press, 1951).

19. Daniel Bell, *The Cultural Contradictions of Capitalism* (New York: Basic, 1976).

20. Joseph Schumpeter, *Capitalism, Socialism, and Democracy* (1943; repr., London: Routledge, 2010).

21. Fredric Jameson, "Periodizing the Sixties," in *The Sixties, without Apology*, ed. Sohnya Sayres, Anders Stephanson, Stanley Aronowitz, and Frederic Jameson (Minneapolis: University of Minnesota Press, 1984).

22. Margaret Kohn and Keally McBride, *Political Theories of Decolonization: Postcolonialism and the Problem of Foundations* (New York: Oxford University Press, 2011), 3.

23. See "The United Nations and Decolonization," available at http://www.un.org/en/decolonization, accessed July 9, 2012.

24. Ngũgĩwa Thiong'o, *Decolonising the Mind: The Politics of Language in African Literature* (London: James Currey, 1986).

25. Mandel, *Late Capitalism*; Fredric Jameson, *Postmodernism, or, The Cultural Logic of Late Capitalism* (Durham, NC: Duke University Press, 1991); David Harvey, *The Condition of Postmodernity: An Enquiry into the Origins of Cultural Change* (Cambridge: Blackwell, 1991); Jean-François Lyotard, *The Postmodern Condition: A Report on Knowledge* (Minneapolis: University of Minnesota Press, 1979).

26. The key texts here are Michel Foucault, *The Order of Things: An Archeology of the Human Sciences* (1966; repr., New York: Random House, 1970); Michel Foucault, *The Archaeology of Knowledge* (New York: Pantheon, 1972).

27. John Martin, *The Modern Dance* (1933; repr., Brooklyn: Dance Horizons, 1965).

28. Kurt Sachs, *World History of the Dance* (New York: W. W. Norton, 1937).

29. The notion of a distributed aesthetics is typically referenced to digital media and network cultures. The shift here to embodied performance practices is meant to enable consideration of the kinesthetics of distribution as such: see, e.g., *Fibreculture Journal* 7 (2005), a special issue edited by Lisa Gye, Anna Munster, and Ingrid Richardson, available at http://seven.fibreculturejournal.org, accessed June 10, 2010.

30. Mark Franko, *The Work of Dance: Labor, Movement and Identity in the 1930s* (Middletown, CT: Wesleyan University Press, 2002), 167. Franko here is speaking about the particular affinity between modern dance and labor movements in the 1930s United States, but his notion of a non-reflective performative economy located

in a refusal of a laboring body to submit to industrial rationalization resonates with a more supple approach to discerning the work of dance in a range of circumstances.

31. Susan Leigh Foster, *Choreographing Empathy: Kinesthesia in Performance* (London: Routledge, 2011), 218.

32. This reading of *La Sylphide* is based on the Royal Danish Ballet's performance in 1988 of the Bourneville version of 1836, with Lis Jeppesen as La Sylphide, Nikolaj Hübbe as James, and Sorella Englund as Madge: *La Sylphide*, DVD Kultur International Films, West Long Branch, NJ, 1988.

33. See Susan Leigh Foster, *Choreography and Narrative: Ballet's Staging of Story and Desire* (Bloomington: Indiana University Press, 1996); Mark Franko, *The Dancing Body in Renaissance Choreography (c. 1416–1589)* (Birmingham, AL: Summa, 1986); Mark Franko, *Dance as Text: Ideologies of the Baroque Body* (Cambridge: Cambridge University Press, 1993).

34. For a longer view of the articulation of military drill and dance, see William H. McNeill, *Keeping Together in Time: Dance and Drill in Human History* (Cambridge, MA: Harvard University Press, 1995). Victoria Peyton Anderson has made very perceptive links between the discipline of the studio and war as they emerged through ballet training in her Victoria Peyton Anderson, "Reflecting Modernity: The Dance Studio as a Performative Space," Ph.D. diss., New York University, 2012.

35. I have explored some of these links between technology of warfare and visualization in Randy Martin, *An Empire of Indifference: American War and the Financial Logic of Risk Management* (Durham, NC: Duke University Press, 2007). The problem of the fog of war and the need for a visual mastery in the form of command and control is formulated most famously by the Prussian military strategist Carl von Clausewitz, based on his experience of the Napoleonic Wars (1816–1830; he died in 1831, and his study was published posthumously): Carl von Clausewitz, *On War* (1832; repr., London: Routledge and Kegan Paul, 1968). The contradictions of pursuing such clarity are described for a number of conflicts in Martin Van Creveld, *Command in War* (Cambridge, MA: Harvard University Press, 1985).

36. For an overview, see Iain Mackintosh, *Architecture, Actor, Audience* (London: Routledge, 1993).

37. For discussions of dance sexualities, see Sally Banes, *Female Bodies on Stage* (London: New York, Routledge, 1998); Peter Stoneley, *A Queer History of the Ballet* (London: Routledge, 2006); Rachel Vigier, *Gestures of Genius: Women, Dance and the Body* (Stratford, Canada: Mercury, 1994); Ramsay Burt, *The Male Dancer: Bodies, Spectacle, Sexualities* (London: Routledge, 1995).

38. Immanuel Kant, *Observations on the Feeling of the Beautiful and Sublime* (Berkeley: University of California Press, 1960); Paul Crowther, *The Kantian Sublime: From Morality to Art* (Oxford: Clarendon, 1989).

39. Mark Franko, *Martha Graham in Love and War: The Life in the Work* (New York: Oxford University Press, 2012).

40. See Janice Ross, *Moving Lessons: Margaret H'Doubler and the Beginning of Dance in American Education* (Madison: University of Wisconsin Press, 2000); Jack Anderson, *The American Dance Festival* (Durham, NC: Duke University Press, 1987); Julia L. Foulkes, *Modern Bodies: Dance and American Modernism from Martha Graham to Alvin Ailey* (Chapel Hill: University of North Carolina Press, 2002).

41. Alice J. Helpern, *The Technique of Martha Graham* (Dobbs Ferry, NY: Morgan and Morgan, 1994); Martha Graham, *The Notebooks of Martha Graham* (New York:

Harcourt Brace Jovanovich, 1973). These observations are also informed by my study of Graham's technique with David and Marnie Wood at the University of California, Berkeley.

42. For documentation, see the performance of the ballet Appalachian Spring from 1957 included in Nathan Kroll, dir., *Martha Graham in Performance*, Kultur International Films, Long Branch, NJ, 1988.

43. Orientalist tropes in Ruth St. Denis's work are discussed in Suzanne Shelton, *Divine Dancer: A Biography of Ruth St. Denis* (Garden City, NY: Doubleday, 1981). Graham called African and Native American dance the "primitive sources" that she "adopts" in her work: Martha Graham, "Affirmations, 1926–37," in *Martha Graham*, ed. Merle Armitage (1937; repr., Brooklyn: Dance Horizons, 1966), 99–100. For a counter-history of Native American dance that includes a discussion of Graham's appropriation of "absent Indians," see Jacqueline Shea Murphy, *The People Have Never Stopped Dancing: Native American Modern Dance Histories* (Minneapolis: University of Minnesota Press, 2007). Thomas de Frantz has written crucial critical engagements with dance modernism and African American culture: see Thomas de Frantz, *Dancing Many Drums: Excavations in African American Dance* (Madison: University of Wisconsin Press, 2002); Thomas de Frantz, *Dancing Revelations: Alvin Ailey's Embodiment of African American Culture* (Oxford: Oxford University Press, 2004).

44. For documentation, see Ernestine Stodelle, *The Dance Technique of Doris Humphrey and Its Creative Potential* (Princeton, NJ: Dance Horizons, 1978); Murray Louis, *The Nikolais/Louis Dance Technique: A Philosophy and Method of Modern Dance* (New York: Routledge, 2005). On Hanya Holm's work, see Claudia Gitelman, *Dancing with Principle: Hanya Holm in Colorado, 1941–1983* (Boulder: University of Press of Colorado, 2001).

45. Andre Lepecki has provided a forceful critique of this modernist imperative for forward movement that is also part of a larger postcolonial critique: see Andre Lepecki, *Exhausting Dance: Performance and the Politics of Movement* (New York: Routledge, 2006). For an elaboration of his project through a range of global sites and practices, see Andre Lepecki and Jenn Joy, eds., *Planes of Composition: Dance, Theory and the Global* (London: Seagull, 2009), which orients dance studies around the critique of mobilization rather than of representation.

46. Sally Banes, *Terpsichore in Sneakers: Post-Modern Dance* (Middletown, CT: Wesleyan University Press, 1979).

47. Susan Leigh Foster, "Choreographing Your Move," in *Move. Choreographing You: Art and Dance since the 1960s*, ed. Stephanie Rosenthal (Cambridge, MA: MIT Press, 2011), 36.

48. This association is established most convincingly in Sally Banes, *Greenwich Village, 1963: Avant-Garde Performance and the Effervescent Body* (Durham, NC: Duke University Press, 1993). In the book, Banes describes the rich intersections of various artistic practices.

49. Cunningham's reflections on his work are in Merce Cunningham, *Changes: Notes on Choreography* (New York: Something Else, 1968).

50. Sally Banes, *Democracy's Body: Judson Dance Theater, 1962–1964* (Ann Arbor, MI: UMI Research Press, 1983), 70.

51. Eugene Fama, "Random Walks in Stock Market Prices," *Financial Analysts Journal* 21, no. 5 (September–October 1965): 55–59; Burton Malkiel, *A Random Walk down Wall Street* (1973; repr., New York: W. W. Norton, 1985).

52. Mabel Todd, *The Thinking Body: A Study of the Balancing Forces of Man* (1937; repr., Princeton, NJ: Princeton Books, 1997).

53. See Genevieve Stebbins, *The Delsarte System of Expression* (New York: Dance Horizons, 1977); Rebecca Nettl-Fiol, *Alexander Technique: Exploring the Missing Link* (Urbana: University of Illinois Press, 2011).

54. It should be noted that the nomenclature of postmodern is now often displaced by the term "contemporary," which ranges from experimental to large-scale ballet. For documentation including that of Pilobolus, see Martha Bremser, *Fifty Contemporary Choreographers* (London: Routledge, 1999). For a situation of 1970s dance improvisation in relation to feminist performance art more broadly, see RoseLee Goldberg, *Performance: Live Art since the 1960s* (London: Thames and Hudson, 2004). On Grand Union and Yvonne Rainer, see Margaret Hupp Ramsay, "Grand Union (1970–1976), an Improvisational Performance Group (Dance, Yvonne Rainer)," Ph.D. diss., New York University, 1986.

55. Mark Franko, *Dancing Modernism/Performing Politics* (Bloomington: Indiana University Press, 1995).

56. On the contexts of dance improvisation more broadly, see Ann Cooper Albright and David Gere, *Taken by Surprise: A Dance Improvisation Reader* (Middletown, CT: Wesleyan University Press, 2003); Danielle Goldman, *I Want to Be Ready: Improvised Dance as a Practice of Freedom* (Ann Arbor: University of Michigan Press, 2010); Susan Leigh Foster, *Dances That Describe Themselves: The Improvised Choreography of Richard Bull* (Middletown, CT: Wesleyan University Press, 2002). For a cultural account of contact improvisation, see Cynthia Jean Novack Bull, *Sharing the Dance: Contact Improvisation and American Culture* (Madison: University of Wisconsin Press, 1990). Accounts of contact improvisation technique are in Cheryl Pallant, *Contact Improvisation: An Introduction to a Vitalizing Dance Form* (Jefferson, NC: McFarland, 2006); Justine Reeve, *Dance Improvisations: Warm-Ups, Games and Choreographic Tasks* (Champaign, IL: Human Kinetics, 2011). This discussion is also informed by my exposure to contact improvisation in New York during the 1980s.

57. The de-centerings of modernism's esthetic universalism have been undertaken by postcolonial dance studies: see, e.g., Marta Savigliano, *Tango and the Political Economy of Passion* (Boulder, CO: Westview, 1995); Ananya Chatterjea, *Butting Out: Reading Resistive Choreographies through Works by Jawle Willa Jo Zollar and Chandralekha* (Middletown, CT: Wesleyan University Press, 2004); Yutian Wong, *Choreographing Asian America* (Middletown, CT: Wesleyan University Press, 2010); Susan Leigh Foster, *Worlding Dance* (New York: Palgrave Macmillan, 2009); Yvonne Daniel, *Caribbean and Atlantic Diaspora Dance* (Urbana: University of Illinois Press, 2011); Priya Srinivasan, *Sweating Saris: Indian Dance as Transnational Labor* (Philadelphia: Temple University Press, 2011).

58. Gil Scott-Heron's poem "Whitey on the Moon" was first recorded live on *Small Talk at 125th and Lenox*, Flying Dutchman Records, 1970, and was rereleased on *The Revolution Will Not Be Televised*, Flying Dutchman Records, 1974.

59. See *Trisha Brown: Early Works, 1966–1979*, DVD, Artpix, San Francisco, 2004.

60. Documentation Trisha Brown's complete repertoire from the 1960s to the present is available at http://www.trishabrowncompany.org, accessed July 13, 2012.

61. Elizabeth Streb, *Streb: How to Become an Extreme Action Hero* (New York: Feminist Press, 2010).

62. Elizabeth Streb discusses Trisha Brown's "Man Walking down the Side of a Building," Whitney Museum of Modern Art, 2010, available at http://www.youtube.com/watch?v=9kxWm31jh3Q, accessed June 14, 2012.

63. Brown, quoted in Douglas Rosenberg, dir., *Speaking of Dance*, film, American Dance Festival, Oregon, WI, 1993.

64. Susan Klein's website, available at http://www.kleintechnique.com/about .html, accessed July 12, 2012.

65. For more on Trisha Brown's formation and work, see Peter Eleey and Philip Bither, *Trisha Brown: So That the Audience Does Not Know Whether I Have Stopped Dancing* (Minneapolis, MN: Walker Art Center, 2008); Lydia Yee, *Laurie Anderson, Trisha Brown, Gordon Matta-Clark: Pioneers of the Downtown Scene, New York 1970s* (Munich: Prestel 2011); Hendel Teicher, *Trisha Brown: Dance and Art in Dialogue, 1961–2001* (Cambridge, MA: MIT Press, 2002); and Trisha Brown, "Trisha Brown on Pure Movement," *Dance Magazine*, May 1, 2013.

66. Gries, quoted in Gabriele Wittmann, Sylvia Scheidl, and Gerald Siegmund, "Lance Gries—Release and Alignment Oriented Techniques," in *Dance Techniques 2010 Tanzplan Germany*, ed. Inigo Diehl and Friederike Lampert (Leipzig, Germany: Henschel, 2011), 269–270.

67. Ibid., 270.

68. Ibid., 274.

69. This passage is from a study of dance techniques undertaken by the German TanzPlan, a five-year national governmental initiative to organize dance comprehensively as a sector of performance, pedagogy, and knowledge. The large study assembled research teams to investigate a range of dance techniques. Lance Gries and release technique, taught at the Frankfurt University of Music and Performing Arts, was one of seven techniques that received intensive focus (see ibid., 285).

70. Donald MacKenzie and Taylor Spears, "'The Formula That Killed Wall Street'? The Gaussian Copula and the Material Cultures of Modelling," June 2012, 64, available at http://www.sps.ed.ac.uk/__data/assets/pdf_file/0003/84243/Gauss ian14.pdf, accessed July 10, 2012. The paper was made available in Lisa Pollock, "The Formula That Wall Street Never Believed In," June 15, 2012, available at http:// ftalphaville.ft.com (blog), accessed June 15, 2012. Before the crisis, MacKenzie had applied Austin's notion of locutionary performativity to explain the social construction of financial markets. See Donald MacKenzie, *An Engine, Not a Camera: How Financial Models Shape Markets* (Cambridge, MA: MIT Press, 2006).

71. On the broader strokes of gentrification in New York, see Neil Smith, *The New Urban Frontier: Gentrification and the Revanchist City* (New York: Taylor and Francis, 1996). For a focus on the dynamics of artists in residence in Soho, see Sharon Zukin, *Loft Living: Culture and Capital in Urban Change* (New Brunswick, NJ: Rutgers University Press, 1989).

72. The potency of hip-hop to draw audiences has not been lost on the art world, as is evident in the sweeping show under Jeffrey Deitch's direction at the Los Angeles Museum of Contemporary Art, which, nonetheless, documented the bicoastal influences and globally dispersed esthetic range of forms. Deitch calls hip-hop "arguably the most influential art movement since Pop": see Jeffrey Deitch, *Art in the Streets* (New York: Skira, Rizzoli, 2011), 10.

73. Associated with the criminologist James Q. Wilson and later developed into a book, broken windows theory was used to justify vigilant community policing of minor crimes in the hope that small infractions against property would not escalate into urban decay: see George Kelling and Catherine Coles, *Fixing Broken Windows: Restoring Order and Reducing Crime in Our Communities* (New York: Martin Kessler, 1996).

74. See Maris Vinovskis, *From a Nation at Risk to No Child Left Behind: National Education Goals and the Creation of Federal Education Policy* (New York: Teachers College Press, 2009).

75. See Robert Fitch, *The Assassination of New York* (London: Verso, 1993); Kim Moody, *From Welfare State to Real Estate: Regime Change in New York City, 1974–Present* (New York: New Press, 2007).

76. Juan Flores, *From Bomba to Hip Hop: Puerto Rican Culture and Latino Identity* (New York: Columbia University Press, 2000).

77. For video documentation of early hip-hop, see Tony Silver, Linda Habib, and Henry Chalfant, prods., *Style Wars*, documentary film, Public Art Films, Los Angeles, 1983.

78. Quoted in Mohanalakshmi Rajakumar, *Hip Hop Dance* (Santa Barbara, CA: Greenwood, 2012), 21.

79. Aram Sinnreich, *Mashed Up: Music, Technology and the Rise of a Configurable Culture* (Amherst: University of Massachusetts Press, 2010).

80. For an overview of these issues, see Kimbrew McLeod, *Freedom of Expression: Resistance and Repression in the Age of Intellectual Property* (Minneapolis: University of Minnesota Press, 2007).

81. Moncell Durden and Rennie Harris, "History and Concept of Hip Hop," 2009, available at http://daiv.alexanderstreet.com/View/1630501.

82. Tricia Rose, *The Hip Hop Wars: What We Talk about When We Talk about Hip Hop and Why It Matters* (New York: Basic, 2008), 1.

83. Joseph G. Schloss, *Foundation: B-Boys, B-Girls, and Hip-Hop Culture* (New York: Oxford University Press, 2009), 3.

84. Ibid., 4.

85. For an emblematic volume of cultural criticism on these issues, see Andrew Ross and Tricia Rose, *Microphone Fiends: Youth Music and Youth Culture* (New York: Routledge, 1994). On the impact of rap music on the music video, see Lisa Lewis, *Gender Politics and MTV* (Philadelphia: Temple University Press, 1990).

86. On the ring shout, see Sterling Stuckey, *Slave Culture: Nationalist Theory and the Foundations of Black America* (New York: Oxford University Press, 1987). On the rhythmic lineages, see Gary Stewart, *Breakout: Profiles in African Rhythm* (Chicago: University of Chicago Press, 1992). On black musicality, see Fred Moten, *In the Break: The Aesthetics of the Black Radical Tradition* (Minneapolis: University of Minnesota Press, 2003). On jookin' and the history of house parties, see Katrina Hazzard Gordon, *Jookin': The Rise of Social Dance Formations in African American Culture* (Philadelphia: Temple University Press, 1990). And on genealogies of blackness in dance, see Brenda Dixon Gottschild, *The Black Dancing Body: A Geography from Coon to Cool* (New York: Palgrave Macmillan, 2005); Brenda Dixon Gottschild, *Digging the Africanist Presence in American Performance: Dance and Other Contexts* (Westport, CT: Praeger, 1996).

87. See John Lowell Lewis, *Ring of Liberation: Deceptive Discourse in Brazilian Capoeira* (Chicago: University of Chicago Press, 1992); Maya Talmon-Chvaicer, *The Hidden History of Capoeira: A Collision of Cultures in the Brazilian Battle Dance* (Austin: University of Texas, 2007). On the diasporic spread of rhythm, see Barbara Browning, *Infectious Rhythm: Metaphors of Contagion and the Spread of African Culture* (New York: Routledge, 1998).

88. For an account of suburban pastoralism, see John R. Stilgoe, *Borderland:*

Origins of the American Suburb, 1820–1939 (New Haven, CT: Yale University Press, 1989). The relation of gender and labor to the emergence of amusement parks is described in Kathy Peiss, *Cheap Amusements: Working Women and Leisure in Turn-of-the-Century New York* (Philadelphia: Temple University Press, 1986). The revisionist turn in suburban history that examines racial and class diversity and the impact on governance and political economy is in Kevin M. Kruse and Thomas J. Sugrue, *The New Suburban History* (Chicago: University of Chicago Press, 2006). The placement of postwar U.S. suburbanization in the context of globalization, which situates the limits to expansion in the 1970s, is in Robert A. Beauregard, *When America Became Suburban* (Minneapolis: University of Minnesota Press, 2006).

89. Jeffrey Stanton, *Venice, California: Coney Island of the Pacific* (Venice, CA: Donahue, 2005).

90. F. T. Marinetti, "The Futurist Manifesto," available at http://cscs.umich .edu/~crshalizi/T4PM/futurist-manifesto.html, accessed July 12, 2012.

91. John Tierney, "24 Miles, 4 Minutes and 834 M.P.H., All in One Jump," *New York Times*, October 14, 2012, available at http://www.nytimes.com, accessed July 12, 2012. Baumgartner broke records set fifty years earlier by Joe Kittinger, when such feats were part of research and training for government-organized space travel. Baumgartner's feat, at which Kittinger, eighty-four, was present to talk the younger man through the jump, was also touted as having research purposes for rescue and bailout of travelers and tourists on commercial space expeditions.

92. Garrett Soden, *Falling: How Our Greatest Fear Became Our Greatest Thrill—A History* (New York: W. W. Norton, 2003), 138–139.

93. Ibid., 247.

94. For an account that entertains multiple indigenous sources (Hawaiian and Peruvian) of surfing and outlines major developments, see Matt Warshaw, *The History of Surfing* (San Francisco: Chronicle Books, 2010).

95. Jamie Brisick, *Have Board, Will Travel: The Definitive History of Surf, Skate, and Snow* (New York: HarperCollins, 2004), 69, quoted in Holly Thorpe, *Snowboarding Bodies in Theory and Practice* (Houndmills, UK: Palgrave Macmillan, 2011), 23. Thorpe's book, based on her own participation, complicates some of the masculinist and homosocial frameworks that frequently inform boarding culture.

96. For an overview of the emergence of skateboarding that makes the transposition from surfing explicit, see Michael Brooke, *The Concrete Wave: The History of Skateboarding* (Toronto: Warwick, 1999). For other insider accounts, see Jocko Weyland, *The Answer Is Never: A Skateboarder's History of the World* (New York: Grove, 2002); Tony Hawk, *Hawk: Occupation Skateboarder* (New York: HarperCollins, 2000); Cole Louison, *The Impossible: Rodney Mullen, Ryan Scheckler and the Fantastic History of Skateboarding* (Guilford, CT: Lyons, 2011).

97. Patrick Laviolette, *Extreme Landscapes of Leisure: Not a Hap-Hazardous Sport* (Surrey, UK: Ashgate, 2011), 176.

98. For documentation of these practices at their inception and for a treatment of the cultural and geopolitical surround, captured on film by the participants, see Stacy Peralta, dir., *Dogtown and Z-Boys*, Columbia Tri-Star, Culver City, CA, 2001.

99. Iain Borden, "Another Pavement, Another Beach: Skateboarding and the Performative Critique of Architecture," in *Reclaiming the Streets*, ed. Ariadne Urlus and Clint Van Der Hartt (Rotterdam, Netherlands: Post Editions, 2011), 31–51.

100. Jeff Howe, "Drawing Lines: A Report from the Extreme World (*sic*)," in *To the Extreme: Alternative Sports Inside and Out*, ed. Robert E. Rinehart and Synthia Sydnor (Albany: State University of New York Press, 2003), 367–368.

101. "HNWIs Thrill Seekers Enjoy Extreme Sports in Bahamas," *Bahamas Investor*, January 2012, available at http://www.thebahamasinvestor.com, accessed January 2012.

102. Susan Casey, *The Wave: In Pursuit of Rogues, Freaks, and Giants of the Ocean* (New York: Doubleday, 2010), 6.

103. Ibid., 17.

104. The California African American Museum's "How We Roll," an exhibition about the history of African American skateboarding culture, surveyed the four decades of the art, photography, and culture of skateboarding as an all-inclusive sport. For documentation, see the short film *How We Roll*, directed and edited by Suziie Wang, available at http://skateboarding.transworld.net, accessed September 15, 2012.

105. Emily Chivers Yochim, *Skate Life: Re-imagining White Masculinity* (Ann Arbor: University of Michigan Press, 2010), 15, 23.

106. Gilles Deleuze "Postscript on Control Societies," in *Negotiations, 1972–1990*, trans. Martin Joughin (New York: Columbia University Press, 1995), 181.

107. The problem of incorporation is raised in Iain Borden, *Skateboarding, Space and the City: Architecture, the Body and Performative Critique* (Oxford: Berg, 2001). Similar issues are raised for extreme sport more generally by some of the contributors to Robert E. Rinehart and Synthia Sydnor, eds., *To the Extreme: Alternative Sports Inside and Out* (Albany: State University of New York Press, 2003). See esp. Robert E. Rinehart's chapter "Dropping into Sight: Commodification and Co-optation of In-Line Skating" (27–51) and Duncan Humphreys's "Selling Out Snowboarding: The Alternative Response to Commercial Cooptation" (407–428). The racial politics of whiteness in such extreme sports are analyzed in Kyle Kus, *Revolt of the White Athlete: Race, Media and the Emergence of Extreme Athletes in America* (New York: Peter Lang, 2007). Yochim, *Skate Life*, examines identity negotiation in boarding cultures.

108. Guy Debord, *Society of the Spectacle* (New York: Zone, 1995).

109. See Annette Michelson, ed., *Kino-Eye: The Writing of Dziga Vertov* (Berkeley: University of California Press, 1984).

110. Don Power, "YouTube versus Vimeo: Which Video Site Is Best for Business? *Sprout Social*, August 31, 2011, available at http://sproutsocial.com, accessed July 15, 2012.

111. See Tiziana Terranova, *Network Culture: Politics for the Information Age* (London: Pluto, 2004).

112. For a critical look at the advent of self-help as a vast cultural industry that displaces forms of organizational association such as labor unions, see Micki McGee, *Self-Help, Inc.: Makeover Culture in American Life* (New York: Oxford University Press, 2006).

113. The notion of moral panic was developed in British cultural studies of youth culture and crime and has morphed into a generalized trope of war on domestic populations. The seminal study is Stuart Hall, Chas Critcher, Tony Jefferson, John Clarke, and Brian Roberts, *Policing the Crisis: Mugging, the State and Law and Order* (New York: Holmes and Meier, 1978). The updated reflection in the U.S. context of generational abandonment is in Larry Grossberg, *Caught in the Crossfire: Kids, Politics and America's Future* (Boulder, CO: Paradigm, 2005).

114. For an account of this elaborate but unseen and undervalued mass of creative labor that underwrites the art world, see Gregory Sholette, *Dark Matter: Art and Politics in the Age of Enterprise Culture* (London: Pluto, 2010).

115. For a productive complication of the polarity between network and organization, see Ned Rossiter, *Organized Networks: Media Theory, Creative Labour, New Institutions* (Rotterdam: Netherlands Architecture Institute Press, 2006).

116. The *Oxford English Dictionary* provides this double etymology of prayer and debt, the latter of which takes on meaning as a claim to inhabit a space through the will of others—hence, a "right, tenancy, etc.: held or enjoyed by the favour of and at the pleasure of another person; vulnerable to the will or decision of others": *OED Online*, s.v. "precarious, adj.," available at http://www.oed.com/view/Entry/149548?redirectedFrom=precarious#eid, accessed January 9, 2006. This internal movement of precarity with respect to linguistic as well as labor and exchange value is exquisitely established by Angela Mitropoulos. She observes, "Precarity might well have us teetering, it might even do so evocatively, for better and often worse, praying for guarantees and, at times, shields that often turn out to be fortresses. But it is yet to dispense with, for all its normative expressions, a relationship to the adjective: to movement, however uncertain": Angela Mitropoulous, "Precari-us?" *Mute Magazine*, January 9, 2006, available at http://www.metamute.org, accessed January 9, 2006. Also insightful are *Fibreculture Journal*, no. 5 (2005), a special issue titled "Precarious Labor" edited by Brett Neilson and Ned Rossiter, available at http://five.fibreculturejournal.org, accessed October 3, 2007; Gerald Raunig, "The Monster Precariat," Translate website, October 3, 2007, available at http://translate.eipcp.net, accessed November 11, 2011; Franco Berardi, *After the Future* (Oakland, CA: AK Press, 2011); Julieta Aranda, Brian Kuan Wood, and Anton Vidokle, *Are You Working Too Much? Post-Fordism, Precarity and the Labour of Art* (Berlin: Sternberg, 2011).

CONCLUSION

1. See Campbell Jones, *Can the Market Speak?* (London: Zero Books, 2012).

2. Jessica Silver-Greenberg and Susanne Craig, "JPMorgan Trading Loss May Reach $9 Billion," *New York Times*, June 28, 2012, available at http://dealbook.nytimes.com/2012/06/28/jpmorgan-trading-loss-may-reach-9-billion/. Dimon, considered the Obama administration's favorite banker, called the use of federally insured deposits for high-risk derivatives trading a one-off stupid mistake, even as he fought federal regulations that might have provided preventative oversight for such errors. Jon Corzine, similarly positioned as an insider, oversaw the bankruptcy of investment house MF Global to bankruptcy through high-risk debt: Ben Protess, Michael J. De la Merced, and Susanne Craig, "Regulators Investigating MF Global for Missing Money," *New York Times*, October 31, 2011, available at http://dealbook.nytimes.com/2011/10/31/regulators-investigating-mf-global.

3. Andrew W. Lo, "Reading about the Financial Crisis: A 21-Book Review," *Journal of Economic Literature* 50, no. 1 (March 2012): 151–178.

4. Gayatri Chakravorty Spivak, *An Aesthetic Education in the Era of Globalization* (Cambridge, MA: Harvard University Press, 2012).

5. Gregory Bateson, Don D. Jackson, Jay Haley, and John H. Weakland, "Toward a Theory of Schizophrenia," *Behavioral Science* 1, no. 4 (1956), reprinted in Gregory Bateson, *Steps toward an Ecology of Mind* (San Francisco: Chandler, 1972), 156.

Index

accountability: how to restore, 27; lack of, 15, 33; of nonprofit organizations, 92–93; TARP and, 16, 17
achievement versus ascription, 163–166
Aerosmith, 188
African American community, skate-boarding in, 204, 250n104
African dance, 165, 192, 245n43
"after," 214–215
agnotology, 49
agricultural prices, derivative contracts for, 51
AIG (American International Group), 13
air quality, pricing of, 53–54
Akula, Vikram, 97–98
Alexander, F. Matthias, 173
Allport, Floyd, 111, 115
Allport, Justen, 203
alternative computing, 138
alternative currency, 223
Alva, Tony, 200
American Dance Festival, 164
American Enterprise Institute, 93–94
American International Group (AIG), 13
"the American people," 110
Anderson, Benedict, 102
antagonism, 213–215
anthropomorphizing of finance, 216
antiheroes, 196
Apache Line, 188

Appalachian Spring (Copland/Graham), 165, 166
approval ratings, 120
Arab Spring, 141
arbitrage, 57, 216–217; and dance, 147; regulatory, 58–59
architectural modernism, 149–150, 242n9
Armstrong, Neil, 179
Arnold, Matthew, 152
Arrighi, Giovanni, 242n6
artistic labor, subsidy of, 146, 242n5
ascription versus achievement, 163–166
"Aspects of the Downward Slide" (Stecyk), 200
assemblage of public, 107–108
automobile manufacturing, 61
automobile workers, wages of, 63, 231n78
autonomy of culture, 153, 155–157
Ayache, Elie, 31–32

backing out, 66
bailout program, 2, 5, 8–9, 13–17, 68
Bair, Sheila, 18
Balanchine, George, 164
ballet, 161–163, 244nn34–35
Bambaataa, Afrika, 189, 191, 193, 207
Banes, Sally, 170
Bank for International Settlements (BIS), 227n27, 230n63
bank reserves after bailout, 17

Bartels, Larry, 117–118
Basel Accords, 59
Bataille, Georges, 48–50, 75, 160, 222
Bateson, Gregory, 224
Battery Park City, 150
Baumgartner, Felix, 196, 249n91
b-boys, 187, 189, 193
Beauchamp, Pierre, 167
Beck, Ulrich, 47–48
behavioral finance, 26
belief, 26
Bell, Daniel, 153
bell curve, 31
benchmark, 63
Bennett, Tony, 152
Bernanke, Ben: bailout plan of, 13–14,
    18–21; and failure of predictions, 27,
    32–33; and knowledge failure, 23; and
    market failure, 26; and neoclassical
    paradigm, 25
Berrer, Danny, 198
Berry, Chuck, 192
Beunza, Daniel, 66
b-girls, 189
Bill and Melinda Gates Foundation, 102
BIS (Bank for International Settlements),
    227n27, 230n63
Black, Fischer, 68–69, 144
"black swans," 28–33
Blumer, Herbert, 111
boarding culture, 10–11, 194–205; gravity
    hero in, 196; logic of appropriation in,
    203; populations at risk and, 202–205;
    skateboarding in, 197–202; snowboard-
    ing in, 197; surfing in, 196–197; urban
    getaways and, 194–195; urban ruins
    and, 205; women in, 204–205
Bomba, 187
"Bonapartism," 36
boom boxes, 188
Borden, Iain, 201
bounded rationality, 58
Bourdieu, Pierre, 111
Bournonville, August, 161
Bower, Bryan ("Slink"), 187
Braudel, Fernand, 242n6
break, 189
breakdancing, 187–188, 193
breaking in hip-hop, 192–193
Bretton Woods, 149, 156, 178

bridge, 189
Brilliant, Eleanor, 87
broken windows theory, 186, 247n73
Brown, James, 187, 189
Brown, Michael, 76
Brown, Trisha, 169, 179–185, 186, 207
Bryan, Dick, 59–67, 69, 76, 114
Buffett, Warren, 102
Burke, Colin B., 233–234n4
Burnside, Cara Beth, 204
Burt, Ronald, 115
"Burt," 200
Burtleman, Larry, 200
Bush, George W., 118
Bush, Vannevar, 137

Cage, John, 168
calculative agent, 39, 43
California, Proposition 13 in, 103
California Master Plan, 34
Callon, Michel, 39–40
Campbell, Clive (DJ Kool Herc), 189
Cam'ron, 190
cap and trade, 54
Capital (Marx), 76
capitalism: with derivatives, 59–67; as
    means of privatizing wealth through
    socializing production, 22
capital reserve requirements, 71
capoeira, 193
"carbon democracy," 127–128
Cardona, Wally, 181
Carmines, Al, 169
Carnegie, Andrew, 102
Case Shiller index, 64
Casey, Susan, 203–204
celebrity complex, 119–120
celebrity in public opinion polling, 9–10
centralized planning, 23, 24
centrifugal forces, 171
centripetal forces, 171
CGAP (Consultancy Group to Assist the
    Poor), 99–100
charismatic leaders, 130–131
charitable giving: amount of, 94, 234–
    235n15; corporate tax rates and, 94–95;
    and economic growth and general well-
    being, 93–94
charitable organizations, 88, 233–234n4
charitable trusts, 83

charter schools, 101
Childs, Lucinda, 169
choice in politics, 122
choreography, 167–168, 207–208
church attendance, 134
cipher in hip-hop, 190
circle in hip-hop, 190
civic participation, 132–134; versus contentious political activity, 139, 241n102; trajectories of, 139
class decomposition, 36
classical kinestheme, 161–163, 171
Clausewitz, Carl von, 244n35
clearinghouses, 52
climate change and extreme surfing, 203–204
Clinton, Bill, 91
clustering around the mean, 31
Code of Federal Regulations, 55
cognitive surplus, 137
Coleman, Gabriella, 136, 240n94
collaboration, 172–174
collateral damage in Iraq, 46
collectivity, 172–174
college education, 33–34, 221
Colon, Richard "Crazy Legs," 187, 193
colonial mimesis, 126–128
colonization, 77; and culture, 153–155
Commission on Foundations and Private Philanthropy, 87
Commission on Private Philanthropy and Public Needs, 87
commodity, fundamental logic of, 76
commons, caring for, 84
Compartamos, 97
competition, 23, 24, 26
complaint, culture of, 125–126
computer technology and politics, 136–138
Coney Island, 194
conflicted conservatives, 117
Congressional Oversight Panel, 16–17
conjuncture: in dance, 148–161; in finance, 223
Conley, Dalton, 89–90
consensus in politics, 121
conservatives, conflicted, 117
constructive rest, 183
Consultancy Group to Assist the Poor (CGAP), 99–100

consumer confidence, 120
consumption taxes, 85
contact improvisation, 173, 177, 246n56
contemporary dance, 246n54
contentious political activity versus civic participation, 139, 241n102
contestability of fundamental value, 62–63
contraction in dance, 164–166
"Contract with America," 91
control, language of, 205
Copland, Aaron, 165
Cornelius, Don, 192
corporate tax rates and charitable giving, 94–95
Corzine, Jon, 222, 251n2
counterculture, 153–154
counter-performativity, 228–229n45
Countrywide, 72
"Crazy Legs" (Richard Colon), 187, 193
creative capitalism, 98
credit, 223
credit liquidity, bailout and, 68
crises, 1–2, 5–6, 20
criticality, excess of, 123–126, 130–133, 140–142
critical participation, 82–83
Crossley Center for Public Opinion Research, 110
crowdsourcing, 136–137
cultural differentiation, 152
"cultural discount," 242n5
cultural experiences, derivatives of, 156–157
cultural knowledge, 220
cultural processes, cyclic versus periodic nature of, 156
cultural scenes from people in movement, 157–158
culture, 151–154; autonomy of, 153, 155–157; of configurability, 188; of measure, 112, 120
culture jamming, 138
culture wars, 10, 126, 239n82
Cunningham, Merce: and abstract objects, 175; and Trisha Brown, 181; and collectivity, 172; and master-apprentice model, 171; and modern kinestheme, 164; and pastiche of styles, 174; and postmodern kinestheme, 168
currency, alternative, 223

currency exchange, 148–149
currency sovereignty, 148–149
cycle, 223

dance, 10–11, 143–212; and arbitrage, 147;
    boarding culture as, 194–205; Trisha
    Brown and, 179–185; classical, 161–163,
    171; colonization and decolonization in,
    145; toward conjuncture in, 148–161;
    definition and use of term, 143–144; as
    derivative, 147, 206–212; ethology of,
    158; and finance, 143–144; generative
    risk in, 206–212; hip-hop, 185–194;
    learning from, 144–145; mobiliza-
    tion through, 145–146, 148; modern,
    163–166, 171; and moving derivatives,
    177–179; multiplicities in, 144–145;
    particularity versus universalism of,
    241n2; as political, 159; postmodern,
    166–177; and skateboarding, 201–202;
    social kinesthetics of, 158–161
dance collectives, 173–174
dancers, wages of, 146, 241–242n4
dance studies, 241n2
"dark pools," 58
The DAS Swaps and Financial Derivatives
    Library, 71
Davis, William, 169
Debord, Guy, 207
debt ceiling, 42–43
de-centered social kinesthetics, 10–11,
    143–212; boarding culture in, 194–205;
    Trisha Brown in, 179–185; classical
    kinestheme in, 161–163, 171; toward
    conjuncture in, 148–161; generative
    risk in, 206–212; hip-hop in, 185–194;
    modern kinestheme in, 163–166, 171;
    movement sensibilities in, 171–173,
    177–178, 246n57; moving derivatives in,
    177–179; postmodern kinestheme in,
    166–177
decolonization, 77, 126; and culture,
    154–155, 157; in postmodern dance,
    171–172
decolonization movement, 10–11
decolonizing kinesthesia, 215
deconstruction, 224
Deep Song (Graham), 176
Deepwater Horizon well, 1–2, 37, 228n39
de-familiarization, 180
Deitch, Jeffrey, 247n72

delegation in politics, 121
Deleuze, Gilles, 32, 205
deliberation in politics, 122
Delsarte, François, 173
demanding capital, 98
democracy, 82–83; "carbon," 127–128; and
    colonial mimesis, 126–128; and culture
    wars, 126; defined, 122; democratization
    as enemy of, 126–128, 131; and energy
    flows, 126–130; and excess of critical-
    ity, 123–126, 130–133, 140–142; oil
    extraction and, 127–129; and pluralism,
    124–125; positing of ideal or origi-
    nal model of, 126–127; technological
    innovation and, 136–138; voluntary
    associations and, 86
Democracy in America (Tocqueville), 86
Democratic affiliation, 116–117
democratic deficit, 125–126
democratization: as enemy of democracy,
    126–128, 131; of knowledge, 33–37;
    limits of, 125–126
Denishawn, 165
Depression, 87
depth of modern dance, 166
deregulation, 55, 104–106
derivative(s), 4–5; capitalism with, 59–67;
    for committing to one decision while
    keeping open others, 58; and contest-
    ability of fundamental value, 62–63; of
    cultural experiences, 156–157; dance as,
    147, 206–212; defined, 51; and distinc-
    tion between money and capital, 61–62;
    as double unbind, 224; as end of econ-
    omy, 74; exchange-traded, 227n27; as
    financial instruments to manage risks,
    7; guidelines for constructing, 71; his-
    tory of, 50–51, 229n61; as meta-capital,
    60–61; moving, 177–205; as "off-balance
    sheet" investments, 64; over-the-coun-
    ter, 227n27; politics as, 121–123, 141;
    regulation of, 71; regulatory capacity
    of, 64–65, 70–71; social logic of, 4, 6–7,
    52–53, 73–79; and treating people in
    parts, 67–68; as un-knowledge of the
    future, 32; unmanageable risk generated
    by, 4; value at risk and, 29–31
derivative contracts, 51, 227n27; for
    agricultural prices, 51; on both sides of
    transaction, 51; clearinghouses for, 52;
    records of, 230n63; value of, 52, 56

derivative knowledge, 213–224
derivative logics, from nonknowledge to, 50–53
derivative trading, 51–52; volume of, 222, 251n2
derive, etymological root of, 121
Derrida, Jacques, 32
DeSoto-Carr, replacement of tenements in, 149–150, 242n9
de Vlamingh, Willem, 31
Dewey, Thomas E., 111
differentiation, cultural, 152
digital platforms, 135–138, 240n94
Dimon, Jamie, 222, 251n2
disasters, 1–2, 5–6
discourse, 110
dis-embeddedness, 38
disintermediation, 56–57, 70
dissensus, 121–122
distributed aesthetics, 243n29
diversification for risk reduction, 27
diversity of hip-hop, 191–192
DJ(s), 188, 189
DJ Kool Herc (Clive Campbell), 189
Dodd, Chris, 13
Dogtown and Z-Boys (film), 200
do-it-yourself movements, 221
dollar, currency exchange rates pegged to, 148–149
donor exemptions, 85–86, 89
double bind, 224
downrock, 187
downward mobility, 228n41
Dudley, Jane, 176
Duncan, Isadora, 176
Dunn, Judith, 169
Dunn, Robert, 168, 169, 171, 180, 183
Durden, Moncell, 190
Dynamic Rockers, 188

Earned Income Tax Credit, 118
economic growth, private giving and, 93–94
Economic Recovery Tax Act (1981), 90–91
economics, embeddedness of, 39–40
economy, 8–9, 13–79; before, 67–73; breach of delimiting boundaries of, 13–14; capitalism with derivatives in, 59–67; chancing prediction in, 27–33; crisis of, 77–78; ends of, 37–43, 74; far from equilibrium regulation in, 53–59;

government intervention in, 21–23; inclusion and exclusion in, 67; knowledge and price in, 23–43; lost expertise in, 33–37; nonknowledge in, 43–73; from nonknowledge to derivative logics in, 50–53; and sociality of derivatives, 73–79; as system of interdependent parts working together, 22; as ungovernable, 21
education: measures of, 101; postsecondary, 33–34, 221
Einstein on the Beach (Glass/Childs), 169
election outcomes, forecasting of, 110–111
Elizabeth II (Queen of England), 18, 20, 27, 226n11
embeddedness, 39–40
Emergency Economic Stabilization Act (2008), 15
Emerson, Ruth, 169, 170, 172
energy flows and democracy, 126–130
Engblom, Skip, 200
An Engine, Not a Camera (MacKenzie), 42, 228–229n45
Enron, 35, 56, 70, 228n36
entitlement programs, 94
epistemic movement, 158
equilibrium regulation, 53–59
euro-dollars, 149
exceptions: culture of attachment to, 119–121; in public opinion polling, 9–10
excess in politics, 123–126
exchange rates, 148–149
exchange-traded derivatives, 227n27
"exhibitionary complex," 152
expert(s), mistrust of, 33
expertise, 221–222; lost, 33–37
expert knowledge, 24
external forces, 40, 41
externality, 40, 41
"extreme action choreographer," 180
extreme sports, 198–199, 202–203
extreme surfing, 203–204

faith-based organizations, 91
fallacy of the group mind, 111
Fama, Eugene, 172
Fanon, Franz, 77
FASB (Financial Accounting Standards Board), 56
fascism, 38

Federal Deposit Insurance Corporation, 18
Federal Housing Administration, 68
Federal Register, 55
Federal Reserve, 20
feeling, structure of, 242n7
Feldstein, Martin, 89
feminist performance art, 246n54
Feuillet, Raoul Auger, 167
Filer Commission, 87
finance: as antagonym, 213–215; anthropomorphizing of, 216; dance and, 143–144; etymology of, 11, 214; sociality of, 216–217
financial accounting, 56–57
Financial Accounting Standards Board (FASB), 56
financial bailout, 2, 5, 8–9, 13–17, 68
financial crisis, 7–8, 14–23; aftermath of, 20–22; criticism of bailout for, 16–17; as emergency, 18–19; as knowledge failure, 20, 23; metaphors for, 22; need of bailout for, 15–16; negotiation of bailout for, 13–15; as reset button, 22; restoring faith after, 20; versus self-correction, 18, 19–20
financial engineering, 56–57, 71
financialization, 55–56, 69–73, 178, 232n86
Fisher, Irving, 144
501(c)(3) organizations, 83–84, 85
501(c)(4) organizations, 91
flare, 187
Flores, Juan, 187
Florida, high-speed rail line in, 68, 231–232n84
Ford Foundation, 86
Forti, Simone, 180
forward movement, 166, 245n45
Foster, Susan, 160, 167–168, 174
Foucault, Michel, 39, 40, 158, 205
fractals, 28, 115
frame, 40, 41
Frank, Thomas, 117
Franko, Mark, 159, 164, 176, 243–244n30
Freeth, George, 197
Fried, Amy, 111
Frisby, Heath, 199
Fukushima Daiichi nuclear reactor, 37, 228n39
Fuller, Loie, 176
Futurist Manifesto, 195
futurity, 142

Gallup, George, 110
Gallup, Inc., 110
Garnerin, André-Jacques, 196
Gates, Bill, 98
GDP (gross domestic product), private giving and, 93–94
Geithner, Timothy, 21
Gelfand, Alan ("Ollie"), 201
General Agreement on Tariffs and Trade (1948), 55
generational shifts in politics, 134–136
generative risk, 206–212
Gerlach, Brad, 203
"Get on the Good Foot" (James Brown), 187
Gingrich, Newt, 91
Glass, Philip, 169
global war on terror, 2, 46, 47
Goldberg, Steven, 100–101
Goldman Sachs, 13, 30, 100, 222
Google, 97–98
Gordon, David, 169
government intervention in economy, 21–23
grading software, 114, 238n63
graduation rates, 101
Graham, Martha: Trisha Brown and, 180; Merce Cunningham and, 168; versus Judson Dance Theater, 172, 173, 174; and modern kinestheme, 164–166; political citation by, 176; use of folk idioms by, 203; use of "primitive sources" by, 245n43
Grameen Bank, 96, 99
Grandmaster Flash (Joseph Saddler), 189
Grand Union, 173
grant making, 96
gravity hero, 196
"great moderation," 72
Great Society programs, 86
"The Great Transformation," 38
Greenspan, Alan, 18, 19, 20, 58–59
Gries, Lance, 183, 184, 247n69
gross domestic product (GDP), private giving and, 93–94
group mind, fallacy of, 111
Grunberg, Emile, 58

Habermas, Jürgen, 110
Hais, Michael D., 135
Hall, Peter Dobkin, 88, 233–234n4

Halprin, Anna, 180
Hamilton, Laird, 203
happiness indices, 120
Harris, Rennie, 190
Harvey, David, 76, 155–156
Hawk, Tony, 198
Hawkins, Erick, 164, 174
Hay, Alex, 169
Hay, Deborah, 169
Hayek, Frederick, 23–26, 27, 33, 48
health insurance benefits, 90
hedging, 57
"Helper's High," 93
Herbst, Susan, 113
herd mentality, 31
Herko, Fred, 169, 170
"hidden welfare state," 104
hierarchy of preferences, 23
higher education, 33–34, 221
high-speed rail line in Florida, 68, 231–232n84
hip-hop, 10–11, 185–194; bounces in, 193; and breakdancing, 187–188; break in, 189; breaking in, 192–193; circle or cipher in, 190; commercialization of, 193–194; diffusion of, 193–194; diversity of, 191–192; East Coast versus West Coast, 193; homophobia and misogyny in, 190–191; Ring Shout in, 192; sampling in, 188–190; and tagging, 186; and urban ruins, 185–186
Ho, Jeff, 200
holistic approach, 181
Holm, Hanya, 164, 166
home mortgage interest deduction, 90
homophobia in hip-hop, 190–191
Hoover, Herbert, 86
horizontal propulsion, shift from vertical lift to, 208–209
Horst, Louis, 168, 171, 180
house parties, 192
Howe, Jeff, 135, 201–202
Hultman, Irene, 183
humanity, concept of, 218–219
Humphrey, Doris, 164, 166, 184
Hurricane Katrina, 2

IASB (International Accounting Standards Board), 56
identity, 77, 126–127
ideokinesis, 173

ignorance and social order, 25–26
income taxes, 85
independent voters, 116–117
indexing, 100–102
inequality, 118–119
information, privileging of, 25
information asymmetry(ies), 26; non-knowledge as, 44; private, 58
information science, 137–138
instability in postmodern dance, 184–185
"Instant Chance," 170
intellectual property, 53, 55–56; in music industry, 188, 189–190
intelligence information, 45
interdependence, 220
interdisciplinarity, 223
interests in pluralism, 124
intergenerational downward mobility, 228n41
Internal Revenue Service (IRS), 84, 85, 88
International Accounting Standards Board (IASB), 56
International Monetary Fund, 149
Internet and democracy, 136–137
investment clubs, 73
Iraq, U.S. invasion of, 45–46, 47
IRS (Internal Revenue Service), 84, 85, 88
Ithaca dollars, 223

Jameson, Frederic, 154–156, 242n6
Japan, earthquake and tsunami in, 2
Johnson, Torger, 198
Jooks, 192
journalism, participatory, 138
JPMorgan Chase, 33, 222, 251n2
Judson Dance Theater, 168–177, 180–181, 201, 208
JumpRope, 238n63
Jung, Karl, 165
Juralewicz, Nicole, 183

Kaahumanu (Queen), 197
Kamehameha (King), 197
Kant, Immanuel, 163
Kaplan Fund, 87
Karczag, Eva, 183
Kelly, Thomas, 33
Keynes, John Maynard, 149
kinestheme(s), 158; classical, 161–163, 171; modern, 163–166, 171; postmodern, 166–177

kinesthetics, 158
Kinney, Abbot, 194
Kinsey, Alfred, 87
kite surfing, 202–203
Kittinger, Joe, 249n91
Klein, Naomi, 236n43
Klein, Susan, 181–182
Klein Technique, 182
Knight, Frank, 28–29
knockdowns, 187–188
knowledge: as credit, 4; cultural, 220; democratization of, 33–37; equal dispersal of, 24; expert versus nonexpert, 24; industrialization of, 3; as intellectual labor, 221; of power, 220; and price, 23–26; private, 58; public, 58, 107–121; of the social, 4; utility of, 23–24; value of, 34
knowledge-based productivity, 3
knowledge economy, 3
knowledge equilibrium, 26
knowledge failure: economic crisis as, 20, 23; and war, 45–47
knowledge limitations, 2, 219, 222
knowledge practice, professionalization and formalization of, 221
knowledge production, 3
knowledge society, 4
knowledge surplus, 3–4
known unknown, 44–45
Kohn, Margaret, 154
Kondratieff, Nikolai, 242n6
Krippendorff, Klaus, 112–113
Krippner, Greta, 232n86
Krugman, Paul, 29

Laban, Rudolf, 173
labor costs, 73
labor movements, modern dance and, 159–160, 243–244n30
Laclau, Ernesto, 77
language of control, 205
Lara, Gregory, 183
Last Poets, 188
La Sylphide (Taglioni/Bournonville), 161–163, 167
lateral mobility, 10, 208–209
Latino dance, 187
Laviolette, Patrick, 199
Lazarsfeld, Paul, 110
Lehman Brothers, 13

LETS (Local Exchange Trading Schemes), 223
liberal arts, disciplines of, 217–218
Lievrouw, Leah, 138
Lippmann, Walter, 111
Literary Digest, public opinion polls by, 110–111
Little Richard, 192
Lo, Andrew, 222
lobbying by 501(c)(4) organizations, 91
Local Exchange Trading Schemes (LETS), 223
locking, 188
logic, 159
Long-Term Capital Management hedge fund collapse, 70, 228n36
Losh, Elizabeth, 137
Louis XIV (King), 162, 167, 176
Lucas, Carolyn, 183
Lyotard, Jean-François, 155–156

MacKenzie, Donald, 42, 184–185, 228–229n45
Madden, Diane, 183
Malkiel, Burton, 172
managers, 24
Mandel, Ernest, 156, 242n6
Mandelbrot, Benoit, 28, 115
"the man on the spot," 24
"Man Walking down the Side of a Building" (Trisha Brown), 179–180, 181
Man with a Movie Camera (Vertov), 208
Marinetti, Filippo Tommaso, 195
market: emergence of, 37–38; as self-correcting, 18, 19–20, 38
market equilibrium, 53–59
market failure, 26
market research, 110
"marking," 170
Marsh, James, 151
Martin, Isaac William, 104
Martin, John, 158
Marx, Karl: and capitalism with derivatives, 60; on class decomposition, 36; and knowledge of the social, 4; and operations in finance, 5; and sociality of derivatives, 75–76, 79; and temporal cycles, 242n6
mash up, 188
Maslow, Sophie, 176
mass culture, 153
mass media, public opinion and, 113

master-apprentice model, 171–172
McBride, Keally, 154
McCain, John, 21, 135
McCarthy, Anna, 137–138
McCarthy, Joseph, 87
McKinsey and Company, 230n63
McNamara, Garrett, 203
measurable assessment, 221
mechanism in neoclassical approach, 25
mediated mobilization, 138–139
Medicaid, 94
Medicare, 89, 94
Merton, Robert, 228n36
"metakinetic exchange," 159
Mettler, Suzanne, 90
microcredit, 96–100
microfinancing, 96–100
middle-class decline, 89–90, 228n41
Milgram, Stanley, 112
military drill and ballet, 163, 244nn34–35
millennials, 135–136
Mirowski, Philip, 25, 44, 226–227n23
mirror, 175
misogyny in hip-hop, 190–191
Mitchell, Tim, 40–41, 43, 127
Mitropoulos, Angela, 251n116
mobilization: critique of, 216; through
    dance, 145–146, 148; mediated,
    138–139; versus representation, 145
models: limitations of, 31; overreliance
    on, 27
modernism versus modernity, 152–153
modern kinestheme, 163–166, 171; and
    labor movements, 159–160, 243–244n30
Modigiliani, Franco, 58
MoMing, 173
Monk, Meredith, 169
the Monkees, 189
monopoly, 23
Moore, Jim, 150
moral hazard, 16
moral panic, 210, 250n113
Morgan Stanley, 13
Morrison, Jim, 194
mortgage(s), securitization of, 72
mortgage interest tax deductions, 104
mortgage relief program, 68, 231–232n84
Motley Fool, 73
Mouffe, Chantal, 77, 121–122
movement practices, 10–11, 143–212;
    boarding culture as, 194–205; Trisha

Brown and, 179–185; classical kinestheme as, 161–163, 171; toward conjuncture in, 148–161; epistemic, 158;
generative risk in, 206–212; hip-hop
as, 185–194; modern kinestheme as,
163–166, 171; moving derivatives in,
177–179; postmodern kinestheme as,
166–177
Movement Research, 175
moving derivatives, 177–205; boarding
    culture as, 194–205; Trisha Brown as,
    179–185; hip-hop as, 185–194
multiculturalism, 77
Mumford, Lewis, 150
music downloading, 189–190
music industry, intellectual property in,
    188, 189–190
music sharing, 189–190

Napolitan, Anthony, 198–199
Nasworthy, Frank, 199
National Income Accounts, 88
National Philanthropic Trust, 234–235n15
Native American dance, 165, 245n43
neoclassical paradigm, 25, 226–227n23
neoliberalism, 8, 104–106, 236n43, 237n44
"new economy," 72
New York Times on debt ceiling, 42–43
NGO (nongovernmental organization),
    84, 96, 100, 131
Nikolais, Alwin, 164
Nocera, Joe, 29–31
Noguchi, Isamu, 165, 175
noise, 68–69
noncharitable nonprofits, 83
noncharitable organizations, 88, 233–
    234n4
nonexpert knowledge, 24
nongovernmental organization (NGO),
    84, 96, 100, 131
nonknowledge, 43–73; and capitalism with
    derivatives, 59–67; and derivative logics,
    50–53; and before economy, 67–73;
    equalization of expert and nonexpert
    decision-making preferences by, 48;
    and equilibrium regulation, 53–59; as
    information asymmetry, 44; as "knowl-
    edge that brings me to nothing," 48–50;
    known unknown as, 44–45; unknown
    known as, 44, 45; unknown unknown
    as, 45–48; and world risk society, 47–48

nonprofit organizations, 9, 83–107; accountability of, 92–93; amount of charitable giving to, 94, 234–235n15; categories of, 83–84, 88, 233–234n4; and coalitions between public and private sources of funding, 86–87; corporate tax rates and, 94–95; defined, 83; as distinct institutional sector, 88; and economic growth and general well-being, 93–94; fundraising capacity of, 102; indexing of, 100–102; large, 100; and microcredit, 96–100; midsized, 100–101; and move from public entitle-ment to self-management, 102–103; number of, 95; privatization of, 104–106; public and government scrutiny of, 87–88; during Reagan years, 90–91, 234n11; recipients of, 95; small, 100; for social justice, 101–102, 236n33; stock market–based approach to sup-porting, 100–101; "submerged state" of, 90; tax exemption of, 83, 84–86, 88–89; and venture philanthropy, 84, 96, 97, 98, 102; voluteerism in, 95–96

nonresponse bias, 112
nonviolent resistance, 169
normal distribution, 27–28
Norris, Pippa, 125

Obama, Barack: charisma of, 131; first campaign of, 121; generational support of, 135; and policies in submerged state, 90; and racism, 143
Occupy Wall Street, 141, 223
Office of Financial Stability, 15
oil extraction and democracy, 127–129
Oki, Peggy, 200, 204
"ollie," 201
Omidyar, Pierre, 98
"Once or Twice a Week I Put on Sneakers to Go Uptown" (Herko), 170
Orange County government, near-bank-ruptcy of, 70
The Order of Things (Foucault), 39
Orientalism, 165, 168, 245n43
OTC (over-the-counter) derivatives, 227n27
outliers: culture of attachment to, 119–121; public as, 109; in public opinion polling, 9–10

outperformers, culture of attachment to, 119–121
overflows, 40
over-the-counter (OTC) derivatives, 227n27

Pacific Ocean Park (POP), 194–195
parachute jumping, 196, 249n91
Parsons, Mike, 203
Parsons, Talcott, 153
participatory journalism, 138
partisanship, 116–117
party affiliation, 116–117, 238n66
pastiche of styles in postmodern dance, 174–175
Paulson, Henry, 13, 14–15, 18–21, 30
"Pax Americana," 177
Paxton, Steve, 169, 170, 174
Pelosi, Nancy, 13
Peralta, Stacy, 200, 207
performance outcomes, 221
performativity, 228–229n45
Peterson Commission, 87
Petit, Philippe, 150–151, 185, 186
petro-dollars, 149
Petronio, Stephen, 181, 183
Pew Charitable Trusts, 86
Pew Research Center, 119
"phantom public," 111
philanthropy, 84; as investment, 91–92; venture, 84, 96, 97, 98, 102
Picasso, Pablo, 165
Pilobolus, 173–174
P.&L. (profit and loss), 30
planning in economic systems, 23
Plato, 33
pluralism, 117, 124–125
Polanyi, Karl, 38, 67
political as production of sensibility, 239n78
political citation in postmodern dance, 176–177
political economy, 54
politics, 121–142; charismatic leaders in, 130–131; and civic participation, 132–134; and colonial mimesis, 126–128; consensus and delegation in, 121–122; deliberation and choice in, 122; and democratization as enemy of democracy in, 122, 126–128, 131; as derivative, 121–123, 141; excess of criticality in,

123–126, 130–133, 140–142; generational shifts in, 134–136; means to mobilize political sentiment in, 123; and pluralism, 124–125; and professional managerial class, 131–132, 240n86; proliferation of issues in, 122; social movements and, 138–139; subjects eligible to exercise rights in, 122–123; surplus and excess in, 123–126; technological innovation and, 136–138; temporality in, 142
polling industry, 9–10, 109–115
polling saturation, 112
poor, share of government benefits for, 89
POP (Pacific Ocean Park), 194–195
popping, 188
popular knowledge and celebrity complex, 119–120
popular sovereignty, 118
"populate," 211
population, etymology of, 11
portfolio insurance and stock market crash of 1987, 70
portfolio theory, 27
possessive individualism, 65–66, 231n82
postmodern architecture, 149–150, 242n9
postmodern kinestheme, 10–11, 166–177; availability to audience in, 172; and choreography, 167–168; contact improvisation in, 173; de-centered movement sensibilities in, 171–173, 177–178, 246n57; and decolonization, 172; emphasis on collectivity over individuality in, 172–174; mirror in, 175; origins of, 168–172; pastiche of styles in, 174–175; randomization in, 172; reference to what lies outside movement space in, 175–176; release technique in, 173, 181, 183–184; scores and scoring in, 169, 171–172; social and political citation in, 176–177; stability/instability in, 184–185; as turn to pedestrian, 167
postsecondary education, 33–34, 221
poststructuralist theory, 32, 224
poverty rates, 71–72, 232n89
power, knowledge of, 220
precarity, 210, 211, 212, 251n116
prediction, 27–33
preemptive action, 47
preference hierarchy, 23
presentism, 142
price, knowledge and, 23–26

price volatility, 27–28
primitives, 126
"print capitalism," 102
private knowledge, 58
privatization, 104–106
probabilities, 27, 31
Proctor, Robert, 49
professional managerial class, 34–36, 131–132, 240n86
profit and loss (P.&L.), 30
Progressive Era, 87
Proposition 13 in California, 103
proprietary trading, 64
prosopopoeia, 216
Pruitt-Igor housing complex, 149–150, 179, 242n9
public, 9–10, 80–83; assemblage of, 107–108; attributes of, 82–83; defined, 121; genealogy of, 80–81; origin of term, 107; as outlier, 109; as people, 82; "phantom," 111; versus private, 81
public gathering. See politics
public good(s), 82, 83–107; institutional expression of, 9; measuring quality of, 53–54. See also nonprofit organizations
public interest, 25
public knowledge, 58, 107–121; and partisanship, 116–117; and popular sovereignty, 118; and public opinion polling, 109–115; and representation, 107–110; and social capital, 115; and tolerance for rich, 118–119
public opinion, 82, 111; and mass media, 113
public opinion polling, 9–10, 109–115
public service television, 138
public will, 112

quants, 28, 31, 185

race, 152
racism and election of Obama, 143
Rafferty, Mike, 59–67, 69, 76, 114
Rainer, Yvonne, 169, 173
Rancière, Jacques, 139, 239n78
"The Random Characters of Stock Market Prices" (Fama), 172
randomization, 172
A Random Walk down Wall Street (Malkiel), 172
rap, 188

"Rapper's Delight" (Sugar Hill Gang), 188
rational choice, 55, 230n68
rationality, bounded, 58
Rauschenberg, Robert, 175
Reagan, Ronald, 34, 91, 103
reductionism, 44–45
reflexive modeling, 66
regulation(s), 54–57, 69–70; as specula-
    tive, 19
regulatory arbitrage, 58–59
regulatory capacity of derivatives, 64–65,
    70–71
regulatory disintermediation, 56–57
rehearsal, 207
Reinhart, Charles, 180
release technique, 173, 181, 183–184,
    247n69
representation, 107–110; versus mobiliza-
    tion, 145
Republic (Plato), 33
Republican affiliation, 116–117; revenue
    flows and, 132, 240n87
rescue without recovery, 20–21
reserve requirements, 58–59
resonance, 66–67
resource allocation, 23–24
retirement, 38–39
retirement benefits, tax-free, 90
revenue flows and Republican affiliation,
    132, 240n87
rich, tolerance for, 118–119
Ring Shout, 192
risk(s), 19; conversion to uncertainty of,
    231n76; generative, 206–212; as own
    reward, 209; versus uncertainty, 28–29;
    value at, 29–31
risk-based movement, 150–152
risk benefit, 55
risk management: derivatives in, 7; maxi-
    mizing returns on risk and, 35; versus
    security provision, 55–56; volatility due
    to, 3
risk reduction, diversification for, 27
robot, 188
Rockefeller, David, 150
Rockefeller, John D., III, 87–88, 89, 102,
    110
Rockefeller, Nelson, 150
Rock Steady Crew, 187, 188, 201
"Roof Piece" (Trisha Brown), 180

Roosevelt, Franklin, 86, 87
roots, 152
Roper Center for Public Opinion
    Research, 110
Rose, Tricia, 190
Ross, Bertram, 174
Roubini, Nouriel, 70, 156
Rove, Karl, 120
Roy, Ananya, 98–100
rule(s), 54–57
The Rule of Experts (Mitchell), 40–41
Ruml, Wentzl, 200
Rumsfeld, Donald, 45–46, 47
Run DMC, 188
Rye Playland, 194

Sachs, Kurt, 158
Saddler, Joseph (Grandmaster Flash), 189
sampling, 115; in hip-hop, 188–190
Santa Monica, California, 194–195,
    196–197
Schlichter, Joseph, 179–180, 181
Schloss, Joseph, 190–191
Schmidt, Lisa, 183
Schoenberg, Bessie, 181
Scholes, Myron, 144, 228n36
School of American Ballet, 164
Schumer, Charles, 13
Schumpeter, Joseph, 153
scores and scoring, 169, 171–172
Scott, Rick, 231–232n84
Scott-Heron, Gil, 179, 188
securitization, 69; of mortgages, 72
security provision versus risk manage-
    ment, 55–56
Select Committee to Investigate Tax-
    Exempt Foundations and Comparable
    Organizations, 87
self-correction, 18, 19–20, 38
self-help industry, 210, 250n112
self-limitation, 26
self-liquidation, 17
self-production, sovereignty as, 211–212
Senter, Shelley, 183
September 11, 2001 terrorist attacks, 2
"Set and Reset" (Trisha Brown), 184
"shadow banks," 58
Shannon, Claude, 137
Shawn, Ted, 174
Shelby, Richard, 13

Shick, Vicky, 183
Shiller, Robert, 64
Shirky, Clay, 137
shock, 236n43
Sidford, Holly, 95
Sievers, Bruce, 92–93
Sinnreich, Aram, 188
Sissel, Sandi, 151
Sixteenth Amendment, 85
skateboarding, 197–202; in African American community, 204, 250n104; banning of, 198; and dance, 201–202; do-it-yourself roots of, 198; as extreme sport, 198–199; new equipment and styles of, 199–200; new moves in, 201; origins of, 197–198; skate parks for, 198; teams in, 200–201; volcano boarding as, 202–203
skate parks, 198
SKS Microfinance, 97
slams, 187–188
Slemrod, Joel, 42–43
"Slink" (Bryan Bower), 187
"the smartest ones in the room," 35, 228n36
Smith, Adam, 91, 92
snowboarding, 197
social capital, 115
social citation in postmodern dance, 176–177
social entrepreneurialism, 221
social impact bonds, 100
social justice, nonprofit organizations for, 101–102, 236n33
social kinesthetic(s), 158–161; de-centered (see de-centered social kinesthetics); defined, 148
social logic of derivatives, 4, 6–7, 52–53, 73–79
social media, 135–137
social movements and politics, 138–139
Social Science Research Council (SSRC), 110, 111
society(ies), 219–220; of control, 205; of the spectacle, 207
socioeconomic mobility, 102, 236n37
Soden, Garrett, 196
Soho, Trisha Brown and, 179–185
Sokolow, Anna, 176
Soul Train, 192

sovereignty: principle of, 37; as self-production, 211–212; techno-scientific, 44
spectacle, society of the, 207
spectatorship, 119, 239n74
speculative investment, 57–58
Spivak, Gayatri, 224
SSRC (Social Science Research Council), 110, 111
stability in postmodern dance, 184–185
Standard and Poor's, 43, 229n47
Stannard, Russell, 44
Stark, David, 66
state planning, 23, 24
St. Denis, Ruth, 174
Stecyk, Craig, 200
Stimson, James A., 116–117
Strauss, William, 135
Stravinsky, Igor, 165
Streb, Liz, 180
string theory, 44
structure of feeling, 242n7
Student Debt Refusal campaign, 223
"submerged state," 90
subprime credit market, 99
subprime mortgage crisis, 7–8, 14–23, 72
subsidy of artistic labor, 146, 242n5
Sugar Hill Gang, 188
Summers, Elaine, 169, 170
Summers, Lawrence, 64
Sunder, Shyam, 56–57
surfing, 196–197; extreme, 203–204; kite, 202–203
surplus, 74–75; in politics, 123–124
Swanson, Wil, 183
Swap Financing, 71
system in neoclassical approach, 25

tagging, 186
Taglioni, Filippo, 161
Taglioni, Marie, 161, 167
"Take It to the Bridge" (James Brown), 189
Taleb, Nasim Nicholas, 28, 31
Tamaris, Helen, 176
TanzPlan, 247n69
target countries, 45
tariffs, 85
TARP (Troubled Asset Relief Program), 15–17, 68, 231–232n84
tax exemption, 83, 84–86, 88–89, 106–107

tax incentives, 71
Tax Reform Act (1969), 88, 89
tax revolt, 103
Taylor, Paul, 164
Tea Party, 22, 43, 57, 220
technological innovation and politics, 136–138
techno-scientific sovereignty, 44
television watching, excessive, 137
temporal cycles or waves, 148, 242n6
temporality, 142
terror, global war on, 2, 46, 47
terrorism, 45
Tet Offensive, 179
Thatcher, Margaret, 34, 105
The Thinking Body: A Study of the Balancing Forces of Dynamic Man (Todd), 173
Thiong'o, Ngūgīwa, 154–155
third sector, 9, 83
Thomson, David, 183
Tilly, Charles, 241n102
"Timepiece" (Emerson), 170
Tocqueville, Alexis de, 86
Todd, Mabel, 173, 181
toprock, 187
Tragedy (Graham), 176
"Transit" (Paxton), 170
transparency, 54, 57, 58
Treasury Department, 20
"Trillium" (Trisha Brown), 181
triplet, 215–216, 217
Troubled Asset Relief Program (TARP), 15–17, 68, 231–232n84
Truman, Harry, 111
tsunamis, 204

uncertainty, 19; conversion of risks to, 231n76; versus risk, 28–29
unemployment: coercive impact of heightened, 63; and politics of millennials, 135
universalism, 220
university education, 33–34, 221
unknowability, contestability and, 63
unknown: as debt, 4; horizon of the, 2–3; as waste in knowledge production, 3
unknown known as nonknowledge, 44, 45
unknown unknown as nonknowledge, 45–46
uprock, 187

urban getaways and boarding culture, 194–195
urban ruins: and boarding culture, 205; and hip-hop, 185–186
U.S. government debt, downgrading of, 43, 229n47

value at risk (VaR), 29–31
value creation and circulation, emergent forms of, 6
Van Bastolaer, Raimana, 203
Venice, California, 194–195
venture philanthropy, 84, 96, 97, 98, 102
verticality: of classical dance, 166; collapsed, 10; shift to horizontal propulsion from, 208–209
Vertov, Dziga, 208
Vimeo, 208
Viniar, David, 30
virtuous cycle, 30
volcano boarding, 202–203
voluntary associations, 83, 86, 134
volunteerism, 95–96, 135, 136
voter turnout, 134

wages of dancers, 146, 241–242n4
"Walk This Way" (Aerosmith/Run DMC), 188
Wallenda, Karl, 196
Wallerstein, Immanuel, 242n6
Walsh Commission, 87
war: and ballet, 163, 244nn34–35; knowledge failure and, 45–47; on terror, 2, 46, 47
War Revenue Act (1917), 85
Warshaw, Randy, 183
weapons of mass destruction, 45–46
Weidman, Charles, 164
Weisbrod, Burton J., 234n11
Welfare Reform Act (1996), 91
well-being, private giving and, 93–94
What's the Matter with Kansas? (Frank), 117
White, Alex, 204
white flight, 179
"Whitey on the Moon" (Scott-Heron), 179
Wiener, Norbert, 137
Williams, Raymond, 152, 242n7
Wilson, James Q., 247n73
Wilson-Gorman Tariff Act (1894), 84–85

windmill, 187
Winograd, Morley, 135
women: in boarding culture, 204–205; microcredit loans to, 96–100
women's alternative health practices, 181
Wood, David, 174
Woodward, Woody, 198
Worker's Dance League, 176
World Bank, 149
world risk society, 47–48
World Systems Analysis, 242n6
World Trade Towers, 150–151
Wright, Frank Lloyd, 165

X-Games, 198–199

Yamasaki, Minoru, 149, 150, 151
Yochim, Emily Chivers, 204–205
YouTube, 208
Yunus, Muhammad, 96
Yuriko, 174

Zephyr Boys (Z-Boys), 200, 204
Zephyr Surfboard Productions, 200
Zuckerberg, Mark, 102
Zulu Nation, 191
Zunz, Olivier, 91, 102

Randy Martin (1957–2015) was Professor of Art and Public Policy at New York University and founder of the graduate program in arts politics. He published many books, as author or editor, including *Financialization of Daily Life* and *Under New Management: Universities, Administrative Labor, and the Professional Turn* (both Temple); *An Empire of Indifference: American War and the Financial Logic of Risk Management*; *On Your Marx: Relinking Socialism and the Left*; *Critical Moves: Dance Studies in Theory and Politics*; *Socialist Ensembles: Theater and State in Cuba and Nicaragua*; and *Performance as Political Act: The Embodied Self.*